Palgrave Macmillan Studies in Banking and Financial Institutions

Series Editor
Philip Molyneux
University of Sharjah
Sharjah, United Arab Emirates

The Palgrave Macmillan Studies in Banking and Financial Institutions series is international in orientation and includes studies of banking systems in particular countries or regions as well as contemporary themes such as Islamic Banking, Financial Exclusion, Mergers and Acquisitions, Risk Management, and IT in Banking. The books focus on research and practice and include up to date and innovative studies that cover issues which impact banking systems globally.

More information about this series at
http://www.palgrave.com/gp/series/14678

Federica Poli

Co-operative Banking
Networks in Europe

Models and Performance

Federica Poli
Università Cattolica del Sacro Cuore
Milano, Italy

ISSN 2523-336X   ISSN 2523-3378 (electronic)
Palgrave Macmillan Studies in Banking and Financial Institutions
ISBN 978-3-030-21698-6   ISBN 978-3-030-21699-3 (eBook)
https://doi.org/10.1007/978-3-030-21699-3

Cover illustration: © Alexander Spatari / Moment / Getty

This Palgrave Macmillan imprint is published by the registered company Springer Nature
Switzerland AG
The registered company address is: Gewerbestrasse 11, 6330 Cham, Switzerland

To my beloved son

PREFACE

Over the past 20 years, the increasing dominance of the shareholder ownership model in banking, with its main purpose of maximizing financial returns to shareholders, has proved to be a toxic combination with financial deregulation, the creation of new financial instruments, and the concomitant rising levels of bank leverage that have taken place. Despite the growing role of private joint-stock banks around the world, co-operative banking is still a credible and high-performing alternative way of doing banking. This is especially true in Europe where co-operative institutions have historical roots dating back to the nineteenth century.

This book focuses on a sample of European co-operative banks (CBs), which nowadays perform universal banking activities, adopting a business model which is fundamentally based on mutuality, community development, not-for-profit, and stakeholder orientation. From a lifecycle perspective, most European CBs have reached an advanced level of maturity. Many modern CBs have evolved into large firms which mainly transact with customers who are not co-operative members and which are run by professional managers.

Many of the CB networks have turned into large, complex, financial conglomerates that have little in common with the small-scale self-help organizations from which they are descended. Forming networks allows the pursuit of economies of scale and scope while also providing a safety net or mutual support mechanism that can compensate for the risks associated with being an individual co-operative whose activities are concentrated on a homogeneous member base. The few empirical research studies, conducted prior to and after the outbreak of the global financial crisis (GFC), into the effects on performance measures of the level of integration of financial co-operatives' systems find that integration tends to reduce the volatility of efficiency and performance measures; it appears to help control managers' expense preferences; and notwithstanding the high costs of running hub-like organizations in highly integrated systems, these systems operate at lower costs than less integrated systems.

Additionally, some authors have recently pointed out that the hybridization process of CBs has exposed them to severe losses following the financial crisis, mainly due to their apex institutions and their highly diversified activities in financial assets which have been harshly hit by the international financial turmoil. This raises the following question: are their stability and resilience to financial shocks threatened by an overexposure to risk and the introduction of the shareholder value logic into hybrid networks? Considering the situation outlined above, it seems that there is still plenty of scope to conduct further investigations into the resilience and profitability of CBs in Europe, properly taking into account the organizational forms of their networks and governance.

The vast majority of European CBs are organized in networks, which vary from loose associations to cohesive groups where membership may or may not be compulsory. Forms of membership vary from country to country, as do governance structures and risk management mechanisms. Given the significance of co-operative banking in certain European countries (e.g. France, the Netherlands, Germany, Austria, and Finland) and, by contrast, its decreasing importance in others (e.g. Italy), and also in light of the events following the outbreak of the financial crisis and the implementation of the Banking Union, it seems that further empirical consideration of the co-operative sector is warranted.

With these considerations in mind, this book presents a survey of the characteristics of different forms of integration of CB networks across several European countries and provides an assessment of their impact on several performance measures for the networks and their co-operative components. With a few exceptions, the existing empirical studies neglect to examine the features of the networks to which the banks belong. Surprisingly, there is little evidence on the extent to which diverse organizational forms of networks determine differences in individual banks' and networks' performances across different countries. The principal objective of this book is to fill this gap in the literature. The European countries investigated are Austria, Finland, France, Germany, Italy, and the Netherlands. In all of these countries CBs have a significant presence, while the organizational forms of their networks vary widely. Therefore, focusing on this sample of European countries may allow us to draw out some insights and policy implications about the role that network organizations play in determining the performance of CBs.

The book is organized into nine chapters. The first chapter outlines co-operative banking's historical roots, with its ground-breaking practices of self-help, solidarity between members and financial inclusion irrespective of social condition or wealth; its ongoing conceptualization; the principles and values associated with co-operative banking; and its role in modern economies. It offers a review of the empirical evidence on the performance of the sector relative to commercial alternatives and its contribution to financial stability in the European context. The second chapter examines the rationales for and structures of co-operative banking networks both from a theoretical perspective and as exemplified in the European countries under investigation. Networks facilitate the building of relationships between CBs that have joined together for mutual benefit or to achieve a common purpose. The need to build alliances tends to increase in relation to the number of CBs existing in a territory, offering benefits in terms of supply alliances, monitoring functions, and the creation of social capital. From Chaps. 3, 4, 5, 6, 7, and 8, the banking co-operative networks that exist in each of the six European countries surveyed are examined, respectively: Austria, Finland, France, Germany, Italy, and the Netherlands.

In relation to each country, we analyze the positioning of the co-operative system, its historical evolution, and the organizational model of its network, and, finally, present an empirical analysis which covers two research areas. The purpose of the first one is to verify empirically the effects of the ongoing hybridization in co-operative banking over the period 2005–2017, answering the following questions: have the mitigation of the principles of mutuality pursued by CBs and the growing complementarity with markets as places of investment and funding meant that the results achieved by CBs have become more similar to those of shareholder-oriented banks? Which areas record analogies and differences in results? Can a convergence in their respective performances be observed over time? To answer these important questions, a set of commonly employed indicators in the form of ratios proxying bank performances is identified and tested. The second area of research aims to verify on a comparative basis the contributions that the central institutions of the networks and the available sample of the individual CBs were able to generate during the period 2008–2017. To deal with this empirical issue, we examine some of the performance indicators selected, comparing the results achieved by central institutions with those of their networks of CBs.

In Chap. 9, we use the entire sample of European countries analyzed and, over different time periods between 2005 and 2017, test for the existence of significant differences between the co-operative banking sector and the purely shareholder-oriented banks which have been selected. In addition to this empirical assessment, the following research question is also addressed: which of the network models seen so far enhances the performances of the CBs that are part of them? Or in other words, which of the types of networks analyzed has the most positive effect on the results of their owners: the local CBs? To answer this question, we return to the classification of co-operative networks introduced in Chap. 2 and examine, on a comparative basis, the performances of the different networks of the individual CBs. The chapter concludes with a brief analysis of the most important challenges that, in the opinion of the author, the CBs are called to face in the coming years.

Milano, Italy   Federica Poli

ACKNOWLEDGMENTS

I am grateful to Phil Molyneux for his helpful comments and to Tula Weis for her patience and assistance in preparing this book. I thank Giorgia Simion, Judy Nagle, and Giorgia Bresciani for their constructive help and Sergio De Angeli and Marco Oriani for their firm encouragement.

Contents

LIST OF FIGURES

LIST OF TABLES

CHAPTER 1

The Theoretical Background of Co-operative Banking

1 HISTORICAL ROOTS OF CO-OPERATIVE BANKING IN EUROPE

The roots of co-operative banking can be traced back to the second half of the nineteenth century in Germany, where it was inspired by the English Rochdale Society of Equitable Pioneers (1844),[1] whose ideas of collective self-help among and to the benefit of working people allowed them to withstand the unemployment and deprivation experienced by its members. The birth of these credit co-operative entities in Germany is linked to the dissemination of a widespread theoretical debate at the time about which social models of development could support the political and economic turnaround that Germany was experiencing. Since the Middle Ages, Germany had been a fragmented political territory, made up of several autonomous political units, which were federally coordinated (Colombo 2012). This structural organization of the as yet non-unified German State—Germany would become a nation state in 1871 through the unification efforts of the ambitious Prussians—influenced the design of the primitive credit co-operatives, which were conceived as independent local entities, coordinated within associations or federations. In

---

[1] The Rochdale Society of Equitable Pioneers was the co-operative enterprise founded by the Rochdale Pioneers in Rochdale, England, which commenced trading on 21 December 1844.

© The Author(s) 2019
F. Poli, *Co-operative Banking Networks in Europe*, Palgrave Macmillan Studies in Banking and Financial Institutions,
https://doi.org/10.1007/978-3-030-21699-3_1

parallel, the development of co-operative banking was sustained by philosophical avant-gardes following the theories of Marx, whose view of politics and the economic life greatly affected the start-up and spread of credit co-operatives within Germany and beyond, in neighboring countries, such as France, Italy, and the Netherlands.

As reconstructed by Birchall (2013), unlike the more industrialized Britain, in the early nineteenth century, Germany was taking its first steps toward industrial growth through the creation of a network of new internal railways and a customs system, designed to facilitate free trade between the various German aristocratic states within the German lands. The abolition of serfdom favored the rise of independent farmers, who were required to act more and more within a market-based framework, although lacking the necessary monetary resources and competence skills. At the same time, artisans, whose production capabilities were mainly channeled toward serving local communities, were still the most productive paradigm in the country.

The arrival of the famine which hit Germany and the whole of Europe in 1846–1847 further exposed the problem of the lack of capital which not only was a cause of the sluggish German economic growth (Kemp 1985) but was leading to the disappearance of small businesses, artisans, and farmers. There was an urgent need to find ways to give credit to those who were able to use it in a productive form but were unable to offer any type of security in exchange (Birchall 2013). As honesty was the only moral guarantee (Luzzatti 1863) that could be given by those aspiring to take advantage of the new markets emerging from the fledgling industrialization process taking place in Germany and across Europe, there was a consequent need to identify organizational models that would allow for the "capitalization of honesty" and the "democratization of credit" suggested by the French liberal economists Leon Say and Leon Walras (1866).[2] Initially production and consumer co-operatives and soon after credit co-operatives were the tools used to release the production and consumption potential of the working classes which would otherwise have remained untapped. As is well defined by Wolff (1893), the lack of capital

---

[2] Referring to Goschen in England and Luzzatti in Italy, two committed liberals and firm believers in *laissez-faire*, Say wrote, "They perfectly know what democracy may call into life, and what it may destroy; they take it as it is. What they want to demonstrate, is that liberty, self-help and foresight are able to find a principle of development and to breathe in the very atmosphere of democracy". See Inglis Palgrave (2015).

determined the persistent condition of poverty of small entrepreneurs and self-employed workers who could not obtain credit from commercial banks as the latter were only targeting wealthy customers.

Credit co-operatives as the solution to the problems of consumption and production was identified by two leading German figures: Franz Hermann Schulze-Delitzsch and Friedrich Wilhelm Raiffeisen. However, their organizational models differed in several ways. For Franz Hermann Schulze-Delitzsch (1808–1883), a Prussian lawyer and liberal politician, British friendly societies were effective associative models to enable self-employed individuals to purchase raw materials on better terms, thus increasing their profits. Having set up a production co-operative for shoemakers in his home town of Delitzsch in 1849, Schulze-Delitzsch soon realized that the availability of credit was at the heart of the consumption activities of urban workers as well as being the fuel that supported the productive efforts both of new entrepreneurs and of already existing manufacturing and trading businesses, which were facing growing competition from the start-up of industrial production on a larger scale. Credit co-operatives "a la Schulze-Delitzsch", also known as Volksbanks or people's banks or popular banks, were means of "financial inclusion", inspired by the founding ideas of savings banks which were already widespread throughout Europe (the first savings bank was established in Hamburg in 1778) (Colombo 2012) and whose main aims were to educate poor people to save for precautionary purposes. Unlike savings banks, which were closely tied to local and national public administrations, credit co-operatives were private ventures, whose foundation was initially supported by rich promoters as well as workers, artisans, and the forefathers of small and medium enterprises (SMEs).[3] Irrespective of their condition or wealth, every member was of equal importance and entitled to one vote per head, exactly in line with the principle of economic democracy followed by Schulze-Delitzsch and shared by the emerging middle class in the large German cities. Members were required to purchase shares issued by the credit co-operatives which were simply a means of reinforcing the unlimited liability of members, acting as a mechanism to align their incentives as both investors and customers (borrowers and savers). In order to facilitate

---

[3] In 1850 Schulze-Delitzsch founded his first credit co-operative which was initially supported by rich philanthropists and artisans. However, as reported by Birchall (2013), "at the same time, Bernhardi, set up a bank in the nearby Eilenburg that was more genuinely co-operative and so in 1852 Schulze modified his own bank to become self-supporting with members contributing share capital".

members' access to credit associations, shares could be bought by installment which as well as serving to democratize access to the role of members was also a way of educating members to save. In fact, the ability to save was an essential condition to qualify for the status of member. Schulze-Delitzsch's idea of credit co-operatives was nothing short of a socially oriented public company, with the unlimited liability of members tempered by the required paid-up capital, which was built up through the issued shares. Members' remuneration, although not guaranteed or fixed in value, was not excluded but was more oriented toward the idea of sharing unreserved profits in proportion to the investment made by members, as in joint-stock companies.

Indeed, the popular banks theorized by Schulze-Delitzsch constituted a hybrid creation, being designed to allow the ascent of the urban working class and, for the reasons highlighted above, unable to avoid adopting a co-operative nature, but needing some of the reinforcing mechanisms of the joint-stock company, such as the paid-up capital and the distribution of unreserved profits. In this way, Schulze-Delitzsch tried to modernize one of the fundamentals of the co-operative movement: the rebate of profits made by credit unions in sole proportion to the work undertaken by co-operative members. Rebates were at the heart of mutuality, inspiring non-credit and credit co-operatives as, in contrast to shareholders of joint-stock companies, co-operative members had to be compensated according to the volume of business undertaken with their union, or in other words, their participation in the activities carried out by co-operatives in the form of labor. One distinctive feature of the new popular banks was the abolition of the role of directors on a volunteer basis, which was typical of co-operative movements. Directors had to be remunerated with salaries and commission in compensation for their efforts in running sound banking operations and allowing the latter to grow. Additionally, lending made by popular banks was meant to finance the short-term financial needs of urban artisans and small entrepreneurs, which normally arose from the costs of operating the business, such as the purchase of raw materials, and any kind of collateral was accepted as security for the loans (Fay 1938). As reported by Birchall (2013), critics of the Schulze-Delitzsch model of credit co-operatives emphasized that the efforts of popular banks to be inclusive were inadequate as poor people could not afford to provide any kind of security other than their reputation and that their credit needs could not be satisfied by short-term lending, given that they were only able to repay slowly the investments which were financed.

In another part of Germany, in Westerwald on the right bank of the river Rhine, a rural area within the Prussian empire, Friedrich Wilhelm Raiffeisen (1818–1888) was developing his own model of credit co-operatives in parallel to Schulze-Delitzsch's. Both were unaware of the other's ideas and become fierce adversaries when they later came into contact, once their original designs for credit co-operatives became public knowledge. The economic environment observed by Raiffeisen differed in several ways from the urban one which met Schulze-Delitzsch's eyes. In both cases, the terrible famines of 1846–1848 needed to be tackled actively, and each identified co-operative solutions as the means to lower the cost of production, fight against usury, and address the persistent lack of access of low-income people to basic banking services. Raiffeisen was the son of a farmer and mayor of a small rural village, who himself became a mayor and later a wine trader and cigar manufacturer (Birchall 2013). He was a fervent Lutheran who actively engaged in works of charity and social activities aimed at helping and developing the impoverished local community he served as a public servant. He first founded the charitable association of Heddesdorf in 1854 with the aim of educating children, helping the unemployed to find jobs, promoting the increased education of community members through the creation of an open-access library, helping poor farmers to buy cattle and grain, and organizing a system of popular mutual credit (Colombo 2012). However, his initial philanthropic idea was soon replaced by a purely co-operative model, as already enacted by Schulze-Delitzsch (Fay 1938), and entirely founded on the principles of self-help and solidarity between members, who were the sole beneficiaries of the co-operative outputs, whether through production or credit co-operatives. Raiffeisen's thoughts called into question the value of the political and economic community, still vital in Germany at that time, despite the Prussian modernist pressures and their efforts to oppose the legacy of the past corporatism (based on the joint liability of small community members) of the Middle Ages. Raiffeisen based everything on the possibility of asymmetrical exchange, which he saw as necessary to build a new and fairer economic system. In it, solidarity and efficiency were combined with the possibility of giving without receiving anything. As highlighted by Colombo (2012), the charitable and voluntary activity imagined by Raiffeisen is active and communitarian, where a group of people carry out charitable actions to create a community, that is, a cohesive social body, which entirely benefits from an organized system of unlimited solidarity and mutuality between peers. Rural credit associations became the center of the system, playing the role of piggy banks and thereby guaranteeing the freedom of the local community and becoming the driving force for economic development on a co-operative basis. Whereas in England, co-operatives were born with the aim of promoting consumption, in Germany and the other countries where Raiffeisen's ideas spread, credit became one of the pillars of the co-operative structure.

The bank model developed by Raiffeisen differed in many respects from that of popular banks. First, the members were not required to subscribe to shares due to their condition of poverty which made them unable to meet that payment. As in Schulze-Delitzsch's popular banks, members had one vote per head and had unlimited liability for the bank's obligations. This position was fiercely defended by Raiffeisen even when German law allowed the co-operatives to abandon it. The unlimited and joint liability of members was, in fact, believed to be an effective mechanism that promoted the reliance of members on each other and the involvement of all in the repayment of the debt of each (Birchall 2013). This commitment to repayment was reinforced by two factors: the homogeneity of members and their restricted number, being part of small communities, typically at the parish level. Such conditions enabled the mutual knowledge of members, putting them in a better position to exert social monitoring on the behavior of each. One other distinctive feature of the Raiffeisen co-operative banking model lies in the use of profits: these were not distributed among members (as there were no shares, as observed by Prinz [2002]) but retained as reserves to meet future losses, lower the cost of lending, and increase the return on deposits. In the event of the dissolution of a credit co-operative, cumulated reserves were not distributed among members but devolved to community-based charitable activities. In this way, the strong mutual character of rural credit co-operatives could be entirely preserved. Loans granted by credit co-operatives were raised entirely from the savings collected from the members and aimed to finance long-term (up to ten years) investments of members (Birchall 2013) with interest rates as low as possible. In Raiffeisen's view, only long-term financing could empower his impoverished borrowers to plan and meet the costs of the investments, which were designed to improve their productive activities and the quality of their lives. This distinctive feature clearly differentiates the popular banks from rural credit co-operatives in terms of the growth capacity of their lending activity and the bank's incentives to take excessive risks.

Compared to the higher turnover of the loan portfolio of popular banks, which the short-term financing typically available favored, rural banks had a physical limitation on the growth of their loan activity, due to the typically long duration of the financing granted. This could also encourage the adoption of more prudent behaviors in the assessment of lending risks and the consequent granting of loans. As lending was not thought of *per se* as a profit-generating business whose returns had to be distributed to members, the initial co-operative managers' appetite for lending growth was effectively delimited. To further reinforce the adoption of prudent lending practices, Raiffeisen, unlike Schulze-Delitzsch, did not allow the management of the credit union to be remunerated. There was neither salary, nor commission on the activities generated by the management, nor bonuses on the performances achieved. The management activities of the credit union had to be carried out on an exclusively voluntary basis in the full spirit of the principle of charity for the good of the community. Only accountants and cashiers received a salary for their work.

Both Schulze-Delitzsch and Raiffeisen were very active in publicizing their co-operative credit entities, including by publishing guidelines for the set-up and management of their models. They were equally vigorous in their efforts to develop mechanisms for the improvement of credit co-operatives through the creation of associations or federations, on a regional and national basis, with the purpose of coordinating and centralizing certain functions, whether with regard to the technical training of personnel, or the provision of liquidity management services to the federated banks. These second- and third-tier bodies conceived by both founders of co-operative credit in Germany offered strong operational and local specialization and represented effective instruments to minimize the inherent fragility of new financial intermediaries. At the same time, these regional and national organizations transposed the concepts of self-help, mutuality, and solidarity onto a geographic plane much wider than the local one presided over by the individual co-operatives.

There is no doubt that for both founders of co-operative credit in Germany, savings and credit services held a social importance: they were intended to minimize the vulnerability of a large section of the population, allowing them to democratically participate in, and not suffer from, the modernization and industrialization processes taking place. For both, their novel financial intermediaries were meant to reduce the market imperfections that emerged more and more clearly due to the rise of liberal and market-based economic systems, in which the availability of capital became increasingly important. However, the functional value of these new financial entities was fundamentally different. For Raiffeisen, a purely functionalist view of credit unions prevailed, highlighting their social value in their governance and operational mechanisms with disregard for individual self-interest; for Schulze-Delitzsch, the popular bank was also an inclusive instrument in individualistic terms, to the extent that even the most vulnerable groups could become holders of the bank's capital and enjoy its relative fruits. The creation of co-operative banking constituted the concrete embodiment of a revolution entirely organized by individuals with equal conditions and therefore based on the principles of self-help, solidarity, and mutuality. Raiffeisen and Schulze-Delitzsch drew a clear line under the idea that only the state could provide for the individual's needs for social improvement, especially in the case of the most disadvantaged. Unlike scholars such as Proudhon in France and Lassalle in Germany (Colombo 2012), Raiffeisen and Schulze-Delitzsch had conceived mechanisms of financial and economic inclusion that were free of state intervention.

Early co-operative banks (CBs) were in many respects like modern microfinance institutions, specialized in small-scale lending, with the aim of financing the productive activity or the purchase of dwellings (like the British building societies developed during the eighteenth century) of specifically targeted members (often in terms of profession and creed[4]) within a clearly delimited geographic area.

The German co-operative movement spread first to neighboring countries and then across the whole of Europe (Wolff 1893). Credit co-operatives inspired primarily by Schulze-Delitzsch and later by Raiffeisen emerged in France, Italy, and Austria from the 1860s onward. In Scandinavia, however, these co-operatives became significant only in Finland, and even there mostly after the Second World War (Kalmi 2012). Over time, differences and tensions between the two co-operative banking models were resolved, and in Germany, for instance, the banks eventually developed a joint apex organization. However, in many countries (e.g. Austria, France, Italy) the duality within the financial co-operative movement remains to this day (Kalmi 2017). German CBs were forerunners to

---

[4] For instance, Dutch Boerenleenbanks and Italian Casse Rurali (rural co-operative banks) were closely linked with the Catholic Church. In other cases, such as in the UK or in Germany, they were more linked with Protestantism.

a great majority of financial co-operatives (FCs) in North America where they gave rise to the Caisses Desjardins in Canada and the Credit Unions in the United States. From there, the credit co-operative idea spread through most of the Anglo-Saxon world and beyond (Fonteyne and Hardy 2011).

2   Conceptualization of Co-operative Banking

The International Co-operative Alliance (ICA) defines a co-operative as "an autonomous association of persons (natural and/or legal persons) united voluntarily to meet their common economic, social, and cultural needs and aspirations through a jointly owned and democratically-controlled enterprise". Businesses run by a co-operative are owned and managed by and for their members. In an acknowledged context of a variety of legal forms, the co-operative has a precise identity clearly distinguishing it from investor-driven (capitalistic) companies: it is made up of people, it is democratically controlled via non-capitalistic criteria (i.e. one member, one vote vs. one share, one vote), and it is not devoted to the enrichment of its founders and participants, but to the satisfaction of needs other than the pure return on capital[5] (needs which, moreover, may also pertain, to a certain extent, to non-members or the community) (Cooperatives Europe et al. 2010). Co-operatives are primarily groups of persons or legal entities with operating principles that are different from those of other economic agents. These include the principles of democratic structure and control and the distribution of the net profit for the financial year on an equitable basis.[6] The introduction of a European legal form for co-operatives, based on common principles but taking their specific features into account, was the driver for the introduction in 2003 of Regulation 1435/2003 on the Statute for European Co-operative Society (*Societas Cooperativa Europaea—SCE*). In the context of the constant effort to harmonize the European legislative framework, the SCE Regulation also has an essential symbolic and political value. Unequivocally,

---

[5] As stated by ICA (2012), "co-operatives exist to meet the needs of people, not primarily to generate a speculative return on capital invested in them. The primary motive for people forming a co-operative is to be self-reliant". This condition is necessary to assure the autonomy and financial independence of a co-operative.

[6] This definition is provided in the seventh section of the premises to the introduction of the EU Regulation 1435/2003 on the Statute for European Co-operative Society (*Societas Cooperativa Europaea—SCE*).

it testifies to the fact that the capitalistic legal form of organization is not the only one available and that other legal forms may be chosen by economic agents to run businesses at both national and cross-border levels in the European territory (Cooperatives Europe et al. 2010).

The array of activities performed by co-operatives range from production and trading, to the consumption of goods and services. Among them FCs offer different types of financial services: credit, payments, deposits, financial investments, and insurance. Their offer may be specialized by the type of service provided, for example, insurance, or may follow a universal banking model, whereby all kinds of financial services are provided. FCs comprise several types of organizations, including diverse member-owned financial intermediaries such as credit unions,[7] savings and credit co-operatives, and CBs (Cuevas and Fischer 2006). Namely, a CB is a licensed and supervised bank established and run as a co-operative enterprise.[8]

The co-operative and mutual nature of these banks is very evident in their denominations, which aim to highlight their nature over and above their mere function (such as the Italian and French popular banks or the German Volksbanks, or the Italian credit co-operative banks) and to evoke their founding fathers (as, for instance, in the case of the German and Austrian Raiffeisen banks). Despite some exceptions provided by the statutes of CBs, nowadays most of them at the European level are established as limited-liability enterprises, whose members aren't liable for more than the amount they have subscribed. As mature co-operative banking systems, European CBs represent various forms of macro-organizations embedded into networks or groups which exhibit different degrees of cohesion and complexity.

---

[7] Credit unions are fully mutual financial intermediaries as membership is required to become a customer. Membership is defined on the basis of a common bond which mitigates any information asymmetries in the provision of financial services even to the most financially excluded members. As noted by McKillop et al. (2006), credit unions' roots are in the German ideas of Raiffeisen and Schulze-Delitzsch. Outside Europe, they spread first in the Canadian region of Quebec in 1900 thanks to the efforts of Alphonse Desjardins. In the United States, the first credit union was established in New Hampshire in 1909.

[8] Goddard et al. (2016) include savings banks among the vast category of mutual banks. Historically and to this day, several savings banks have been owned by their members, typically depositors, and in many instances also by local or regional public authorities (as in the German case, up to the present day) which sponsored their establishment. Apart from where these banks have been privatized, the pure savings banks have some distinctive features: they are non-profit organizations, and they pursue social aims and are often included within large networks (Ferri et al. 2013).

Together with other long-lasting co-operative financial institutions (Cuevas and Fischer 2006; Goglio and Alexopoulos 2013), CBs ground their *raison d'être* in universal values and principles which are mutually reinforcing, and which firmly differentiate them from investor-owned banks. Faced with the latter, the prudent and not-for-profit conduct of the co-operative banking businesses, along with their limitations on profit distribution, outweighs the pitfalls of potential residual claims by members, thus helping them to maintain the performance of a broad array of corporate goals (Butzbach and Mettenheim 2012).

Following the last banking crisis of 2008, policy makers, academics, experts, and industry and consumer associations have been committed to identifying effective regulatory incentive mechanisms (new capital requirements, rules on managers' compensation and internal controls, new disclosure requirements to foster market discipline) to limit the twin lures of profit maximization, including that achieved through excessive risk-taking, and short-termism which profoundly affects the management of private banks and their strong shareholder orientation. Recently, Birchall (2013) wrote that if CBs "did not exist, over the last few years, they would probably have been invented". A low-risk attitude, care of customers/members, and attention to social and cultural values at a local level are already embedded in the DNA of these alternative financial institutions (Butzbach and Mettenheim 2012). Co-operatives, as recently stated by Paranque (2017), "provide a modern solution to the non-cosmetic problems with the governance and exercise of corporate social responsibility (CSR)".

Other than being "alternative" to the commonly prevailing conventional paradigm of private joint-stock banks with shareholder orientation, CBs belong to the so-called customer-owned banks, so termed by Birchall (2013) as they comprise all financial organizations that make customers into members. This relationship can be more or less stringently applied to different types of financial co-operatives, leaving room for the co-existence of fully or partially mutual organizations. In the case of CBs, membership is not always the *conditio sine qua non* for customers to access the financial services provided by these intermediaries. The possibility for CBs to expand their activities beyond their actual membership is in fact valuable as long as it allows for the exploitation of the benefits arising from the diversification of the customer base. However, in order to safeguard the alternative nature of CBs or, in other words, their common bond with the communities they serve and their not-for-profit calling, there must be in place limitations on the relaxation of the *nexus* between members and customers. De-mutualization, as noted by Davis (2007) and Birchall (2013), springs from the weakening of the common bond with their target communities and the shared missions they pursue.

3   Principles and Values Driving Co-operative Banking

As stated effectively by Carr-Saunders et al. (1938), "the co-operative ideal is as old as human society. It is the idea of conflict and competition as a principle of economic progress that is new. The development of the idea of co-operation in the nineteenth century can best be understood as an attempt to make explicit a principle that is inherent in the constitution of society, but which has been forgotten in the turmoil and disintegration of rapid economic progress".

Transcending their sectoral specialization, co-operatives are not-for-profit institutions whose returns are seen as a means of assuring the viability of the co-operative business over time and the survival of its values. Honesty, openness, social responsibility, and caring for others are the ethical pillars that inspired the initial and modern co-operatives (International Co-operative Alliance, ICA 2012).[9] Founders of co-operatives strongly promoted the values of self-help, self-responsibility, democracy, equality, and solidarity, identifying guidelines or principles with the aim of implementing and possibly reinforcing those values.[10] As affirmed in the *Statement on the Cooperative Identity—Values and Principles* adopted by the ICA in 1995, co-operatives follow the principles of voluntary and open membership; democratic member control; member economic participation; autonomy and independence; education, training, and information; co-operation among co-operatives; and concern for communities.

Membership of co-operatives is voluntary and open to all persons (normally both natural and legal [corporate] persons)[11] able to use their services and willing to accept the responsibilities of membership (e.g. by exercising voting rights, participating in meetings, using the co-operative's

---

[9] The Statement on the Co-operative Identity—Values and Principles was adopted in 1995 during the gathering of the international co-operative movement at the general assembly of the International Co-operative Alliance (ICA) in Manchester, England. The United Nations General Assembly recognized the essential nature of co-operative enterprise in resolution 56/1145 of 2001.

[10] Ibidem.

[11] Depending on the type of co-operative business.

services, providing capital, and, in some cases, where members' liabilities are not limited by law or design, sharing losses), without any type of discrimination or restrictions that impede the membership (such as the fixing of a high-value threshold of shares to be paid to become a member).

Nowadays, in many co-operatives, for example, in the financial sector, the offer of co-operative services exclusively to members has been widely abandoned, mainly for reasons of both economics and stability. The provision of co-operative services to a larger population of users, other than members, may indeed increase the economic sustainability of the co-operative business (via a higher exploitation of economies of scale), favor the diversification of risks borne by the co-operative financial intermediary (e.g. in the credit sector or in the insurance sector), and encourage the approach of non-members to the co-operative business model idea.[12]

Whatever the members' status—whether customers, employees, or residents—they hold an equal voice in the administration of the business (democratic participation in the governance of the business) and share in the surplus (profits) in both indirect ways (i.e. rebates) and direct ways (i.e. profits distribution, although this is typically restricted, and democratic participation in the co-operative's surplus). Co-operatives are organizations democratically controlled by their members, who actively participate in setting policies and making decisions. Members usually have equal voting rights (one member, one vote), especially in primary co-operatives, which are exercised in annual meetings. In multi-stakeholder or hybrid primary co-operatives[13] different voting schemes may apply. For

---

[12] As recommended by ICA (2012) if non-member trade exceeds trading with members, or members' usage of co-operative services is low, the reasons should be examined, and new measures should be adopted to encourage non-members to become members, or to stimulate members to use services. There is no doubt that when these circumstances arise, some of the motivations that gave rise to the co-operatives are therefore weakened, such as the exclusivity of the offer made to the shareholders in the absence of a profit incentive. Members' incentives can be significantly altered when the offer of co-operative services is increasingly made in favor of subjects other than members. Membership may become more driven by the achievement of profits in the form of dividends, where this is allowed and not appropriately counterbalanced by appropriate mechanisms (e.g. through limits on the distribution of profits, accumulated reserves).

[13] The following terms are defined by ICA (2012): a primary co-operative is a co-operative that operates a co-operative enterprise for the benefit of its members. A multi-stakeholder co-operative is a co-operative with more than one class of legal persons as members. A hybrid co-operative is a co-operative that has issued equity shares to non-member investors. A secondary co-operative is a co-operative whose members are primary co-operatives. Tertiary

instance, in order to increase members' participation in annual meetings, in November 2017, the Finnish OP Financial Group's CBs successfully held the election of their Representative Assemblies electronically.

The strict link between member shares and voting rights has been challenged in recent decades. Many FCs have started to issue shares to non-members, which are listed and without voting rights. ICA (2012) states that these arrangements give rise to hybrid co-operatives that merge two organizational models: a co-operative and investor ownership. While the development of these equity structures is mainly regulatory driven as CBs seek to increase their capital adequacy ratio to fulfill regulatory requirements, these hybrid co-operative/equity investor businesses may challenge the co-operative's leading principles of conduct. For instance, in France, since the 1980s, the capital-related instruments available to CBs have been enhanced by new financing tools, offering returns higher than shares (in accordance with provisions set by the by-laws) but without voting rights.

Capital or long-term investments without voting rights usually offer guaranteed compensation at a "fair market rate or compensatory rate" in order to provide a reasonable return on investment without being granted increased control. Likewise, this remuneration serves as an inducement to members to invest more than their minimum voting share or to attract new non-member investors, thus limiting the contribution of existing members in the event of the co-operative needing to increase its own patient capital. An adequate level of capital is essential for co-operatives, in particular FCs, not only for capital regulatory purposes, but also because reliance on external financing may induce higher risk-taking and compromise the independence of the co-operative enterprise through the financial and compliance covenants imposed on it by lenders or non-member capital investors. For these reasons, the collection of capital from members and the prevailing retention of earnings with the consequent limitation of their distribution represent essential safeguards to the autonomy of the co-operative, regardless of its specialization. However, as external capital may be necessary to finance the growth of the business, as recommended by ICA (2012), co-operatives should always privilege funding provided by institutions with homogeneous values (i.e. from other co-operatives and co-operative financial institutions, and social investors) over capital mar-

co-operatives are national co-operatives, co-operative unions, or co-operative federations that represent the interests of its member co-operatives nationally and internationally.

kets in order to minimize any possible strain on the co-operative conduct that may compromise its original nature. In this regard, the creation of co-operative financial networks, well-developed in countries with a strong co-operative banking history, may be thought of as an effective mechanism that, through facilitating the collection of funding (via capital or debt), has enabled the survival of the co-operative business model and secured its success over time.

In Raiffeisen's original organizational paradigm, the involvement of members in the governance and management of the co-operative was assured by the unlimited liability of members for any losses made by their co-operative. By fostering an attitude of self-responsibility among all members, this principle of unlimited liability was undoubtedly designed to ensure the prudent allocation of common resources on a long-term basis, avoiding any speculative perspective which might harm the entire co-operative project. Despite this latter potential outcome, many national legislations have long since replaced the unlimited liability with a limited one. FCs are at the forefront of those who have widely abandoned the principle of the unlimited liability of members without nevertheless replacing them with effective mechanisms other than those simply aimed at promoting member participation via the offer of different forms of benefits and rewards. In evaluating the usefulness of the unlimited liability clause as a mechanism for self-responsibility and participation, one cannot avoid the conclusion that its value is primarily challenged by the actual competence of members in exercising an effective hands-on monitoring of the co-operative's operations. The provision of a broad educational program for members, enabling them to become more responsible and aware of the managerial complexity of the co-operative and its embedded risks, is therefore the necessary counterbalance to the absence of the unlimited liability burden. Unfortunately, this has not always translated into concrete and lasting educational actions.

Besides, one should note that the unlimited responsibility of members may reduce the attractiveness of participating in these forms of socially organized entrepreneurial activities, when members risk seeing their wealth undermined by the co-operative entity's losses. One can also imagine that in precisely those cases where the threshold for capital participation is kept low enough to make it more affordable to members, the existence of unlimited liability may, unsurprisingly, deter membership. The creation of reserves out of the undistributed earnings or in observance of strict national legislation limiting the distribution of profits (for instance, in Italy, 70% of

CBs' profits must be placed in reserves) serves as a tool to mitigate the economic burden on members should the co-operative experience losses. However, as the business of the co-operative grows, it becomes difficult to maintain the unlimited personal responsibility clause for members, due, in the opinion of the writer, to the fear of the burden borne by members which the presence of this clause creates. For this reason, its maintenance should not only be subject to careful assessment as the co-operative's activities increase in volume, but it should also be flanked by the simultaneous establishment of inter-co-operative financial solidarity instruments that make the membership's position of unlimited liability less burdensome, psychologically as well as financially. To this end, in the various co-operative banking systems, institutional protection systems have been developed over time, which concretely implement the principle of solidarity among co-operatives, thus making the acquisition of the status of member less "unsafe".

The detractors of these protection mechanisms may object that they may give rise to moral hazard phenomena in the management of the co-operatives. However, the design of these devices in preserving their function and credibility over time must insulate them in this regard. In fact, in the most deeply rooted co-operative banking systems, access to the mechanisms of solidarity is regulated as it is not without costs and managerial burdens for the entities that use them.

Two principles which characterize the co-operative business concern the redemption of shares, which is subject to adequate notice, and the indivisibility of reserves. Different rules for the withdrawal of capital may be applied to voting and non-voting capital, but the withdrawal of any members' capital needs to be under very strict conditions (i.e. whenever the CB shows a distributable surplus), so as not to endanger the co-operative's financial stability and ultimately its *raison d'être* for the remaining members.[14] These conditions are even stricter in the case of FCs (i.e. CBs) as the redemption of shares in response to members' requests for withdrawal must be approved by the national supervisory authority.

The indivisibility of reserves implies that withdrawing members or in the event of the co-operative's dissolution, all members agree to forgo part of the co-operative's surpluses (co-operative's annual profits) which are a

---

[14] See, for instance, European Association of Co-operative Banks (EACB), 2012, The Process for the Redemption of Shares in CBs in different EU Countries; a Comparative Overview, Brussels.

common property built up over time and therefore not forming part of the individual property of any current member.[15] The protection of reserves varies from country to country. In some cases, there is a legal asset-lock in place which prevents their distribution to members on the winding-up or dissolution of a co-operative enterprise: reserves must be transferred to another co-operative, a co-operative fund, or a charity. In countries without a legal asset-lock, co-operatives protect indivisible reserves from distribution to members through provisions in their rules or by-laws which cannot be amended (ICA 2012).

In contrast to shareholder-oriented firms, in co-operatives the limitations on the financial remuneration of members in monetary terms (where allowed by national legislations or by by-laws) may take different forms. What in investor-owned firms is known as a dividend is better known in co-operatives as a patronage refund and can be made either in cash, in the form of discounts on the price of products or services, or as non-voting capital (ICA 2012).

Self-help has been a distinctive feature of co-operatives since their inception and enabled them to lift and keep people out of the oppressive poverty prevalent in the nineteenth century. Naturally connected with this principle of self-help is the concept of independence which implies the freedom to act independently in the best interests of its members. Therefore, any influence that may threaten the autonomy of co-operatives calls into question the same principle of self-help that has given rise to these long-lasting types of organizations. As already mentioned, independence is potentially weakened any time co-operatives, for example, seeking to raise capital from financial markets and financial institutions, or as a result of the burden of financial covenants and compliance obligations, gradually grant more control to investors. The lure of growth is indeed perilous to the autonomy of co-operatives as it may induce an excessive dependence on external investor-based financing. This risk is constantly in play in the case of FCs that, over time, due to widespread deregulation processes, have increasingly resorted to financial market instruments to finance their growth. The same can be said of the opening up of the offer of the co-operative's services to non-members. The increasing misalignment between the values and incentives of client-members and those of independent customers can alter the prudent and long-term vision of

---

[15] Redemption of shares is sometimes at nominal value or may include a limited compensatory return.

co-operatives' businesses. In order to mitigate such risks, many national legislations or statutes concerning FCs have imposed restrictions on the ability of these institutions to deviate significantly from their founding elements as it may endanger their financial stability. Thus, the governance and management of co-operatives play a crucial role in assuring not only the viability of co-operatives but also the preservation of their values and principles. Observing the principle of the democratic participation of members means that the latter may be involved in the direction and supervision of co-operatives, even though they may lack the necessary skills required to preserve the soundness of the co-operatives over time, and thus their autonomy. In many circumstances, the failures of co-operatives have been attributed to the lack of managerial and supervisory competence of the elected members, who proved unable to safely guide such social organizations over time and through changes in the economic environment. At the same time, the appointment of directors from outside the co-operative movement, with the proper skills and expertise to run enterprises in the modern economy, may introduce into the co-operatives managerial incentives which are not aligned with their values, ultimately driving the organizations toward a process of de-mutualization, as has been quite widespread in the financial sector. Reconciling the conflicting needs arising from these phenomena is not always easy and is indeed one of the most critical exercises required of co-operative organizations. In addition, in the financial sector, the authorities' regulatory and supervisory powers translate into actions regarding the management of financial co-operatives that often concern the sphere of control of the co-operative activity. Although dictated by the superior need to ensure the stability and efficiency of financial intermediaries, regardless of the business model followed, it is evident that potential misalignments may emerge between the solutions required of supervised intermediaries by the authorities and the principles and values followed by the co-operatives. The answers to the demand for expertise in the management of co-operatives, on the one hand, and the preservation of their guiding values, on the other, are different. In some cases, as often happens in the financial sector, an instant solution can be found in the appointment of more independent non-executives, who bring with them the skills that the democratically elected board members lack. In the financial sector, the presence of a certain proportion of independent non-executive board members is also required by regulators and supervisors. However, as already mentioned, it is not *per se* a mechanism that is totally neutral with respect to the principles followed by co-operatives, such as the operation of a not-for-profit business, its strong social orientation, and its autonomy over time. The founding fathers of the co-operative movement were well aware of the valuable role that member education could play in bridging any gaps in the know-how that was required to manage the co-operative enterprise safely. Schulze-Delitzsch and Raiffeisen were fully mindful of the need to put members in a position where they could fully exercise the management and control functions of co-operatives. For this reason, they worked actively on the drafting of technical and popular publications and developed second- (regional) and third- (national) level bodies with the specific function of training the existing and prospective board members of the entities they created, enabling them to have the knowledge and capacity to fulfill the corporate governance role. Apex regional and national co-operative organizations (in various forms[16]) play a pivotal role in providing advice and managerial know-how to co-operatives on how to avoid and/or manage the risks to the autonomy and independence of member co-operatives (ICA 2012) posed by the dominant market-based banking model. Over time, regional and national apex organizations have acquired what in investor-owned companies is best known as the role of holding companies, but in the form of inverted group models where the ownership of the apex belongs to member co-operatives. Indeed, several apexes of FCs act as delegated providers of a wide range of services that offer single co-operatives affordable access to specific qualified functions (such as training, auditing, promotion) as well as to more sophisticated financial products and services (e.g. liquidity management, risk management) that are aimed to strengthen their ability to compete with investor-based firms while still protecting their independence and survival. At the same time, the top organizations are called upon to represent the interests of the co-operative organizations to legislators and regulators in order to ensure that enacted norms are appropriate and not detrimental to the co-operative nature of these social enterprises.[17]

In fact, co-operation between co-operatives through the creation of apex bodies is a strategic mechanism that has enabled the self-preservation

[16] As federations, or as co-operative or even non-co-operative enterprises, they are used by first-tier member co-operatives to gain access to different types of activities, including training, managerial advisory, auditing, and financial services.

[17] As stated by Cuevas and Fischer (2006), "mutual financial intermediaries require a specialized regulatory environment that supports the special nature of the contracts imbedded in the institutions".

of the species, as it would be called in biological terms, reinforcing the fundamental idea that has guided the establishment of co-operatives: making the weak strong. In this case, the top organizations have the task of keeping member co-operatives safe, strengthening their capacity to serve their communities.

4   THE ROLE OF CO-OPERATIVE BANKING IN MODERN DEVELOPED ECONOMIES

The emergence and wide acceptance of the theoretical proposition that financial systems should privilege the analysis of the services provided (the functional perspective), rather than focus on the activities and roles of existing markets and intermediaries, such as banks (the institutional perspective) (Merton 1995), seems to have dimmed the relevance, in dynamic terms, of the institutional design[18] of financial systems. The argument in favor of the functional perspective relies on the persistence over time of "functional financial needs of agents, although packaged differently and delivered in substantially different ways" (Allen and Santomero 1997). By contrast, institutions such as intermediaries, but also markets, are spatially and temporarily variable components of financial systems which arise, change, and die (Merton 1995).

As argued by Merton (1995), "for a variety of reasons—including differences in size, complexity, and available technology, as well as differences in political, cultural, and historical backgrounds the most efficient institutional structure for fulfilling the functions of the financial system generally changes over time and differs across geopolitical subdivisions". Thus, the blend of banks and other financial intermediaries and markets, as intermediation channels of funds and ultimately devices for economic growth, varies across countries and time, being the endogenous outcome of several drivers of change.

The variability and transience of financial institutions and their combination is possibly one of the motivations for disregarding the debate on the optimal design or, in other words, the institutional structure that financial systems should adopt in order to realize their functions efficiently. It is no accident, however, that the minor role played by financial institu-

---

[18] The term "institutional structure", as introduced by Merton and Bodie (2005), includes financial institutions, financial markets, products, services, organization of operations, and supporting infrastructure such as regulatory rules and the accounting system.

tions, and explicitly intermediaries, is consistent with the neoclassical view of the irrelevance of specific financial institutional structures in terms of setting prices and allocating economic resources. The academic disaffection for the discussion concerning the institutional structure of financial systems seems also to stem from the growing "financialization" of modern economies[19] which unsurprisingly favor investor-owned institutions over member-owned ones. Additionally, since 1980, reforms and regulations have sought to reinforce the former as being better suited to delivering a market-based banking, reducing financial repression, and freeing market forces (Butzbach and Mettenheim 2012).

Critical reconsideration of the neoclassical theory, where price-setting is nothing but a "natural" and inevitable phenomenon (Fligstein and Calder 2015) which allows the allocation of resources under utility and profit maximization paradigms, has led to the diagnosis that the existence of frictions and inefficiencies in financial markets as well as the irrationalities of market participants (Merton and Bodie 2005) lead financial systems to perform their functions sub-optimally, thus threatening economic development.

Using the existence of market imperfections (which stem from the weaknesses of the neoclassical assumptions of full information, individual rationality, and the absence of transaction costs) as its basis, the modern theory of financial intermediation, influenced by the New Institutional Economics, proposes the presence of financial intermediaries as the solution to the above market failures (for a review see Allen and Santomero 1997; Merton and Bodie 2005). Financial markets and intermediaries such as banks compete, although not perfectly, to offer the financial solutions that are best suited to satisfy the evolving needs (not simply in purely financial terms) of end-users: savers and borrowers. The *pros* and *cons* of systems more oriented to one of the aforementioned channels have been debated at length without any convincing conclusive outcome.

Market-based financing turns out to outpace bank lending if borrowers have relatively good credit reputations (Diamond 1991), exhibit high levels of disclosure, and attach great value to the feedback role of market prices (Boot and Thakor 1997). For instance, markets seem inadequate to finance those borrowers who require a lot of monitoring because their output is pledged as collateral (Gambacorta and Mistrulli 2014) or

---

[19] Konczal and Abernathy (2015) define financialization as "the growth of the financial sector, its increased power over the real economy, the explosion in the power of wealth, and the reduction of all of society to the realm of finance".

because, on the other hand, they have few tangible assets to offer as collateral and pose particularly onerous moral hazards (Boot et al. 1991). Additionally, the innovative efforts of firms seem better accomplished by markets than banks as the latter may be tempted to extract informational rents and insulate firms closely tied to banks from competition (Rajan 1992). Market-based financing tends to grow in parallel where legal and judicial frameworks are strong and efficient. The "law and finance view" developed by La Porta et al. (1998) has pointed out that since common law systems offer higher protection to investors in securities and minority shareholders, they foster the development of market-based finance, which depends on the efficiency of arm's-length relationships between issuers of securities and investors (Gambacorta and Mistrulli 2014). Rajan and Zingales (1998) contend that, where laws are weak and contract enforcements are lacking, banks step in to internalize the transactions because they can enforce contracts, extra judicially, via their market power. In other words, banks compensate for the weaknesses of the national legal infrastructure in protecting investors, especially in French civil law countries.[20]

Aoki and Dinç (2000) maintain that market- and bank-based financing differ significantly in how borrowers renegotiate debt during recessions. While in market-based financial systems, forces of supply and demand set the price of credit "at arms' length", in bank-centric systems, credit is shaped by "face-to-face" relationships and ways of collaboration that are fundamentally driven by the type of business model adopted by banks.

Financial markets are viewed as efficient institutional alternatives to intermediaries when financial products are highly standardized, they can address the needs of a large number of customers, and they are well-enough "understood" for transactors to be comfortable in assessing their prices (Merton 1995). Focusing on transactions rather than relationships, financial markets represent an arm's-length provider of finance. Indeed, the fundamental difference between the latter and banks is similar to that between the qualitative asset transformation performed by banks and the brokerage of standardized financial contracts in anonymous financial market settings (Boot and Thakor 2000). As competition from financial mar-

---

[20] Commercial laws originate from two broad legal traditions. The first is the common law which has English origin, while the second is the civil law, which comes from Roman law. Within the civil tradition, there are only three major families that modern commercial laws originate from: French, German, and Scandinavian. Legal systems in the German and Scandinavian law traditions fall between common law and French civil law traditions in terms of the protection they offer to arm's-length investors (La Porta et al. 1998).

kets increases, banks' ex ante rents from lending diminish, which in turn decreases entry into banking and lowers interbank competition. The result, as predicated by Boot and Thakor (2000), is that the costly relationship lending will decline as well as banks.

Financial markets and intermediaries, namely, banks, are not valuable only for borrowers *per se*. Theoretical and empirical contributions have shown that the two intermediation channels may be significantly relevant to agents insofar as they concern, for example, risk management, corporate control, and information. The market-based view underlines the positive role of markets in enhancing risk management (Levine 1991),[21] information production (Holmström and Tirole 1993),[22] capital allocation by means of more effective ways to aggregate and transmit information to investors (Boot and Thakor 1997),[23] and corporate control by easing takeovers and making it easier to tie managerial compensation to firm performance (Jensen and Murphy 1990). However, the value of reducing the uncertainty of information in investment decision-making may be challenged by well-developed financial markets where, as argued by Stiglitz (1985), information is publicly revealed quickly, thus reducing the incentive for participants to acquire information on firms. Opponents of the market-based view stress that liquid markets create a myopic investor climate (Bhide 1993). In liquid markets, investors can sell their shares cheaply, so that they have fewer incentives to exert rigorous corporate control. Accordingly, greater market development may deter corporate control and economic growth (Levine 2002).

---

[21] According to Levine (1991), "stock markets arise to help agents manage liquidity and productivity risk, and, in so doing, stock markets accelerate growth. In the absence of financial markets, firm-specific productivity shocks may discourage risk-averse investors from investing in firms. Stock markets, however, allow individuals to invest in a large number of firms and diversify against idiosyncratic firm shocks. This raises the fraction of resources allocated to firms, expedites human capital accumulation, and promotes economic growth".

[22] Holmström and Tirole (1993) indicate the stock market's role in monitoring managerial performance. They show that a firm's stock price incorporates performance information that cannot be gained from the firm's current or future profit data, and that this information is useful in structuring managerial incentives.

[23] As stated by Boot and Thakor (1997), "a key attribute of the financial market, and one that delineates its role from that of a bank, is that there is valuable information feedback from the equilibrium market prices of securities to the real decisions of firms that impact those market prices. This information loop provides a propagation mechanism by which the effects of financial market trading are felt in the real sector. Bank financing does not have such an information loop. Hence, real decisions are not impacted by the information contained in bank credit contracts".

In view of these analyses, it is clear that the assessment of the role of co-operative banking in modern financial systems is a multifaceted theoretical and empirical issue. Let's start with the theoretical arguments supporting co-operative banking reported in the following pages. However, before starting this review, it is worth mentioning that the establishment up until now of CBs and, at a higher level, their networks, constitutes a form of "grouping" recognized in biology. This was and still is driven by the human capability to feel empathy or, in other words, to understand what others feel, and to adopt consequent altruistic behaviors. Citing the ethologist De Waal (2009), Birchall (2013) convincingly points out that these human abilities led Raiffeisen and Schulze-Delitzsch to establish the former credit co-operatives as "survival" devices that represent the intrinsic tendency of human beings toward groupings. For these reasons, CBs should not be retained philanthropic organizations but rather as dual bottom line institutions whose profitability, efficiency, and stability objectives are knotted with deeply rooted local and social goals (Ayadi et al. 2010).

4.1   The Mitigation of Market Imperfection and the Promotion of Financial Inclusion

As social organizations, CBs qualify as entities that originally and still now depend on their ability to create and give direction to communities (Arvidsson 2009). The basis of this power lay initially in their ability to allow people to participate in something that was more powerful than themselves and that enabled them to become financially and socially included. In fact, co-operative banking developed to overcome market failures identified in the money supply monopoly of commercial investor-owned banks. This monopoly was explained by market imperfections caused by the informational asymmetries of potential borrowers whose limited formal knowledge prevented them from accessing credit in investor-owned banks. As already pointed out, banks, and especially those local in nature like CBs, play a key role in lending to those borrowers who require substantial state verification, such as small- and medium-sized enterprises, and for this reason may find it difficult to obtain credit from larger and less regionally focused banks. Traditionally, co-operatives played a vital role in granting adequate financing to SMEs and helping them through economic downturns.

CBs may be in a better position to provide credit to low-income borrowers and businesses with little or no collateral due to two distinct motivations. First, thanks to their limited geographical scope, CBs may exploit their close proximity to borrowers, which enables them to collect more and cheaper "soft" information than can be collected by intermediaries, headquartered at a distance from borrowers' locations. Repeated interactions (in different forms) become easier at the local level, which favors co-operative behavior and mutual trust (Uzzi and Lancaster 2003).

As pointed out by Hansmann (1996), local banks, like CBs, are able to economize on the transaction costs associated with screening borrowers as well as monitoring and enforcing repayments. Hauswald and Marquez (2003) maintain that the severity of the asymmetric information problem itself increases with distance and that this affects the cost of lending. Analogously, monitoring costs rise with borrower–lender distance because of extra costs incurred by banks, that is, visiting the borrowers' premises (Degryse and Ongena 2005). Sussman and Zeira (1995) state that as banks face an increase in monitoring costs with distance, close lenders are possibly able to extract rents from borrowers because more distant competing banks take into account their own higher monitoring costs in their loan rate offers. One of the results of this strand of literature is that banks which are able to observe borrowers at close quarters may engage in spatial price discrimination.

In the case of not-for-profit banks like CBs, their proximity with borrowers, together with a substantial overlap between members and borrowers, not only alleviates informational asymmetries and their related risks, but allows these banks to adopt price discrimination strategies in favor of their members. As noted by Fonteyne and Hardy (2011), such price discrimination can be implicit and tax-efficient if CBs underprice the services offered to their member-customers and may thereby avoid several types of taxes (e.g. VAT or taxes on profits).

The efficiency of co-operative banking in minimizing the costs of managing informational asymmetries further derives from substituting the screening and monitoring role played by a bank's lending officers with peers (Ghatak 2000). Geographical closeness between co-operative members and bank borrowers allows the former to exert some forms of social control that banks cannot perform. For instance, in a tightly knit community, social sanctions on non-paying borrowers serve as a valuable alternative to formal enforcement devices (Stiglitz 1990).

The ability to collect soft information on the one hand, and exploit mechanisms that allow the reduction of the costs associated with the exposure to informational asymmetries on the other, seems to determine the competitive advantages of these banks (Oliver Wyman 2008; Ayadi et al. 2010; Fonteyne 2007) and their ability to continue to operate in markets (such as low-income areas) where information asymmetries discourage private banks (McKillop and Wilson 2011).

4.2   The Inter-temporal Risk Smoothing Effect

Inter-temporal risk smoothing implies that adjustments to shocks avoid dramatic downturns in the business cycle. Banks and markets have traditionally been viewed as having different abilities to smooth inter-temporal risk. For Allen and Gale (1997), banks retain a superior ability over capital markets as they are designed and required through regulations to accumulate capital in good times for use in bad, especially after the release and adoption of the Basel 3 regulations in 2010. As well as increasing the amount of capital that banks must hold to face risks, this new set of capital adequacy rules requires banks to build up capital conservation and countercyclical capital buffers that are naturally present in the CB business model. The emergence and the crisis of market-based banking, where banks intensively use markets for funding and contribute to their growth through the adoption of originate-to-distribute (OTD) strategies, has cast a shadow over the idea that banking is superior in terms of inter-temporal risk smoothing.

But not all banks are the same. Unlike investor-owned banks, CBs do not feel the pressure to realize profits to be distributed or to adopt a short-term view of their whole business and their customer relationships. For instance, an empirical study by Stefancic and Kathitziotis (2011) on Italian commercial and CBs during the 2006–2009 period shows that the latter were able to accumulate capital and provide credit to customers despite the ongoing crisis. Additionally, on average, CBs were able to manage their loan portfolio better than commercial banks. Findings suggest that co-operative banking in Italy should be encouraged due to its positive contribution to economic development and possibly financial stability. Groeneveld and de Vries (2009) show that European CBs were able to demonstrate their "impact presence" in financially and economically turbulent times, such as the recent financial crisis, due to their characteristics, structure, and financial solidity, which help to back their customers for longer periods. Ayadi et al. (2010) and more recently Oliver Wyman (2014) find that European CBs are naturally prone to establishing long-term relationships with their customers, mainly SMEs, non-profit institutions, and households, and that this is reinforced by their fundamental retail banking orientation and their focus on their local community. This attitude may contribute to the adoption of a more countercyclical view of these banks in lending terms.[24] According to Groeneveld (2011), co-operative banking "is not a panacea for post-crisis banking in general but should be viewed as an interesting alternative to the shareholder value banking model, or the private/commercial banking model, which has been in the spotlight much of the time in recent decades".

One of the distinctive features of co-operative banking is the role played by reserves. Their formation is naturally linked to members' disposition to renounce the cashing-in of dividends in exchange for better future resilience guaranteed by the retention of earnings. This prudent attitude is consistent with the paternalistic view of the co-operative firm, which accumulates reserves to take care of its members and stakeholders in difficult and unforeseen circumstances. Reserves are also a necessary tool to accomplish the long-term view of relationships with members, borrowers, and depositors, which characterizes co-operative banking (Birchall 2013). Reserve unlocking may become necessary in times of difficulty when customers and indeed peers may get into financial distress. However, as stated by Ayadi et al. (2010), the distinctive feature of the institutional design of co-operatives is that neither earnings pressure nor stock market pressure prevents them from performing the socially valuable function of inter-temporal risk management.

The statutory indivisibility of reserves, or in other words the impossibility of members to hold any residual claim on them to emphasize their value as a risk management strategy, serves to further accomplish this aim, removing any potential for the opportunistic usage of the reserves.

Holding reserves, as already stated, ultimately smooths the effect of economic shocks on the community served, that is, by limiting the phenomena of credit crunches and helping to preserve the independence of the co-operative. It is the prudent behavior embedded in the creation of reserves that provides competitive advantages to CBs in periods of financial stress. A sort of inter-sectoral flight to quality in periods of crisis has proved to favor this business model, enabling it to attract deposits from

---

[24]According to a survey by Oliver Wyman (2014), two-thirds of the European CBs surveyed have initiatives to help less favored client segments, including alternative repayment schemes, educating clients about personal finance and money management, and dedicating branches to restoring the financial health of customers in financial distress.

private banks during banking crises and reinforcing its capacity to provide counter-cyclical lending and inter-temporal risk smoothing. The avoidance or limited usage of originate-to-distribute (OTD) practices has facilitated their inter-temporal smoothing ability as it limits issues of adverse selection and moral hazard. Coco and Ferri (2010) show that European CBs were able to maintain higher and more stable earnings throughout the 2007 financial crisis.

4.3   Reducing Conflicts of Interest

As shareholder-oriented banks, co-operatives are subject to some potential sources of conflicts of interest with regard to the relations between members and depositors or borrowers and those between members and managers. The potential for a misalignment of interests between members or stockholders (holders of equity) and depositors (holders of debt) stems from the limited downside risk exposure of shareholders compared with their ability to capture any potential profit from the investments undertaken, over and above the remuneration contractually granted to the debtholders (i.e. depositors). CBs mitigate equity holders' incentive to leverage the banks via the debt raised from depositors by unifying these roles. As long as members and depositors are one and the same, members are not incentivized to leverage their bank and promote unsound business practices, as their own deposits may be at risk.[25] In cases such as this, where the roles coincide, borrowers are also less incentivized to default on their debtor commitments, since their insolvency can endanger that of their bank and therefore the capital invested in the co-operative shares or in bank deposits. This is especially true when loans granted by CBs are relatively small and with shorter terms (Fonteyne and Hardy 2011).[26]

---

[25] In contemporary banking, where the presence of deposit insurance has made deposits safer, it might have contributed to breaking the alignment between the interests of depositors and members in sound banking, stimulating the risk appetite of the latter. The same can be assumed with regard to the increasing reliance of modern CBs on funding (in the form of deposits and other funding instruments) from non-members.

[26] There is an inherent challenge in the way democratic membership is still realized in many CBs: traditionally and to date, co-operatives have set low levels of shareholdings in order to boost membership among the poorest and/or established limitations to individual shareholdings in order to favor diffuse membership. This can favor a member-borrower's moral hazard as the misalignment between the value of the shares held and the size of the loans obtained increases. In co-operative banking several remedies are in play to mitigate this potential conflict, including the transfer of large borrowing demands to specialized entities

Any kind of organization, whether co-operative or not, may be a victim of managerial inefficiencies resulting from potential conflicts of interest between managers and owners (Berle and Means 1932), which the theory categorizes as principal–agent problems producing so-called agency costs (Jensen and Meckling 1976; Grossman and Hart 1983). As the management runs businesses under a delegation provided by shareholders or members while not being subject to the consequences of its decisions, its behavior may be more oriented toward pursuing its own interests (increasing personal income and prestige at the expense of firm owners) rather than those of shareholders or members. The conflicts of interest stem from the separation of the functions of decision-making by managers and risk-taking by shareholders in commercial banks or members in the case of CBs. Such conflicts are amplified in circumstances where the observability and consequent discipline of managers' behaviors is limited, as it is when the ownership of a business is highly fragmented, being dispersed among many shareholders/members with generally inadequate managerial knowledge and, above all, the inability to impose full discipline on the management due to possible limitations in the voting power of owners (i.e. the "one head, one vote" principle followed by CBs).[27]

The theory predicts that the magnitude of managerial inefficiency,[28] and thus related agency costs, increases as the degree of shareholder dispersion increases. The latter is especially true in ownership structures which are purely exogenous, as is theorized in the case of co-operative banking (Gorton and Schmid 1999). The exogeneity of the ownership structure of CBs is due to two reasons. In the first instance, institutional restrictions do not generally allow for the trading of co-operative shares

---

within the co-operative groups, or to the apex institutions of the co-operative networks. In this way, the involvement of entities with superior capabilities of screening and monitoring of large borrowers helps to reduce the risk to local banks of exposure to the phenomena of adverse selection and moral hazard in lending, even to members.

[27] In this regard, Coco and Ferri (2010), speaking about the increasing role of shareholder-oriented banking from the 1980s, write, "the model of the co-operative bank—the prototype of stakeholder value banks—was depicted as archaic since, assigning value (also) to objectives different from maximising short-term profit and putting on the same par (at least in their statutes)—especially via the principle "one head one vote", irrespectively of the amount of shares actually held—the weight of each shareholder in the bank's choices, allows representing a larger set of the bank's stakeholders".

[28] The theory predicts that the expense preferences of managers increase with institutional size but that this is less pronounced in networks (Fama and Jensen 1983) as multiple levels of monitoring are at work.

which, in practice, insulate these banks from any hostile takeover. The second restriction is the impossibility of accumulating votes into blocks, because of the adoption of the democratic principle of "one head, one vote", regardless of the amount of stock owned by each member. As already stated, the absence of block shareholders is believed to prevent the effective monitoring and disciplining of managerial behaviors. Equally, Rasmussen (1988) argues that the managers of co-operatives are completely insulated from any monitoring due to the absence of block shareholders. For these reasons, co-operative banking is often regarded as a weak business model, a victim of its own democratic distinctive governance (Ayadi et al. 2010). The limitations of the co-operative banking business model in terms of disciplinary power also seem to emerge in relation to managerial turnover. In an empirical study on management turnover in Italian banks using the survival analysis method, Stefancic (2012) tests whether top managers in non-commercial banks are more likely to stay on in their managerial position, "surviving" longer than top managers in commercial banks (over the period 1993–2003). The results confirm that there is a direct correlation between the juridical form of banks and management turnover, with CB managers tending to survive longer than their counterparts in commercial banks, even when bank performance is below average. This result seems to provide evidence of the limited monitoring ability embedded in stakeholder-oriented banks.

As shown in the following pages, empirical results are far from conclusive on the effects of limited control issues and related agency costs caused by the high fragmentation of ownership in co-operative banking. Additionally, it is worth mentioning that this issue of fragmentation is not just a problem for co-operative banking *per se* but for any organization whose ownership is held by many small and potentially unsophisticated shareholders. The capacity of the CB business model, in various and evolving forms, to survive and flourish seems to testify that the supposed weaknesses of its ownership structure are a source of concern but are not the most important: co-operative banking exhibits compelling features in reducing conflicts of interest arising from its governance that seem to outweigh its apparent weaknesses. Co-operative banking possesses intrinsically different ways to resolve management-member conflicts.

It may be argued that the original unlimited liability of members which characterized early CBs acted as a powerful monitoring mechanism on the behavior of bank management but this was soon abandoned as it deters membership and can be replaced with other powerful devices, such as internal and external auditing, the introduction of outside board directors who may exercise a check on management in non-profit firms (Fama and Jensen 1983), and the creation of supervisory boards.

In the first instance, as in co-operative banking, there is, at least in theory, a significant overlap between the roles of members, depositors, and borrowers. This implies an extensive risk-sharing among the bank stakeholders which favors a more careful monitoring by members of management behaviors whenever these may hinder the maximization of members' total returns[29] (Fonteyne and Hardy 2011). This is especially true in the following circumstances: where there is benefit to the member-customer, for example, in cases where lending rate mark-downs and deposit rate mark-ups are tightly linked to the bank's profitability and efficiency; in the case of non-negligible shareholdings held by members which motivate them to monitor the bank management more carefully; or when members are actively involved in the management of the bank and are properly educated to perform their monitoring role.

In principle, CBs already have governance mechanisms to align the interests of members and management, which, in some ways, act as threats of partial takeover or liquidation (Fama and Jensen 1983) of the bank business: the ability of the members to ask for the redemption, on demand, of their shares, thus depriving the management at any given moment of control over assets. Despite statutory or legislative limitations on the redemption of members' shares for reasons of bank stability, such a device is widely present in co-operative banking and may effectively work as a deterrent against management opportunism (Ayadi et al. 2010). Additionally, members of CBs can exercise the option of exit at the nominal value invested, at minimum, thus being protected from the risk of downward losses. In a sense, the power of the members to ask for the redemption of their shares is a more powerful discipline mechanism on

---

[29] Members' total return includes the explicit remuneration of capital, where adopted, the return on savings, and the so-called consumer surplus which results from the difference between the price he/she is willing to pay and the price actually paid (Fonteyne and Hardy 2011). Surpluses in co-operative banking can be explained as differences in lending rates paid by members-borrowers versus market rates, in price differentials enjoyed in other financial services provided by CBs (i.e. payments, asset management, etc.), or, *ceteris paribus*, in more remunerative deposits than those collected by commercial banks.

managers than the sale of equity stakes in investor-owned banks. The latter does not directly alter the total resources of the bank as the former does.[30]

CBs and other customer-owned banks may additionally rely on networks and shared wholesale activities for discipline, for example, local bank managers (Butzbach and Mettenheim 2012). In this regard, the system of auditing entities created by the German and Austrian CBs at the regional level and coordinated nationally represents a prime example. Additionally, co-operatives can diminish managers' opportunistic use of bank free cashflows through dividends or compulsory contributions to mutual guarantee funds (Fonteyne 2007) as well as reduce agency conflicts that may arise from input procurements at network level (Desrochers 2005).

4.4   Developing of Competitive Skills

Theoretical modeling on the effects of financial market growth tends to underline that banks will lose their importance. For instance, Boot and Thakor (1997) affirm that "unless the actions of banks are coordinated … it is unlikely that financial market growth can be retarded. Thus, it is possible that a critical factor in the development of the financial market is the fragmentation of the banking industry, which in turn may depend on the number of banks in the industry". In other words, the fragmentation of the banking sector and the consequent difficulties in coordination would favor financial market growth. For which kinds of banks is this true? While investor-owned banks might find it difficult to co-operate, as hypothesized by Boot and Thakor (1997), given their competitive nature determined by their for-profit orientation, there are some banking organizations which have built their *raison d'être* around the idea of co-operation and have

---

[30] This disciplinary effect may, however, be mitigated by the concomitant intervention of two main aspects. On the one hand, by the superior need to preserve bank stability through limiting redemptions of shares which can hurt its financial stability (as stated by bank capital regulation and bank by-laws), and, on the other hand, by the slow speed with which the redemption may take place according to the provisions of by-laws and bank regulations.

A further solution comes from the creation of governance structures founded on the presence of powerful supervisory boards, truly enabled to monitor and intervene in management conduct. In the major European co-operative banking groups, there are, along with executive boards, supervisory boards which are responsible for protecting the co-operative vocation of banks and containing any phenomena of opportunism and moral hazard on the part of management.

developed successfully thanks to their abilities to create networks of co-operatives. The creation of these was not aimed, in the first instance, at making CBs more competitive; for them networking was written into their DNA and represented nothing short of a remedy to preserve their independence and their principles and values. Through the development of two- and three-tiered structures, independent CBs overcame the weaknesses arising from their small size. Shared central entities offering centralized liquidity and asset management, wholesale divisions, and the creation and/ or acquisition of specialized financial intermediaries allow them to reap economies of scale and benefit from a more diversified banking offer, thus making local banks more competitive and fostering retail and relationship banking. The creation of coordinated networks within joint liability and/or mutual guarantee agreements safeguards against volatile returns (Boot 2000; Degryse and Van Cayseele 2000). Integration makes CBs an interest group, bringing several additional benefits to the competitive skills of CBs, encompassing political influence, greater visibility as a group of banks dedicated to local communities, and coordinated business and communication strategies (Birchall 2013). The creation of central institutions may also contribute to a reduction in the risks for local banks serving homogeneous customer bases. They help to stabilize the profitability of the co-operative group as a whole by expanding and diversifying the lending business. Depending on the type of integration at the national level, the apex body (the national federation and/or the apex intermediary) may assume supervisory powers over the local banks, represent them vis-à-vis the supervisory authorities, and provide consultancy and training activities to improve the managerial quality of the local banks. Undeniably, the formation of federations and groups with central institutions exposes new types of agency problems in the relationship between the center and the periphery. For instance, local banks have been asked to bear the losses of the central institutions which arose during the recent financial crisis relating to businesses not traditionally supported by CBs. Local banks lose their autonomy due to compliance with a common set of managerial standards defined by the central body and may feel unable to monitor their top institution. As stated by Ayadi et al. (2010), central institutions of highly integrated networks have stronger incentives than local banks to safeguard common resources, such as the common brand, the pooled reserve fund, and their political influence.

Undoubtedly, the historical restriction on intra-sector competition, that is, aimed at avoiding competition at the local level among contiguous CBs, has acted as a powerful device to preserve opportunistic forms of "cannibalism" which could alter the spirit of co-operation between the members of the networks. Hence, co-operation between these kinds of banks is a strategy that is super-imposed on the interests of individual members, guaranteeing the competitiveness of the whole group in dynamic environments.

4.5   Economic and Social Engagement

Biologists have already widely recognized that the popular idea of the theory of evolution, dominated by the struggle for survival and for individual affirmation, does not fully recognize all the mechanisms that are present in nature. The scenario of extreme competition among individual entities stands in stark contrast to the widespread forms of co-operative behaviors existing in nature, in particular to those deemed altruistic, where individuals work for the good of the community. In fact, in order to understand the evolution of co-operation and its embedded value of altruism, we must abandon the simplistic view of natural selection that identifies it with the individual struggle for survival, and instead consider the subtler mechanisms through which existence is guaranteed.

The invention of customer-owned banks, working as production and consumption FCs, has historically minimized market imperfection, enabling the formation of social organizations that are indeed driven by a paradoxical combination of community-oriented sharing and the rational and reflexive pursuit of the self-interest of members to improve their economic and social conditions within and on behalf of a community. Unlike investor-owned banks, co-operatives were created and still act to foster local economic growth, providing accessible financial services in disadvantaged areas and reinvesting their capital in the communities where it was generated. As stated by Gutknecht (2008), since CBs "give their surplus revenue back to their members, they keep wealth in their communities. Stock companies do the reverse. By distributing profits to shareholders, they take capital out of the community".

Minsky (1993) in his theoretical support for community banks observes that the emergence of large banks drives small- and medium-sized businesses and marginal communities away from financial services because big banks love big business. Long before the 2007 financial crisis, he embraced the idea of a financial system on a human scale that is deeply rooted in its local territory and aims to stimulate local economic activities and pursue social equity and cohesion in the local community (De Antoni 2013), as was the original mission of CBs.[31] The literature has identified different channels through which the presence of local banks, that is, CBs, has contributed to local growth. For instance, Ayadi et al. (2010) show that co-operative presence in some European countries has had a significant impact on regional growth (measured in GDP growth terms), despite some variations between countries. Gagliardi (2009) reports in an empirical study on the creation of new businesses in Italy that a less concentrated banking system, as exists in many Italian provinces where many small CBs are located, strengthens the activities of co-operative entities. Kalmi (2013) tests whether the co-operative formation rates are higher in depressed economic conditions in Finland. His results indicate that co-operatives, both financial and non-financial, play a useful role in reducing unemployment and that the formation of co-operatives is positively influenced by the existence of dedicated advisory services, such as those provided by local CBs.

The clear focus on the community and its growth renders CBs different from shareholder-oriented banks in terms of social engagement through donations. According to Oliver Wyman's report (2014), on average CBs donate three times more to social action than their shareholder-owned counterparts (respectively 0.47% vs. 0.12% as a share of revenues in 2012). There is a difference between the two business models not just in terms of quantity but also in terms of targets: co-operatives tend to support many small local social projects, such as schools, hospitals, or sports and cultural clubs. By contrast, shareholder-owned banks tend to finance a limited number of national or even sometimes international initiatives.

5   Empirical Evidence on Co-operative Banking: Performance and Contribution to Financial Stability

The European banking system is characterized by a substantial degree of diversity in its business models. CBs are particularly prominent in Austria, France, the Netherlands, Italy, and Finland, as well as in Germany, as we

---

[31] Indeed, the kind of community bank supported by Minsky (1993) was a profit-seeking community development bank, thus apparently different from a co-operative bank. However, as stated by De Antoni (2013), in Minsky's view profit maximization had to be considered just as an instrument rather than as a target. His community banks shared all the remaining aims of CBs and are part of that alternative financial system which in grounded in a *shared-prosperity capitalism* (Minsky and Whalen 1996).

will show in the following chapters. Since the 1980s and over recent decades, the liberalization and deregulation of European banking systems have encouraged, among other things, restructurings which have brought about the emergence of large-scale national and pan-European banks with a marked shareholder orientation. CBs have also been part of these rearrangements through a pervasive process of intra-category consolidation and the formation of large integrated co-operative banking groups with various degrees of hybridization (i.e. with specialized joint-stock subsidiaries and/or apex institutions and, in some cases, listed companies). This trend has led some scholars (Jaeger et al. 2016) to affirm that co-operative banking groups are, to some extent, converging toward the conventional and dominant (joint-stock) model in the banking sector. This, in turn, will lead to a decrease in banking diversity which is believed to be necessary for the economy as a whole.[32] This is due to a number of different reasons.

From an evolutionary standpoint, Birchall (2013) remembers that diversity is important for society, enabling it to respond to uncertain future changes, and points out that "if we see the global economy as a kind of evolutionary, adaptive system then we can expect one type of business to thrive at the expense of another. However, if one type dies out completely then the stock of existing solutions will have declined". Banking diversity can be appreciated in portfolio theory terms. If we look at the banking system of a country or a larger geographical area (e.g. a continent) as a portfolio of different business models, we may retain that, *ceteris paribus*, the greater the diversification, the lower the risk of the banking and financial systems and the stronger the inter-temporal risk smoothing effect due to diversity. Different bank business models (private, co-operative, savings, etc.) are also important as they represent alternative solutions to the problem of producing a set of collective outcomes (Freeman and Hannan 1989).

Diversity in banking is in fact relevant for the promotion of a diverse kind of capitalism, one in which there is a shared prosperity (Minsky and Whalen 1996). CBs have traditionally focused on retail services: providing savings products and credit lending to consumers and SMEs, segments which are more neglected by large shareholder-oriented banks.

---

[32] According to the Likanen Report (2012), while many not-for-profit banks have undeniably expanded their activities over time and become almost indistinguishable from their commercial bank competitors, co-operative and savings banks have also preserved their focus on local retail business.

Additionally, they do not discriminate against marginal customers and the areas which traditionally motivated their existence and adopt a long-term view of the banking relationship due mainly to their not-for-profit nature. Diversity is also significant as it represents an institutional heritage that governs or facilitates the coordination of relationships between individuals or groups, under common sets of formal (laws, contracts, political systems, etc.) and informal (norms, traditions, value systems, religions, etc.) rules. This is particularly true in Europe, which, as a political and economic project, aims to preserve all kinds of diversity.

Ultimately, the theoretical and empirical arguments supporting one specific form of banking model (the joint-stock bank) are far from conclusive. Therefore, further investigations are necessary to have a better view of which, if any, may be the superior business model in the long run, the one best able to adapt to economic and social changes.

In the next pages, we therefore examine the most relevant empirical evidence on the performances and contribution of CBs, viewed as organizations that may favor diversity and all its consequent outcomes. In particular, we will focus on the empirical literature which considers the relevance of different business models for stability, competition, efficiency, and growth.

5.1   Co-operative Banking and Financial Stability

According to empirical evidence, CBs have generally lower incentives to adopt risk-taking activities and this makes them, and the systems in which they operate, more financially stable. For instance, Rajan (1992) maintains that the lack of profit maximization targets and the absence of many factors that lead rational managers in joint-stock banks to assume short-term horizons discourage CBs from taking on risk. Hansmann (1996) shows that during the US savings and loans crisis, investor-owned savings and loans associations fared much worse than mutual savings and loans associations because the former tended to pursue more speculative investment policies. Chaddad and Cook (2004) also find that de-mutualized financial institutions follow riskier strategies. In France and Switzerland, CBs performed better than commercial banks during the banking difficulties of the early 1990s. Iannotta et al. (2007) highlight that the better loan quality and lower asset risk of CBs was a source of stability in 15 European countries during the period 1999–2004.

Hesse and Čihák (2007) compare the stability of co-operative, savings, and commercial banks in 29 major advanced economies over the period 1994–2004 and provide evidence that savings banks and CBs are more stable than commercial banks. They also specify that the higher stability of CBs is due to the much lower volatility of their returns, which more than offsets their relatively lower profitability. Garcia-Marco and Robles-Fernández (2008), Beck et al. (2009, 2010), Groeneveld and de Vries (2009), and Liu et al. (2013) provide further evidence that stakeholder-oriented banks appear to be safer than their commercial counterparts. Garcia-Marco and Robles-Fernández (2008) reveal major differences in the risk-taking patterns of Spanish commercial and savings banks during 1993–2000: commercial banks are more risk-inclined than savings banks while small institutions appear to assume lower risks. Beck et al. (2009) report that in Germany private banks are less stable than savings banks or CBs, using three different measures of bank stability: the Z-score (distance from insolvency), the proportion of non-performing loans, and distress probabilities. Groeneveld and de Vries (2009) suggest that European co-operatives tend to be more stable than commercial banks due to their lower volatility of returns and involvement in less risky activities.

Groeneveld and Sjauw-Koen-Fa (2009), Llewellyn (2009), Ayadi et al. (2010), Stefancic (2012), Groeneveld (2011), and Stefancic and Kathitziotis (2011), although using different datasets, time periods, and countries, argue that CBs promote the stability of national banking systems by contributing to the diversity of business models and ownership structures adopted by bank intermediaries. Ayadi et al. (2012) finds that retail-oriented banks have generally outperformed their peers in terms of cost efficiency and performance measures. Wholesale banks and to a lesser extent investment banks have suffered substantial trading losses amidst the crisis, which has contributed to their less stable performances. As regards risks, the study advocates that the retail-oriented models appear to be safer than others, as measured by the distance to default (Z-score) and the long-term liquidity risks (net stable funding ratio). Chiaramonte et al. (2015) show that the role of CBs in a sample of OECD countries varies considerably over time and according to their market share. They show that co-operatives exert a stabilizing effect during the crisis years, subject to them exceeding a certain market share threshold. Moreover, their results indicate that a greater presence of co-operative banking exerts a positive and increasing influence on the stability of large banks in the same banking system, but only during the financial crisis. They suppose that banking instability phenomena may be lesser and spread more slowly in more mutualized banking systems, since the interconnections between large commercial banks and CBs are certainly weaker than those between large commercial banks (due to the latter's extensive involvement in wholesale funding, and derivatives). Köhler (2015) finds that CBs may become significantly sounder through the benefits of income diversification and that retail-oriented credit institutions become less stable if they increase their share of non-deposit funding. Ferri et al. (2015) investigate the loan quality of a sample of European banks over the period 1996–2011 and report that stakeholder banks had better loan quality during the pre-crisis (1996–2007) and crisis period (2008–2011), and that this relative advantage is strengthened during the crisis.

Becchetti et al. (2016) analyze different ownership models in a sample of 32 banking systems over the period 1998–2010. According to their results, CBs exhibit a significantly lower earnings volatility, which contributes to higher end of period net loans/total assets ratios. They argue that the inter-temporal risk of CBs (especially during a turbulent period including the years of the financial crisis) contributes to their higher levels of net loans/total assets ratios. However, an interesting finding is that the difference in terms of loan intensity between co-operative and non-CBs does not increase (and in fact contracts a little) during the global financial crisis (GFC) and slowly converges in the overall sample period.

Jaeger et al. (2016) compare the resilience of a sample of co-operative and joint-stock peer banking groups in certain European countries and Canada before and after the global financial crisis. Interestingly, they categorize co-operative groups according to their degree of hybridization and report that CBs were better able to face the financial crisis but that their degree of resistance to the crisis depended on their features. More specifically, highly hybrid co-operative groups exhibited a degree of financial stability (proxied by the Z-score) no different to that of joint-stock groups. Mid-hybrid groups were the most able to face the financial crisis, while low-hybrid groups were weakened during the financial crisis.

Groeneveld (2017) argues that the global financial crisis has demonstrated that banks operating with less equity were more likely to fail or to be in need of state support. Since then, regulatory requirements have become stricter to prevent a recurrence of such a crisis. The reforms raised the regulatory capital base and enhanced the risk coverage of the capital framework. At a European level, CBs were better capitalized than their conventional competitors both before and after the financial crisis, and this is one of the reasons for their resilience to it. In this regard, also Fiordelisi and Mare (2013) showed that capital is a key determinant of CBs' soundness.

Maroua (2015) empirically addresses CBs' financial stability (proxied by the Z-score) and introduces explanatory variables at the bank level: the governance ratio (number of members over total customers) and the number of members. The author employs a panel group of CBs in 12 countries, both within and outside the European Union, namely, France, Greece, Bulgaria, Germany, Denmark, Luxembourg, Portugal, Poland, Cyprus, the Netherlands, Australia, and Finland over the period from 2004 to 2011. He reports that the governance of CBs has a significant influence on its performance, while the membership variable has a negative impact on individual CB's financial stability. The author explains the latter result by the increasing level of information asymmetry and the conflicts of interest between a large number of members.

Among the voices contrasting with the above findings, Goodhart (2004) suggests that financial crises may be more likely in countries with higher proportions of state-owned banks and other non-profit-maximizing banking entities, since they may reduce interest margins in traditional banking and push private sector banks toward engaging in riskier activities. Brunner et al. (2004) note that the Swedish co-operative banking sector did not survive the crisis of the early 1990s in a co-operative form, since it faced high marginal costs of capital and the need to restore capital was a major factor in its decision to de-mutualize. Far from contributing to the stability of financial systems, CBs would be causes of instability according to Fonteyne (2007) because of their higher vulnerability to shocks in credit quality and interest rates. The reason behind this vulnerability lies in their strong focus on traditional financial intermediation, which renders them more exposed to credit and interest rate risk. In this regard, a recent empirical analysis undertaken by Milani (2017) finds that a higher incidence of community banks in Italian local markets increases overdue loans, in the middle of a very deep economic and financial crisis. The author interprets this outcome as the consequence of local banks' general lower efficiency in loan underwriting procedures, mainly due to their closer relationships with borrowers living in small towns, where the competition from medium–large banks is lower. Whether competition can act as a stimulus to improving CBs' selection processes is still an empirically open question. Of course, it cannot be forgotten that historically and even today CBs pursue the financial and economic inclusion of sections of the population which are otherwise excluded. And in preparing for the potential risks that might arise, CBs develop and adopt solutions that would not naturally be contemplated by commercial banks, such as the provision to reserve a large proportion of their profits and the creation of intra-sectoral solidarity. In this regard, Meriläinen (2017) has investigated the discretionary cyclical component of loan loss provisions (LLPs) and the timeliness of LLPs in a sample of Western European banks over the 2004–2015 period, taking into account different banking business models. The results show that LLPs have an unexplained component that decreases during economic booms and increases during recessions, thus amplifying the volatility of returns. This could be caused by factors such as exaggerated loan losses, over-optimism, or other subjective reasons. This amplifies the cyclical pattern of LLPs. The outcomes of the estimates suggest that CBs' LLPs have a much smaller cyclical component than those of the other ownership types. Olszak et al. (2017) also report similar empirical results. Stakeholder-oriented banks are found to recognize larger and timelier LLPs than shareholder banks, possibly as a result of lower pressures on the profits of the former banks. As Beatty and Liao in an earlier study (2011) found loan loss recognition to be positively related to lending dynamics in recessionary times, this could provide empirical support to the results of Ferri et al. (2014) and Meriläinen (2016) who observed that lending in the EU by stakeholder banks, especially CBs, is less cyclical than that of commercial banks. Therefore, a larger proportion of CBs in the banking systems could help to smooth the financial instability caused by lending cyclicality.

Overall, the empirical findings suggest that CBs, as a whole, stabilize the financial system, even following the outbreak of the 2007 financial crisis. During 2008–2009, the co-operative sector helped to maintain the stability of the financial system by continuing to provide financial services to both retail and business clients, even reducing the cost (Akinsoyinu 2017). This should not be surprising as it is in their DNA.[33] However,

---

[33] For instance, Behr et al. (2017) investigate whether the cyclical nature of lending to SMEs is dependent on government involvement in banking. To this aim, they investigate a sample of German savings banks, which have a public mandate, and CBs, which have no public mandate, over the period 1987–2007. The authors find that SME lending by savings banks is on average 25% less sensitive to GDP growth than that of CBs from the same area. The effect is found to be statistically highly significant. They claim that this result is relevant for regulatory purposes (i.e. prudential regulation) as well as for the definition of the optimal

their degree of hybridization matters. This finding deserves further empirical analysis to understand whether the relaxation of some differences between conventional and co-operative banking groups aligns their contribution to the stability of financial systems, thus depriving them of the beneficial role of ownership diversity in banking.

5.2   Co-operative Banking and Efficiency

Efficiency represents an essential condition for the survival of any kind of business model, whether profit or non-profit oriented. As CBs do not have strong incentives to translate their profits directly to shareholders but rather to maximize the surplus to member-customers, the conventional view tends to label them as low efficient businesses. Additionally, CBs and their management are viewed as insulated from capital markets since the management seems freer to pursue its own agenda and has fewer incentives to be efficient (Altunbas et al. 2001). The latter authors investigate scale economies, inefficiencies, and technical progress in a sample of private, mutual, and publicly owned banks in the German market over the period 1989–1996 and find little evidence to suggest that privately owned banks are more efficient than their mutual and public-sector counterparts. This finding is attributed to the slight cost and profit advantages enjoyed by non-private banks over their private counterparts, due to their lower cost of funds. While Altunbas et al. (2001) conclude that no agency problems were identified for non-private banks operating in the German banking market, two further studies, almost contemporaneous, investigate the operational efficiency of CBs, taking into account membership as a measure of ownership dispersion and control over bank management.

Gorton and Schmid (1999) report from a sample of Austrian CBs over the period 1987–1990 that their performance (proxied by the return on assets, ROA) declines as the number of members increases, and that mean wages rise as membership becomes more diffuse. Similar results are found by Leggett and Strand (2002). By contrast, Jones and Kalmi (2015) in a more recent study on a sample of Finnish CBs over the years 2001–2005

local banking structure. Other considerations aside, the greater prudence of CBs over a long and relatively tranquil period may have enabled them to continue to sustain the economy, without facing the severe financial difficulties which the German system of savings banks experienced in the aftermath of the global financial crisis (GFC). As stated by Behr and Schmidt (2015), "being less involved in structured finance and capital markets products than the savings banks, the CBs survived the financial crisis better than any other banking group".

find that increases in membership ratios are associated with better bank performance, which is linked with faster growth rates in membership than in the rise of customers.[34] Iannotta et al. (2007) employ a number of profitability and cost-efficiency measures (return on assets and the ratio of costs to assets) to compare the performances and risk characteristics of European banks with more than € 10 billion of assets in 15 European countries from 1999 to 2004. Their results indicate that the profitability of banks with more dispersed ownership is not significantly different to that of more concentrated banks. An additional empirical contribution from Iannotta et al. (2007) is the similarity found between mutual and private banks in terms of higher loan quality and lower operating costs. The resulting lower profitability of mutual banks is explained as a consequence of a smaller average size and different kind of asset mix, as these banks are typically involved in more traditional financial intermediation activities than large private banks.

Girardone et al. (2009) compare efficiency levels for a large sample of commercial, savings, and co-operative banking institutions operating in the EU-15 over the period 1998–2003. Their results reject the agency theory hypothesis that managers of privately owned banks are more cost-efficient than those of mutual banking institutions because of capital market devices as it is found that mutual banks operating in the EU-15 countries are significantly more cost-efficient than commercial banks.

In the empirical study of Ayadi et al. (2010) on European CBs during the years 2000–2008, customer-owned banks turn out to be slightly less profitable (in terms of ROA and return on equity [ROE]), with the exception of Germany, Spain, and Finland. In relation to cost efficiency (proxied by cost-to-income ratio), the differences between co-operatives and other banks are mixed. Co-operatives seem to enjoy significant cost benefits in Finland, France, Italy, and Spain, while scoring lower in Austria, Germany, and the Netherlands.

---

[34] In a Japanese empirical study on the effect of governance-related variables on firm performance across stock and CBs (Shinkin banks) over the period 2009–2013, Yamori et al. (2017) find that having a large number of board members has a negative effect on efficiency measures (obtained from stochastic frontier analysis) for both stock and CBs. On the other hand, the presence of outside directors exerts a significant effect on the efficiency of the individual CBs. These results suggest that outside directors' discipline is more necessary for CBs than for stock banks, which are under extreme pressure from shareholders. Additionally, the authors show that a high ratio of representative council members in CBs, which is the most important decision-making body for Shinkin banks, has negative effects on efficiency measures.

Considering only France, Ory and Lemzeri (2012) examine whether all French co-operative banking groups have suffered in a similar way during the crisis, or whether different organizational and strategic features or choices may explain different levels of resilience to the financial turmoil. First, the authors compare the efficiency of the French co-operative networks (comprising the individual primary banks) and groups (on a consolidated basis, considering all the entities) relative to each other and then compare them with the efficiency of plc banks, during the period 1995–2007. The tests performed show that personal expenses/total assets are significantly lower in the co-operative groups than in the CBs; this seems to confirm the incentive to control costs and improve productivity in organizational schemes where the shareholder value approach coexists with the co-operative model. Globally speaking, although the operational efficiency of the French co-operative groups is not weak compared to that of French plc banking groups, it remains lower than those of the European joint-stock banks. According to the authors, the emergence of the financial crisis has highlighted that the hybridization of the original co-operative model was not neutral, and the impact of the crisis has spread from investment banking activities and subsidiaries held by the co-operative networks to impact on all the stakeholders within the groups.

Focusing on a large sample of Italian CBs between 1997 and 2009, Fiordelisi and Mare (2013) show that more efficient banks (efficient either in terms of cost saving or in terms of revenue maximization) have a higher probability of survival. They also find that the joint consideration of a bank's managerial ability to minimize costs and maximize revenues increases the bank's survival time. Aiello and Bonanno (2016) evaluate the impact of local market conditions on small Italian mutual co-operative banks' efficiency over the period 2006–2011. The estimation of efficiency is made through stochastic frontiers and is the explained variable, while individual and environmental factors are the explanatory variables. Results show that CBs have performed better than other banks in the present crisis, although efficiency has decreased over time. CBs' efficiency is found to increase with market concentration and demand density, and decline with a rise in the number of bank branches in local markets. Local development negatively affects cost efficiency, while BCCs generate more profits with more diversified assets.

Ferri et al. (2015) analyze the role of ownership structures in European banking before and after the crisis, using the time span 1996–2011 to provide clear results for banking in "normal times" and search for possible performance changes during the crisis. They first distinguish between shareholder value and stakeholder value in banking and then, seeking to unveil the heterogeneity within these two types of bank groups, they divide stakeholder banks into four subcategories: tightly integrated co-operative banks, loosely integrated co-operative banks, public savings banks, and private savings banks. The authors find that shareholder banks have better profitability than stakeholder banks on average, but that this advantage disappears during the crisis period. Cost efficiency is rather similar for both types of business models, except for tightly integrated co-operative banks and public savings banks: these are more cost efficient than general shareholder banks during the crisis time, although the statistical significance is relatively weak.

Over the period 2011–2015, the profitability of European CBs had on average outperformed all other banks in terms of return on equity (ROE) (Groeneveld 2017). The ROE of CBs was also more stable over a longer time period due to their higher involvement in retail banking. In 2015, the average ROE of both clusters of banks was 6%. As regards cost efficiency, measured by the cost-to-income ratio, co-operative banking groups had significantly higher ratios only in 2011. In 2012 and 2013, the ratios were not statistically different. In 2014, CBs posted significantly more efficient results, while in 2015, the ratios were identical again with a value of around 61%.

To conclude, the empirical literature on the profitability and cost efficiency of European CBs does not seem to support a clear weakness of these banks compared to conventional ones. Their underperformance in some circumstances, besides being caused by their main focus on less profitable businesses such as retail banking, should also be contrasted with some other determinants. For instance, Bossler and Schild (2016) examine the employment structure of CBs from 2003 to 2010 and find that CBs in comparison with otherwise similar private and savings banks are characterized by more stable employment, an older workforce, more extensive training activities, and a more homogeneous composition of employees. The authors claim that their results are in line with the hypothesis of CBs as internally homogeneous organizations closely tied to local society and culture. Yet, to our knowledge, homogeneity and an aging workforce may lead to lower cost efficiency. The authors' findings are interesting as they open up other ways of looking at the determinants of the local CBs' performances.

However, some findings lead us to think that the increasing similarity, especially between large institutions, despite the different ownership models, exposes them to the same problems at the same time, thus complicating the policy response (Brunnermeier et al. 2009; Llewellyn 2009; Goodhart and Wagner 2012). Real diversity suggests that diverse institutional forms, and different business models and earnings models coexist, being strong enough to compete effectively with each other (Llewellyn 2009).

5.3   Co-operative Banking and Competition

Another empirical area of analysis relates to the role that competition exerts on CBs' performances measured in terms of banking activity (lending, deposit taking, etc.), prices on loans and deposits, or as forms of rents. The theoretical literature has suggested that competition produces different effects. According to the competition-fragility view, monopoly rents gained by banks in less competitive markets discourage excessive risk-taking and enhance a bank's ability to bear supply/demand shocks (Allen and Gale 2004; Carletti 2008). According to this view, competitive markets limit the ability of banks to gain informational advantages from their relationships with borrowers, reducing their incentives to properly screen borrowers, thus increasing the risk of fragility (Beck et al. 2013). For instance, Weill (2013) shows that bank competition (measured in different ways) did not increase during the 2000s in European banking markets. He also clearly supports the view of a convergence in bank competition across European countries. Similar results are found by Apergis et al. (2016) over the period 1996–2011.

The alternative view, the competition-stability view (Boyd and De Nicolò 2005), maintains that more competitive banking systems result in more, rather than less, stability. If competition reduces the cost of financing, bank borrowers are better able to repay their loan obligations, thus reducing the risk to bank stability due to credit risks. By contrast, in more concentrated markets, incumbent banks exert their market power by setting high interest rates on lending, driving borrowers to finance only high-risk projects and ultimately undermining their ability to repay loans, thereby negatively affecting bank stability. Less competitive markets also represent breeding grounds where too large, complex, and highly interconnected banks have better access to subsidies from national safety nets and pursue excessive risk-taking activities consistent with morally hazardous behavior (Chiaramonte et al. 2015).

Additionally, when CBs hold large market shares, especially at the local level, and put in place transactions based on tied relationships, as is the case in some European countries, they may exploit a certain degree of monopoly power in recurring transactions with local customers which may lock customers into relationships at non-competitive interest rates.

As far as the measurement of bank competition involving CBs is concerned, empirical studies are few and limited to the single country level, mainly due to the intensity of local banking data needed. Structural and non-structural models have been employed: the former typically uses the Herfindahl-Hirschman Index, while the latter utilizes measures such as the Panzar-Rosse H-statistic, the Lerner Index, and the Boone Indicator. Hempell (2002) uses the Panzar-Rosse model and finds that in the case of Germany, private banks (excluding large banks) seem to operate more competitively than co-operative and savings banks (excluding their head institutions), and that savings banks appear to have behaved more competitively than CBs over the period 1993–1998. The author contends that regional demarcation for co-operative and savings banks might be responsible for these findings in comparison with private banks as this—at least theoretically—prevents co-operative and savings banks from competing with other banks pertaining to the same group in regional markets. A similar study by Gutiérrez (2008) on the Italian banking system from 2000 to 2006 shows that Italian co-operatives enjoy a greater degree of market power than their commercial peers. By contrast, Lopez and Di Colli (2013) use structural and non-structural measures of competition over the period 1995–2004 and show that the market power of CBs is not greater than that of the conventional banks.

There is an interesting area of empirical investigation in the measurement of switching costs in different bank business models and the relationship between these costs and bank competition. Switching costs are incurred by customers when they change suppliers (relating to time, effort, and money). These costs may arise where repeated purchases are made from a single supplier or may be associated with informational costs. As bank lending is informationally intensive, switching from one bank to another may expose borrowers to unfavorable lending conditions because the new bank is more exposed to adverse selection than their existing one. Possible divergences in switching costs between CBs and commercial banks can explain differences in the market power of banks between banks and countries. Egarius and Weill (2016) propose a means of measuring switching costs in banking derived from Shy (2002). The authors report that switching costs exert a positive influence on the market power of European banks. Additionally, they report that CBs have lower switching costs than commercial banks and suggest that this result may be due to the fact that, as CBs are owned by their clients, their managers have lower incentives to implement switching costs. They conclude that CBs represent a significant business model in limiting switching costs and favoring consumers' welfare.

In terms of the implications for CBs' market power, there are several strands of empirical literature at the European level. Fiordelisi and Mare (2014) analyze the nexus competition (measured by the Lerner Index) and financial stability of a large sample of CBs in the EU between 1998 and 2009, obtaining three main results. They show the existence of a positive relationship (both in the short and long terms) between competition and stability, in line with the competition-stability view proposed by Boyd and De Nicolò (2005). This result still holds in the wake of the 2007 financial crisis. They also find a statistically significant relationship between the herding measure[35] and bank stability and, contrary to the view supporting diversity in banking, they state that the level of industry homogeneity has a positive influence on CBs' stability. Chiaramonte et al. (2015), using an OECD sample of commercial banks, CBs, and savings banks over the period 2001–2010, show that the growing market power of CBs is beneficial to single banks' financial stability, especially during a crisis period and in Europe. They find evidence of a U-shaped relationship between CBs' market shares and bank stability.

Using a single sample of CBs over the period 2006 to 2014, Clark et al. (2018) estimate the relationship between market power and stability and demonstrate that market power increases individual bank stability, but that the relationship is non-linear. The authors analyze the market for loans and deposits separately and find that most of the individual bank stability derives from market power in the loan market. There is no conclusive evidence for market power in the deposit market. Furthermore, they indicate that there is a positive relationship between CBs' solvency and the degree of diversification in both assets and liabilities.

---

[35] This is a measure of banking industry heterogeneity computed, as in Beck et al. (2013), as the within-country standard deviation of the percentage non-interest income (with respect to total assets) per year and per country. The higher the value of this indicator, the lower the herding behavior in the co-operative banking sector.

A further area of study is the effect of CB competition on their traditional business. Barbetta et al. (2016) focus on the banking market of the Italian province of Trento between 2000 and 2009, which is characterized by a significant presence of CBs and contains a variety of different local competitive environments. The authors introduce three groups of CBs: a group composed only of the mutual banks competing among themselves, a group formed by the mutual banks competing both with each other and with non-mutual banks, and a group including all the mutual banks that compete only with non-mutual banks. They find that the mutual banks competing only with non-mutual banks are better able than the latter to transform savings into loans at the local level (i.e. indicating a higher local effectiveness) and, at the same time, are better able to control local credit risk (i.e. showing a higher mission efficiency) and reduce the proportion of bad loans to the total loans. The authors suggest that competition between mutual banks is not socially beneficial from a welfare perspective because competition between federations or associations of CBs contrasts with co-operation within federations of CBs (Barbetta et al. 2016). This happens particularly when CBs join alternative associations and may be induced to cease co-operating with their former partners in order to exploit (higher) short-term benefits (Grillo 2013). Further evidence of the negative effects of internal competition in co-operative banking in Italy can be found in the empirical works of Coccorese et al. (2016) and Ferri and Coccorese (2016). The analysis of the effects of competition on CBs' performances is of particular interest in terms of policy. Traditionally, CBs have been subject to territorial restrictions in the supply of their services. In many European legislations, including Italy, the principle of territorial exclusivity has been mitigated as a result of an increased acceptance of the benefits of competition, including intra-sectoral competition. The empirical evidence, although limited, nevertheless, seems to put a brake on overly simplistic causal relationships between competition and efficiency. Moreover, what emerges from these studies is that taking into account the identity of the competitors makes a discernible difference. Nevertheless, this area of investigation may be deserving of further empirical analysis in order to better understand the competitive role of CBs and the implications of this, as the overall contribution appears to be considerable.

5.4   Co-operative Banking and Economic and Social Growth

Customer-owned banks adopt a local focus which aims to improve the mobilization of savings and their transformation into lending to local borrowers (mainly SMEs, households, and local public authorities). Thus, they minimize the capital flight that can occur for savings mobilized in one less developed region and loaned in more active regions, causing migration and lower economic growth (Sfar and Ben Ouda 2016).[36]

In doing this, CBs ultimately pursue two interrelated purposes: favoring financial inclusion on a long-term basis and fostering economic and social growth at the local level. Is this empirically supported? What are the channels through which CBs may contribute to growth at the local level? Can their support consistently maintain their strong orientation toward relationship banking? The empirical literature has tried to address these issues in different countries, over different time periods and adopting various estimation approaches that try to overcome the potential for endogeneity issues. It has already been established that financial development exerts a positive impact on economic growth (Guiso et al. 2004). With this in mind, it is interesting to investigate the role played by CBs. For instance, in Italy, the analyses of Usai and Vannini (2005) exploit the peculiarities of the Italian banking system with its different bank business models and analyze the role of intermediaries in economic growth[37] across 20 Italian regions over the 1970–1993 period. They report that the overall size of the financial sector has a weak impact on growth, but that some intermediaries are better than others in promoting growth. Specifically, CBs and special credit institutions are found to play a positive role in fostering regional growth. The authors provide support for the idea that smaller and less complex banking institutions are better equipped than large hierarchical banking corporations to fund the performance of information-intensive SMEs. A similar result is found by Hakenes et al. (2014) in a sample of 457 German savings banks and corresponding regional statistics between 1995 and 2004. Similarly, Caporale et al.

---

[36]The importance of localism in banking is addressed by Presbitero et al. (2014) who find that during the global financial crisis in Italy, the contraction of credit was more severe in provinces with larger shares of branches owned by distantly managed large banks. Large and "good-quality" firms in functionally distant credit markets suffered relatively more rationing than those in credit markets largely populated by functionally close banks.

[37]Economic growth is measured in two ways: the growth rate of gross domestic product per capita and the growth rate of regional value added per worker.

(2016) show that local banking (measured by CBs' share of loan markets) had a positive effect on local growth (proxied by the annual change of total value added per capita), especially in Northern Italy, from 1998 to 2009.

In a cross-country study of Austria, Finland, France, Germany, Italy, and the Netherlands from 2000 to 2008, Ayadi et al. (2010) evaluate the impact of institutional diversity (measured by the total assets of co-operative banks divided by regional GDP) on economic growth (proxied by the growth of GDP per capita). The estimations reveal that the presence of CBs has a significant positive impact on growth rates in four countries (Austria, Germany, Finland, and the Netherlands) as well as for the pooled sample (EU-7).

In terms of the link between relationship banking and competition, Presbitero and Zazzaro (2011) document, in line with Degryse and Ongena (2007), the existence of a U-shaped effect of market concentration on relationship lending and indicate that this non-monotonicity can be better explained by the organizational structure of local Italian credit markets. They find that marginal increases in interbank competition are detrimental to relationship lending in markets (measured as a dummy variable equal to 1 if a firm obtains more than 33% of banking credit from its main bank and has credit lines with no more than four banks) where large and out-of-market banks predominate. Conversely, where a large group of small mutual banks already widely make use of relational lending technologies, harsher interbank competition may drive banks to further cultivate their extensive ties with customers.

In France, Sfar and Ben Ouda (2016) investigate the contribution of French CBs to regional economic growth (change in annual real GDP per capita). They employ a system-generalized method of moments approach and use a sample of 88 regional CBs in France across 26 different regions for the period 2006–2012. The empirical results confirm that the presence of CBs (measured as a ratio of co-operative bank assets to regional GDP) is positively associated with economic growth after controlling for various determinants. In fact, the development of co-operative banks, through improving their own financial situation, can promote regional economic development.

Using a dataset on bank branch locations in Poland and organization-, county-, and bank-level data from 2008 to 2012, Hasan et al. (2017) provide evidence that a strong position for local co-operative banks enables access to bank financing and lowers financial costs for SMEs. Additionally, the authors find that CBs positively affect boost investments and growth for SMEs. Wherever CBs maintain a strong position in the market, a more rapid pace of new firm creation is observed, contrary to what happens in local markets dominated by foreign-owned banks. The authors warn about the effects that industry consolidation may have on SME prospects in emerging economies. This warning is echoed by Ryan et al. (2014) who argue that the restructuring of the European banking sector led to an increase in financing constraints for SMEs, which may negatively affect investment and output.

The empirical literature on the relationship between CBs and the accumulation of social capital is quite limited. According to Pastor and Tortosa-Ausina (2008), social capital can be defined as "the social networks, the reciprocities that arise from them, and value of these for achieving mutual goals". Due to their potential for creating long-term relationships, for instance, trust and inequality are found to explain the development of co-operation (Jones and Kalmi 2009). Ostergaard et al. (2015) reveal that Norwegian savings banks had better survival propensities in areas with higher social capital. Catturani et al. (2016) investigate the relationship between social capital and CBs in Italy, despite not resolving endogeneity concerns, over the period from 2003 to 2011. They find that there is a positive link between the social capital and market shares of Italian CBs and that the associations are stronger when banks lend to small enterprises. As, by definition, social capital favored the creation of the early co-operatives (Guinnane 2005) it may also explain their generally more stable banking practices which are fundamental to the promotion of economic growth. Further empirical research is needed to better understand the underlying relationships, their direction, and their strength.

6   Conclusion

Variations of the two founding models of co-operative banking instigated by Schulze-Delitzsch and Raiffeisen to foster financial inclusion still today constitute a significant presence in the banking ecology of European and other countries worldwide.

Despite taking a variety of legal forms, the co-operative identity retains elements which clearly differentiate it from investor-driven (capitalistic) banks: voluntary and open membership; democratic member control; member economic participation; autonomy and independence; education, training, and information; co-operation between co-operatives; and concern for communities. The low-risk attitude, concern for members/customers, and attention to social and cultural values at a local level that are embedded in their DNA make co-operatives particularly apt and effective in combating the twin lures of profit maximization and short-termism that in recent years have often been seen to affect the management of shareholder-oriented banks.

Nevertheless, in the face of such competition, many co-operative institutions have evolved, consolidating to form large co-operative banking groups which merge co-operative and investor ownership through specialized joint-stock subsidiaries and/or regional and national apex institutions which provide specific functions across the group. While some scholars contend that this marks a convergence with the conventional joint-stock model, in fact, as well as enables the co-operative sector to meet capital adequacy requirements introduced in the wake of the global financial crisis, these hybrid structures can be viewed as a strategic attempt to strengthen co-operatives' ability to compete with the dominant, market-based banking model while still protecting their independence and ensuring their survival.

Although the co-operative model is viewed as having limitations in terms of governance and the monitoring and disciplining of management due to the high fragmentation of its ownership, periods of crisis have proved to favor this business model. Overall research shows that co-operative banks generally have lower incentives to adopt risk-taking activities and this makes them, and the systems in which they operate, more financially stable. Indeed, empirical evidence points to the positive contribution of co-operative banks across a number of areas, including inter-temporal risk smoothing and fostering local and regional growth, while their performance in terms of cost efficiency and profitability compare favorably with that of joint-stock groups.

REFERENCES

Aiello, F., & Bonanno, G. (2016). Bank Efficiency and Local Market Conditions. Evidence from Italy. *Journal of Economics and Business, 83,* 70–90.

Akinsoyinu, C. A. (2017). Cooperative Banks: Is Demutualization an Answer? The Experience of Building Societies in the UK. In E. Miklaszewska (Ed.), *Institutional Diversity in Banking – Small Country, Small Bank Perspectives.* Palgrave Macmillan.

Allen, F. & Gale, D. (1997). Financial Markets, Intermediaries, and Intertemporal Smoothing. *Journal of Political Economy, 105*(3), 523–546.

Allen, F., & Gale, D. (2004). Competition and Systemic Stability. *Journal of Money, Credit and Banking, 36,* 453–480.

Allen, F., & Santomero, A. M. (1997). The Theory of Financial Intermediation. *Journal of Banking and Finance, 21*(11), 1461–1485.

Altunbas, Y., Evans, L., & Molyneux, P. (2001). Bank Ownership and Efficiency. *Journal of Money, Credit and Banking, 33*(4), 926–954.

Aoki, M., & Dinç, S. (2000). Relational Financing as an Institutional and Its Viability Under Competition. In M. Aoki & G. R. Saxonhouse (Eds.), *Finance, Governance, and Competitiveness in Japan* (pp. 19–42). Oxford: Oxford University Press.

Apergis, N., Fafaliou, I., & Polemis, M. L. (2016). New Evidence on Assessing the Level of Competition in the European Union Banking Sector: A Panel Data Approach. *International Business Review, 25*(1), 395–407.

Arvidsson, A. (2009). The Ethical Economy: Towards a Post Capitalist Theory of Value. *Capital and Class, 33*(1), 13–29.

Ayadi, R., Schmidt, R. H., Llewell, D. T., Arbak, E., & De Groen, W. P. (2010). *Investigating Diversity in the Banking Sector in Europe. Key Developments, Performance and Role of Cooperative Banks.* Brussels: Centre for European Policy Studies.

Ayadi, R., Arbak, E., De Groen, W. P., & Llewellyn, D. (2012). *Regulation of European Banks and Business Models: Toward a New Paradigm.* Brussels: Centre for European Policy Studies.

Barbetta, G. P., Colombo, L., Colombo, S., & Grillo, M. (2016). Intra-Competitiveness and Inter-Competitiveness Among Mutual Banks: The Case of Trento. *International Review of Economics, 63*(3), 195–214.

Beatty, A., & Liao, S. (2011). Do Delays in Expected Loss Recognition Affect Banks' Willingness to Land? *Journal of Accounting and Economics, 52*(1), 1–20.

Becchetti, L., Ciciretti, R., & Paolantonio, A. (2016). The Cooperative Bank Difference Before and After the Global Financial Crisis. *Journal of International Money and Finance, 69,* 224–246.

Beck, T., Hesse, H., Kick, T., & Von Westernhagen, N. (2009, February). *Bank Ownership and Stability: Evidence from Germany.* Working Paper, Tilburg University.

Beck, T., Coyle, D., Dewatripont, M., Freixas, X., & Seabright, P. (2010). *Bailing Out the Banks: Reconciling Stability and Competition: An Analysis of State-Supported Schemes for Financial Institutions.* London: Centre for Economic Policy Research (CEPR).

Beck, T., De Jonghe, O., & Schepens, G. (2013). Bank Competition and Stability: Cross-Country Heterogeneity. *Journal of Financial Intermediation, 22*(2), 218–244.

Behr, P., & Schmidt, R. H. (2015). *The German Banking System: Characteristics and Challenges*. White Paper No. 32. SAFE.

Behr, P., Foos, D., & Norden, L. (2017). Cyclicality of SME Lending and Government Involvement in Banks. *Journal of Banking and Finance, 77*, 64–77.

Berle, A. A., & Means, G. C. (1932). *The Modern Corporation and Private Property*. New York: Macmillan.

Bhide, A. (1993). The Hidden Costs of Stock Market Liquidity. *Journal of Financial Economics, 34*(1), 31–51.

Birchall, J. (2013). *Finance in An Age of Austerity*. Edward Elgar Publishing.

Boot, A. W. A. (2000). Relationship Banking: What Do We Know? *Journal of Financial Intermediation, 9*, 7–25.

Boot, A. W. A., & Thakor, A. V. (1997). Banking Scope and Financial Innovation. *The Review of Financial Studies, 10*(4), 1099–1131.

Boot, A. W. A., & Thakor, A. V. (2000). Can Relationship Banking Survive Competition? *The Journal of Finance, 55*(2), 679–713.

Boot, A. W. A., Thakor, A. V., & Udell, G. (1991). Secured Lending and Default Risk: Equilibrium Analysis, Policy Implications and Empirical Results. *Economic Journal, 101*(406), 458–472.

Bossler, M., & Schild, C. (2016). The Employment Structure of Cooperative Banks: A Test of Institutional Hypotheses. *Annals of Public and Cooperative Economics, 87*(1), 79–92.

Boyd, J., & De Nicolò, G. (2005). The Theory of Bank Risk Taking and Competition Revisited. *Journal of Finance, 60*, 1329–1343.

Brunner, A., Decressin, J., Hardy, D., & Kudela, B. (2004). *Germany's Three-Pillar Banking System: Cross-Country Perspectives in Europe*. Occasional Paper 233, International Monetary Fund (IMF) Working Paper, Washington, DC.

Brunnermeier, M., Crockett, A., Goodhart, C., Persaud, A., & Shin, H. S. (2009). The Fundamental Principles of Financial Regulation. *Geneva Reports on the World Economy, 11*.

Butzbach, O., & Mettenheim, K. V. (2012). Alternative Banking: Theory and Evidence from Europe. *Brazilian Journal of Political Economy, 32*(4), 580–596.

Caporale, G. M., Di Colli, S., Di Salvo, R., & Lopez, J. S. (2016). Local Banking and Local Economic Growth in Italy: Some Panel Evidence. *Applied Economics, 48*(28), 2665–2674.

Carletti, E. (2008). Competition and Regulation on Banking. In A. Boot & A. Thakor (Eds.), *Handbook of Financial Intermediation and Banking*. Amsterdam: Elsevier.

Carr-Saunders, A. M., Sargant Florence, P., & Peers, R. (1938). *Consumers' Co-operation in Great Britain* (1st ed.). London: George Allen and Unwin.

Catturani, I., Kalmi, P., & Stefani, M. L. (2016). Social Capital and Credit Cooperative Banks. *Economic Notes, 45*(2), 205–234.

Chaddad, F. R., & Cook, M. L. (2004). Understanding New Cooperative Models: An Ownership-Control Rights Typology. *Applied Economic Perspectives and Policies, 26*(3), 348–360.

Chiaramonte, L., Oriani, M. E., & Poli, F. (2015). Are Cooperative Banks a Lever for Promoting Bank Stability? Evidence from the Recent Financial Crisis in OECD Countries. *European Financial Management, 21*(3), 491–523.

Clark, E., Mare, D. S., & Radić, N. (2018). Cooperative Banks: What Do We Know About Competition and Risk Preferences? *Journal of International Financial Markets, Institutions and Money, 52*, 90–101.

Coccorese, P., Ferri, G., Lacitignola, P., & Lopez, J. (2016). Market Structure, Outer vs. Inner Competition: The Case of Italy's Credit Coop Banks. *International Review of Economics, 63*(3), 259–279.

Coco, G., & Ferri, G. (2010). From Shareholders to Stakeholders Finance: A More Sustainable Lending Model. *International Journal of Sustainable Economy, 2*(3), 352–364.

Colombo, E. C. (2012). Radici, consolidamento e crescita del credito cooperativo tra Ottocento e Novecento. In A. Carretta (Ed.), *Il credito cooperativo. Storia, diritto, economia, organizzazione*. Il Mulino Editore.

Cooperatives Europe, Euricse, and Ekai. (2010). *Study on the Implementation of the Regulation 1435/2003 on the Statute for European Cooperative Society. Final Study*, Contract No SI2.ACPROCE029211200 of October 8, 2009.

Cuevas, C. E., & Fischer, K. P. (2006). *Cooperative Financial Institutions: Issues in Governance, Regulation, and Supervision*. Herndon: World Bank Group.

Davis, K. (2007). Australian Credit Unions and the Demutualisation Agenda. *Annals of Public and Co-operative Economics, 78*(2), 277–300.

De Antoni, E. (2013). Cooperative Banking: A Minskyan Perspective. In S. Goglio & Y. Alexopoulos (Eds.), *Financial Cooperatives and Local Development*. Routledge: Abingdon.

De Waal, F. (2009). *Primates and Philosophers*. Princeton, NJ: Princeton University Press.

Degryse, H., & Ongena, S. (2005). Distance, Lending Relationships, and Competition. *The Journal of Finance, 60*(1), 231–266.

Degryse, H., & Ongena, S. (2007). The Impact of Competition on Bank Orientation. *Journal of Financial Intermediation, 16*(3), 399–424.

Degryse, H., & Van Cayseele, P. (2000). Relationship Lending Within a Bank-Based System: Evidence from European Small Business Data. *Journal of Financial Intermediation, 9*(1), 90–109.

Desrochers, P. (2005). Learning from History or from Nature or Both? Recycling Networks and Their Metaphors in Early Industrialisation. *Progress in Industrial Ecology, 2*(1), 19–34.

Diamond, D. W. (1991). Debt Maturity Structure and Liquidity Risk. *The Quarterly Journal of Economics, 106*(3), 709–737.

Egarius, D., & Weill, L. (2016). Switching Costs and Market Power in the Banking Industry: The Case of Cooperative Banks. *Journal of International Financial Markets, Institutions and Money, 42*, 155–165.

Fama, E. F., & Jensen, M. C. (1983). Agency Problems and Residual Claims. *Journal of Law and Economics, 26*(2), 327–349.

Fay, C. R. (1938). *Co-operation at Home and Abroad* (4th edition in two volumes). London: PS King.

Ferri, G., & Coccorese, P. (2016). *Is Competition Among Cooperative Banks a Negative Sum Game?* Working Paper No. 19 March 2017. Center for Relationship Banking and Economics Working Paper Series.

Ferri, G., Kalmi, P., & Kerola, E. (2013). Governance and Performance: Reassessing the Pre-crisis Situation of European Banks. In S. Goglio & Y. Alexopoulos (Eds.), *Financial Cooperatives and Local Development.* Routledge: Abingdon.

Ferri, G., Kalmi, P., & Kerola, E. (2014). Does Bank Ownership Affect Lending Behavior? Evidence from the Euro Area. *Journal of Banking and Finance, 48*, 194–209.

Ferri, G., Kalmi, P., & Kerola, E. (2015). Organizational Structure and Performance in European Banks: A Reassessment. In A. Kauhanen (Ed.), *Advances in the Economic Analysis of Participatory & Labor-Managed Firms* (Vol. 16, pp. 109–141). Emerald Group Publishing Limited.

Fiordelisi, F., & Mare, D. S. (2013). Probability of Default and Efficiency in Cooperative Banking. *Journal of International Financial Markets, Institution and Money, 26*, 30–45.

Fiordelisi, F., & Mare, D. S. (2014). Competition and Financial Stability in European Cooperative Banks. *Journal of International Money and Finance, 45*, 1–16.

Fligstein, N., & Calder, R. (2015). Architecture of Markets. In R. A. Scott & S. M. Kosslyn (Eds.), *Emerging Trends in the Social and Behavioral Sciences* (pp. 1–14). Hoboken, NJ: John Wiley & Sons Inc.

Fonteyne, W. (2007). *Cooperative Banks in Europe: Policy Issues, WP/07/159.* Washington, DC: International Monetary Fund (IMF) Working Paper.

Fonteyne, W., & Hardy, D. C. (2011). Cooperative Banks and Ethics: Past, Present and Future. *Ethical Perspectives, 18*(4), 491–514.

Freeman, J., & Hannan, M. T. (1989). Setting the Record Straight on Organizational Ecology: Rebuttal to Young. *American Journal of Sociology, 95*(2), 425–439.

Gagliardi, F. (2009). Banking Market Structure, Creation and Activity of Firms: Early Evidence for Cooperatives in the Italian Case. *Annals of Public and Cooperative Economics, 80*(4), 605–640.

Gambacorta, L., & Mistrulli, P. E. (2014). Bank Heterogeneity and Interest Rate Setting: What Lessons Have We Learned Since Lehman Brothers? *Journal of Money, Credit and Banking, 46*(4), 753–778.

Garcia-Marco, T., & Robles-Fernández, M. D. (2008). Risk-Taking Behaviour and Ownership in the Banking Industry: The Spanish Evidence. *Journal of Economics and Business, 60*(4), 332–354.

Ghatak, M. (2000). Screening by the Company You Keep: Joint Liability Lending and the Peer Selection Effect. *Economic Journal, 110*(465), 601–631.

Girardone, C., Nankervis, J. C., & Velentza, E. (2009). Efficiency, Ownership and Financial Structure in European Banking: A Cross-Country Comparison. *Managerial Finance, 35*(3), 227–245.

Goddard, J., McKillop, D. G., & Wilson, J. O. S. (2016). Ownership in European Banking. In T. Beck & B. Casu (Eds.), *The Palgrave Handbook of European Banking*. London: Palgrave Macmillan.

Goglio, S., & Alexopoulos, Y. (2013). Introduction: Cooperative Finance and Sustainable Local Development. In S. Goglio & Y. Alexopoulos (Eds.), *Financial Cooperatives and Local Development*. Routledge: Abingdon.

Goodhart, C. A. E. (2004). Money, Stability and Growth. In C. A. E. Goodhart (Ed.), *Financial Development and Economic Growth. Explaining the Links* (pp. 183–206). Palgrave Macmillan.

Goodhart, C. A. E., & Wagner, W. (2012, April). Regulations Should Encourage More Diversity. *Voxeu*.

Gorton, G., & Schmid, F. (1999). Corporate Governance, Ownership Dispersion and Efficiency: Empirical Evidence from Austrian Cooperative Banking. *Journal of Corporate Finance, 5*(2), 119–140.

Grillo, M. (2013). Competition Rules and the Cooperative Firm. *Journal of Entrepreneurial and Organizational Diversity, 2*(1), 36–53.

Groeneveld, J. M. (2011). Morality and Integrity in Cooperative Banking. *Ethical Perspectives, 18*(4), 515.

Groeneveld, J. M. (2017). *Snapshot of European Co-operative Banking 2017*. TIAS School for Business & Society, Tilburg University.

Groeneveld, J. M., & de Vries, B. (2009). European Co-operative Banks: First Lesson of the Subprime Crisis. *The International Journal of Cooperative Management, 4*(2), 8–21.

Groeneveld, J. M., & Sjauw-Koen-Fa, A. (2009, October). *Cooperative Banks in the New Financial System*. Rabobank Group Report for the Duisenberg Lecture, Annual Meeting of the IMF and World Bank, Istanbul.

Grossman, S., & Hart, O. (1983). An Analysis of the Principal-Agent Problem. *Econometrica, 51*, 7–45.

Guinnane, T. W. (2005). Trust: A Concept Too Many. *Jahrbuch für Wirtschaftsgeschichte/Economic History Yearbook, 46*(1), 77–92.

Guiso, L., Sapiensa, P., & Zingales, L. (2004). Does Local Financial Development Matter? *Quarterly Journal of Economics, 119*(3), 929–969.

Gutiérrez, E. (2008). *The Reform of Italian Cooperative Banks: Discussion of Proposals, WP/08/74.* Washington, DC: International Monetary Fund (IMF) Working Paper.

Gutknecht, D. (2008). Thinking Outside the Coop. *Cooperative Grocer, 136*(May–June).

Hakenes, H., Hasan, I., Molyneux, P., & Xie, R. (2014). Small Banks and Local Economic Development. *Review of Finance, 19*(2), 653–683.

Hansmann, H. (1996). *The Ownership of Enterprise.* Cambridge, MA: Harvard University Press.

Hasan, I., Jackowicz, K., Kowalewski, O., & Kozłowski, Ł. (2017). Do Local Banking Market Structures Matter for SME Financing and Performance? New Evidence from Emerging Economy. *Journal of Banking and Finance, 79*, 142–158.

Hauswald, R., & Marquez, R. (2003). *Competition and Strategic Information Acquisition in Credit Markets.* Mimeo, University of Maryland.

Hempell, H. S. (2002). Testing for Competition Among German Banks. *Deutsche Bundesbank Discussion Paper Series 1: Economic Studies*, No. 04/02.

Hesse, H., & Čihák, M. (2007). *Cooperative Banks and Financial Stability, WP/07/2.* Washington, DC: International Monetary Fund (IMF) Working Paper.

Holmström, B., & Tirole, J. (1993). Market Liquidity and Performance Monitoring. *Journal of Political Economy, 101*(4), 678–709.

Iannotta, G., Nocera, G., & Sironi, A. (2007). Ownership Structure, Risk and Performance in the European Banking Industry. *Journal of Banking and Finance, 31*(7), 2127–2149.

Inglis Palgrave, R. H. (2015). *Dictionary of Political Economy.* Cambridge University Press.

International Co-operative Alliance (ICA) (2012), *Guidance Notes to the Co-operative Principles.*

Jaeger, M., Lemzeri, Y., & Ory, J. (2016). Cooperative Versus Conventional (Joint-Stock) Banking in Europe: Comparative Resistance and Resilience During the Recent Financial Crisis. *Journal of Applied Business Research (JABR), 32*(5), 1341.

Jensen, M. C., & Meckling, W. H. (1976). Theory of the Firm: Managerial Behavior, Agency Costs and Ownership Structure. *Journal of Financial Economics, 3*, 305–360.

Jensen, M. C., & Murphy, K. J. (1990). CEO Incentives – It's Not How Much You Pay, but How. *Journal of Applied Corporate Finance, 3*(3), 36–49.

Jones, D. C., & Kalmi, P. (2009). Trust, Inequality and the Size of the Co-operative Sector: Cross-Country Evidence. *Annals of Public and Cooperative Economics, 80*(2), 165–195.

Jones, D. C., & Kalmi, P. (2015). Membership and Performance in Finnish Financial Cooperatives: A New View of Cooperatives? *Review of Social Economy, 73*(3), 283–309.

Kalmi, P. (2012). Finnish Cooperative Banks and the Crisis of Early 1990s. In W. W. Boonstra & J. Mooij (Eds.), *Raiffeisen's Footprint: The Cooperative Way of Banking.* Vrije University Press.

Kalmi, P. (2013). Catching a Wave: The Formation of Co-operatives in Finnish Regions. *Small Business Economics, 41*(1), 295–313.

Kalmi, P. (2017). The Role of Stakeholder Banks in the European Banking Sector. In E. Miklaszewska (Ed.), *Institutional Diversity in Banking – Small Country, Small Bank Perspectives.* Palgrave Macmillan.

Kemp, T. (1985). *Industrialization in the Nineteenth Century Europe.* Longman.

Köhler, M. (2015). Which Banks Are More Risky? The Impact of Business Models on Bank Stability. *Journal of Financial Stability, 16,* 195–212.

Konczal, M., & Abernathy, N. (2015). *Defining Financialization.* Roosevelt Institute Report.

La Porta, R., Lopez-de-Silanes, F., Shleifer, A., & Vishny, R. W. (1998). Law and Finance. *Journal of Political Economy, 106,* 1113–1155.

Leggett, K. J., & Strand, R. W. (2002). Membership Growth, Multiple Membership Groups and Agency Control at Credit Unions. *Review of Financial Economics, 11*(1), 37–46.

Levine, R. (1991). Stock Markets, Growth, and Tax Policy. *The Journal of Finance, 46*(4), 1445–1465.

Levine, R. (2002). Bank-Based or Market-Based Financial Systems: Which Is Better? *National Bureau of Economic Research,* No. W9138.

Likanen, E. (2012, October 2). *High-Level Expert Group on Reforming the Structure of the EU Banking Sector.* Final Report, Brussels.

Liu, H., Molyneux, P., & Wilson, J. O. S. (2013). Competition and Stability in European Banking: A Regional Analysis. *The Manchester School, 81*(2), 176–201.

Llewellyn, D. T. (2009). A Perspective from the UK. In R. Ayadi & R. Schmidt (Eds.), *Investigating Diversity in the Banking Sector in Europe: The Performance and Role of Saving Banks.* Centre for European Policy Studies.

Lopez, J. S., & Di Colli, S. (2013). Competition and Market Power Within the Italian Banking Industry. In S. Goglio & Y. Alexopoulos (Eds.), *Financial Cooperatives and Local Development.* Routledge: Abingdon.

Luzzatti, L. (1997). *La diffusione del credito e delle banche popolari.* Venezia – Istituto di Scienze, Lettere ed Arti, Original Edition 1863.

Maroua, B. (2015). The Impact of the Multi-Stakeholders Governance on the Performance of Cooperative Banks: Evidence of European Cooperative Banks. *Procedia – Social and Behavioral Sciences, 195,* 713–720.

McKillop, D. G., & Wilson, J. O. S. (2011). Credit Unions: A Theoretical and Empirical Overview. *Financial Markets, Institutions and Instruments, 20*, 79–123.

McKillop, D. G., Goth, P., & Hyndman, N. (2006). *The Structure, Performance and Governance of Irish Credit Unions*. Dublin: Institute of Chartered Accountants in Ireland.

Meriläinen, J. M. (2016). Lending Growth During the Financial Crisis and the Sovereign Debt Crisis: The Role of Bank Ownership Type. *Journal of International Financial Markets, Institutions and Money, 41*, 168–182.

Meriläinen, J. M. (2017). Western European Stakeholder Banks' Loan Loss Accounting. *Journal of Financial Services Research*. https://doi.org/10.1007/s10693-017-0283-4.

Merton, R. C. (1995). A Functional Perspective of Financial Intermediation. *Financial Management, 24*(2), 23–41.

Merton, R. C., & Bodie, Z. (2005). Design of Financial Systems: Towards a Synthesis of Function and Structure. *Journal of Investment Management, 3*(1), 6–28.

Milani, C. (2017). Community Banks and Lending Technologies: Evidence from the Italian Retail Market. In E. Miklaszewska (Ed.), *Institutional Diversity in Banking – Small Country, Small Bank Perspectives*. Palgrave Macmillan.

Minsky, H. P. (1993). Community Development Banks: An Idea in Search of Substance. *Challenge, 36*(2), 33–41.

Minsky, H. P., & Whalen, C. J. (1996). Economic Insecurity and the Institutional Prerequisites for Successful Capitalism. *Journal of Post-Keynesian Economics, 19*(2), 155–171.

Oliver Wyman. (2008). *Co-operative Banks: Customer Champion*. New York.

Oliver Wyman. (2014). *Cooperative Banking. Leveraging the Cooperative Difference to Adapt to a New Environment*. New York.

Olszak, M., Pipień, M., Kowalska, I., & Roszkowska, S. (2017). What Drives Heterogeneity of Cyclicality of Loan-Loss Provisions in the EU? *Journal of Financial Services Research, 51*(1), 55–96.

Ory, J., & And Lemzeri, Y. (2012). Efficiency and Hybridization in Cooperative Banking: The French Case. *Annals of Public and Cooperative Economics, 83*(2), 215–250.

Ostergaard, C., Schindele, I., & Vale, B. (2015). Social Capital and Availability of Stakeholder-Oriented Firms: Evidence from Savings Banks. *Review of Finance, 20*(5), 1673–1718.

Paranque, B. (2017). The Need for an Alternative to Shareholder Value Creation? The Ethomed Student Experience. *Research in International Business and Finance, 39*, 686–695.

Pastor, J. M., & Tortosa-Ausina, E. (2008). Social Capital and Bank Performance: An International Comparison for OECD Countries. *The Manchester School*, 76(2), 223–265.

Presbitero, A. F., & Zazzaro, A. (2011). Competition and Relationship Lending: Friends or Foes? *Journal of Financial Intermediation*, 20(3), 387–413.

Presbitero, A. F., Udell, G. F., & Zazzaro, A. (2014). The Home Bias and the Credit Crunch: A Regional Perspective. *Journal of Money, Credit and Banking*, 46(S1), 53–85.

Prinz, M. (2002). *German Rural Co-operatives, Friedrich Wilhelm Raiffeisen and the Organization of Trust*. Manuscript, University of Bielefeld.

Rajan, R. G. (1992). Insiders and Outsiders: The Choice Between Informed and Arm's-Length Debt. *The Journal of Finance*, 47(4), 1367–1400.

Rajan, R. G., & Zingales, L. (1998). Which Capitalism? Lessons from the East Asian Crisis. *Journal of Applied Corporate Finance*, 11(3).

Rasmussen, E. (1988). Stock Banks and Mutual Banks. *Journal of Law and Economics*, 31, 395–422.

Ryan, R. M., O'Toole, C. M., & McCann, F. (2014). Does Bank Market Power Affect SME Financing Constraints? *Journal of Banking and Finance*, 49, 495–505.

Say, L., & Walras, L. (1866). *Les Obligations Populaires*. Guillamin Et C.

Sfar, F. E. H., & Ben Ouda, O. (2016). Contribution of Cooperative Banks to the Regional Economic Growth: Empirical Evidence from France. *International Journal of Economics and Financial Issues*, 6(2), 508–514.

Shy, O. (2002). A Quick-and-Easy Method for Estimating Switching Costs. *International Journal of Industrial Organization*, 20, 71–87.

Stefancic, M. (2012). Governance Specifics in Cooperative Banks: Or, Why Do Managers in Italian Cooperative Banks "Survive" Longer. *Studi Economici*, 67(107), 85–105.

Stefancic, M., & Kathitziotis, N. (2011). An Evaluation of Italian Banks in the Period of Financial Distress. *The International Business and Economics Research Journal*, 10(10), 103–113.

Stiglitz, J. E. (1985). Credit Markets and the Control of Capital. *Journal of Money, Credit and Banking*, 17(2), 133–152.

Stiglitz, J. E. (1990). Peer Monitoring and Credit Markets. *World Bank Economic Review*, 4(3), 351–366.

Sussman, O., & Zeira, J. (1995). *Banking and Development*. C. E. P. R. Discussion Papers, No. 1127.

Usai, S., & Vannini, M. (2005). Banking Structure and Regional Economic Growth: Lessons from Italy. *The Annals of Regional Science*, 39(4), 691–714.

Uzzi, B., & Lancaster, R. (2003). Relational Embeddedness and Learning: The Case of Bank Loan Managers and Their Clients. *Management Science*, 49(4), 383–399.

Weill, L. (2013). Bank Competition in the EU: How Has It Evolved? *Journal of International Financial Markets, Institutions and Money, 26,* 100–112.

Wolff, H. (1893). *People's Banks: A Record of Social and Economic Success* (1st ed.). P.S. King.

Yamori, N., Harimaya, K., & Tomimura, K. (2017). Corporate Governance Structure and Efficiencies of Cooperative Banks. *International Journal of Finance and Economics, 22*(4), 368–378.

CHAPTER 2

Co-operative Banking Networks: Rationalities and Models

1 The Rationale for the Formation of Co-operative Banking Networks

Networks build relationships between co-operative banks (CBs) that have joined together for mutual benefit or to achieve some common purpose, whether or not an explicit agreement has been worked out between them. From a more formal perspective, a network is a set of links connecting agents (nodes), not always directly through bilateral relations, but often making use of intermediaries who provide "knots". The types of links existing can be described as both formal contract and informal social mechanisms, such as trust, shared values and norms, as well as implicit sanctions. These links also contribute to defining the common purpose of the networks, which may be based on a combination of shared values and/ or aligned strategies (Klein and Mangan 2005). Through the prism of networks, it is possible to find inter-organizational arrangements like strategic alliances, consortia, joint ventures, geographical areas, or social networks (Ebers 1999).

Within networks the position of each CB may be different. It can be a simple member, sometimes with a single link to another entity (e.g. a provider of given services); it can function as a bridge for a series of partners, performing a more strategic role (i.e. being an intermediate production entity between its controlling company and the network members or having a regional coordination role); or it can be the key enterprise for the

© The Author(s) 2019   65
F. Poli, *Co-operative Banking Networks in Europe*, Palgrave
Macmillan Studies in Banking and Financial Institutions,
https://doi.org/10.1007/978-3-030-21699-3_2

entire network, with all the other enterprises depending on it, performing the role of overall network coordinator (Menzani and Zamagni 2010). Links between the components can be tighter or looser and more or less hierarchical, giving rise to various degrees of centralization. Business networks, similar to those between CBs, combine elements of markets (based on contracts or arm's-length transactions) and hierarchies (where resources are pooled under a common command and relational contracts are in place) (Greve 2009). They represent hybrid structures (Williamson 1985) which can also be viewed as an extension of Coase's theory of the firm (Granovetter 1995) and founded on co-operation in production, outsourcing, and the standardization of common activities performed on a frequent basis.

The economic activities which arise from these structures produce several benefits for members, ranging from better and less costly information, to enhanced reputation, a greater ability to serve the members and customers of local CBs, and the exploitation of both a common brand and a coordinated presence in the market. CBs in Europe are organized into networks or various forms of alliances that imply several arrangements for collaboration and the sharing of resources. As stated by Cuevas and Fischer (2006), the degree of complexity of CB networks, at least of those that have been able to withstand an adaptation process, is far from unsophisticated: "these arrangements are as or more sophisticated in their organizational features, play a similar role to, and are as vital to the functioning of co-operatives … and ways to control market risk facing the enterprise members of the alliance".

From a market perspective, networks are effective organizational devices enabling CBs to continue to serve their member-customers with an adequate array of products and services at competitive and fair prices. The need to build networks (as unions, federations, consortia, etc.) tends to increase with the number of local CBs established in a territory and that of the member-customers served and the homogeneity of their financial needs. Taken individually, local CBs share similarities in their weaknesses which are driven by their small-scale demand for inputs, their low bargaining power with suppliers, and the lack of specialized personnel to make informed decisions about the procurement and management of a large set of complex inputs and outputs (Cuevas and Fischer 2006). Scholars have primarily rationalized the creation of networks by focusing on the availability (or lack thereof) of the prevailing resources and competences that may push firms to form or enter into alliances (Andrews 1971). From a market standpoint, it is the degree of competitiveness in product or supplier markets that leads to the formation of formalized networks. Other than being triggered by market forces, the propensity of firms, and of CBs in particular, to form networks has been theoretically explained by some forms of isomorphism present in a given industry or market segment which create a drive toward a homogenization of organizational arrangements in certain organizational fields (i.e. due to common marketing efforts or shared risk management activities) (Di Maggio and Powell 1983).

Viewing the transaction costs from a theoretical angle (Williamson 1985), for instance, in a low competitive environment, firms are exposed to "small numbers bargaining" and other forms of opportunistic behavior (Gulati 1998) which may be reduced through the set-up of networks specialized in the cost-efficient procurement of goods and services on behalf and in favor of the members (i.e. the individual CBs). The procurement activity may encompass the supply of technology for delivering the financial intermediation services provided by CBs, raw materials (i.e. stationery material, computers, etc.), professional services (i.e. auditing, legal advisory, personnel training, etc.), and financial products (i.e. insurance, credit cards, derivatives, etc.) and services (i.e. risk management, liquidity management, marketing, etc.). Therefore, the need to benefit from economies of scale (Littlechild 1975) and to decrease the uncertainty in the acquisition of inputs drives the realization of networks among CBs.

Resource dependence theorists maintain that when firms experience high levels of competitive uncertainty, they are likely to mitigate this competitive inter-dependence by entering into forms of co-operation that are aimed, for instance, at reducing the uncertainty faced on the supply side (Pfeffer and Nowak 1976). Solidarity financial arrangements among CBs (i.e. simple systems of guarantee and solidarity or institutional protection schemes [IPSs]) may be thought of as an organizational device to mitigate the risk associated with the lack of bank capital or the decline in traditional funding (i.e. deposits). As a collective of peers, CBs tend to face the same constraints, leading them to form contractual alliances, known in organizational theory as "supply alliances" (Cuevas and Fischer 2006). The creation of networks further represents an organizational device for CBs to acquire and share knowledge (Berg and Friedman 1981) on technologies, processes, and activities which in turn may enable CBs to become more effective in building their own relationship banking and thus their social networks. From a theoretical standpoint, these alliances provide individual members with direct and repeatable access to their partners' organizational routines, which diminishes the ambiguity about a partner's knowledge and increases the efficacy of its transfer and assimilation (Jensen and Szulanski 2007).[1]

Marin (2016) recalls that networks of CBs may act as an effective monitoring tool on banks involved in the alliance, as members of local banks may count on the supplementary and perhaps more effective monitoring and discipline functions of the network itself or the entity specialized in the supervising function. The latter, thanks to large investments in information systems, is able to decrease the level of uncertainty by detecting or closely monitoring the individual organization's behavior and performance (Eisenhardt 1989). In other words, CB networks exert, *per se*, a complementary monitoring effect that becomes formalized when a given entity within the network is placed in charge of this task, both through the autonomous choice of the network's members and for regulatory reasons.

Networks are also important in generating social capital which in turn is vital in banking to minimize adverse selection and moral hazards and to impose discipline on the bank management. The extant literature has provided evidence that the density of the networks and the degree of connection between members are seen as devices which produce social capital: dense structures, a feature of co-operative banking in several European countries, generate trust, reciprocity norms, and a shared identity, which increase co-operation and knowledge sharing (Coleman 1988; Portes 1998). Two effects of the trust generated by CBs, for instance, can be observed in two areas: the large share of retail deposits held by CBs in some European countries (e.g. France, the Netherlands, and Germany), which demonstrate their ability to generate trust in both good times and bad; and the loyalty of employees who, through their additional membership, tend to be involved in decision-making and are encouraged to invest more in firm-specific human capital (Becht et al. 2002).[2]

---

[1] According to Teece (1992), alliances are better suited than market transactions to the repeated exchange of tacit, routine-embedded knowledge because of the increased social interaction and enhanced incentive alignment and monitoring features on which they are grounded.

[2] However, as noted by Fonteyne (2007), the lower turnover in CBs as well as their main focus on traditional retail banking activities may lessen their attraction to top talent. This, in turn, may limit the ability of CBs to enter and develop more sophisticated financial market activities. A remedy to these sources of potential limitations has been found by large CB networks in the segregation of more innovative financial businesses into separate entities, more often with a joint-stock legal nature.

Some empirical research has also suggested that mutual trust and reciprocity norms between partners provide effective and efficient informal governance and serve as social control mechanisms that mitigate opportunism in alliances (Dyer and Singh 1998). By contrast, the increase in the size of networks may have some drawbacks. Kay (2006) observes that when mutual financial institutions and their related networks become large and pursue growth and diversification, they tend to lose their trust advantage because they start to act like commercial institutions. As already pointed out when highlighting the disadvantages of a wide membership in co-operative banking, a high level of fragmentation in CB networks may produce consequences analogous to CBs' decreasing ability to monitor and discipline the management of the entities governing the alliances and/or delivering specialized financial products and services. At this point, Di Salvo (2002) recalls that since the 1960s the search for scale economies has led CBs to outsource functions and production processes to higher-level organizations, giving rise to a concentration of power at the higher levels and greater risk of facing organizational costs as explained by the expense preferences theory (Fonteyne 2007). Ultimately, forming networks between CBs, especially if they are close-knit, may improve the ability of this business model to dialogue with a bank's regulators and supervisors and to lobby for the preservation of its own values, principles, and related interests.

2   THE TYPOLOGIES OF CO-OPERATIVE BANKING NETWORKS

The selection of the precise contractual form of networks is based on the activities performed, and the consequent concerns relating to appropriation that they perceive at the outset. The literature on the formation of alliances (Pisano et al. 1988) highlights that the greater the criticality of the activities included in the alliances and the related contracting hazards and behavioral uncertainty at the time of their formation, the greater the use of hierarchical controls as an effective response to these anticipated concerns. The reason for hierarchical controls as a response to appropriation fears lies in their capacity to enable monitoring and align incentives between network members and the organizational entities resulting from the set-up of the alliance. The historical experience of German CBs forming coalitions in the mid-twentieth century in order to establish regional central banks for the purpose of liquidity management is a clear example of the use of hierarchical control. As noted by Greve (2009), the ownership of the regional central banks enabled CBs to prevent the banks from investing their money in a risky manner or refusing to pay out money at the time it was needed.

Furthermore, the need to introduce formal control mechanisms to manage an alliance increases when the alliance encompasses multiple parties, as is clearly the case in some European countries with national co-operative banking networks (Canal et al. 2003) comprising hundreds of small local banks.

2.1   The Structures of CBs' Networks

Looking at networks in organizational terms, two distinct focuses can frequently be distinguished: the structure of the networks and their composition. The former concept refers to the pattern of the relationships existing among a set of entities, while the network composition identifies the types of actors in a network characterized in terms of their stable traits, features, or resource endowments (Wasserman and Faust 1994). With regard to the structure, we will adapt the taxonomy used by Menzani and Zamagni (2010) and draw distinctions between horizontal and vertical networks, networks of networks, and financial safety nets.

Horizontal networks were the pioneers in co-operative banking in Europe. In this type of network, CBs create entities at a regional or national level with the aim of rationalizing some internal functions (e.g. liquidity management, auditing, and managerial advisory). In so doing, they reap economies of scale and put in place "symmetrical integrations", which can also facilitate future mergers. Each local bank interfaces with the new entity which manages all the individual relationships. Historically, the entities created to perform the outsourced functions were legal forms of associations of co-operatives who performed an instrumental role for the associated companies. In fact, individual CBs expected some form of benefit from the association, both in terms of an increase in profits and through their being a device which would preserve their existence. Now, as then, these forms of networks perform an activity whose beneficiaries are at least predominantly, if not wholly, the individual CBs. The resulting network of CBs makes use of formal governance mechanisms—such as detailed contracts and the use of equity as a "hostage" in commonly owned structures—to restrain opportunism and accomplish co-operation.

Within the network, certain obligations are imposed on members that will be kept mutually under observation by the organization as a whole. In the case of almost every country examined in this book, we show that the development of these types of networks emerged soon after the advent of the co-operative banking movement in that country. In Italy, however, the establishment of a horizontal network among small rural CBs took place later and dates only to 1963 when a specialized service institution— Istituto di Credito delle Casse Rurali Artigiane (ICCREA)—was created specifically to support rural CBs and to finally make them independent from other commercial banks which had formerly provided certain specific services (e.g. payments, liquidity management).

Horizontal networking may have different levels, including multilevel networks or networks of networks (Menzani and Zamagni 2010), with local banks joining regional networks, and the latter being part of a super-regional or national network which undertakes productive and coordina-tion functions for the individual regional networks.

In Germany, a notable example of a network of networks can be found in the development of regional coalitions between local credit co-operatives that gave rise to regional central banks owned by local CBs (Greve 2009). In order to manage the liquidity between regional co-operative central banks, the Preußische Zentral-Genossenschaftskasse was created in Berlin in 1895 as the predecessor of DZ Bank (Deutsche Zentral-Genossenschaftsbank) based in Frankfurt am Main (Faust 1977). The three-tier network of networks comprised local CBs, regional central banks, and a national institution at the top. This model lasted several decades until it was modified in the 1980s, with several regional central banks being taken over by the top institution, and later ended in 2016 with the merger of DZ Bank with Westdeutsche Genossenschafts-Zentralbank (WGZ Bank) headquartered in Düsseldorf.

In several cases, the old associations or *consortia* were absorbed or replaced by other more complex organizations, often with a national structure, as in the case of the Italian ICCREA—which was transformed into a joint-stock company held by CBs and later positioned as the hold-ing company of the group of specialized subsidiaries servicing CBs.

In European co-operative banking networks, it is possible to find differ-ent levels of tiering, with two or three levels that, besides existing for his-torical reasons, seem to be designed to distribute the degree of specialization between the levels. The first-tier entities, local CBs or primary banks, are primarily engaged in the conduct of retail banking in their local territory, building and holding relationships with customers whose financial needs are satisfied by a mix of financial products and services that are produced directly by local banks or by specialized companies that are either part of the network or from suppliers outside the network. Second-tier structures (such as regional banks and/or regional federations or associations), where they exist, provide specialized services and fulfill some oversight functions, while the third-tier structures feature an apex entity, which performs the strategic and operational coordination of regions and is often active in financial markets also at the international level. Frequently, the apex acts as the holding company of the specialized financial subsidiaries, not necessarily having a co-operative legal nature. With some variation, these forms of tiering exist in all the countries examined in this book. In addition to being designed to exploit economies of scale, the formation of these multilevel structures may enable the different levels to enjoy the benefits of risk diversification and unite the advantages of the co-operative structure with the flexibility and discipline of financial markets (Fonteyne and Hardy 2011). For instance, CBs usually suffer from limited flexibility in adjusting their own capital in good times when it could be used advantageously to foster growth. This is because, traditionally, retained earnings are the major source of capital increase. By combining co-operative and apex joint-stock entities within the same network, the latter companies can be used to raise capital more easily on the financial markets. Ultimately, tiering can be thought of as a device to specialize and improve the monitoring role of co-operative members. While members of local CBs may focus on and discipline the local management, the upper levels (i.e. local banks and regional banks), by becoming shareholders of regional and apex institutions, may be better equipped to control and discipline the management of their top entities for the benefit of the ultimate shareholders: the members of local CBs (Fig. 2.1).

Multi-tiering can also be functional in preserving the identity of subgroups of members, thus favoring the construction of differently distributed trust schemes within the network. On the other hand, multi-tiering can be burdensome. At an economic level, the need to keep expensive institutions alive (e.g. regional banks and the intermediary bodies themselves), when they are no longer operated on a voluntary basis as in the past, impacts on the overall efficiency of the network. On the relational level, there is the risk that the multiplicity of relationships that are established within schemes that are not always purely hierarchical may give rise to possible conflicts that undermine the effectiveness of the action of the

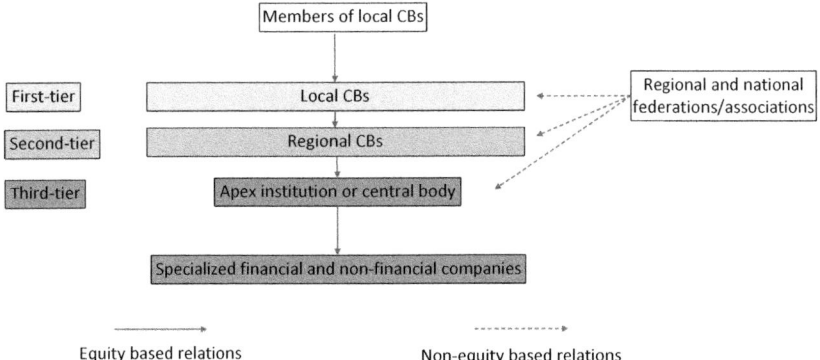

Fig. 2.1 Macro-structure of a co-operative banking network. Source: Author's elaboration

network as a whole. Over recent decades, the original multi-horizontal forms of networks have been largely replaced by simplified tiering in networks or have led to the mergers of some individual or regional CBs which had previously operated within horizontal networks, or indeed of all the CBs in a territory, as in the case of the Dutch Rabobank.

Vertical networks in co-operative banking imply the existence of relations between supplying and purchasing/distributing entities. For instance, in top-down relationships, local CBs act as distributors of specialized financial services produced by other firms involved in the network (e.g. investment funds, insurance contracts, credit cards) through both equity and non-equity relationships (i.e. via distribution agreements); in bottom-up relationships, CBs may be committed to supplying funds to the regional and/or apex institutions through deposits and/or the underwriting of bonds issued by the second- or third-tier level. The verticalization of CB networks has been more often achieved through the set-up or the purchase of specialized entities. The latter may diverge from the co-operative legal form, being joint-stock companies, whose capital is often controlled by a holding company owned by local CBs. Control of the product companies is common in major European co-operative banking systems and assumes a strategic relevance, aimed *inter alia* at ensuring the maintenance of income flows within the networks. Relationships between suppliers and the distributors, CBs, may or may not be exclusive. For example, both partners may be bound to carry out exclusive exchanges through distribution agreements that do not allow for other external partners, suppliers, or distributors. In other cases, it may be that the specialized companies also offer their products to entities outside the network and/or that local banks have the option of independently choosing to distribute financial products and services from third-party producers. The presence of exclusivity constraints faced by primary banks (or at a higher level by regional financial institutions) gives rise to closed networks consisting of fixed units primarily interacting among themselves. In an open network, on the contrary, units may ideally interact with the environment.

High levels of verticalization in co-operative banking networks can lead them to structure themselves as integrated groups with a holding company which has the function of coordinating the controlled specialized subsidiaries and/or the non-equity agreements with selected third parties for the benefit of the CBs. In even more integrated networks, an apex entity (a financial intermediary or a national federation) is formally "delegated" by its owners, the local CBs, to perform strategic and operational coordination functions for the whole network of CBs and specialized subsidiaries. By virtue of sets of agreed rules, the apex institution is thus empowered to establish top-down relationships with its owners, the CBs, exerting control over them by means of binding instructions and their powers of intervention in local banks, which are in fact the owners of the apex in this inverted group scheme.

Within non-financial co-operative networks (i.e. in the retail sector), it is common to find financial arrangements featuring organizations that perform a financial function for their members (e.g. funding on capital markets and financing to members) (Menzani and Zamagni 2010). Likewise, in co-operative banking, the establishment of financial arrangements to create an internal safety net is a natural consequence of the relationships based on solidarity that historically characterizes the networks of CBs in Europe and in the countries where these institutions are most widespread.[3] These are financial arrangements which are founded on the principle of solidarity within the network, implemented via contractual mutual support schemes that aim to ensure the liquidity and solvency of the participating institutions and are beyond the coverage provided by the actual mandatory deposit insurance schemes (Ayadi et al. 2010). Their formalization depends on the degree of centralization of the CBs' network.

---

[3] With some notable exceptions. Italian popular banks, for instance, do not have in place any form of mutual support.

The resulting structures are internal safety nets which make the CBs more effective in managing capital, liquidity, or insolvency problems without external aid, while maintaining full observance of the principles of self-help, independence, and solidarity that distinguish the co-operative banking world.

Among member institutions which opt to stay largely autonomous, these mutual support schemes may take the form of institutional protection schemes (IPSs) which were formerly introduced under the European Directive 2006/48 and further regulated under Regulation (EU) 575/2013 of the European Parliament and of the Council (the Capital Requirements Regulation—CRR), in the context of European banking supervision.[4] Pursuant to Art. 113(7) of the CRR, IPSs are defined as contractual or statutory liability arrangements which are designed to protect member institutions[5] and where necessary to ensure them prompt liquidity and solvency in order to avoid bankruptcy.[6] These schemes may also be recognized as statutory deposit guarantee schemes. An additional benefit of forming IPSs is the permission granted by the European Central Bank under Art. 113(7) of the CRR to apply, for capital regulation purposes, a 0% risk weight to exposures to other counterparties[7] which are members of the same IPS.[8] In addition, the exposures in question are exempt from the rules on large exposure limits (Art. 395[1] of the CRR). Furthermore, the application of Art. 113(7) is one of the preconditions for granting additional waivers to IPS members, namely (1) exemption from the deduction of holdings in own funds (as provided for in Art. 49[3] of the CRR); (2) the granting of a liquidity waiver (Art. 8[4] of the CRR);

---

[4] See also European Central Bank (ECB) (2016), Guide on the approach for the recognition of institutional protection schemes (IPS) for prudential purposes, July.

[5] Under Art. 113(6) undertakings included in the scope of IPS are institutions such as financial holding companies or mixed financial holding companies, financial institutions, asset management companies, or ancillary services undertaken subject to appropriate prudential requirements (Art. 113[6] point a). Furthermore, the institutions must be established in the same Member State as the institution. See ECB (2016), Guide on the approach for the recognition of institutional protection schemes (IPS) for prudential purposes, July.

[6] The IPSs are different from the solidarity schemes that have long been present in the sector. An IPS is subject to ECB authorization and enjoys more lightened prudential requirements.

[7] The counterparties must be established in the same Member State as the institution which applies the 0% risk weight.

[8] With the exception of exposures giving rise to Common Equity Tier 1, Additional Tier 1 and Tier 2 items (ECB 2016).

and (3) the application of lower outflow and higher inflow percentages for the calculation of the liquidity coverage ratio (LCR) (Arts. 422[8] and 425[4] of the CRR). The assumption underlying the creation of an IPS is the maintenance of relatively loose connections between member institutions, who are free to join the IPS and leave it with an advance notice of at least 24 months. Examples of IPS can be found in Spain and among German and Austrian Raiffeisen banking networks. In line with the provision of Art. 113(7), point h of the CRR, IPS shall be based on a broad membership of credit institutions of a predominantly homogeneous business profile, since broad membership should ensure the diversification of individual risks and increase the common capital base at the IPS level. Besides, a predominantly homogeneous business profile of IPS members has the benefit of (probably) more coherent risk measuring metrics at the IPS level (Stern 2014).

An IPS is not a legal entity but a civil law arrangement between specific financial undertakings to mutually protect each other from financial distress (Stern 2014). Although not clearly stated, the provision of Art. 113(7) assumes the existence of a legal entity within the network, which has ongoing responsibility for the regulations relating to the established IPS (i.e. providing the IPS risk review, the consolidated report of the IPS, and exerting influence over the conduct of the IPS members). The IPS must have an ex ante fund to ensure that it has readily available resources to undertake the necessary support measures. Contributions to the ex ante fund are clearly defined and are only invested in liquid and safe assets, which can be liquidated at any time (ECB 2016). For instance, the national association of German co-operative banks (Bundesverband der Deutschen Volksbanken und Raiffeisenbanken—BVR) has set up an IPS with a paid-up guarantee fund and a guarantee scheme based on guarantee bonds provided by affiliated institutions. The German IPS is managed by BVR Institutssicherung GmbH (BVR-ISG) whose sole shareholder is BVR. It is worth noting that IPSs do not have a dominant influence, such as that of parent institutions in relation to their subsidiaries, but as specified in Art. 113(7) must be able to exert influence over the conduct of the IPS members by for instance making their support conditional on the implementation of certain recovery and restructuring measures by a particular institution (ECB 2016). In operational terms, the establishment of an IPS may be seen as a relevant device for risk management which fosters coordination within the network. Additionally, due to its exclusivity, it allows the co-operative sector to further differentiate its value proposition. When the degree of integration between members of a co-operative banking network increases, the mutual support linkages implied in the financial network are founded on a system of joint and several liabilities and cross-guarantees which must be in place between the members (CBs and other specialized entities) and the entity which has responsibility for the management of mutual support. The latter is typically a financial institution, performing several operational and strategic functions in addition to the management of the mutual support scheme as provided for in Art. 10 and in Art. 113(6) of the CRR.

Another way of examining the structure of networks is to look at their components. In this case, two criteria can be used. The first takes into consideration the legal nature of the various companies that make up the networks and their degree of openness to the capital markets through their possible listing on the stock exchange. The second criterion concerns the extent of financial activity carried out within the network.

In some of the co-operative networks, the apex institution has a conventional joint-stock legal nature, whose capital is under the control of the first-tier or where present the second-tier banks. This insulates the apex company from the threat of takeover. According to Ory and Lemzeri (2012), the transformation of some European central bodies into joint-stock companies began during the 1990s, restructuring in response to the deregulation and increased competition in banking markets (e.g. in France and Germany). Scholars and bank managers alike have identified the underlying motivations for this strategic decision, highlighting the superior effectiveness of these legal structures to carry out other banks' acquisitions, to control other joint-stock subsidiaries and take decisions over their possible divesture or merging (Ory and Lemzeri 2012), and their broader ability to raise capital in the financial markets. Our analysis of the co-operative networks active in six European countries, namely, Austria, Finland, France, Germany, Italy, and the Netherlands, reveals the taxonomies listed in Table 2.1. Out of 13 co-operative networks, 8 have chosen to set up a central institution in the form of joint-stock companies; these are active in Austria, Germany, France, and Italy. While in the first three countries the networks have had an apex in the form of a joint-stock company for many years, in Italy this has occurred only recently (in 2016), due to a legislative intervention that has made the granting of a banking license contingent on belonging to a banking group co-operative governed by a joint-stock company. In some cases, the apex or some of its controlled subsidiaries are listed on the stock exchange which is believed to be a

Table 2.1 Taxonomy of co-operative banking networks in some European countries

Co-operative network	Macro-structure of the network	Legal nature of the central institution	Listed apex	Listed subsidiaries of the central institution	Specialization of subsidiaries of the central institution or the institution itself	Type of network	Number of tiers	Governance ratio % (2017)
Austria								
Raiffeisen banks	Local CBs, regional banks and federations; national federation, central institution, IPS	Joint stock	Yes	No	CIB, AM, I, SFS	Quasi-strategic	Three	47.2% (1.7 mln members, 3.6 mln clients)
Volksbanks	Regional banks, national federation, central institution	Joint stock	No	No	CB, AM, SFS	Strategic	Two	58.3% (0.69 mln members, 1.1 mln clients)
Finland								
OP Financial Group	Local CBs, regional federations, central institution	Co-operative	No	No	CIB, AM, I, SFS	Strategic	Two	41.7% (1.8 mln members, 4.4 mln clients)
POP Bank Group	Local CBs, central institution	Co-operative	No	No	I	Strategic	Two	34.9% (0.087 mln members, 0.25 mln clients)
France								
Crédit Agricole	Local CBs, regional banks and federations, national federation, central institution	Joint stock	Yes	Amundi	CIB, AM, I, SFS	Strategic	Three	18.6% (9.7 mln members 52 mln clients)

BPCE	Regional CBs, national federations, central institution	Joint stock	No	Natixis	CIB, AM, I, SFS	Strategic	Two/three[a]	29.4% (9.1 mln members, 31 mln clients)
Crédit Mutuel	Local CBs, regional banks, regional and national federation, central institution	Co-operative	No	No	CIB, AM, I, SFS	Strategic	Three	24.7% (7.8 mln members, 31.6 mln clients)
Germany	Local CBs, regional associations, national federation, central institution, IPS	Joint stock	Yes	No	CIB, AM, I, SFS	Quasi-strategic	Two	61.7% (18.5 mln members, 30 mln clients)
Italy								
Banche di credito cooperativo[b]	Local CBs, regional federations, national federation, central institution	Joint stock	No	No	CIB, AM, I, SFS	Strategic and quasi-strategic	Two	21.7% (1.3 m members, 6 mln clients)
Banche Popolari	Local CBs, national association	Association	No	No	Legal and regulatory advisory, statistics and economic research	Atomized network	Two	8.2% (500,000 members, 6.1 mln clients)
Netherlands	Merger of all CBs from 2016	Co-operative	Yes	No	CIB, I, SFS	Formal banking group	–	22.5% (1.9 mln members, 8.5 mln clients)

Source: Author's elaboration

CIB, corporate and investment banking; *AM*, asset management; *I*, insurance; *SFS*, special financial services (i.e. payments, leasing, etc.)

[a]A two-tier system is in place for Banque Populaire while Caisse d'Epargne is organized with a three-tier system

[b]In 2016 local CBs were required by law to join a co-operative banking group with a parent company, incorporated as a joint-stock company. Two co-operative banking groups resulted from the reform and commence operation in 2019. One small network of CBs formed an IPS

better way of conveying information to the markets and introducing market discipline compared to the monitoring exerted by CBs and/or their regional central entities as shareholders. More specifically, the central institutions of the Austrian Raiffeisen network, the French CBs belonging to the Crédit Agricole network, and the network of German CBs are listed. The Finnish co-operative banking group, the OP Financial Group, took the decision to delist its main body in 2014 to again become a financial services group fully owned by customers/members, while the network of Dutch Rabobanks agreed to merge all its CBs in 2016 and listed its member certificates in 2014. Among the networks owning a listed subsidiary, there are two French groups: Crédit Agricole with Amundi and the network Banques Populaire and Caisses d'Epargne (BPCE) with Natixis. Both these companies are particularly active in national and international capital markets, offering services ranging from asset management to corporate and investment banking. The Crédit Mutuel network decided to delist its corporate and investment banking subsidiary, Crédit Industriel et Commercial (CIC), in 2017. The decision was motivated by the need to simplify the group's structure and eliminate some of the regulatory and administrative constraints associated with the listing of the CIC shares as well as the related costs.

All networks are particularly active in offering a diversified range of financial services, which sometimes also include those relating to real estate (not shown in Table 2.1). These are mainly carried out through specialized companies which are themselves a public limited company. Some of them have a large international presence, as in the case of Crédit Agricole. Some of the co-operative networks analyzed were classified as financial conglomerates in 2017.[9] This is the case for the three French groups, the German apex, the Finnish group OP Financial Group, and the Rabobank group. The analysis carried out so far allows us to state that the main European co-operative groups, despite the diversity of the structural choices they have adopted, now make extensive use of hybrid structures which no longer feature a co-operative company at their head. Only in two countries, Finland and France, where it is limited to the Crédit Mutuel group, does a strong co-operative component remain. However, these

---

[9] As reported in the list of financial conglomerates for the year 2017 published by the Joint Committee of the European Supervisory Authorities. Available at https://esas-joint-committee.europa.eu/Publications/Guidelines/List%20of%20financial%20conglomerates%20 2017.pdf.

groups are smaller and seem to have chosen to delist their components, perhaps to avoid market mechanisms that are incompatible with their co-operative vocation and principles.

2.2 The Governance of Co-operative Banking Networks

According to Greve (2009), co-operative banking networks, like any other form of organization, have to protect their key strategic resources against competitors. For this reason, strategic resources should be integrated into the network both to extract and retain any relative economic advantage (i.e. a reduction of transaction costs) and to defend them against imitation. Recalling Picot and Hardt (1998), three types of competencies are integrated within the network: core competencies, complementary competencies, and peripheral competencies. Core competencies are very specific in nature, demanding a higher level of protection. In co-operative banking, these kinds of competencies can be identified in an organization's deep local knowledge, and its closeness to its customers, its good relationships with small- and medium-sized enterprises, the collaborative attitude existing within the network, and the individuality of its membership and self-government (Hellinger 1999). The boundary within which these core competencies can be developed and must be protected is primarily that of local CBs, the first tier, where the larger share of the whole network's business and profitability originates (Greve 2009). Therefore, core competencies at the first-tier level can be protected as long as effective organizational arrangements are found to contractually and economically defend them. In fact, given the small size of local banks and the ban on engaging in intra-sector competition, individual CBs need to reap economies of scale and scope. This becomes fundamental at the sector level because of their expensive decentralized structures that still tend to require a large staff.

Complementary competencies are important in enabling the effective use of CBs' core competencies in the long run; they are specific to their medium and are of strategic importance. Such competencies are found in specialized financial intermediaries (e.g. special credit intermediaries, asset management companies, corporate and investment banking, regional CBs) and in entities (such as a financial intermediary and/or a political body like a federation) delivering support activities (e.g. personnel training, auditing, advice, risk monitoring and measurement, strategic planning) which are internalized within networks through hierarchical forms, for the purposes of limiting both transaction costs and the risk of appropriability arising from the specificity of assets held by providers of specialized products and services. Depending on the degree to which the criteria are fulfilled, the institutional response could range from joint ventures to long-term contracts between the member of the network and the entities providing the complementary competences.

Finally, peripheral competencies complement the activity of CBs, despite not being strategically vital or specific. They do not expose CBs to the risks of hold-up and moral hazard as they are functions and activities which can be outsourced in the name of efficiency, as for instance with data processing and facilities management. Where they are internalized within a network, it is purely due to an economic imperative. Combining the theoretical contributions of Greve (2009) and Desrochers and Fischer (2005), we report in Table 2.2 the complementary and peripheral competencies that enable CBs to make their core competencies effective and efficient. One interesting parallel that we find between the competencies reported in Table 2.2 relates to the so-called "support activities" within Porter's value chain model (1998). These represent all those activities which can create value for individual CBs and consequently competitive advantage in several areas, such as human resources (e.g. with selection and training of employees), technology (e.g. technological developments which enable improvement in financial products and processes), procurement (relating to the purchase of inputs to be used in the firms' value chain, ranging from stationery to wholesale funding), and infrastructure (comprising several activities including planning, risk management, auditing, legal, accounting, representation, etc.). Support activities underpin the primary activities CBs perform in creating and managing relationships with customers, members, and communities, producing or distributing financial products (i.e. loans to households or SMEs, insurance contracts, deposits and other savings products), and providing after-sales assistance. Continuing the parallel between the Porter vision (1998), based on activities, and that of Greve (2009), founded on skills, we can identify in the primary activities the core competencies to which Greve (2009) refers. These reside in local banks and create value for individual banks and the network as a whole, to the extent that they are supported by adequate complementary and peripheral skills. Because of the resource constraints faced by small CBs, as by any other small firm, support activities may be outsourced to entities within the networks with the aim of reaping scale economies, promoting innovation, and assuring market orientation within

Table 2.2 Complementary and peripheral competencies supporting networks' members

Network competencies	Description	Type of network
Human resources		
Training and education	A central institution delivers training activities for bank employees and board members (supervisory and managerial boards) and forms co-operative members, customers, and other stakeholders	AN; CN; SN
Procurement		
Non-strategic goods and services	A central institution or contractual arrangements are in place with their parties to offer non-strategic goods and services to the members of the networks (e.g. data processing, facility management)	AN; CN; SN
Marketing, communication, and strategic planning		
Common branding	A central institution is in charge of common brand image management and communication	CN; SN
Marketing mix	A central institution is in charge of the product design, pricing, distribution channels, and communication	CN; SN
Strategic planning	The central institution is in charge of the definition of the mission and the strategic planning of the network. It monitors the implementation of the strategic planning and take actions	CN (limited to planning); SN
Risk management and reporting		
Liquidity and funding management	A central institution provides services for the pooling and investment of CBs' liquidity	CN; SN
Risk measure and reporting	A central institution defines common risk evaluation tools for several financial and non-financial risks and reporting	SN
Auditing, control, and supervision		
Advisory	A central institution is in charge of the provision of legal, tax, regulatory, and managerial advisory services	AN; CN; SN
Representation	A central institution represents the system in common issues	AN; CN; SN
Consolidation	The activities of the member of the network are monitored and reported on a consolidated basis	SN
Supervision	A central institution is empowered to supervise the network and to issue instructions	SN
Internal safety net mechanism		
Solidarity mechanisms	A system of joint and cross-guarantees is in place to guarantee the commitments of all the members of the network	SN

Source: Adapted from Desrochers and Fischer (2005)

AN, atomized network; *CN*, consensual network; *SN*, strategic network

a co-operative vision of banking and the economy in general. How well each value activity is performed and governed determines the contribution to members' and customers' needs in terms of returns or differentiation.

As with any firm, governance plays a key role in the creation of value for CBs because it influences transaction costs, as well as the willingness of alliance partners to engage in value-creation initiatives. Two types of mechanisms may be in play, both individually and jointly, to make governance effective (Dyer and Singh 1998). A first set of mechanisms rely on contractual agreements (e.g. legal contracts, by-laws) and third-party enforcement tools, whereas the second relies on self-enforcing agreements. The former fall primarily within the theoretical perspective of transaction cost economics and enlist third parties (i.e. courts or legitimate authorities such as a national supervisor) to enforce contractual agreements and resolve disputes between network partners (Williamson 1991). By contrast, self-enforcing agreements, also known as "private ordering" in the economics literature, call for safeguards that allow for self-enforcement. The latter agreements may encompass formal mechanisms, such as "financial and investment hostages" (Williamson 1983), and informal ones, such as trust and reputation (Gulati 1995). Examples of financial and investment hostages are, for instance, equity participations in jointly held specialized companies within the networks or safety net tools, such as an IPS. All of them are designed to align the economic incentives of network partners and minimize opportunistic behaviors which may threaten the individual partner and the network as a whole. On the other hand, informal mechanisms, such as trust and reputation, represent less costly means of safeguarding against opportunistic behaviors which may endanger, for instance, the jointly developed complementary competencies and ultimately the core competence of CBs: their ability to build and hold reliable relationships with members and customers. Scholars such as Uzzi (1997) maintain that trust and reputation are effective in creating value for networks because they reduce the transaction costs related to bargaining and monitoring the jointly held resources and competencies within the networks. Allies are more inclined to invest resources (i.e. pooling their liquidity) if they trust that they will be managed safely in the common interest of partners. Monitoring costs will be lower in a context of reciprocal trust, especially if common values and beliefs pervade the institutions responsible for the governance of the network's complementary competencies. Equally, unlike contracts, trust and reputation do not have any fixed duration. They might increase over time as interactions within the network augment, both spontaneously and through scheduled situations (i.e. meetings, committees, etc.).

In the governance of co-operative banking networks, both formal and informal enforcement mechanisms are employed but as a network becomes more complex and shared competencies more specialized, formal mechanisms and financial hostages tend to prevail over the development of self-enforcing mechanisms like trust.

The governance of these competencies requires organizational mechanisms that can be designed along a continuum of hybrid organizations (Greve 2009) ranging from the formation of atomized networks to consensual networks and strategic networks (Desrochers and Fischer 2005).

In atomized networks (ANs), according to Desrochers and Fischer (2005), the ties between network members are weak. Member autonomy is high and responses to changing environments tend to be the result of individual efforts to adapt. Some shared competencies may exist, as for instance in the procurement of non-strategic goods and services, representation, and advisory services. These functions are usually performed by associations or federations of CBs, which in some ways do assume a central role without having any formal hierarchical role and tool to strengthen coordination. An example of AN is the popular banks' sector in Italy (Table 2.1).

Consensual networks (CNs) imply the establishment of consensual multilateral agreements between first-tier entities, local CBs, that are designed to develop and produce activities for all its members. They are another type of co-operative banking network where member banks retain strategic and managerial control. An apex organization (the national federation or association) or a central body (i.e. a financial intermediary with some controlled specialized subsidiaries) may be in place but only performs limited operational functions (e.g. treasury services, payment systems, IT solutions, employee training), while also having some strategic planning and advisory capacities, and, sometimes, taking on the role of representing the network (Table 2.2). In CN, the pooling of resources and standardization is voluntary and, in most cases, partial, as some members opt out for a variety of reasons while still remaining members of the network (Desrochers and Fischer 2005). These networks usually develop a unique brand and image, which over time require delegation to a central entity to develop and coordinate the institutional communication and marketing campaigns. This will introduce some delegation of strategic planning from CBs to a central hub that will, however, be powerless to take any actions against the individual CBs. CNs may enable CBs to improve their offer through the joint production of financial activities and instruments which the individual CBs may not produce alone due to their lack of scale. As the importance of these financial activities grows, standardization increases within the networks along with the need to delegate to one entity the provision of product design, marketing, and planning services.

The pooled resources are subject to low risks of hold-up and hazard as they typically comprise peripheral and/or few complementary competencies. Given the high degree of decentralization in such networks and the autonomy of members in using the network resources, they are characterized by weak governance mechanisms to assure members' compliance with the contractual rules embedded in the network. Mutuality and trust are the prevailing mechanisms for enforcing the contractual relationships within these networks. However, lock-in and lock-out effects are also in place (Gulati et al. 2000), which arise from resource constraints that typically affect small-size CBs.

CNs can be very atomistic, comprising many small CBs which might enjoy a degree of market power in their own territory and are therefore less exposed to competitive pressures, and/or might include some larger CBs which, having a greater ability to control contractual hazards, are less inclined to adhere to more intrusive networks. For the latter, their presence in the network might simply be a consequence of their being part of the sector or alternatively might be a way of expressing their influential power over the decision-making processes of the network. There are no financial ties linking members as is the case when liquidity pooling or safety net mechanisms are in place. Such ties, where they exist, promote coordination and the development of private ordering mechanisms to ensure compliance and the existence of credible checks to prevent opportunism in activities where the risk of appropriability is highest (Desrochers and Fischer 2005). According to the European Association of Co-operative Banks (EACB) (2017), in basic forms of CNs, local CBs are associated in accordance with statutory or legal provisions and co-operation is limited. CBs jointly own a central institution, which manages the liquidity of the network, and provides cash clearing and access to the national central bank and to financial markets. Pursuant to Art. 400(2)(d) and Art. 422.8 of the CRR, member CBs individually enjoy some regulatory reliefs relative to the capital requirements for large exposures against their central institution and the calculation of the liquidity risk requirements. Examples of basic models of CNs can be found in Poland or Hungary (EACB 2017). Taken as a whole, a CN exhibits some fragility in adapting to changes in market conditions caused by modifications in demand or technological shifts (Desrochers and Fischer 2005). Often, aggregations take place within the network, both for purely strategic reasons and in order to resolve cases of distress. Spain and Italy were also good examples of CNs. The reform of the co-operative banking sector in Italy during 2016 (Law 49/2016) introduced the compulsory formation of strategic networks which are still in the process of being completed. In Spain an IPS among CBs has been approved by the ECB (2016).

The presence of an IPS improves network integration as in the case of the Austrian Raiffeisen banks, and the German and Spanish co-operative banking sectors (ECB 2016). IPSs are significant liability arrangements in absolute terms, given that about 50% of credit institutions in the Euro area are members of an IPS, corresponding to around 10% of the total assets of the Euro area banking system (ECB 2016). In fact, pursuant to Art. 113(7) (c) of the CRR, the recognition of an IPS for regulatory purposes requires that it operates suitable and uniformly stipulated systems for the monitoring and classification of risk. These provide a complete overview of the risk situations of all its individual members and the institutional protection scheme as a whole, with the accompanying possibility of exerting influence in well delimited areas. In fact, the set-up of an IPS introduces more standardization across the network with regard to the way risks are assessed and monitored. The IPS also demands additional integration within the network through its requirement to publish an annual financial report for the IPS as a whole (Art. 113[7][e]) including the balance sheet, the profit-and-loss account, the situation report, and the risk report. As such, the IPS ends up holding some coordination, control, and intervention functions over CBs.

However, as already mentioned, the existing central body does not have the power to issue instructions to first-tier banks (Groeneveld 2015), which still enjoy a large degree of strategic and operational autonomy (EACB 2017) and are directly supervised by national supervisory authorities. We may classify these networks as quasi-strategic networks (QSNs) due to their higher degree of integration in comparison to CNs. Since risk management represents the essence of banking activity, conditioning its operational dimension and its evolution, it is clear that the establishment of an IPS gives rise to a network in an intermediate position between the consensual and the strategic ones.

Strategic networks (SNs) may be viewed as long-term institutional arrangements between distinct but related organizations that are based upon an extensive inter-firm division of labor and intensive inter-firm co-operation but are different to other types of inter-firm networks run by a hub firm (Jarillo 1988, 1993). In SNs, the degree of integration is high, and decisions taken according to defined governance mechanisms become mandatory for all the CBs for as long as they belong to the network (Desrochers and Fischer 2005). This is because individual CBs cede control of their strategic and operational decisions that have become strategic to the network as a whole (Table 2.2). Additionally, the cession of strategic and operational decisions may be in response to national regulations that make the granting of a banking license conditional on the compulsory affiliation to a co-operative banking network (for instance, as in Italy) with affiliation being either permanent or impermanent, depending on current national regulations. The cession of first-tier banks' decisional powers in favor of an apex institution or central body is embedded in several hierarchical and non-hierarchical devices, such as equity investments in the apex, approval of legal arrangements, and changes in the by-laws and statutes of CBs. The apex resembles a real "hub" with meta-coordination functions (Greve 2009), agreed upon by vote by the collective, and including both complementary and peripheral competencies as well as core competencies (i.e. the relationships with local CBs' members become standardized). SNs are grounded in the extensive use of private ordering mechanisms— internal regulatory and control bodies—to enforce the collective contract, rendering them very similar to hierarchies.

For Greve (2009), in changing and more competitive environments, SNs are essential to protect the core competencies of local CBs, as well as the brand and its reputation. Moreover, as the degree of financial sophistication increases, and the array of joint productions of financial products and activities multiplies, the network ties become tighter and the resources that have been invested in developing the capacity to produce those services, and the risks of loss of investments, also grow (Gulati et al. 2000). Finally, prudential regulation can require and indeed provides incentives for the development of SNs, as in the case of the previously mentioned CRR waivers on liquidity and credit risk prudential requirements. Co-operative banking networks in Finland and France do have a clear strategic nature. The Dutch Rabobank was also a strategic network before the amalgamation of all the local CBs in 2016. The influence and control exercised by the members of the former CBs is now assured by each having direct representation on the highest body of the co-operative: the general members' council which, among other things, defines the strategy of Rabobank.

According to Desrochers and Fischer (2005), SNs are created to control appropriability hazards (Oxley 1997), namely, the risk arising from the difficulties in adequately specifying the outcomes of relevant activities, monitoring their execution, and/or enforcing contracts through the courts. Networks' activities which are subject to meta-coordination have increased over time. Over time, the centralized running of certain activities outsourced by CBs (IT support, data processing, training, and accounting) has been joined by other functions such as treasury management, marketing, product development, risk management, and representation. Some functions are performed directly by the network's central body (e.g. treasury management, risk management, marketing) or through subsidiaries (e.g. asset management, special types of lending), usually controlled by the institution acting as a central hub. In some cases, regional and national associations of local CBs are responsible for the provision of services such as training, advisory, representation, and auditing. As the extent of integration within CB networks rises, the level of centralization of individual CBs' activities also increases, as does the power of the central body to strategically coordinate and control the local CBs and the many financial and non-financial undertakings taking place across the network (Fig. 2.2).

The highest levels of integration can be found in those networks that fall into the category circumscribed by Art. 10 of the CRR. In these cases, CBs are permanently affiliated to the central body they control, which is empowered to supervise them and issue instructions for the management of local CBs. The autonomy of subsidiaries and permanently affiliated CBs is severely limited with regard to their business strategies and decisions,

	ATOMIZED NETWORK	CONSENSUAL NETWORK	QUASI-STRATEGIC NETWORK	STRATEGIC NETWORK
	HIGH AUTONOMY OF CBs			LOW AUTONOMY OF CBs
Centralized competences	Low	Low-medium	Medium-high	High
Power of the apex to issue instructions	No	No	Limited and held by the IPS	Yes
Supervision of CBs	National autority	National autority	National autority and ECB	National autority and ECB
Consolidated reporting and monitoring	No	No	Yes	Yes

Fig. 2.2   From atomized to strategic networks. Source: Author's elaboration

but in return for this they are exempt from banking regulations, reconciling the fact of their limited independence (Stern 2014). According to EACB (2017), this model is applied in Finland by the co-operative banking network OP Financial Group, in Austria by the Volksbanks Verbund, in Portugal by Credito Agricola, by Raiffeisen Luxembourg, and in Italy by two newly formed highly integrated networks of credit cooperative banks.

An intermediate situation foreseen in the CRR is prescribed by Art. 113(6) of the CRR where local/regional CBs and the central body are linked by a parent-subsidiary relationship, which is characterized by a high level of control of the central institution: the local/regional banks are the owners and hold the political control of the central institution. They have however delegated some control powers to their central institution to ensure oversight. In this case, local CBs' affiliation is not permanent as is required by Art. 10 of the CRR. The central body is subject to the same risk evaluation, measurement, and control procedures as the local CBs. EACB (2017) considers the French Crédit Agricole, Crédit Mutuel, and BPCE as examples of networks falling within the remit of Art. 113(6) of the CRR. Both networks regulated in Art. 10 and Art. 113(6) of the CRR may be regarded as strategic networks according to the interpretation of Desrochers and Fischer (2005). In cases of networks regulated by Arts. 10 and 113(6) of the CRR, a system of joint liabilities and cross-guarantees is in place between the members (CBs and other specialized entities); the central body is required to publish consolidated accounts. For solvency and liquidity purposes, the central body and its affiliates are monitored on a consolidated basis by the national supervisory authority or by the European Central Bank should the network fall into the category of the so-called "significant entities".[10]

According to our interpretation of the publicly available data on the networks under investigation, EACB's classification and reported references to the CRR articles in the individual networks' annual reports and

---

[10] In accordance with Art. 49(1) of Regulation (EU) No 468/2014 and of the European Central Bank (ECB/2014/17) (the Single Supervisory Mechanism Framework Regulation), the ECB has direct supervision of significant entities and significant groups. To be considered significant, at least one of the following criteria must be met: (1) the total value of assets above € 30 billion, (2) relevance at the country level, (3) total value of assets above € 5 billion and high cross-border assets/liabilities in more than one other participating Member State; request or granting of funding from the European Stability Mechanism or the European Financial Stability Facility.

presentations, out of the co-operative banking networks displayed in Table 2.1, strategic networks (SNs) dominate; three networks, namely, the German one, the Austrian Raiffeisen banks, and a handful of Italian credit co-operative banks are quasi-strategic networks (QSNs), while only one, the network of Italian popular banks, is an atomized network (AN) (Table 2.1). Both SNs and QSNs are highly hybridized with apex institutions and controlled subsidiaries and a joint-stock legal form. Hybridization seems to go hand in hand with increased specialization within the networks, being not strictly linked to the type of network. Both SNs and QSNs are highly hybridized and specialized. It is interesting to note that two QSNs enjoy the largest governance ratios, measured by the ratio of the total number of members to that of customers (Table 2.1). Since the governance ratio proxies roughly the degree of concentration of bank offer to members, we could conjecture that resistance to transforming QSNs into SNs may be higher when independence is considered an important value by the members of the co-operative banks. The strategic and managerial independence of local CBs may, in fact, magnify their focus on the needs of members and communities while, on the contrary, this could be prevented in highly integrated SNs. Ory and Lemzeri (2012) maintain that the evolution of co-operative banking networks toward more strategically designed models calls for a clear distinction in terminology between co-operative networks and co-operative groups. While the former are essentially equivalent to consensual networks, co-operative groups also include a large number of joint-stock subsidiaries, with a wide range of businesses (asset management, CIB, insurance, wholesale banking, forex, etc.) at the national and often international levels. Additionally, using the expression co-operative banking group seems more appropriate where the central institution performs relevant financial activities but also centralizes the definition of the group strategy, controls the activities of the subsidiaries, and performs some processes to a standardized level (e.g. data processing and reporting, training, risk management) (Ory and Lemzeri 2012). In our understanding, co-operative banking groups correspond to what we have identified as, *strictu sensu*, strategic networks. In these networks joint competencies are highly specialized, make substantial use of governance mechanisms that mimic those of formal groups of firms, and consolidate their results. They also adopt the joint-stock legal form to undertake in a more convenient way a number of specialized activities, which however remain largely under the control of CBs. It is true that both the networks themselves and the regulators use the term "group" in place of "network" putting the emphasis, it seems to us, on the analogy between the controlling powers of the holding company toward its subsidiaries and those of the strategic network apex toward its own shareholders, the CBs. In this case, however, the powers of the apex to define strategy and exercise control were delegated by the same subjects who were involved in creating it to better meet the interests of the co-operative members. Although we use the word "group" frequently, the definitions of its use must be very clear.

3   Conclusion

Driven by the need to overcome issues such as low bargaining power and lack of specialization, as well as the desire to benefit from shared knowledge, reduced risks, and a greater ability to serve their members, individual co-operative banks in the European countries examined in this work are seen to be bound together in a variety of forms of sophisticated network, ranging from the atomistic to the strategic. The precise contractual form that these networks take depends primarily on the activities they perform, the degree of concern relating to their appropriation, and the number of members involved.

The networks, whether horizontally or vertically structured, feature two or three tiers of organization: the first-tier entities, local co-operative banks, are engaged in providing a mix of financial products and services in their local territory; the second-tier structures, which are regional banks or regional federations or associations, provide specialized services and fulfill some oversight functions; while third-tier organizations, frequently joint stock in nature but owned by the first-tier co-operative banks, consist of an apex entity which performs the strategic and operational coordination of regions and is often active in financial markets. These hybrid structures are extensively used in the majority of countries analyzed in this work.

In keeping with the co-operative principle of solidarity, networks have historically developed internal safety nets to protect their member institutions from bankruptcy, in the form of protection schemes, which ensure prompt liquidity and solvency.

In terms of the governance of co-operative banking networks, a range of informal and formal mechanisms are employed to protect the core, complementary, and peripheral competencies of members. In atomized networks, where ties between members are relatively weak, informal mechanisms are widely used while consensual networks typically feature more formal multilateral agreements. Where there is a higher level of integration including an IPS, the networks can be classified as quasi-strategic but in the most complex, highly hybridized, and specialized networks where long-term institutional arrangements between distinct but related organizations exist, these can be classified as strategic networks. In this analysis, strategic networks constitute the dominant model.

REFERENCES

Andrews, K. (1971). *The Concept of Corporate Strategy*. Homewood: Irwin.

Ayadi, R., Schmidt, R. H., Llewell, D. T., Arbak, E., & De Groen, W. P. (2010). Investigating Diversity in the Banking Sector in Europe. In *Key Developments, Performance and Role of Cooperative Banks*. Brussels: Centre for European Policy Studies.

Becht, M., Bolton, P., & Röell, A. (2002). Corporate Governance and Control. *European Corporate Governance Institute – Finance Working Paper, 2*, 168.

Berg, S., & Friedman, P. (1981). Impacts of Domestic Joint Ventures on Industrial Rates of Return: A Pooled Cross Section Analysis. *Review of Economics and Statistics, 63*, 293–298.

Canal, E. G., Lianeza, A. V., & Arino, A. (2003). Effectiveness of Dyadic and Multi-Party Joint Ventures. *Organization Studies, 24*, 743–770.

Coleman, J. S. (1988). Social Capital in the Creation of Human Capital. *American Journal of Sociology, 94*(supplement), S95–S120.

Cuevas, C. E., & Fischer, K. P. (2006). *Cooperative Financial Institutions: Issues in Governance, Regulation, and Supervision*. Herndon: World Bank Group.

Desrochers, M., & Fischer, K. P. (2005). The Power of Networks: Integration and Financial Cooperative Performance. *Annals of Public and Cooperative Economics, 76*(3), 307–354.

Di Maggio, P. J., & Powell, W. W. (1983). The Iron Cage Revisited: Institutional Isomorphism and Collective Rationality in Organizational Fields. *American Sociological Review, 48*(2), 147–160.

Di Salvo, R. (2002). La "Governance" des Systèmes Bancaires Mutualistes et Coopératifs en Europe. *Revue d'Economie Financière, 67*, 165–180.

Dyer, J. H., & Singh, H. (1998). The Relational View: Cooperative Strategy and Sources of Interorganizational Competitive Advantage. *Academy of Management Review, 23*, 660–679.

Ebers, M. (1999). Explaining Inter-Organizational Network Formation. In M. Ebers (Ed.), *The Formation of Inter-Organizational Networks* (pp. 3–40). New York: Oxford University Press.

Eisenhardt, K. M. (1989). Agency Theory: An Assessment and Review. *The Academy of Management Review, 14*(January), 57–74.

European Association of Co-operative Banks (EACB) (2017). Models of groups and networks of co-operative banks. Retrieved from http://www.eacb.coop/en/co-operative-banks-models-groups-and-networks.html.

European Central Bank (ECB). (2016, July). *Guide on the Approach for the Recognition of Institutional Protection Schemes (IPS) for Prudential Purposes.*

Faust, H. (1977). Geschichte der Genossenschaftsbewegung: Ursprung und Aufbruch der Genossenschaftsbewegung in England. In *Frankreich und Deutschland sowie ihre weitere Entwicklung im deutschen Sprachraum* (3rd ed.). Frankfurt am Main: Fritz Knapp Verlag.

Fonteyne, W. (2007). *Cooperative Banks in Europe: Policy Issues, WP/07/159.* Washington, DC: International Monetary Fund (IMF) Working Paper.

Fonteyne, W., & Hardy, D. C. (2011). Cooperative Banks and Ethics: Past, Present and Future. *Ethical Perspectives, 18*(4), 491–514.

Granovetter, M. (1995). Coase Revisited: Business Groups in the Modern Economy. *Industrial and Corporate Change, 4,* 93–130.

Greve, R. (2009). The German Cooperative Banking Group as a Strategic Network. *Canadian Journal of Development Studies/Revue Canadienne D'Études du Développement, 29,* 1–2, 65–100.

Groeneveld, J. M. (2015). *Governance of European Cooperative Banks: Overview, Issues and Recommendations.* TIAS Working Paper.

Gulati, R. (1995). Does Familiarity Breed Trust? The Implications of Repeated Ties for Contractual Choice in Alliances. *Academy of Management Journal, 38,* 85–112.

Gulati, R. (1998). Alliances and Networks. *Strategic Management Journal, 19*(4), 293–317.

Gulati, R., Nohria, N., & Zaheer, A. (2000). Strategic Networks. *Strategic Management Journal, 21*(3), 203–215.

Hellinger, C. (1999). *Kernkompetenzbasiertes Outsourcing in Kreditgenossenschaften: Eine transaktionskostenökonomische Analyse unter besonderer Berücksichtigung von Netzwerkstrukturen.* Regensberg: Münster.

Jarillo, J. C. (1988). On Strategic Networks. *Strategic Management Journal, 9*(1), 31–41.

Jarillo, J. C. (1993). *Strategic Networks: Creating the Borderless Organization.* Oxford: Butterworth Heinemann.

Jensen, R. J., & Szulanski, G. (2007). Template Use and the Effectiveness of Knowledge Transfer. *Management Science, 53,* 1716–1730.

Kay, J. (2006, April 26). The Mutual Interest in Building Trust Still Remains. *Financial Times.*

Klein, S., & Mangan, A. (2005). Stability in Times of Change: A Strength of Co-operatives. In T. Theurl (Ed.), *Economics of Inter-Firm Networks* (pp. 89–117). Tübingen: Mohr Siebeck.

Littlechild, S. C. (1975). Common Costs, Fixed Charges, Clubs and Games. *Review of Economics Studies, 42,* 117–124.

Marin, M. (2016). Organizational Form and Financial Stability: Lessons from Cooperative Banks in the US and UK. *Banking and Finance Law Review, 31*(3), 513.

Menzani, T., & Zamagni, V. (2010). Cooperative Networks in the Italian Economy. *Enterprise and Society, 11*(1), 98–127.

Ory, J., & And Lemzeri, Y. (2012). Efficiency and Hybridization in Cooperative Banking: The French Case. *Annals of Public and Cooperative Economics, 83*(2), 215–250.

Oxley, J. E. (1997). Appropriability Hazards and Governance in Strategic Alliances: A Transaction Cost Approach. *Journal of Law, Economics and Organizations, 13,* 387–409.

Pfeffer, J., & Nowak, P. (1976). Joint Venture and Interorganizational Interdependence. *Administrative Science Quarterly, 21*(3), 398–418.

Picot, A., & Hardt, P. (1998). Make-or-Buy-Entscheidungen. In A. Meyer (Ed.), *Handbuch Dienstleistungsmarketing* (Vol. 1, pp. 625–646). Stuttgart: Schäffer-Poeschel.

Pisano, G. P., Russo, M. V., & And Teece, D. (1988). Joint Ventures and Collaborative Arrangements in the Telecommunications Equipment Industry. In D. C. Mowery (Ed.), *International Collaborative Ventures in U.S. Manufacturing* (pp. 23–70). Cambridge: Ballinger Pub. Co.

Porter, M. (1998). *Competitive Advantage: Creating and Sustaining Superior Performance.* New York: Free Press.

Portes, A. (1998). Social Capital: Its Origins and Applications in Modern Sociology. *Annual Review of Sociology, 24,* 1–24.

Stern, T. (2014). Regulating Liquidity Risks Within "Institutional Protection Schemes". *Beijing Law Review, 5,* 210–239.

Teece, D. (1992). Competition, Cooperation, and Innovation: Organizational Arrangements for Regimes of Rapid Technological Progress. *Journal of Economic Behavior and Organization, 18,* 1–25.

Uzzi, B. (1997). Social Structure and Competition in Interfirm Networks: The Paradox of Embeddedness. *Administrative Science Quarterly, 42,* 35–67.

Wasserman, S., & Faust, K. (1994). *Social Network Analysis: Methods and Applications.* Cambridge, UK: Cambridge University Press.

Williamson, O. E. (1983). Credible Commitments: Using Hostages to Support Exchange. *American Economic Review, 73,* 519–535.

Williamson, O. E. (1985). *The Economic Institutions of Capitalism.* New York: Free Press.

Williamson, O. E. (1991). Strategizing, Economizing, and Economic Organization. *Strategic Management Journal, 12,* 75–94.

CHAPTER 3

Co-operative Banking in Austria

1 Brief Overview of the Austrian Banking System

The Austrian banking system plays a significant role within the national financial system although, as in other European countries, it is declining in importance. As demonstrated by certain traditional indicators which are used to analyze the structure and development of financial systems, at the end of 2016, the ratio of Monetary Financial Institutions'[1] (MFIs) total assets to national GDP stood at 2.3 (3.6 in 2008) (as compared to 2.6 in Germany, 3.7 in France, 2.3 in Italy, and 2.4 in Spain in 2016),[2] while the assets held by MFIs as a percentage of the total assets of the financial sector equaled 61.4% (70.2% in 2008) (61.1% in Germany, 63.5% in France, 63.8% in Italy, and 67.2% in Spain in 2016) (ECB 2017).[3] Between 2015 and 2016, Austria experienced one of the biggest declines in banking assets in Europe, −10.5%,[4] which was driven by the restructure of Unicredit

---

[1] According to the definition provided by the ECB, MFIs form the money-issuing sector of the Eurozone. These include the Eurosystem, resident credit institutions, and all other resident financial institutions whose business is to receive deposits and/or substitutes for deposits from entities other than MFIs and, on their own account (at least in economic terms), to grant credit, and/or invest in securities. The latter group consists predominantly of money market funds.

[2] Excluding the data of the European System of Central Banks (ESCB).

[3] These two indicators were 3.6% and 70.2%, respectively, in 2008 (ECB 2017).

[4] Banking asset declines were recorded in Greece (−13.9%), Ireland (−8.9%), Cyprus (−8%), Latvia (−7.9%), and Portugal (−5.3%) (ECB 2017).

© The Author(s) 2019   97
F. Poli, *Co-operative Banking Networks in Europe*, Palgrave Macmillan Studies in Banking and Financial Institutions, https://doi.org/10.1007/978-3-030-21699-3_3

Bank Austria, and the consequent transfer of its central, eastern, and south-eastern European subsidiaries to the Italian Unicredit Group (ECB 2017). The banking industry predominantly comprises domestic banks who held a 74% share of total banking assets in 2016 although this is steadily decreasing (having dropped from 80% in 2009); foreign subsidiaries and branches, mostly from other European countries, held 20% of national banking assets in 2009 versus 26% at the end of 2016 (ECB 2017).

The domestic banking sector has a fundamental role in the financing of non-financial companies (NFCs), which rely heavily on domestic banks. At the end of 2016, the total financing provided by the domestic financial sector amounted to € 175 billion, almost 87% of which was granted by MFIs, mainly banks, while 8.46% came from Other Financial Intermediaries (OFIs) (excluding insurance companies and pension funds). In parallel, MFIs' financing to NFCs in other countries of the Eurozone totaled € 36.8 billion, following a decreasing trend (€ 38.7 billion in 2014) due to the ongoing restructuring of the major Austrian banking groups' foreign assets.[5]

Austria has a universal banking system, with a large number of banks adopting a variety of business models. Structural changes to the Austrian banking system began in the 1990s, facilitated by new sets of rules which permitted savings banks, co-operative banks (CBs), and state mortgage banks to incorporate their banking activities into stock corporations, and allowed the sale of state-owned banks (Braumann 2004). These legislative changes gave rise, as in other European member states, to a process of bank aggregations and regroupings within the country. Although a few domestic mergers and acquisitions took place involving the country's then largest banks (i.e. Erste Bank and Girocredit, Bank Austria, and Creditanstalt), as well as one major cross-border acquisition (Bank Austria-Creditanstalt being taken over by the German HypoVereinsbank and subsequently by Unicredit), this did not obscure the fundamental nature of the national consolidation process under way, which was characterized by domestic mergers between small- to medium-sized regional banks, primarily within the group of CBs and within the savings banks group (Egger and Hahn 2010). At the same time, this wave of privatization facilitated the growth of larger Austrian banks beyond their national boundaries, particularly into Eastern Europe. Further restructuring of the banking system occurred in response to the 2008–2009 crisis which led to significant

---

[5] ECB's data reported in the Report on Financial Structures (ECB 2017).

financial sector distress in Austria, due to strains that developed both domestically and in Central Europe and South-Eastern Europe (CESEE), where Austrian banks had gained a systemic role. More recently, the consolidation process of banks and branches has gained extra momentum due to the trend toward self-service and online banking which has further speeded up the rationalization of both credit institutions and banking outlets.

The outburst of the global financial crisis (GFC) led to banking distress in Austria. The internationally active banks' high exposure in CESEE weakened market confidence and boosted borrowing costs for both Austrian banks and the sovereign issuer (IMF 2014). In response to the crisis, the government and financial authorities took several steps to support the banking system and to strengthen financial oversight. A "banking package" was put in place in October 2008 that included bank recapitalization measures,[6] bank funding guarantees, unlimited deposit insurance until the end of 2009, and the creation of a federal entity to manage public participation in the banking system[7] (IMF 2014).

The Austrian banking sector was made up of 534 banks and 3759 branches at the end of 2017 (Table 3.1), making it one of the densest in Europe (14,210 inhabitants per credit institution compared to 67,341 per institution across the Eurozone in 2016) (ECB 2017). Like the German banking system, the Austrian one is highly competitive as a whole, probably more so than most others in Europe. As in Germany, one reason for this high level of competition is that banking concentration is extremely low by international standards: the five largest credit institutions' share of total assets has shown a downward trend in the last decade, standing at 34% at the end of 2016 (31% in Germany compared to 48% in the Eurozone in 2016) (ECB 2017). From 1980 onward, almost all Austrian

---

[6] In October 2008, the recapitalization of systemically important financial institutions up to € 15 billion was allowed by the Financial Market Stabilization Act (FinStaG). Capital injections reached € 5.9 billion in December 2012 (IMF 2014), while bank funding guarantees were introduced up to € 75 billion (IMF 2013).

[7] A nationalization of Austrian banks took place during 2008–2009. Kommunalkredit Austria AG, Austria's eighth largest bank held by Österreichische Volksbanken AG and the Belgian-French Dexia Crédit Local, with a total balance sheet of € 34.5 billion, was the first company to be acquired under the Financial Market Stabilization Act. It was followed by the Hypo Group Alpe Adria, the country's sixth largest bank by assets with about € 40 billion (held by BayernLB, a state-controlled German bank) and by the partial nationalization of Österreichische Volksbanken which will be detailed in the following pages.

Table 3.1 Number of banks and branches in Austria

Year	Joint-stock banks and private banks		Savings banks		State mortgage banks		Raiffeisen banks		Volksbanks		Building and loan associations		Total	
	Banks	Branches	Banks	Branches	Banks	Branches	Banks	Branches	Banks	Branches	Banks	Branches	Banks	Branches
2000	61	751	70	1397	9	154	625	1741	71	472	5	34	841	4549
2004	47	907	59	1019	10	169	581	1712	68	488	4	52	769	4347
2008	51	836	55	1007	11	167	551	1695	68	482	4	45	740	4232
2012	45	1108	51	956	11	159	520	1680	64	461	4	87	695	4451
2016	41	908	49	877	10	142	448	1505	20	407	4	76	572	3915
2017	39	871	49	866	9	141	419	1458	14	350	4	73	534	3759

Source: Author's elaboration on data extracted from the National Bank of Austria's statistics

banks greatly expanded their domestic branch networks, leading to over-banking. Consequently, with the opportunities for national expansion having been so limited for so long, private commercial banks, savings banks, and networks of CBs expanded significantly into the neighboring countries of Central and Eastern Europe.

The prevailing "alternative nature" of the Austrian banking sector is well demonstrated by the number of savings banks and CBs, as well as building and loan associations (Table 3.1): the number of joint-stock and private banks accounts for just 7.3% of the market, although their share of branches is higher at 23% at the end of 2017. However, almost 82% of the total number of banks are in the co-operative banking sector: popular banks or Volksbanks, and Raiffeisen banks that together hold about 48% of total branches.

The drive for efficiency, together with the increasingly pervasive role of technology in delivering banking services, has had a clear effect on the number of banking outlets held by the two co-operative banking networks. The Raiffeisen banks possess the largest branch network in Austria (Table 3.1), more than four times larger than that of the Volksbanks sector. The Volksbanks Verbund, the strategic network of popular banks which aggregates the majority of these types of CBs in Austria, held 340 branches, or 97% of the total Volksbanks branches in 2017. Both co-operative banking networks have undergone a process of deep restructuring since 2000. From 2000 to 2017, intra-sectoral aggregations led to a decrease in the number of banks, equating to almost 33% of Raiffeisen banks and 80% of Volksbanks, due to the severe crisis faced by the latter after the outbreak of the GFC. It is worth mentioning that despite the undoubted trend toward a rationalization of banking outlets across different banking business models in Austria (Table 3.1), the total reduction in the number of Raiffeisen banks' branches amounts to only 16% (down from 1741 to 1458 branches) (Table 3.1). This figure represents a much smaller decrease than that of their main domestic competitors, the savings banks, at 38%, and the Volksbanks, at about 26%. Therefore, it seems that proximity to members and customers is still of value to the Raiffeisen banks.

Among the most important banking groups, the co-operative Raiffeisen banking group (RBG) with its central institution and network of local and regional CBs is the largest in terms of assets, followed by the savings banking sector represented by the Erste Bank Group and the commercial Unicredit Bank Austria Group.

2   The Role of CBs Within the Austrian Banking Sector

The individual positions of Raiffeisen banks and Volksbanks within the country are quite different. While the former hold a leading position with mostly favorable growth trends, the latter retain a minor role at the national level, largely as a result of the more severe effects exerted on them by the GFC and their exposure to CESEE countries. At the end of 2017, the RBG ranked as Austria's largest banking group, representing around 30% of the Austrian banking system in terms of assets[8] as compared to the Volksbanks which held just under 2.7%.[9]

Data publicly disclosed by the European Association of Co-operative Banks (EACB) on the membership of the two co-operative banking groups documents about 1.7 million Raiffeisen members versus almost 661,000 Volksbanks members at the end of 2017. Both groups have displayed the ability to retain their membership numbers over time, with Raiffeisen faring better than the popular banks (Table 3.2). The Volksbanks experienced strong growth in their customer base from 2004 to 2010, followed by a decrease due to the financial distress faced by the network during most of the GFC, and then a renewed recovery in 2014 and 2016. Raiffeisen's customer base has apparently remained very stable with about 3,600,000 customers, a figure more than three times higher than that of the Volksbanks.

The Austrian co-operative banking system's strong operational focus on its members is demonstrated by its high governance ratios (in %). These are calculated as the proportion of the total number of members to customers, and represent one of the highest of the European samples considered in this book. Only Germany, with a rate of about 60%, ranked higher than Austria in 2017. Considering the two networks, Raiffeisen banks have held a nearly constant ratio at about 47% since 2010, with a slight increase after the GFC. By contrast, Volksbanks have shown considerable variability with a marked decrease between 2004 and 2006 (from 92.86%

[8] Own calculations on data disclosed by Raiffeisenlandesbank Niederösterreich-Wien (2018) for the RBG's assets and consolidated banking assets of Austria as reported in the National Bank of Austria's statistics at the end of 2017.

[9] Own calculations on consolidated banking assets reported in the Annual Report of the Association of Austrian Volksbanks at the end of 2017 and consolidated banking assets of Austria as reported in the National Bank of Austria's statistics at the end of 2017.

Table 3.2 Members, customers, and governance ratios of Raiffeisen banks and Volksbanks

Year	Volksbanks			Raiffeisen banks		
	Members	Customers	Governance ratio (%)	Members	Customers	Governance ratio (%)
2004	650,000	700,000	92.86	1,654,970	3,600,000	45.97
2006	673,158	1,500,000	44.88	1,657,186	3,600,000	46.03
2008	674,000	1,500,000	44.93	1,650,000	3,600,000	45.83
2010	701,643	1,500,000	46.77	1,720,000	3,600,000	47.78
2012	687,902	900,000	76.43	1,720,000	3,600,000	47.78
2014	688,000[a]	1,161,000	59.26	1,700,000	3,600,000	47.22
2016	688,000[a]	1,180,000	58.31	1,700,000	3,600,000	47.22
2017	660,807	1,134,339	58.25	1,700,000	3,600,000	47.22

Source: EACB. Author's calculations of the governance ratios

[a] Data reported on members of Volksbanks for 2014 and 2016 refer to 2013

Table 3.3 Domestic market shares of Raiffeisen banks and Volksbanks

Year	Loans (%)		Deposits (%)	
	Raiffeisen banks	Volksbanks	Raiffeisen banks	Volksbanks
2004	22.17	5.78	25.91	6.27
2006	23.42	7.70	27.78	7.10
2008	24.60	7.50	28.60	8.00
2010	25.50	7.30	29.30	7.20
2012	26.10	6.40	29.80	7.20
2014	28.40	5.34	29.60	5.55
2016	28.60	4.30	30.20	3.50
2017	28.90	4.50	30.60	5.30

Source: EACB

to 44.88%) due to the expansionary growth undertaken by the network, and a subsequent increase in 2012 due to the reduction in customer numbers caused by the severe financial distress and the restructuring which resulted. Volksbanks' governance figures in 2014, 2016, and 2017 look more consistent and are well above those of Raiffeisen, with a governance ratio of over 58% at the end of 2017 (Table 3.2).

Analysis shows that almost one-third of loans and deposits are intercepted by the deeply locally rooted Raiffeisen CBs (Table 3.3). These exhibit a steady growth in both sides of their credit intermediation function over time, while the same cannot be said of Volksbanks, whose shares have generally been decreasing since the GFC as a result of the financial difficulties faced by the network but with a return to growth in 2017.

The growing competition and wider diversification opportunities brought about by the deregulation of the European banking industry seem not to have lured Raiffeisen CBs, whose orientation toward traditional banking intermediation, making loans, and attracting deposits has even grown over time. From 2004 to 2017 their percentages of loans to customers to total assets reached 67.18%, which is lower than the 78.26% reported for the more focused Volksbanks (Table 3.4). Certainly, the severe episodes of distress encountered by the Volksbanks group after the outbreak of the financial crisis, which culminated in the breakup of Oesterreichische Volksbanken AG (ÖVAG), historically the central bank of the group, may have contributed to strengthening the market share of their natural competitor, Raiffeisen CBs (Table 3.3). The larger share of loans and deposits to total assets exhibited by Volksbanks at the end of 2017, besides reflecting their return to traditional lending and deposit activities, is purely the result of the asset downsizing undertaken by the group in light of the already mentioned distress phenomena experienced.

In fact, the total assets of Volksbanks, having tripled between 2004 and 2008 (from € 33,733 to € 94,571 million), have been constantly diminishing since the onset of the GFC, dropping to € 24,466 million and

Table 3.4 Credit intermediation orientation of Raiffeisen banks and Volksbanks

Year	Customer loans to assets (%) (A)		Customer deposits to assets (%) (B)		Customer loans to deposits (%) (A/B)	
	Raiffeisen banks	Volksbanks	Raiffeisen banks	Volksbanks	Raiffeisen banks	Volksbanks
2004	59.37	52.16	59.14	65.30	100.39	79.88
2006	57.88	55.53	55.71	66.16	103.90	83.93
2008	62.16	55.80	54.25	66.26	114.58	84.21
2010	63.78	69.08	58.68	45.40	108.70	152.16
2012	66.50	48.73[a]	59.06	20.54[a]	112.59	237.22[a]
2014	66.70	72.36	60.99	65.78	109.36	110.00
2016	66.85	79.24	67.74	81.82	98.70	96.84
2017	67.18	78.26	69.31	82.41	96.93	94.96

Source: Author's calculations on data reported by EACB

[a]Figures refer to domestic/local banks only

€ 25,323 million at the end of 2016 and 2017, respectively, a figure lower than the amount recorded in 2004. Conversely, in the same period the Raiffeisen network's total assets grew from € 145,530 million in 2004 to € 286,063 million in 2017, almost doubling (EACB, various years).

Table 3.4 shows the ratio of loans to deposits (in %) which represents a proxy of the so-called "funding gap" broadly measuring the dependence of banks on market-based funding (Hardie and Howarth 2013). The values recorded by the two networks at the end of 2017 are very similar (96.93% for Raiffeisen banks and 94.96% for Volksbanks), although with very dissimilar preceding amounts. Volksbanks' ratio grew substantially during 2008–2012 principally due to suffering a contraction in deposits: in 2008 deposits totaled € 94,571 million while in 2012 they fell to € 11,793 million as reported in the EACB's statistics. More recently, both co-operative groups appear to be more insulated from the risks arising from a substantial reliance on market funding, thanks to their ability to attract and mobilize the savings of customers and members.

3 CO-OPERATIVE BANKING: HISTORICAL DEVELOPMENT IN AUSTRIA

The co-operative banking system in Austria is characterized by two autonomous co-operative banking groups: Volksbanks, also known as people's banks or popular banks, inspired by the German Schulze-Delitzsch's ideas; and Raiffeisen banks, following the Christian-inspired principles of its German founder, Raiffeisen. The development of co-operative banking in Austria began in the middle of the nineteenth century, originally following the founding ideas of Schulze-Delitzsch. The first example of a credit co-operative was the "Aushilfskassenverein in Klagenfurt" which was created in 1851 (Brazda et al. 2016). Initially CBs were founded thanks to the guarantees provided by wealthy sponsors. However, they soon adopted models based on the principle of "self-help". The spread of CBs across the territories of the Austrian monarchy took place quite rapidly: in little more than 30 years the number of CBs reached 1133, most of them located in small villages and towns and not organized into any kind of association. A general federation was established in 1872, while in the following year the co-operative law (Genossenschaftsgesetz) was enacted,[10] granting co-operatives substantial flexibility to adapt the norms through their statutes.

[10] Law April 9, 1873, n. 70/1873, on purchase and economic co-operatives.

In these years, credit co-operatives' activities developed in a heterogeneous manner: in fact, while in the small rural centers, the spirit of the founding principles of the credit co-operatives (Kreditgenossenschaften) remained intact, in the cities many of them were transformed into small banks that focused mainly on the business of the wealthy middle class, and on promoting the transformation of large traders into genuine entrepreneurs. This had led to strong criticism of the Schulze-Delitzsch banking sector, to the point that the Ministry of Commerce contemplated, toward the end of the century, introducing new rules requiring state approval for the establishment of a credit co-operative, or the expansion of an existing business.

Just a few years after the foundation of the Schulze-Delitzsch CBs, the Raiffeisen co-operatives started to be popular in Austria as financial vehicles that aimed to reduce the rural population's difficulties in obtaining credit. The first Raiffeisen bank in Austria was founded in 1886 by Ernst Vergani (1848–1915) in Mühldorf, near the village of Spitz an der Donau. Its members included farmers, craftsmen, workers, and traders. The co-operative's foundation was preceded by a number of congresses which had sought solutions to the agrarian crisis.[11] As in Germany, development occurred rapidly, with the help of public entities. As reported by Brazda et al. (2016), "the public sector took over the revision, monetary settlement, the starting aid, supported with training courses, the publication of manuals and the organization of study tours". The growth of the Raiffeisen co-operative banking was even faster than that of popular banks, as documented by Brazda et al. (2016). Inspired by the German model, a central association of Raiffeisen co-operatives was established, preparing the ground for the birth of the Austrian Raiffeisen banking network.

The years following the First World War proved fundamental for the strengthening of sectoral networks, which had already been hit by episodes of crisis which favored aggregation between banks. In 1922, the Schulze-Delitzsch credit co-operatives established what became known as Österreichische Volksbanken AG (ÖVAG) as their central bank. This was a legally constituted co-operative, providing clearing services and liquidity support for the Volksbanks. In 1927, Genossenschaftliche Zentralbank, later renamed Raiffeisen Zentralbank (RZB), was established as the co-operative central bank for Raiffeisen banks.

---

[11] See the history of the network reported on the website of Raiffeisen Bank International (RBI) https://www.rbinternational.com/.

The development of co-operative banking was accompanied by several reforms which established specific regulations on co-operatives and the banking sector. Following the German model, in 1903 the co-operative auditing law (Revisionsgesetz) was enacted, making the regular auditing of co-operative companies by co-operative auditing unions mandatory. The reformulation in 1974 of the Co-operative Law, followed by the subsequent introduction in 1979 of the new Credit Law (Kreditwesengesetz), was a significant step in the history of Austrian co-operative banks. The new regulation on co-operatives, in particular, redefined the founding values of these entities, allowing them for the first time to operate with those who were not members of the co-operative. This meant that the banking co-operatives could significantly expand their customer base. However, this option of having non-member clients remained subordinate to the ultimate goal of the co-operative form, which is to promote the economic conditions of its members. To the same end, co-operatives were also allowed to participate in undertakings in other legal forms.

The Credit Law introduced the requirement to have at least two directors working full-time on the management of local banks' activities. It should be considered that at the time not all of the small local banks were particularly structured in their organization and, often, the administration of banks was undertaken by local professionals as a kind of second job.

As a result of the Credit Law, there was a significant wave of mergers between small operational entities, substantially reducing their number. At the end of 2005, 66 popular banks and 576 Raiffeisen banks were recorded, which was about a third of the number existing in the 1970s (Crespi 2008).

Tax benefits at the corporate and member level were eliminated during the 1970s and 1980s, thus putting more competitive pressures on the co-operative banking sector.

During this period, the popular and Raiffeisen banks followed a path that transformed them into truly universal banks, with a broad supply of production and services. To get an idea of the evolution of these institutions, consider that, until the beginning of the 1950s, the majority of Raiffeisen banks opened their doors only on Sundays, after Mass. Over a period of about 20 years, and especially after the liberalization of branches in 1977, the Raiffeisen banking network became the premier banking group in terms of geographical spread.

Since the 1980s, with the process of modernizing the co-operative banking sector completed and the creation and continuous expansion of specialized institutions (and the related services they offer) under way, synergies within the two networks have been strengthened, thanks to the strategic management of national associations and overseas expansion, mainly by Raiffeisen banks, especially into the neighboring countries of Eastern Europe.

ÖVAG became a private co-operative limited company in 1974 and a commercial bank in 1991, after which it developed a life of its own, lending on its own account and acquiring interests not only within Austria but in CESEE countries. In 1996 the German central institution of the co-operative banking network, DZ Bank, bought a 25% stake, apparently to improve "co-operation" between the Austrian and German co-operative banking systems. In 1997, ÖVAG founded an international division, strategically aimed at streamlining banking activities in CESEE countries and deploying capital more effectively. Volksbanks International AG (VBI) became a joint-stock company in 1999.[12] ÖVAG itself remained in majority ownership by the Volksbanks. The onset of the 2007–2008 financial crisis in Europe initially damaged ÖVAG due to the failure of Austria's infrastructure bank Kommunalkredit AG, of which ÖVAG was the largest shareholder.[13] It was bailed out several times by the Austrian federal government and part-nationalized by means of a debt-equity conversion of Austrian federal government's subordinated debt holding. Nonetheless ÖVAG continued to make losses.[14] In light of the difficulties faced by the entire Volksbanks system, it agreed to restructure, adopting a legal framework in line with Art. 10 of the Capital Requirements Regulation (CRR) (as transposed by Art. 30a of the Austrian Banking Law). The new integrated system of banks, the so-called "Volksbanks Verbund", is based on a contract of association (Verbundvertrag) with a joint-liability and joint-liquidity scheme and authorization for the central organization within the association (initially ÖVAG) to issue instructions to the affiliated credit institutions, the Volksbanks (Art. 30a [1]).

In October 2014, following its downgrade by Moody's to one notch above junk and the lack of further support from the Austrian federal

---

[12] As part of the resulting restructuring process undertaken by the sector, Volksbank International AG was sold to Russian Sberbank in February 2012.

[13] The stake in Kommunalkredit AG was sold to the Austrian Federal Government in November 2008 for a symbolic € 1. As several CESEE countries slid into deep recession in 2008 (e.g. Romania, Hungary, and Latvia), banks exposed to CESEE suffered collapsing asset values and the destruction of shareholder value. OVAG was largely hit by the CEE crisis.

[14] This historical reconstruction is made by Coppola (2015), https://www.thenews.coop/95508/sector/lesson-behind-austrian-co-op-banking-disaster/.

government, and preempting their expected failure of the European Banking Authority (EBA) stress tests, ÖVAG announced that it was to be broken up. In 2015, the core functions of ÖVAG were transferred to the Volksbank Wien AG (effective since 4 July 2015) with the legal form of joint-stock corporation and the biggest regional bank of the system. At the same time, all property belonging to the non-core segments of ÖVAG was transferred out of the co-operative group. The remaining Volksbanks committed to a strict merger plan, reducing independent credit institutions to fit into a target structure of eight regional banks and one specialized institution, Österreichische Ärzte und Apothekerbank, AG.

Like ÖVAG, the Raiffeisen network started, via its central institution, to expand into Central Eastern countries in 1986, founding its first subsidiary in Hungary. Three years later, the original Genossenschaftliche Zentralbank was renamed Raiffeisen Zentralbank AG (RZB) which continued to enlarge its presence in CESEE countries successfully, especially after the fall of the "iron curtain" in 1989. The group's dynamism led to the listing of Raiffeisen Bank International (RBI) Holding in 2005, a fully consolidated RZB subsidiary, acting as the holding and steering unit for the RZB Group's subsidiaries in CESEE countries. The outbreak of the financial crisis and the consequent financial difficulties forced RZB's main shareholders to make a capital injection to strengthen the bank's resilience and to use Austrian state assistance. From 2010, the group embarked on a program of rationalization. In 2010, RZB's commercial customer business and its related activities were spun off and merged with RBI Holding AG, creating the newly founded institution, RBI AG. Activities related to RZB's function as the central institution of the RBG and those undertakings relevant to this sector were to remain at RZB. In January 2017, the extraordinary general meetings of RZB and RBI approved the merger of the two companies which became effective on 18 March 2017. RBI has become the comprehensive legal successor of RZB. The merger was designed to simplify their organizational structure, improve their capital base (via the regulatory treatment of minority interests), and strengthen their cost basis. Currently, the regional Raiffeisen banks hold approximately 58.8% of the listed shares of the joint-stock company RBI, with 41.2% remaining in free float.[15]

---

[15] The Raiffeisen Landesbanks and direct and indirect subsidiary companies of the Raiffeisen Landesbanks are parties acting in concert within the meaning of section 1 subpara. 6 of the Austrian Takeover Act (Übernahmegesetz) on the basis of a syndicate agree-

4   Austrian Co-operative Banking Networks: Main Characteristics

The organizational models adopted by Austrian CBs are based on the concept of networks, although with different degrees of integration. These networks are made up of legally autonomous local institutions with distinct business models and central institutions at the regional and/or national level whose capital belongs to local banks, thus creating an inverted ownership structure.

According to Austrian Banking Law, banks constituted in the form of a co-operative company are authorized to carry out banking business. The initial capital or endowment amounts of the CB must be freely available to the directors without restrictions or charges in Austria. The shares (Geschäftsanteile) are fully part of the Tier 1 capital of the bank, in accordance with EU capital regulation.

In the legal definition of a co-operative, the concept of the non-closed number of participants is fundamental in allowing members the opportunity to enter and exit the scheme. This implies that the co-operative's capital does not constitute a fixed amount but may vary within limits, provided these do not alter the stability of the bank itself. The idea of open association which exists in the co-operative form does not oblige the association to accept the entry of any natural and/or legal person. Statutorily, it is possible to delimit the type of its members: in fact, the purpose of the co-operative could be to promote the conditions of particular types of members (e.g. residents in the same area as the bank, those occupied in particular productive sectors). Members may ask for the redemption of their shares through a written request to the issuing CB to terminate their membership (or to redeem a member share). In the event of the death of a private member, his/her shares and membership are passed to those

ment in relation to RBI. The syndicate agreement includes inter alia a block voting agreement for all matters subject to a resolution of the RBI shareholders' meeting, agreement with respect to rights of nomination to the Supervisory Board of RBI, and agreement of preemption rights between the parties to the syndicate agreement. Furthermore, it is agreed that for a period of three years following the date on which the merger of RZB and RBI takes effect, sales of RBI shares held by the Raiffeisen Landesbanks (with a few exceptions) are subject to contractual restrictions in the event that as a result the aggregate (direct and/or indirect) shareholding of the Raiffeisen Landesbanks in RBI falls below 50% of the share capital plus one share (thereafter the shareholding threshold reduces to 40% of the share capital of RBI). See RBI's shareholder structure as reported in company's website.

heirs who apply for membership and are accepted by the board. Only in cases where no heir becomes a member within a year of the transfer of the title according to the inheritance proceedings is the membership automatically terminated at the end of the current business year. In this instance, as in the case of the liquidation of a corporate member, no request is required. Termination of membership and redemption of shares is possible only at the end of the business year (EACB 2012). A valid request is subject to a notice period of at least one month before the end of the business year. Partial redemption without termination of membership follows the same procedure. According to the Austrian Co-operative Law, a member leaving in the event of insolvency or liquidation remains liable for his/her co-operative shares and an additional commitment of at least the same amount for a period of three years after his/her withdrawal (EACB 2012). However, CBs' statutes may lay down that the liability of their members is limited to their co-operative share pursuant to Art. 27 of the Austrian Banking Act.[16]

As in the case of banks constituted in the form of joint-stock companies, CBs can issue capital instruments without voting rights[17] (Art. 26a Austrian Banking Law) or contingent convertible bonds which can be converted into Common Equity Tier 1 instruments (Art. 26 Austrian Banking Law) upon the occurrence of a triggering event defined in advance and for which the conversion ratio is determined or can be determined upon issuing the contingent convertible bonds. The co-operative must at the same time obtain from the subscribers an undated and irrevocable declaration of enrollment with regard to the conversion.

The two co-operative Austrian networks operate under different regulated organizational schemes. In both cases, there is a central institution, owned by the local/regional banks, with well-defined roles. While Volksbanks act in line with the provisions of Art. 10 of the CRR with the highest degree of integration and a central institution that has significant power over affiliated banks, the Raiffeisen banks' network features a lower degree of integration and an institutional protection scheme (IPS) in line with the provisions of Art. 113(7) of the CRR. Its central institution retains limited influence over the individual co-operatives. In both cases, the central institution provides services that the local bank cannot provide

---

[16] The Act is available at https://www.fma.gv.at/en/national/supervisory-laws/.

[17] Profits allocated to these instruments shall be a predefined multiple of the dividend on a share of profit attributable to a co-operative share with a voting right.

itself, such as securities trading, financing of export customers and support for their foreign operations, access to hedging products, cash management, and payment methods.

Article 30a of the Austrian Banking Law defines the conditions under which the network of banks affiliated to a central institution enjoys the regulatory prudential requirements waiver pursuant to Art. 10(1) of the CRR. Specifically, banks permanently affiliated to a credit institution established in Austria as a central body can, as credit institutions themselves, join together with the central body to form an affiliation of credit institutions. The affiliation of credit institutions is formed through the establishment of a contract between the central body and the affiliated credit institutions. To be valid in all participating companies, this contract requires the approval of a majority of the shareholders or general meeting, as is the case for an amendment of the articles of association. The companies must also adapt their articles of association accordingly. The establishment of an affiliation of credit institutions is subject to approval by the Financial Market Authority (FMA), with the central body responsible for the submission of the application on behalf of the affiliated entities. The application must be accompanied by documentation detailing the control, monitoring, and risk management processes; the ability of the affiliation to comply permanently with the prudential requirements; and other significant information.

Responsibility for compliance with the provisions of the Austrian Banking Act and EU Regulation No 575/2013 that apply to the affiliation of credit institutions lies with the central body. This must carefully monitor the solvency and liquidity of the affiliation of credit institutions on the basis of consolidated financial statements and of individual financial statements from the affiliated credit institutions. To this end, the central body ensures that the directors of the affiliated credit institutions meet all personal and professional requirements and that the affiliation of credit institutions has in place the appropriate administrative, accounting, and control mechanisms for the capture, assessment, management, and monitoring of commercial and operational banking risks and remuneration policies and practices. The central body's powers to issue instructions under Art. 10(1)(c) of the CRR are established by contract and articles of association.

Pursuant to Article 30a(6), the central body is regarded as a European Economic Area (EEA) parent credit institution while the affiliated credit institutions are subordinate institutions in accordance with Art. 405(2) of the CRR. The central body prepares consolidated financial statements.

Joint-liability schemes are also in place as the central body and all affiliated credit institutions assume liability for the entire assets of any affiliated credit institution.

Members of the affiliation of credit institutions are permitted to resign, subject to observance of the normal notice periods specified in the contractual arrangements between the central body and the affiliated credit institutions and to approval by the FMA. This is granted if compliance with prudential requirements is guaranteed by the affiliation of credit institutions following the resignation of the affiliated credit institution in question (Art. 30a [5a]).

Both co-operative banking networks have in place joint cash-clearing operation systems. The arrangements regarding the actual provision of liquidity between the central institution (or any other credit institution where the liquidity reserve is held) and the other credit institutions participating in the liquidity association must be governed by contractual or statutory means. The contractual or statutory arrangements must include, inter alia, the requirement to provide liquidity to associated credit institutions when necessary; the specific description of the obligation on the central institution or other credit institution where the liquid funds are held to provide liquidity when necessary; and the relevant decision-making process, in particular the requirements for resolutions. The system of liquidity balancing is designed to ensure financial market stability by entitling affiliated banks to receive the liquidity they need in the event of a shortfall. This rule enables Raiffeisen banks and Volksbanks to maintain an appropriate balance between money supply and credit demand; additionally, it eases the maturity transformation of larger amounts through the cash pools managed by central institutions and favors the availability of capital for larger projects financed by central institutions.

Volksbanks and Raiffeisen banks in Austria adopt multi-tier organizational structures. Namely, while Volksbanks adopt a two-tier model (as do Austrian savings banks), Raiffeisen banks have opted for a three-tier form.

In both co-operative systems, one finds traditional elements of co-operatives and features of corporations. For this reason, they are hybrid systems. Banks which are part of the two networks operate under a common brand name and, thanks to the pooling of certain functions, are able to offer their customers a wide array of products while also benefiting from economies of scale.

4.1   The Raiffeisen Banking Group

The RBG is a fairly complex network made up of 407 independent banks which focus on retail banking.[18] The banks at the base of the pyramid, the first tier, act as "primary banks", that is, universal banks that provide a full range of banking services to local customers regardless of whether they are members of the co-operative or not. Each CB operates within a well-defined geographical area and is not allowed to set up branches inside the market territory of a competitor of the same co-operative association.

Above the level of the primary banks, there are eight regional Raiffeisenlandesbanks, which are owned by the primary banks and other co-operative entities. These banks are often corporations held by regional holding companies and serve their members, the primary banks, providing them with a variety of services, ranging from liquidity balancing to other central services, such as transactions on the money market and the foreign exchange market, corporate banking, data processing, consulting, and training services. These regional Raiffeisen banks are also universal banks. However, the Raiffeisenlandesbanks' main area of business lies in the middle-market sector and corporate customers. Although clearly identified in regional organizational structures, the business operations of Landesbanks are not restricted to specific geographical areas.

Regional co-operative banks hold 58.8% of the top institution's capital, with the three major shareholders being Raiffeisenlandesbank NÖ-Wien, Raiffeisenlandesbank Steiermark, and Raiffeisenlandesbank Oberösterreich. Together they hold about 42% of RBI's capital (Fig. 3.1).

RBI has holdings in domestic and international companies operating in the banking and financial sector, as well as in ancillary activities, such as information technology and marketing.

Following the merger with its former majority shareholder RZB in March 2017, RBI acts as the central body of the regional Raiffeisen banks and other financial institutions within the RBG. The merger was motivated by capital reasons and organizational rationalizations. Namely, the aggregation responded to the need to strengthen the regulatory capital ratio of the group in light of the removal of the minority deductions from Common Equity Tier 1 capital at the group level; additionally, it has simplified its decision-making structures, eliminating duplication between RBI and RZB. RBI has positioned itself in CESEE countries as a fully

---

[18] Taken from Investor Presentation of Raiffeisen Bank International (RBI 2018).

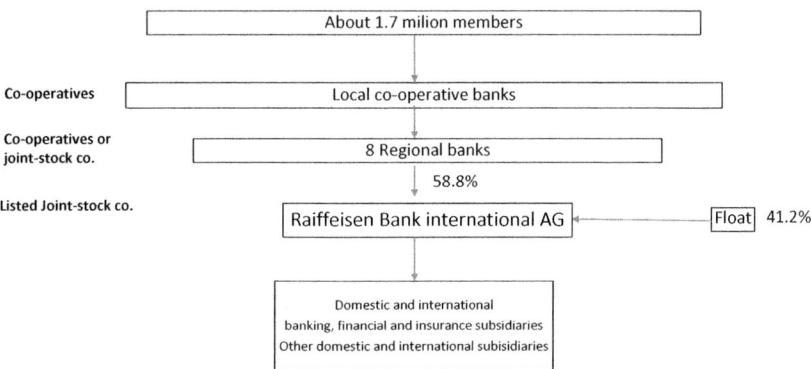

Fig. 3.1 The structure of the Raiffeisen Banking Group. Source: Author's elaboration

integrated corporate and retail banking group with a comprehensive product offering. In Austria, RBI is one of the top corporate and investment banks. It primarily serves Austrian customers, but also has international customers and large multinational corporate customers as well as wealthy private clients operating in CESEE.

In this role, RBI renders essential services for its direct owners, the regional Raiffeisen banks, and provides joint solutions within its own group and the RBG.

According to the articles of association approved by the general meeting of RBI's shareholders on 24 January 2017, RBI is authorized to engage in all activities that become incumbent on it as the central institution of the Austrian RBG. More specifically, RBI is empowered to administer and invest the liquid funds made available to it by primary and regional banks, also offering liquidity to banks that need it. According to the Banking Law (Art. 27a), credit institutions that are associated with a central institution must participate in a joint cash-clearing operation system. They are required to hold a liquidity reserve at the central institution. The liquidity reserve is calculated as being 10% of the savings deposits and 20% of the other euro deposits, subject to a maximum of 14% of the entire euro deposits. The arrangements regarding the provision of liquidity between the central institution or other credit institution with which the liquidity reserve is held and the other credit institutions participating in the liquidity association must be governed by contractual or statutory means. Due to the three-tier structure of the RBG, the liquidity reserve arrangements takes place on two levels: primary banks hold liquidity reserves with their regional Raiffeisen banks (which act as central institutions of the local banks), and the latter place liquidity reserves with their own central body, RBI.

The apex is also tasked with ensuring the consistency of advertising and organization, and the training of the employees of the group's enterprises, irrespective of their legal form. It is responsible for the strategic management of the "Raiffeisen" brand development and for the definition and management of the national advertising and sponsorship strategy. This puts RBI at the top of a so-called quasi-strategic group according to our taxonomy of co-operative banking networks' governance models.

The services that RBI provides to the network include coordinating the maintenance of RBG's minimum reserve held at Austria's central bank by determining and bundling the payment streams and forwarding them to the central bank. According to its articles of association, RBI offers consultancy and management services of all kinds to the business enterprises in which RBI has a holding or which are otherwise linked to it.

RBI is situated at the top of RBG's institutional protection scheme, which was approved by the FMA at the end of 2014. The liability arrangements of the IPS protect the participating institutions, being designed to ensure their liquidity and solvency when required. The IPS is based on uniform, joint risk monitoring pursuant to Article 49(3) and Article 113(7) of the CRR. The whole IPS is designed with two levels (the federal and regional IPSs) to reflect RBG's organizational structure. Contractual and statutory liability arrangements are in place to make the IPS effective in pursuing its goals. Hence, the IPS supplements the RBG system of mutual assistance that comes into effect if a member experiences economic difficulties. As RBG's central institution, RBI is a member of the federal IPS whose members, in addition to the regional Raiffeisen banks, include Raiffeisen-Holding Niederösterreich-Wien, Posojilnica Bank (formerly ZVEZA Bank), Raiffeisen Wohnbaubank, and Raiffeisen Bausparkasse. The federal and regional IPSs are subject to authorization and the regulatory supervision of the ECB.

Financial support (such as capital injections, loans, or guarantees) for RBG's system of IPSs is granted according to conditions determined by the risk council on a case-by-case basis. A hierarchical scheme of intervention is in place with the preliminary involvement of the regional IPS, followed by that of the federal IPS, should the former be unable to cope with the entire financial assistance required. A cross-guarantee scheme has also been designed to cover any lack of funds in the IPS. Members of the IPS are required to contribute to an ex ante fund and to make ex post contributions if necessary.

A voluntary supplementary scheme protects customers up to the level of the economic reserves of the participating banks. The Raiffeisen-Kundengarantiegemeinschaft Österreich (RKÖ) includes the regional banks and RBI was established in 1999.[19] It offers deposit protection supplementary to the legal protection[20] provided by the Österreichische Raiffeisen-Einlagensicherung eGen (ÖRE) that is responsible for the statutory deposit guarantee and investor compensation scheme for the Raiffeisen banks and the regional Raiffeisen banks, as well as RBI. Solidarity mechanisms are also in place at the regional level.

4.2   The Volksbanks Group

The Volksbanks Verbund (Association of Volksbanks) currently comprises a group of eight regional Volksbanks and one specialized financial institution dedicated to physicians and pharmacists, the Aerzte und Apothekerbank AG, in Austria. The primary banks have merged into eight regional entities roughly mirroring Austria's federal structure. Mergers between Volksbanks have taken place throughout the period 2013–2018. Out of the 63 banks that existed in 2013, 43 have undergone mergers, while a few banks have left the Association (FitchRatings 2018). The current Verbund was established in 2015, acts as a strategic network, and grants the central body the power to issue binding orders to all or individual primary banks and to enforce support measures pursuant to Art. 10 of the CRR and Art. 30a of the Austrian Banking Law. The Verbund is assimilated to a banking group in the context of the CRR and, therefore, is regulated as a group with consolidated financial accounts. As a result, the EU's Bank Recovery and Resolution Directive (BRRD) applies to the Verbund, but not to its member entities individually.

The Association stands as a highly integrated inverted financial group and qualifies as a significant entity under the direct supervision of the ECB. At the end of 2017, Volksbank Wien, which acts as the central institution, was the largest member with assets totaling around € 11 billion.

---

[19] As reported in RBI's Annual Report for the year-end 2017.
[20] It includes customer deposits, bonds, and promissory note loans.

On an individual basis, the remaining Volksbanks hold total assets ranging from € 1 to € 3 billion.

Although a few Volksbanks have opted for the legal form of a corporation, their statutes are designed as a co-operative corporation. Most of the Volksbanks still operate in the co-operative form. Rather than adopting the principle of shareholder value, the banks follow the principle of member value and pay a dividend. Generally, one member has a limited number of votes (restricted to a maximum of ten) depending on the number of shares they hold (Blisse 2014). One of the banks in the Association Volksbank Vorarlberg is listed on the Austrian stock exchange. In 2017, Sparda bank, historically the CB for railways workers, merged with Volksbank Wien AG. The brand has been kept independent and continues to exist as a bank with employees and branches throughout Austria (Fig. 3.2).

The implementation of the co-operation agreement between the banks is entrusted to an ad hoc company Volksbank Vertriebs und Marketing eG, which is responsible for the harmonization of sales activities and related processes.

The central body of the group, in addition to its retail business, assumes management and steering functions and is responsible for liquidity and risk management across the association. It is also responsible for the planning process, internal organization, and IT as well as compliance with regulatory requirements, having the power to issue general and individual instructions to affiliated banks. It is also empowered to impose remedial actions on troubled primary banks if early-warning indicators deteriorate materially.

Volksbank Wien's ordinary capital is held (as at the end of 2017) by regional Volksbanks (30%) and the Republic of Austria (25%), with the remainder held by sector-related entities. As part of its restructuring in

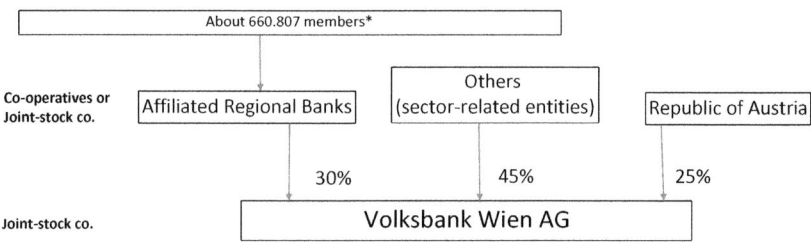

Fig. 3.2 The structure of the Volksbanks Verbund. Source: Author's elaboration

2015, the Austrian government was granted a profit participation right (Genussrecht) and a blocking minority in Volksbank Wien in exchange for a capital injection. The government will recoup its stake when its Genussrecht pays out a cumulative € 300 million (of which € 233 million is still outstanding), based on a binding annual schedule until 2023 (FitchRatings 2018).

The Association of Popular Banks is based on a mutual support scheme, namely, a joint-liability scheme, whereby the members contractually agree to bear the costs and risks of the central institution on a pro rata basis.[21] The scheme comprises a trust fund, the Volksbanks Leistungsfond (VL), established in 2016, which is managed by the central institution and designed to provide financial support, also in the form of recapitalization, to affiliated Volksbanks facing financial distress due to a deterioration in their earnings, their liquidity position, or their capital structure. The apex has the responsibility for defining the VL's target endowment based on the primary banks' average risk position.

Analogously to Raiffeisen banks, the central body participates in and manages the joint cash-clearing operation system of the Volksbanks.

The banks of the Verbund are party to the statutory guarantee of deposits and investor compensation scheme for the Volksbanks sector, which is administered by the Volksbanks Einlagensicherung eG (VEG). Should the mutual support scheme fail to ensure Verbund's viability, VEG will intervene to protect eligible deposits up to a maximum of € 100,000 per depositor. VEG monitors the financial position of Verbund's members using the same early-warning system that the central institution uses for the mutual support scheme (FitchRatings 2018). The auditing and representation of interests of the Verbund is undertaken by the Austrian Co-operative Association which, together with VEG, jointly performs tasks in relation to the early identification of risks incurred by its members.

As a result of the reorganization of the group, which took place in response to several intra-sector aggregations, the Association now appears less complex and more oriented toward achieving higher levels of efficiency. This is further imposed by the persistence of a low interest rate environment in Europe which calls for improvements in productivity and the streamlining of cost structures. Several steps have been taken, such as increasing the standardization of the product mix, the launch of different

---

[21] For further details, see the Annual Report of the Association of Volksbanks for the year-end 2015.

digitization initiatives (i.e. digital desktop banking, banking apps, automation of some credit processes), and the enlargement of the financial offer through external suppliers. Due to its limited size, since 2016, the Verbund has sourced consumer lending and asset management products from DZ Bank, the apex of the German co-operative banking group. This strategic decision allows the Verbund to exploit the leading franchise of their historical partner, acting primarily as a simple distributor and thus diversifying its revenues while limiting its exposure to any credit risk (which is assumed by the German partner).

5   The Performance of Austrian Co-operative Versus Non-Co-operative Banking Groups over the Period 2005–2017

As well as being different in organizational terms, the two co-operative banking networks differ considerably in size. At the end of 2017, the Volksbanks Verbund reported total assets of € 25.3 billion (€ 24.4 billion in 2016) and a strong focus on the national market, while the Raiffeisen banking group's assets totaled € 286 billion (€ 279.6 billion in 2016), of which € 135.1 billion (€ 111.9 billion in 2016)[22] related solely to RBI with its international presence in 13 CESEE countries. Banking assets outside Austria amount to about 64% of RBI's total assets (the most significant being in the Czech Republic, Poland, Slovakia, and Russia which make up about 61% of its assets in foreign holdings) while the remainder consist of non-retail business activities.[23] The network of Raiffeisen CBs and their apex, RBI, constitute the leading banking group in the country, measured by total assets. This is followed by the Erste Group, representing the savings bank sector which, in common with the Raiffeisen group, has had a policy of significant expansion in Central and South-Eastern Europe since the 1990s (with assets amounting to € 220.7 billion at the end of 2017).[24] The third major intermediary is the joint-stock Unicredit

---

[22] Figure reported in the company presentation of Raiffeisenlandesbank Niederösterreich-Wien AG in June 2018.

[23] Our calculations on figures reported in the Annual Report of Raiffeisen Bank International for the year-end 2017.

[24] Data include independent savings banks which are members of the Haftungsverbund (cross-guarantee system) of Austrian savings banks. The Erste Bank Group is a listed joint-

Bank Austria (with total assets of € 102.1 billion at the end of 2017), a shareholder-oriented bank, which is also active in Central Eastern European countries and is controlled by the Italian Unicredit Group. Austria's second co-operative network, the Volksbanks Verbund, is decidedly smaller in size (with total assets of € 25.3 billion at the end of 2017) and focuses almost exclusively on the domestic market.

Both the apex of the Raiffeisen network and the Erste Group enjoy positive long-term ratings (A3 in Moody's Rating Scale in 2017), while Unicredit Bank Austria is slightly lower (Baa1) and the Volksbanks Verbund was assigned a BBB long-term issuer default rating by Fitch in early 2018. This rating has since increased as result of the restructuring efforts undertaken by the network of popular banks to streamline its product range and risk management across the group.

Like other European banking systems, the Austrian banking sector faces significant cost pressures, mostly as a result of exogenous factors such as the low interest rate environment, the growing investment needs arising from the trend toward banking services digitalization, and the increasing competition exerted by new non-banking entrants. As reported by the Österreichische Nationalbank (2018), Raiffeisen Bank International, Unicredit Bank Austria, and Volksbank have undergone remarkable changes in their strategic focus and risk profiles, which have had positive implications for their own financial stability and that of the Austrian banking system. Since the outbreak of the GFC, the Austrian banking sector has been characterized by asset downsizing and a contraction in the foreign exposures held mainly by the RBG, the Erste Group, and Unicredit Bank Austria. According to figures published by the Austrian central bank, the banking sector's total assets decreased by 16% between mid-2010 and 2017, while foreign exposure fell by 26% (from the third quarter of 2008).[25] As already mentioned, the restructuring within the sector encompassed mergers, branch rationalization, and profound and ongoing organizational changes in order to cut costs. These, together with the

---

stock corporation. More than about 53% of its shares are held by institutional investors and the remainder by a foundation, by private investors, by other Austrian savings banks, and by savings bank employees (see Annual Report for the year-end 2017). Thus it is more exposed to the pressure of the stock market than the other institutions in the savings bank system. The principle of "one head, one vote" is applied (see Annual Report).

[25] It is worth mentioning that Austria retains the largest share of the aggregate CESEE-related claims of EU-15 banks, with about 22% at the end of September 2017 (Österreichische Nationalbank 2018).

improvement in loan portfolios, have facilitated the return to profitability (proxied by the return on assets [ROA]) at pre-crisis levels.

The purpose of this section is to verify empirically the effects of the ongoing hybridization in co-operative banking, answering the following questions: have the mitigation of the principles of mutuality pursued by CBs and the growing complementarity with markets as places of investment and funding meant that the results achieved by CBs have become more similar to those of commercial joint-stock banks? Which areas record analogies and differences in results? Can a convergence in their respective performances be observed over time? To answer these important questions, we have identified a set of commonly employed indicators in the form of ratios proxying bank performances. The group of indicators used to run the comparisons includes the capitalization of banks; their activities in lending and investing in securities, including those held for trading on the financial markets; their reliance on deposits from customers; the role they play over time in the interbank market; the riskiness deriving from lending; and, finally, banking profitability and efficiency. In order to verify if, where, and when there have been phenomena of convergence between stakeholder- and shareholder-oriented banking models, a peer national commercial banking group has been identified with which a comparative analysis is carried out. The two Austrian co-operative banking groups are compared with one major shareholder-oriented banking group, Unicredit Bank Austria. We also consider the Erste Group, given its importance, its highly hybridized nature, and its substantial dependence on capital markets.

Year-end figures are used for all the entities. The analysis covers the period 2005–2017, which is particularly helpful since it allows the results obtained by the different business models to be taken before and after the outbreak of the GFC. Data are collected from three databases SNL, BankScope Bureau van Dijk, and Orbis Bank Focus in order to minimize the potential for missing data. We use consolidated data for the Volksbanks Verbund, the Erste Group, and Unicredit Bank Austria as these are available in the databases mentioned. We do not have consolidated public data for the entire RBG, encompassing the apex, its subsidiaries, and the independent CBs, as, for example, in the German case. Therefore, we decided to present two batteries of data for the RBG alone, one referring to the apex, RBI, and the other to the network of independent CBs. In this regard, the sample coverage available in BankScope and Orbis Bank Focus amounts to about one-third of the 419 CBs active in 2017 (Table 3.1). We provide means and standard deviations of the selected indicators in different sub-periods, covering, respectively, the pre-crisis period, 2005–2007; the main GFC period, 2008–2010; the period from 2011 to 2013 during which the sovereign debt crisis severely affected various countries including Austria and important regulatory and monetary policy measures were taken to restore bank financial stability; and the implementation of the CRR, the initiation of the European Banking Union with the implementation of the Single Supervisory Mechanism (SSM) and the Single Resolution Mechanism (SRM), 2014–2017.

In Table 3.5, we report the first set of indicators under investigation. The capital ratios employed consist of a regulatory proxy for the appraisal of the capital adequacy of the banking groups, the Tier 1 (%) ratio, and an

Table 3.5 Comparison of Austrian co-operative vs. non-co-operative banking groups: capital ratios

	RBI		Raiffeisen network CBs		Volksbanks Verbund		Erste Group		Unicredit Bank Austria	
	Mean	SD	Mean	SD	Mean	SD	Mean	SD	Mean	SD
Tier 1 (%)										
2005–2007	9.17	1.26	–	–	–	–	6.23	0.15	9.10	1.78
2008–2010	9.60	1.45	12.93	4.35	–	–	8.45	2.08	8.61	1.77
2011–2013	10.77	0.75	13.78	5.03	10.40[a]	1.22	11.29	0.74	11.09	0.42
2014–2017	12.53	1.35	17.15	6.04	11.79	1.02	12.56	1.49	14.84	4.86
Equity/total assets (%)										
2005–2007	8.46	0.56	8.42	3.02	–	–	5.29	0.97	6.21	1.33
2008–2010	8.25	0.82	8.51	3.22	4.97	0.23	7.27	1.54	7.62	1.34
2011–2013	7.79	0.30	9.56	3.38	5.72	2.02	7.42	0.21	8.43	0.66
2014–2017	7.68	0.75	10.28	3.52	6.84	0.21	7.63	0.63	7.89	0.32

Source: Author's calculations

This table reports descriptive statistics (means and standard deviations [SDs]) of Austrian co-operative and non-co-operative banking groups. Tier 1 (%) is the ratio between primary regulatory capital and risk-weighted assets; equity/total assets (%) is the ratio between total equity and total assets. Our calculations are based on data extracted from SNL for Volksbanks Verbund, Erste Group, and Unicredit Bank Austria; calculations for RBI and the Raiffeisen network are based on data extracted from BankScope and Orbis Bank Focus solely for the year-ends 2016–2017. The sample of Raiffeisen banks consists of 134 CBs until 2015 and 99 CBs in 2016–2017

[a]Only 2012–2013

accounting ratio represented by equity over assets (%). The first one represents a measure of capital adequacy under the Basel rules to address credit risk. Broadly speaking, the Tier 1 ratio is calculated as the shareholder funds plus perpetual non-cumulative preference shares as a percentage of risk-weighted assets and some off balance sheet items. The higher the Tier 1 value, the more capitalized the bank is, which improves its ability to face the risks arising from lending to and financing borrowers. Under the Basel 3 rules introduced in Europe in 2014 (with EU Directive 2013/36 and the EU Regulation 575/2013—CRR) the minimum level of Tier 1 permitted is 6% plus the capital conservation buffer of 2.5%.[26] The ratio of equity to total assets (%) proxies the cushion against banking risks. The higher this figure, the better able the bank is to cope with potential losses arising from its activity.

The Tier 1 ratio has, on average, been increasing over time in all the sub-periods under investigation for all banking models. In the pre-crisis period and during 2008–2010, the Raiffeisen apex and the sample of CBs proxying the network recorded average Tier 1 ratios that were higher than the other groups, resulting in them being better equipped to withstand the financial turbulence that the GFC entailed. After 2010, we observe the regulatory capitalization indicator becoming more closely aligned with average values at close to or slightly higher than 12%. Unicredit achieves the highest average value, equaling 14.84% over the period 2014–2017. However, this value is lower than the average recorded for the sample of Raiffeisen CBs (17.15%). Analysis of the ratio of equity to total assets reveals a similar trend to that already seen for the Tier 1 ratio (Table 3.5). However, what emerges from the reported data is the lower level of capital held by the commercial and savings bank groups before the GFC. The Volksbanks Verbund results indicate it being the least capitalized over the whole period, despite following a growing trend. Only recently have commercial banking and the savings banks groups reported average values in line with those of RBI. The network of CBs continues to record the highest average values (10.28%). Both Raiffeisen CBs and Volksbanks were able to increase their total capital ratios in a similar fashion to other European banking systems. The ECB attributes this increase to higher capital buffers, de-risking, and the reallocation of portfolios toward safer assets. Austria, together with Ireland, France, Latvia, Lithuania, and the

---

[26] Prior to Basel 3 coming into force, the minimum value of the Tier 1 ratio was 4%.

Netherlands, was cited among the countries where the biggest increases in capitalization took place in 2016 (ECB 2017).

The second set of indicators concerns the asset side of the banking groups and aims to shed light on its composition. In this regard, we employ three types of ratios: the ratio of net customer loans to total assets (%) which measures the degree of dedication to traditional lending activity; the ratio of the total securities held to total assets (%) which provides an assessment of the banks' integration with financial markets in investment terms; and finally the ratio of securities held for trading to total assets (%), which shows the degree of banks' active participation in the financial markets through financial instruments (i.e. bonds, derivatives, and stocks) which allows for an assessment of speculative activities within the financial markets (Table 3.6). The lending activity of the Raiffeisen group members is on average slightly higher than that of the other groups in the pre-crisis period. The average value of the network (54.62%) is lower than the apex (61.99%), although the standard deviations reported indicate a high sample variability. Given RBI's significant operations in the CESEE markets, the substantial weight of RBI's credit activity on total assets is not surprising. These average values are well above those recorded by the German apex, DZ Bank: 32.73% in 2014–2017 (Table 6.11) as opposed to RBI's 57.90% in the same period. Over the whole period, however, while the apex reduces the importance of lending on its asset side, the network of Raiffeisen banks, on the contrary, increases its average values, thus showing its steady ability to finance the economy.[27] Volksbanks Verbund's values for net loans to total assets particularly stand out as higher than the rest at 75.98% in 2014–2017. During this period, the average data recorded by all the remaining groups are very close to 60%.

The network of Raiffeisen banks' investments in securities was the lowest in 2014–2017: 9.55% (Table 3.6). However, the allocation of securities by the apex has been growing over time (from 11.85% in 2005–2007 to 19.15% in 2014–2017). On the other hand, the percentages of securities held by commercial banks, and in particular by the Erste Group, are

---

[27] The average customer loan values shown in this section differ from that indicated in Table 3.4. This is particularly evident in the last analysis period, 2014–2017. For both the apex and the network, values of less than 60% are recorded, compared to values above 65% according to data published by EACB (Table 3.4). We believe this may be attributable, for the most part, to the limited sample coverage offered by the BankScope and Orbis Bank Focus databases. In fact, out of the just over 400 Raiffeisen banks existing at the end of 2017, the available databases cover only around 25%.

Table 3.6 Comparison of Austrian co-operative vs. non-co-operative banking groups: lending and securities holdings ratios

	RBI		Raiffeisen network CBs		Volksbanks Verbund		Erste Group		Unicredit Bank Austria	
	Mean	SD	Mean	SD	Mean	SD	Mean	SD	Mean	SD
Net customer loans/total assets (%)										
2005–2007	61.99	3.35	54.62	14.97	–	–	52.58	2.30	53.16	1.77
2008–2010	60.77	5.94	54.52	17.38	–	–	61.29	0.46	63.46	3.99
2011–2013	55.65	2.97	58.67	16.45	63.40	7.19	59.68	1.38	65.77	1.96
2014–2017	57.90	1.44	59.60	15.48	75.98	4.23	62.68	0.75	59.15	1.22
Securities/total assets (%)										
2005–2007	11.85[b]	2.26	–	–	–	–	23.92	2.07	21.20	2.08
2008–2010	16.21[b]	5.52	–	–	17.49	1.18	22.26	1.28	11.66	3.00
2011–2013	18.15[b]	1.29	13.01[a]	10.90	19.16	3.15	27.02	1.16	14.00	1.16
2014–2017	19.15[b]	0.78	9.55[a]	9.82	11.64	3.33	23.76	3.04	17.32	1.34
Total assets held for trading/total assets (%)										
2005–2007	4.30[b]	0.48	–	–	–	–	3.44	0.10	10.36	1.08
2008–2010	5.75[b]	0.72	–	–	4.49	0.68	4.75	1.11	2.13	0.10
2011–2013	7.24[b]	0.98	1.76[a]	5.34	6.08	1.43	6.92	0.69	1.43	0.22
2014–2017	5.33[b]	1.61	1.43[a]	5.75	1.97	2.27	4.11	1.04	1.37	0.42

Source: Author's calculations

This table reports descriptive statistics (means and standard deviations [SDs]) of Austrian co-operative and non-co-operative banking groups. Net customer loans/total assets (%) is the ratio between net loans and total year-end assets; securities/total assets (%) is the ratio between total securities held and total assets; assets held for trading/total assets (%) is the ratio between total assets held for trading on total assets. Our calculations are based on data extracted from SNL for Volksbanks Verbund, the Erste Group, and Unicredit Bank Austria; calculations for RBI and the Raiffeisen network are based on data extracted from BankScope and Orbis Bank Focus solely for the year-ends 2016–2017. The sample of Raiffeisen banks consists of 134 CBs until 2015 and 99 CBs in 2016–2017

[a]Data extracted from Orbis Bank Focus
[b]Data extracted from SNL

on average higher in the last of the analyzed periods. The investment space that the banking groups devote to financial instruments held for trading purposes is rather low and decreasing over time. Among the organizations examined, RBI is the most active in holding financial assets for trading purposes. The apex consistently has average values that are mostly double the corresponding values of the network. This demonstrates mean values above those of the Volksbanks Verbund and Unicredit Bank Austria but with a high degree of variability indicated by the reported standard deviation.

If we calculate the impact of the assets held for trading on the total securities holdings (not reported in Table 3.6), we find, for example, that the commercial banking group Unicredit Bank Austria reports the lowest percentage: about 8% in 2014–2017. In the same period, RBI held the highest average values, which is almost equal at about 28%, while its network of CBs held about 15%. The Volksbanks Verbund and Erste Group show values close to 17%. The trading activity, although limited, therefore absorbs just less than a third of RBG's total investments in securities. To date, the data displayed seem to highlight the emergence of similarities between the groups in terms of the resources dedicated to lending activity, with the exception of the Volksbanks Verbund from 2014 to 2017. However, long-standing differences remain with regard to preferences concerning investment in securities.

A third set of selected indicators concerns the level of traditional funding activity through customer deposits and the role of interbank activity for the most important Austrian banking groups (Table 3.7). The difference between the business models in terms of their dependence on funding in the form of deposits is noteworthy. Traditionally, CBs are more dependent on funding provided by customer deposits. This is verified in the case of the RBG. Both RBI and its network display the highest average values, at, respectively, 58.71% and 67.40% in the pre-crisis period. A high degree of volatility is found in the Raiffeisen CB network in which, for the most part, funds in the form of customer deposits increase over time, due partly to the effectiveness of the deposit protection mechanisms (temporary and permanent) introduced after the onset of the GFC in order to restore depositors' trust.[28] All peer groups display consistent growth in their customer deposits, with the exception of RBI, which only recorded average values up by 60.36% in the period 2014–2017, due in part to the refocusing strategies implemented on the foreign markets. In the most recent period, the two co-operative networks hold the highest values, at 74.24%

---

[28] On 1 October 2008, temporary unlimited coverage was set for individuals (until 31 December 2009); for non-individuals no changes except raising coverage for SMEs to € 50,000. The law of 20 October 2008 set the level for individuals at € 100,000 (from 1 January 2010). The law of 16 June 2009 raised the level for non-individuals to € 100,000 (from 1 January 2011) and discontinued co-insurance (from 1 July 2009). See European Commission (EC) (2010).

Table 3.7   Comparison of Austrian co-operative vs. non-co-operative banking groups: funding and interbank ratios

	RBI		Raiffeisen network CBs		Volksbanks Verbund		Erste Group		Unicredit Bank Austria	
	Mean	SD	Mean	SD	Mean	SD	Mean	SD	Mean	SD
Customer deposits/total assets (%)										
2005–2007	58.71	2.83	67.40	21.24	–	–	49.20	1.32	39.83	4.50
2008–2010	50.50	6.05	66.86	21.87	44.51	0.87	55.54	1.28	48.24	4.76
2011–2013	48.33	2.75	68.40	19.60	51.99	10.12	58.47	2.46	53.81	1.54
2014–2017	60.36	4.25	74.24	17.79	77.85	7.89	65.30	2.60	54.64	1.65
Interbank ratio (%)										
2005–2007	92.97	10.32	192.10	171.51	–	–	45.43	3.80	67.61	3.17
2008–2010	53.04	9.42	218.53	219.35	–	–	50.88	10.16	61.72	6.66
2011–2013	71.36	3.63	213.61	209.02	51.90	11.60	41.81	10.53	87.03	7.72
2014–2017	68.92	5.65	294.03	265.11	117.30	38.93	40.90	14.79	136.37	9.20

Source: Author's calculations

This table reports descriptive statistics (means and standard deviations [SDs]) of Austrian co-operative and non-co-operative banking groups. Customer deposit/total assets (%) is the ratio between customer deposits and total assets; interbank ratio (%) is the ratio between loans to banks and deposits from banks. Our calculations are based on data extracted from SNL for Volksbanks Verbund, Erste Group, and Unicredit Bank Austria; calculations for RBI and the Raiffeisen network are based on data extracted from BankScope and Orbis Bank Focus solely for the year-ends 2016–2017. The sample of Raiffeisen banks consists of 134 CBs until 2015 and 99 CBs in 2016–2017

for Raiffeisen and 77.85% for the Volksbanks Verbund.[29] As found in the case of other European countries analyzed in this book, commercial banks exhibit a greater degree of diversification on the liabilities side of their balance sheets (Unicredit has an average value of 54.64% in 2014–2017), while the apex organization RBI and the Erste Group occupy the middle ground (65.30% in the last sub-period with low volatility in comparative terms).

As a result of Unicredit Bank Austria's lower reliance on deposits from customers, its funding gap appears on average higher than that of the other groups: about 108% and decreasing over time.[30] All the other busi-

---

[29] Once again, our data diverge from what is reported in Table 3.4 but to a lesser extent.

[30] The funding gap is calculated as the ratio between the ratio of net customer loans to total assets (%) reported in Table 3.6 and the ratio of deposits from customers to total assets (%) reported in Table 3.7.

ness models show a funding gap below 100% in 2014–2017 with the lowest held by the Raiffeisen network at about 80%.[31] This makes the Raiffeisen network and its apex less exposed to the risks arising from higher levels of maturity transformation and greater dependence on funding from the financial markets. As regards the role of the various banking models on the interbank market, approximated by the interbank ratio (%), the decisively active role of the RBG in the period 2005–2007 immediately stands out. Its network of CBs, in particular, records average values close to 200% with high levels of variability within the sample. It is interesting to note the complementarity that exists between the apex and its network: the network's growing the supply of funds on the interbank, in favor of the apex, is accompanied by a reduction in the ratio of the apex and vice versa. This demonstrates well the fundamental role played by the network in providing funding to the apex, separate from any other consideration about the potential lack of lending opportunities for the network's banks. By contrast, the interbank position of the Erste Group is the most contained throughout the period of analysis. The increasing average values recorded for Unicredit Bank Austria seem to highlight the important funding role played by foreign subsidiaries, especially in the last of the sub-periods under examination.

Table 3.8 contains a proxy for exposure to liquidity risk, often used in the empirical literature, and two proxies for credit risk. The use of the ratio of liquid assets to total liabilities (excluding equity) (%) was preferred to the prudential ratios relating to liquidity risk since the latter would have been available only for the last of the periods under investigation. The ratio used looks at the amount of liquid assets available to cover all the financial liabilities held by banks. The higher this percentage, the more liquid and generally able to redeem its debts the bank is, and the less vulnerable it is to a classic run on the bank.

The data in Table 3.8 show a common trend over the whole period with liquidity decreasing between the pre-crisis period and 2008–2010, but to a lesser extent for the RBG's entities. Over this and the subsequent phases, the liquidity holdings are constantly higher for both co-operative networks. A decreasing trend in the liquidity ratio is recorded for all the groups with the sole exception of Unicredit Bank Austria between 2011 and 2017. This general reduction of liquidity reserves, albeit on an average basis, reflects, for the most part, banks' greater confidence in the

---

[31] Ibidem.

Table 3.8   Comparison of Austrian co-operative vs. non-co-operative banking groups: liquidity and credit risk ratios

	RBI		Raiffeisen network CBs		Volksbanks Verbund		Erste Group		Unicredit Bank Austria	
	Mean	SD	Mean	SD	Mean	SD	Mean	SD	Mean	SD
Liquid assets/total liabilities (%)										
2005–2007	27.15	1.49	27.21	13.45	–	–	16.71	2.58	29.08	2.32
2008–2010	24.70	0.93	27.09	12.45	–	–	13.78	0.44	14.52	1.93
2011–2013	27.50	2.04	25.26	11.41	24.42	4.50	12.89	0.08	16.50	0.15
2014–2017	26.10	2.66	26.74	11.20	20.52	2.97	12.91	3.02	20.33	1.17
Impaired loans/gross loans and advances (%)										
2005–2007	–	–	–	–	–	–	4.48	0.30	5.02	0.51
2008–2010	7.07	3.53	–	–	–	–	6.40	1.28	7.05	2.18
2011–2013	9.73	1.05	7.42[a]	4.35	6.95[b]	0.70	9.08	0.59	9.60	0.82
2014–2017	9.57	2.83	6.26[a]	4.16	5.01[b]	1.20	6.15	2.02	6.62	2.57
LLR/impaired loans (%)										
2005–2007	–	–	–	–	–	–	71.51	2.15	65.89	1.03
2008–2010	63.35	6.86	–	–	–	–	59.71	0.79	58.66	2.69
2011–2013	66.26	2.56	63.34[a]	17.94	81.59[b]	10.47	62.20	1.18	54.97	4.61
2014–2017	70.13	3.61	52.94[a]	7.51	46.66[b]	6.20	67.82	2.20	67.38	5.61

Source: Author's calculations

This table reports descriptive statistics (means and standard deviations [SDs]) of German co-operative and non-co-operative banking groups. Liquid assets/total liabilities (%) is the ratio between liquid assets and total liabilities; impaired loans/gross customer loans and advances (%) is the ratio between impaired loans and gross customer loans and advances; LLR/impaired loans (%) is the ratio between loan loss reserves and impaired loans. Our calculations are based on data extracted from BankScope and Orbis Bank Focus solely for the year-ends 2016–2017. The sample of Raiffeisen banks consists of 134 CBs until 2015 and 99 CBs in 2016–2017

[a]Data available only for the majority of the regional Raiffeisen CBs
[b]Data extracted from SNL

improvement of the economic situation and consequently their increased willingness to provide credit, thereby holding lower levels of liquidity reserves. In the case of Unicredit Bank Austria, on the other hand, the ratio increase must be interpreted in combination with their simultaneous reduction in lending activity (Table 3.6) and the increase in their inter-bank position (Table 3.7). In terms of the quality of the banking groups' credit portfolios, Table 3.8 reports two proxies: the ratio of impaired loans to gross loans and advances (%) and the ratio of loan loss reserves to impaired loans (%). The first one shows impaired or non-performing loans as a percentage of the bank's gross customer loans and advances (%).

It indicates the weakness of the loan portfolio which increases as the percentage rises. The second of the ratios used relates loan loss reserves to impaired loans. Higher values of this ratio, also known as the "coverage ratio", indicate that the bank is better equipped to face losses on loans. On the other hand, of all accounting considerations, higher levels of the coverage rate are generally indicative of a poorer quality loan portfolio. The data indicate that RBI's riskiness was lowest in the period 2005–2007. In subsequent years, high tension in the credit markets caused a significant increase in the ratio of impaired loans/gross loans and advances (%) for all banking models examined. The average values recorded by RBI are not substantially different from those recorded by the Erste Group and Unicredit Bank Austria. However, while there is a significant reduction in the credit risk indicator for the latter two and for the Volksbanks Verbund over the period 2014–2017, this does not happen to the same extent for RBI. Its average values remain at slightly above 9.5%. Analysis of the annual data reveals a substantial improvement in the ratio from 2016 (9.2%) to 2017 (5.7%).[32] This improvement in the quality of the loan portfolio arises from the implementation in recent years of strategies designed to reduce the incidence of non-performing loans. The average value of RBI remains high compared to the other groups due to the high levels of risk that still exist in some of the CESEE countries in which the apex of the Raiffeisen group is active (i.e. Hungary, Poland, Albania, Ukraine, Croatia).[33] The data shown in Table 3.8 relating to the Raiffeisen CBs network have been calculated using only the part of the group containing most of the regional banks, given that data relating to the first-tier banks is unavailable. The average values recorded are in line with those of the Erste Group and Unicredit Bank Austria in 2014–2017 but they provide a very limited indication of the network's riskiness. After the GFC, the coverage ratio for impaired loans increased for RBI, the Erste Group, and Unicredit Bank Austria (Table 3.8). In 2014–2017, the values for these last two groups stood at 67%, while they were slightly higher for RBI at around 70%. The average coverage rates of the Volksbanks Verbund's and the CBs' network are decidedly lower, the latter represented exclusively by most of the regional banks. Although the data shown in Table 3.8 must be interpreted with caution, the risk of the networks alone is lower and better than the RBI apex. The degree of liquidity of the co-operative banks is also better than the other two banking business models.

---

[32] The ratio was 11.9% in 2015 and 11.4% in 2014.
[33] For further details, see the Annual Report of RBI for the year-end 2017.

The last set of indicators that we examine involves variables that are representative of bank profitability and efficiency, which are widely employed in the empirical literature. With regard to the profitability analysis, three indicators are taken into consideration: the net interest margin (%); the return on average assets (ROAA) (%); and the return on average equity (ROAE) (%). To evaluate the operational efficiency achieved by the bank management, we use a widespread indicator: the cost-to-income ratio (%) (Table 3.9).

Table 3.9 Comparison of Austrian co-operative vs. non-co-operative banking groups: profitability and efficiency ratios

	RBI		Raiffeisen network CBs		Volksbanks Verbund		Erste Group		Unicredit Bank Austria	
	Mean	SD	Mean	SD	Mean	SD	Mean	SD	Mean	SD
Net interest margin (%)										
2005–2007	4.10	0.17	2.25	0.55	–	–	2.15	0.14	1.82	0.30
2008–2010	4.14	0.42	2.05	0.53	2.33	0.51	2.76	0.10	2.61	0.16
2011–2013	2.89	0.17	1.91	0.53	1.78	0.10	2.59	0.17	2.30	0.14
2014–2017	3.04	0.26	1.78	0.71	1.83	0.16	2.23	0.13	1.40	0.63
ROAA (%)										
2005–2007	1.82	0.71	0.80	1.19	–	–	0.71	0.07	1.33	0.65
2008–2010	0.95	0.53	0.42	0.46	−0.46	0.89	0.52	0.05	0.52	0.10
2011–2013	0.56	0.13	0.36	0.38	0.01	1.17	0.04	0.28	−0.15	0.57
2014–2017	0.35	0.61	0.50	0.53	−0.26	0.42	0.37	0.69	0.61	0.15
ROAE (%)										
2005–2007	22.21	8.83	9.33	12.82	–	–	14.13	0.63	22.97	10.58
2008–2010	11.40	6.35	4.70	6.06	−9.63	18.08	7.70	0.83	7.12	2.19
2011–2013	7.22	1.75	3.88	5.20	−0.62	26.01	0.58	3.73	−1.74	6.44
2014–2017	4.49	7.90	5.87	8.19	−3.73	5.91	4.76	9.33	7.83	1.80
Cost to income (%)										
2005–2007	56.06	6.61	66.76	10.19	–	–	62.89	0.41	50.00	8.97
2008–2010	53.74	1.42	65.81	11.18	58.56	3.61	57.28	5.36	52.07	1.73
2011–2013	60.08	3.45	70.10	11.21	63.93	18.70	56.51	2.57	57.98	3.73
2014–2017	59.92	0.59	78.44	47.48	86.38	5.63	62.73	2.36	70.55	16.76

Source: Author's calculations

This table shows descriptive statistics (means and standard deviations [SDs]) of Austrian co-operative and non-co-operative banking groups. Net interest margin (%) is the ratio between net interest income and total earning assets; ROAA (%) is the return on average assets; ROAE (%) is the return on average equity; cost to income (%) is the ratio between operating expenses and intermediation margin. Our calculations are based on data extracted from SNL for Volksbanks Verbund, the Erste Group, and Unicredit Bank Austria; calculations for RBI and the Raiffeisen network are based on data extracted from BankScope and Orbis Bank Focus solely for the year-ends 2016–2017. The sample of Raiffeisen banks consists of 134 CBs until 2015 and 99 CBs in 2016–2017

The net interest margin (%) represents the profitability stemming from the bank's credit intermediation activity. It is expressed as the percentage of net interest income to earning assets. Less diversified banks generally enjoy higher net interest margins. Higher values of the ratio may be indicative of cost advantages in funding or may derive from the exploitation of strong market power positions. The data shown in Table 3.9 indicate a generally decreasing trend in net interest income, caused by both the deterioration in asset quality, at least until recent years, and the effects of a prolonged low interest rate regime. The outcomes of these phenomena however vary between the different business models. For example, the average profitability of the RBI apex is the highest in the period under analysis and far removed from that of Erste Group and Unicredit Bank Austria. In terms of its CB network, its net interest income is generally lower than that of the other groups, except in 2014–2017 (1.78%). Erste Group's profitability is on average better than that of the Unicredit Bank Austria: in the last four years Erste achieved an average value of 2.23% compared to 1.40% for the commercial group. Looking at the ROAA (%) (Table 3.9), the RBG performed better than everyone else on average, especially before the outbreak of the GFC and its aftermath in 2011–2013 (a high degree of variability is recorded for the representative sample of the network's CBs). During the 2014–2017 period, the Raiffeisen CBs network, the Erste Group, and Unicredit Bank Austria all show increasing profitability. This is not the case for RBI however, whose average result is lower (0.35%) in the last of the periods under review than in the previous three-year period (0.56%). In none of the periods examined did the RBG and, to a lesser extent, the Erste Group achieve negative income results. This is also true for the other indicator of profitability selected: ROAE (%). By contrast, average negative results were recorded by the Volksbanks Verbund, reflecting the costs connected to the network restructuring process, and by the Unicredit Bank Austria, although for the latter only in the three-year period from 2011 to 2013. The data on the operating efficiency indicator, the cost-to-income ratio (%), are less gratifying. Here there is on average a generally increasing trend which affects all the groups shown in Table 3.9. In this regard, the Österreichische Nationalbank (2018) attested that the cost-to-income ratio remains high for the Austrian banking system (not including foreign subsidiaries) despite the rationalization and reorganization processes pursued by banks. For instance, in 2016 it stood at around 75% and decreased to almost 65% in 2017 with smaller banks recording above-average cost-income ratios. This phenomenon can be observed in the average cost-income values recorded by the

Raiffeisen CBs network (78.44% in 2014–2017 but with high variability within the sample). Even the Volksbanks Verbund network did not fare any better and, in the last period, recorded an average value of 86.38%, also as a result of the negative profitability results achieved. In comparative terms, the RBI apex is more efficient than its network (59.92% in 2014–2017) and performs similarly to the Erste Group. The worsening of Unicredit Bank Austria's cost-to-income ratio is entirely due to its increase in 2016 alone. Excluding this figure, Unicredit group's cost-to-income ratio would be, on average, better than that of Erste and RBI.

Overall, in the Austrian case, we do find some differences between the co-operative banking model (at least as represented by the RBG) and the shareholder-oriented model, in terms of capital, dependence on customer deposits, their interbank position over time, liquidity, and profitability. Some differences are also found with the other stakeholder-oriented group, the Erste Group. Additionally, in some cases noteworthy differences have been found between the two co-operative banking groups as, for instance, in terms of lending commitment, profitability, operational efficiency, and capital.

In order to verify whether the detected differences between the banking business models are statistically significant, the non-parametric Wilcoxon-Mann-Whitney (WMW) (1947) test[34] is used. This is suitable for small sample sizes and for testing whether observations in one population tend to be larger than observations in the other as it tests the equality of central tendency of two distributions (Fay and Proschan 2010). The selected indicators are subjected to the test for the period 2008–2017 only. It was decided to concentrate the analysis on this ten-year period, because we wanted to check whether, and if so how, the manifestation of the episodes of crisis and the start of the Banking Union in 2014 have affected the performance of the business models, and whether this makes them more similar. In Table 3.10 the test is carried out by first comparing the performances of the sole Austrian co-operative Raiffeisen apex and its network of CBs with the results obtained by the Erste Group, a historically stakeholder-oriented group that has been gradually hybridized over time, and subsequently with the results of the commercial bank Unicredit Bank Austria. The Volksbanks Verbund is excluded due to its smaller size. The medians and the p-values resulting from the test are reported in Table 3.10.

The first of the tests was carried out using the Erste Group as a comparison displays some significant differences in the results achieved, as evi-

[34] This test is also known as Wilcoxon ranksum test or Mann-Whitney U test.

Table 3.10   Wilcoxon-Mann-Whitney test (2008–2017)

	RBG versus Erste Group		RBG versus Unicredit Bank Austria	
	Median	P-value	Median	P-value
Capital ratios				
Tier 1 (%)	12.50–11.08	0.09	12.50–10.85	0.16
Equity/total assets (%)	8.43–7.53	0.00	8.43–9.92	0.09
Lending, securities holdings ratios				
Net customer loans/total assets (%)	57.82–61.55	0.00	57.82–61.85	0.00
Securities/total assets (%)	13.42–24.20	0.00	13.43–14.88	0.10
Total assets held for trading/total assets (%)	3.76–4.90	0.44	3.76–1.61	0.05
Funding and interbank ratios				
Customer deposit/total assets (%)	64.94–59.40	0.45	64.95–53.23	0.02
Interbank ratio (%)	128.95–45.53	0.00	128.95–91.45	0.40
Liquidity and credit risk ratios				
Liquid assets/total liabilities (%)	25.57–13.19	0.00	25.57–18.84	0.00
Impaired loans/gross customer loans and advances (%)	8.57–7.32	0.15	8.57–8.88	0.66
LLR/impaired loans (%)	64.22–62.85	0.86	64.21–60.88	0.38
Profitability and efficiency ratios				
Net interest margin (%)	2.43–2.50	0.83	2.43–2.23	0.23
ROAA (%)	0.46–0.49	0.69	0.46–0.48	0.76
ROAE (%)	5.86–7.22	0.86	5.86–6.37	0.79
Cost to income (%)	65.12–59.99	0.03	65.12–57.23	0.08

Source: Author's calculations

denced by the *p*-values obtained. Capitalization levels in Austrian co-operative banking are significantly higher, while the share of net loans to customers to total assets (%) and their holdings in securities are significantly lower. Statistically significant differences have also been detected in terms of the role played by Raiffeisen banks in the interbank market. CBs are significantly more liquid than the savings bank model, while their exposure to credit risk, approximated by the two indicators of impaired loans to gross loans and advances (%) and loan loss reserves to impaired loans (%), is not significantly different. Finally, looking at the indicators of profitability and operating efficiency, significant differences are found only in terms of cost to income (%). In this case, however, co-operative banks achieve worse results than the Erste Group. Contrary to expectation, the comparison between the co-operative banking model and the commercial (joint stock) Unicredit Bank Austria reveals a lower degree of significant differentiation. CBs are less significantly capitalized than the commercial reference group as proxied by the equity-to-total assets ratio (%). They exhibit a lower median engagement in lending to customers and in the investment in securities while having a significantly higher median share of securities held for trading purposes. Furthermore, they are more dependent on the funding represented by deposits from clients and tend to be more liquid but less efficient from an operational point of view, as evidenced by the higher median cost-to-income ratio (%). In terms of the exposure to credit risk (the ratio of impaired loans to gross loans and advances [%] and that of loan loss reserves to impaired loans [%]) and the measures of profitability, the differences between the two business models are not significant.

Overall, in the period 2008–2017 the co-operative model is different in terms of higher capital and liquidity and lower investment space allocated to securities. It turns out to be slightly less involved in lending to customers when compared with the peer non-co-operative groups. These profiles seem essentially to make the co-operative sector more resilient to market shocks. Additional emerging significant differences depend on the business model with which the Raiffeisen banks are compared. For instance, they are more similar to the sector of savings banks in terms of share of bank deposits but they are definitely different from the commercial shareholder-oriented sector. However, if we turn to the credit risk exposure of the co-operative sector and the profitability results obtained from it, we find that the combination of risks and returns for the various bank models is rather similar over time. CBs maintain a degree of operational inefficiency that is significantly higher than that of their peers among the commercial (joint-stock) and savings banks.

6   THE PERFORMANCE OF AUSTRIAN CO-OPERATIVE BANKING NETWORKS AND THEIR CENTRAL INSTITUTION

To what degree do the performances of the central institutions of co-operative banking networks and the networks of CBs themselves differ? To answer this question, we examine some of the performance indicators analyzed in the previous paragraph, comparing the results achieved by central institutions with those of their networks of CBs, as in Ory and Lemzeri

(2012). To this end, the consolidated data referring to each central institution and its subsidiaries were extracted from the databases previously mentioned; the same data were inserted for the networks of CBs alone. We also accounted for a small number of Volksbanks which are not included in the association, according to the data available in the databases.[35] For the Volksbanks Verbund we considered Volksbanks Wien as the central institution. Over the period 2014–2017, the Verbund disclosed separate data relating only to the section of Volksbank Wien which has responsibility for activities and duties performed on behalf of the Verbund. We will comment on these data but will only report data that refers to Volksbank Austria in order to exploit the greater temporal depth of the data available in the databases. We computed average annual values and standard deviations of the selected indicators for the network of CBs alone. Data on the two networks of Austrian CBs refer to individual banks, usually in unconsolidated form. In a few cases, consolidated data for larger CBs are available and were selected. The data obtained do not cover all the CBs included in the networks over time due to incomplete data in the databases.[36] To minimize the effect of missing data on our analysis, especially before 2008, we chose to limit our analysis to the period 2008–2017 and to restrict the scrutiny to some of the indicators previously examined. These are the equity to total assets (%); the net customer loans to total assets (%); the impaired loans to gross customer loans (%); the customer deposits to total assets (%); the ROAA (%); and the cost-to-income ratio (%). For each of these we replicate the analysis reported in the previous paragraph by calculating averages of results over sub-periods 2008–2010, 2011–2013, and 2014–2017. Figures are reported in Table 3.11.

Most of the local CBs of the Raiffeisen network had an average asset value of less than € 500 million at the end of 2017, while the average size of the banks included in the Volksbanks Verbund is on average larger, but with a total asset that does not exceed € 3 billion.

As regards the first indicator, the ratio between equity and total assets (%), the data in Table 3.11 show that both networks of CBs are much bet-

---

[35] The sample of independent Volksbanks comprises Volkskreditbank AG-VKB Bank, DolomitenBank Osttirol-Westkärnten, Volksbank Marchfeld, and two Volksbanks subject to aggregation (Volksbank Gailtal and Volksbank Gmuend).

[36] Data were extracted from BankScope and Orbis Bank Focus solely for the year-ends 2016–2017. The sample of individual Raiffeisen banks consists of 134 CBs until 2015 and 99 CBs in 2016–2017. The sample of Volksbanks is made up of 29 Volksbanks until 2014, 16 in 2015, 8 in 2016, and 7 in 2017.

Table 3.11 Comparison of Austrian co-operative central institutions and their networks of CBs in terms of capital, lending, funding, and credit risk exposure

	Raiffeisen central institution		Raiffeisen network CBs		Volksbanks Verbund central institution[a]		Volksbanks Verbund network CBs		Independent Volksbanks	
	Mean	SD	Mean	SD	Mean	SD	Mean	SD	Mean	SD
Equity/total assets (%)										
2008–2010	8.25	0.82	8.51	3.22	4.33	0.30	7.12	2.52	8.98	1.64
2011–2013	7.79	0.30	9.56	3.38	4.46	0.21	6.64	2.76	8.71	2.40
2014–2017	7.68	0.75	10.28	3.52	4.96	0.81	7.10	2.87	8.88	2.03
Net customer loans/total assets (%)										
2008–2010	60.77	5.94	54.52	17.38	54.50	4.53	60.50	13.71	61.26	18.23
2011–2013	55.65	2.97	58.67	16.45	58.90	2.07	64.60	13.70	68.08	12.69
2014–2017	57.90	1.44	59.60	15.48	48.73	15.19	71.65	12.64	73.05	8.90
Customer deposits/total assets (%)										
2008–2010	50.50	6.05	66.86	21.87	89.28	0.54	73.22	11.30	76.85	14.84
2011–2013	48.33	2.75	68.40	19.60	86.17	2.13	74.76	11.73	79.78	11.86
2014–2017	60.36	4.25	74.24	17.79	57.77	22.18	79.93	10.54	81.11	7.78
Impaired loans/gross loans and advances (%)										
2008–2010	7.08	3.53	–	–	–	–	–	–	–	–
2011–2013	9.74	1.05	7.42[b]	4.35	–	–	–	–	–	–
2014–2017	9.57	2.83	6.26[b]	4.16	3.89	0.86	–	–	–	–

Source: Author's calculations

This table reports descriptive statistics (means and standard deviations [SDs]) of Austrian co-operative banking networks and their central institutions. Equity/total assets (%) is the ratio between total equity and total assets; net customer loans/total assets (%) is the ratio between net loans and total year-end assets; customer deposits/total assets (%) is the ratio between customer deposits and total assets; impaired loans/ gross customer loans and advances (%) is the ratio between impaired loans and gross customer loans and advances. Our calculations are based on data extracted from BankScope and Orbis Bank Focus solely for the year-ends 2016–2017. The sample of Raiffeisen banks consists of 134 CBs until 2015 and 99 CBs in 2016–2017. The sample of Volksbanks of 29 Volksbanks until 2014, 16 in 2015, 8 in 2016, and 7 in 2017

[a]Volksbank Wien

[b]Data available for the majority of the regional Raiffeisen CBs (Landesraiffeisen banks)

ter capitalized than their respective apexes, with capital holdings increasing over time, at least for the sample of Raiffeisen CBs. In comparative terms, both the network of Raiffeisen CBs and its central institution exhibit consistently higher values than those of the small network of Volksbanks and their top institution. At the end of 2017, the average value of the indicator for the sample of the Raiffeisen CBs network was 10.28%

compared to 7.68% for its apex. The gap between the capital held by the central institution and the sample of CBs has increased over time, unlike what we detected in other European countries, such as France and Germany. In 2014–2017, the average equity to total assets of the network of Volksbanks, which was highly involved in intra-sector aggregations, stood at 7.10% while that of the apex was almost 5% (being also involved in aggregations). Capital held by independent Volksbanks is on average much higher than that of the Verbund but lower than the average values held by the Raiffeisen network of independent CBs.

It is reasonable to assume that networks are more involved in lending activity, in keeping with the specialization of activities common in well-integrated, strategic networks (Table 3.11). In the Austrian case, this is particularly evident for the banking system part of the Volksbanks Verbund, which has seen its commitment to credit increase over time (71.65% in the last four years) while that of the central institution has decreased (48.73% in 2014–2017). According to data reported in the financial statements of the Volksbanks Verbund from 2014 to 2017, lending to customers, relative to the segment responsible for management and control of the association, went from 29% in 2014 to 7% in 2017, highlighting the disengagement from the lending business in favor of more specialized functions, that is, treasury and liquidity management. On the other hand, the differences between RBI and the Raiffeisen CBs network are more limited (both having values close to 60%), even if in the last two sub-periods the network shows average values slightly higher than those of the central institution. This is because, as already highlighted, the latter is involved in credit activity, both directly and through its foreign subsidiaries. For both groups it is worth noting the high degree of standard deviation in relation to the networks. In comparison with Germany, the average lending values of the Bundesverband der Deutschen Volksbanken und Raiffeisenbanken (BVR) network (see Table 6.11) are very similar only to those of the Raiffeisen CBs network. The Volksbanks network's greater tendency toward lending is, instead, similar to that of the CBs that form part of Crédit Agricole and Banques Populaire and Caisses d'Epargne (BPCE) in France (see Table 5.10). However, over time, the independent Volksbanks prove the most involved in the lending business.

Similar to our findings with regard to lending activity, we observe once again that over time the two networks of CBs are more distinctly concentrated in traditional funding in the form of deposits than their central institutions (Table 3.11), with a more diversified structure. In 2014–2017, the Volksbanks network recorded average deposit-to-total assets ratio (%)

of 79.93% while the Raiffeisen ratio was 74.24%. These values are similar to those on average reported for the sample of German CBs: about 75% of customer deposits to total assets (%) (see Table 6.11).[37] The independent Volksbanks' dependence on customer deposits is even higher (81.11% in 2014–2017). Combining this data with that on net lending to total assets, we find that the funding gaps of the two networks are on average below 100% over the whole period, ranging from the highest value of RBI at 96% in 2014–2017 to around 85% for the two components of the Volksbanks Verbund, to 80% for the Raiffeisen CBs in the same period. Due to their high and increasing share of customer deposits over time, individual Austrian CBs appear to be more insulated from the risks arising from a substantial reliance on market funding than their apexes. At the same time, their ability to attract and mobilize the savings of customers and members is a distinctive and strategic element of the two Austrian co-operative groups.

The comparative analysis of the levels and trends of credit risk, approximated by the ratio of impaired loans to gross loans to customers (%) (Table 3.11), relies on a small dataset available for the Volksbanks Verbund. However, at least for the period 2014–2017, we observe a significant difference between the riskiness of the two apexes, with Volksbank Wien AG having the lowest average ratio (3.89% against 9.57% of RBI). Naturally, the differential is affected by the two central institutions' different geographical focuses. While RBI is, as noted, very active in the riskier markets of CESEE, Volksbank Wien is mostly concentrated in the domestic market, which is enjoying a constant improvement in credit quality due to the more favorable economic environment. As reported by the National Bank of Austria (2018), the non-performing loan (NPL) ratio for domestic business dropped to 2.8% in 2017 (it was 3.8% in 2016). A consistent decrease was also recorded for Austrian banks' subsidiaries in CESEE, whose recorded NPL ratio was higher, equaling 4.8% in 2017.

The last two indicators examined concern the profitability and efficiency of the organizations under investigation. For these purposes, ROAA (%) and cost-to-income ratio (%) were selected and are reported in Table 3.12. The values of the first show that on average the central institutions are more profitable than their networks, in contrast to our findings

---

[37] Own calculations on data on customer deposits to total assets (%) refer to the segment of Volksbank Wien responsible for the performance of its activities as the central institution indicates that the percentage of deposits ranges from almost 15% in 2014 to about 10% in 2017.

Table 3.12 Comparison of Austrian co-operative central institutions and their networks of CBs in terms of profitability and operational efficiency

	Raiffeisen central institution		Raiffeisen network CBs		Volksbanks Verbund central institution[a]		Volksbanks Verbund network CBs		Independent Volksbanks	
	Mean	SD	Mean	SD	Mean	SD	Mean	SD	Mean	SD
ROAA (%)										
2008–2010	0.95	0.53	0.42	0.46	0.35	0.12	−0.01	0.45	0.14	0.38
2011–2013	0.56	0.13	0.36	0.38	0.28	0.14	−0.10	0.56	−0.05	0.74
2014–2017	0.35	0.61	0.50	0.53	0.52	0.26	0.08	0.59	0.05	0.33
Cost to income (%)										
2008–2010	53.74	1.42	65.81	11.18	67.22	2.67	69.29	11.19	66.45	9.78
2011–2013	60.08	3.45	69.96	11.21	70.59	8.42	75.26	10.81	71.17	11.85
2014–2017	59.92	0.59	78.44	47.48	85.33	10.91	86.31	14.72	94.97	31.76

Source: Author's calculations

This table reports descriptive statistics (means and standard deviations [SDs]) of French co-operative banking networks and their central institutions. ROAA (%) is the return on average assets; cost to income (%) is the ratio between operating expenses and intermediation margin. Our calculations are based on data extracted from BankScope and Orbis Bank Focus solely for the year-ends 2016–2017. The sample of Raiffeisen banks consists of 134 CBs until 2015 and 99 CBs in 2016–2017. The sample of Volksbanks consists of 29 Volksbanks until 2014, 16 in 2015, 8 in 2016, and 7 in 2017

[a]Volksbank Wien

relating to the German BVR. While the Raiffeisen network posts positive mean results over time, Volksbanks' network returned to a positive average ROAA only in 2014–2017, after a long period of negative results in consequence of the substantial reorganization undertaken in the sector. Negative average profitability was also recorded by the sample of independent Volksbanks but only in 2011–2013.

The different profitability of the apexes reflects their different geographical and business scopes. In the last of the sub-periods examined, Volksbanks Wien AG displayed a higher return (0.52% against 0.35%), thanks both to the positive effects of the reorganization beginning to emerge and to the more favorable economic environment.

Finally, the cost-to-income figures displayed in Table 3.12 show that the benefits of the rationalization of the Austrian banking sector are as yet far from evident. We report, on average, a general trend of increasing cost to income, which particularly affects the network of the Raiffeisen CBs, that of the Volksbanks and their apex. The figures reported for the latter two are very similar in magnitude and timescale. With regard to the Raiffeisen CBs, the increase in the cost-to-income ratio reflects a widespread increase, which does not change even if we remove a dozen CBs with cost-to-income values above 100% (this, however, explains the increase in the standard deviation in 2014–2017). For the RBG, there is a clear parallel with the corresponding performance of BVR in Germany. The latter's network and apex exhibit values that are mostly aligned with those of Austrian Raiffeisen but are far removed from those of the equally important French networks of CBs (see Table 5.11). The independent Volksbanks' cost-to-income (%) values are better than those of the Verbund up until 2013. The worsening in the average level of efficiency reported in 2014–2017 is due to the values recorded by one small Volksbank. When this element is removed from the sample, the average value of the independent Volksbanks' cost to income becomes 84%, which is just slightly better than that of the network of popular banks in the Verbund (86.31% in the last sub-period).

Overall, following a period of substantial and costly transformation, the profitability and operational efficiency of the Raiffeisen group exceeds that of the smaller Volksbanks Verbund and of the independent popular banks. The assets and liabilities allocation strategies pursued by the two networks show similar trends, but the Volksbanks Verbund and the small group of independent Volksbanks concentrate to a greater degree on traditional banking intermediation activity (measured by the percentages of net loans to customers to total assets and that of customer deposits to total assets). The data show that the CBs network is a valuable asset that organizational integration seems to enhance over time.

7   Conclusion

The prevailing "alternative nature" of the Austrian banking sector is confirmed by the number of savings banks and CBs: almost 82% of the total number of banks are in the co-operative banking sector. Popular banks or Volksbanks, and Raiffeisen banks together hold about 48% of total branches. The individual positions of Raiffeisen banks and Volksbanks within the country are quite different. While the former hold a leading position with mostly favorable growth trends, the latter retain a minor role at the national level, largely as a result of the more severe effects exerted on them by the GFC and their exposure to CESEE countries. At the end of 2017, the RBG ranked as Austria's largest banking group, representing around 30% of the Austrian banking system in terms of assets as compared to the Volksbanks, which held just under 2.7%.

The organizational models adopted by Austrian CBs are based on the concept of networks, although with different degrees of integration. These networks are made up of legally autonomous local institutions with distinct business models and central institutions at the regional and/or national level whose capital belongs to local banks, thus creating an inverted ownership structure. The two co-operative Austrian networks operate under different regulated organizational schemes. In both cases, there is a central institution, owned by the local/regional banks, with well-defined roles. While Volksbanks act in line with the provisions of Art. 10 of the CRR with the highest degree of integration and a central institution that has significant power over affiliated banks, the Raiffeisen banks' network features a lower degree of integration and an institutional protection scheme (IPS) in line with the provisions of Art. 113(7) of the CRR. Its central institution retains limited influence over the individual co-operatives. In both cases, the central institution provides services that the local bank cannot provide itself, such as securities trading, financing of export customers and support for their foreign operations, access to hedging products, cash management, and payment methods.

In addition to analyzing the role and organization of co-operative networks in Austria, the chapter offers two empirical investigations, respectively, aimed to verify empirically the effects of the ongoing hybridization in co-operative banking and to assess to what degree do the performances of the central institutions of co-operative banking networks and the networks of CBs themselves differ.

Regarding the first of the two areas of analysis, the data show that overall in the period 2008–2017 the co-operative model is different from non-co-operative banking in terms of higher capital and liquidity and lower investment space allocated to securities. It turns out to be slightly less involved in lending to customers when compared with the peer non-co-operative groups. These profiles seem essentially to make the co-operative sector more resilient to market shocks. Additional emerging significant differences depend on the business model with which the Raiffeisen banks are compared. For instance, they are more similar to the sector of savings banks in terms of share of bank deposits but they are definitely different from the commercial sector. However, if we turn to the credit risk exposure of the co-operative sector and the profitability results obtained from it, we find that the combination of risks and returns for the various bank models is rather similar over time. CBs maintain a degree of operational inefficiency that is significantly higher than that of their peers among the commercial and savings banks.

With reference to the second area of investigation, reported figures show that, overall, following a period of substantial and costly transformation, the profitability and operational efficiency of the Raiffeisen group exceeded that of the smaller Volksbanks Verbund and of the independent popular banks. The assets and liabilities allocation strategies pursued by the two networks show similar trends, but the Volksbanks Verbund and the small group of independent Volksbanks concentrate to a greater degree on traditional banking intermediation activity (measured by the percentages of net loans to customers to total assets and that of customer deposits to total assets). The networks of the sampled individual CBs, compared with their apexes, are normally more capitalized, more involved in lending activities, and more decisively concentrated in traditional funding, represented by customer deposits. On average the central institutions are more profitable than their networks but operational inefficiency remains high. This concerns particularly the network of the Raiffeisen CBs, that of the Volksbanks and their apex.

References

Association of Volksbanks. (2015). Annual Report.

Blisse, H. (2014). Central Cooperative Bank and Local Cooperative Banks on Their Way to an Integrated System of Banks (2009–2012). Position of Points for the Austrian Volksbanks. *International Interdisciplinary Journal of Scientific Research, 1*, 1.

Braumann, B. (2004). Tu Felix Austria: Evidence for a De-Celerator in Financial Reform. *International Economics and Economic Policy, 1*(1), 53–72.

Brazda, J., Jagschitz, F., & Schediwy, R. (2016). Cooperative Banks in the Austrian Banking System. In S. Karafolas (Ed.), *Credit Cooperative Institutions in European Countries*. Springer.

Coppola, F. (2015). The Lesson Behind the Austrian Co-op Banking Disaster. *Coop News*, May 15. Retrieved from https://www.thenews.coop/95508/sector/lesson-behind-austrian-co-op-banking-disaster/.

Crespi, F. (2008). Germania e Austria. In S. De Angeli (Ed.), *Il credito popolare in alcune significative realtà straniere*. Vita e Pensiero.

Egger, P., & Hahn, F. R. (2010). Endogenous Bank Mergers and Their Impact on Banking Performance. *International Journal of Industrial Organization, 28*(2), 155–166.

Erste Group. (2017). Annual Report.

European Association of Co-operative Banks (EACB). (2012). *The Process for the Redemption of Shares in Co-operative Banks in Different EU Member States. A Comparative Overview.* Brussels.

European Association of Co-operative Banks (EACB). *Key Statistics,* Various Years.

European Central Bank (ECB). (2017, October). *Report on Financial Structures.*

European Commission (EC). (2010). *Impact Assessment, Accompanying Document to the Report from the Commission to the European Parliament and to the Council.* Review of Directive 94/19/EC on Deposit Guarantee Schemes, Brussels SEC (2010) 834/2.

Fay, M. P., & Proschan, M. A. (2010). Wilcoxon-Mann-Whitney or T-Test? On Assumptions for Hypothesis Tests and Multiple Interpretations of Decision Rules. *Statistics Surveys, 4,* 1.

FitchRatings. (2018). Volksbanken-Verbund. Full Rating Report, April.

Hardie, I., & Howarth, D. (2013). A Peculiar Kind of Devastation: German Market-Based Banking. In I. Hardie & D. Howarth (Eds.), *Market-Based Banking and the International Financial Crisis.* Oxford University Press.

International Monetary Fund (IMF). (2013). Austria: Financial Sector Stability Assessment, IMF Country Report No. 13/283, September.

International Monetary Fund (IMF). (2014). Austria: Publication of Financial Sector Assessment Program Documentation—Technical Note on Stress Testing the Banking Sector, IMF Country Report No. 14/16, January.

Mann, H. B., & Whitney, D. R. (1947). On a Test of Whether One of Two Random Variables is Stochastically Larger than the Other. *Annals of Mathematical Statistics, 18*(1), 50–60.

National Bank of Austria. (2018, April). *Facts on Austria and Its Banks.*

Ory, J., & And Lemzeri, Y. (2012). Efficiency and Hybridization in Cooperative Banking: The French Case. *Annals of Public and Cooperative Economics, 83*(2), 215–250.

Raiffeisenlandesbank Niederösterreich-Wien. (2018). Company Presentation, June.

Raiffeisen Bank International (RBI). (2017). Annual Report.

Raiffeisen Bank International (RBI). (2018). Investor Presentation, August.

CHAPTER 4

Co-operative Banking in Finland

1 Brief Overview of the Finnish Banking System

The Finnish banking sector has undergone extensive restructuring as a result of the Nordic banking crisis of the early 1990s. Like the banking sectors in many European countries, the Finnish banking system moved during the 1980s from a heavily regulated banking environment to a deregulated one, although banks, especially those co-operative in nature, still play a key role. At the end of 2016, the ratio of Monetary Financial Institutions' (MFIs) total assets to national GDP stood at 2.6 (as compared to 2.6 in Germany, 2.3 in Austria and Italy, and 2.4 in Spain)[1] while the assets held by MFIs as a percentage of the total assets of the financial sector equaled 68.8% (61.1% in Germany, 63.8% in Italy, and 67.2% in Spain) (ECB 2017).[2] While up until 2012, the MFIs' share was almost 80%, from 2013 onward their role began to be reconfigured, mostly due to the growing importance of other financial intermediaries (OFIs) which include finance companies, non-monetary investment funds, and financial vehicle corporations (ECB 2017): between 2008 and 2016, these OFIs' share of assets rose from 10.1% to 21.6%.

Of all the countries examined in this book, Finland has the highest share of assets owned by foreign banks, standing at 57% of total banking

---

[1] Excluding the data of the European System of Central Banks (ESCB).
[2] These two indicators were, respectively, 3.6 and 70.2% in 2008 (ECB 2017).

© The Author(s) 2019
F. Poli, *Co-operative Banking Networks in Europe*, Palgrave Macmillan Studies in Banking and Financial Institutions,
https://doi.org/10.1007/978-3-030-21699-3_4

assets at the end of 2016 (ECB 2017). However, as in the case of other Nordic countries in the Eurozone, such as Latvia, Lithuania, and Estonia,[3] domestic banks in Finland have steadily begun to regain their share, growing from 33% in 2012 to 43% in 2016 (ECB 2017). The vitality of the domestic banking sector is demonstrated by the constant growth of its assets in the years following the international financial crisis (from 2008 to 2016) with an average annual rate of 6.4% versus 3.7% for foreign banks and contrary to the trend in many major European economies.

The domestic banking sector is also vital for the financing of non-financial companies which rely heavily on domestic banks. At the end of 2016, the total financing provided by the domestic financial sector amounted to € 86.2 billion. Of this, almost 74% was granted by MFIs, mainly banks, while 24% came from OFIs (excluding insurance companies and pension funds). In parallel, financing to non-financial companies in other countries of the Eurozone totaled € 13.5 billion, following a growing trend.[4] The competition posed by OFIs can be clearly seen if we compare the growth rates in financing to non-financial companies between 2014 and 2016: during this time Finnish MFIs expanded their lending to domestic non-financial companies by 4.6% compared to an increase of 20.9% on the part of OFIs.[5]

At the end of 2016, there were 275 credit institutions[6] operating in Finland, of which 28 were branches of foreign intermediaries (ECB 2017). This is 81 units fewer than at the end of 2008. The change was mainly due to mergers between co-operative banks (CBs) and savings banks.

Most Finnish credit institutions are part of a banking group or amalgamation, of which there were 12 at the end of 2017. The OP Financial Group is the largest Finnish banking group by market share and falls under the supervision of the European Central Bank (ECB). Among those with the largest market shares, there are also Nordea and Municipality Finance, while Danske Bank Finland plc became the Finnish branch of the Danish Danske Bank in late 2017. The Handelsbanken, Savings Bank Group, Aktia Group, S-Bank Group, Bank of Åland plc, POP Bank Group, and

---

[3] The share of domestic banks in Latvia, Lithuania, and Estonia was 49%, 26%, and 7%, respectively, in 2016 (ECB 2017).

[4] Our calculations on ECB's data in the Report on Financial Structures (ECB 2017).

[5] Ibidem.

[6] Credit institutions include deposit banks and other credit institutions that do not take deposits, such as finance houses, credit card companies, mortgage credit banks, and Municipality Finance plc.

Oma Savings Bank (Finance Finland 2018) make up the smaller intermediaries. The OP Financial Group and POP Bank Group are the only two
co-operative networks currently in existence, the former having a leading
role in the Finnish banking sector. Another small bank, S-Bank Ltd, is not
a true CB but is owned by the S-Group (S-Ryhmä), a Finnish consumer
co-operative. It was established at the end of 2007[7] due to changes in
regulations regarding personal accounts at co-operatives that made them
uncompetitive (Kalmi 2016).

The Finnish banking system is one of the most concentrated in the
European Union. At the end of 2016, the five biggest credit institutions
held a 66% share (83% in 2008) of total assets (compared with 31% in
Germany, 43% in Italy, 85% in Netherlands, and 62% in Spain) (ECB
2017). The number of bank branches throughout the country is one of
the lowest in Europe due to an extensive rationalization of branch networks in parallel with the growth in the digitalization of banking services.
Looking at the population density per bank branch, Finland recorded
5289 inhabitants per branch at the end of 2016 (3178 in 2008), as compared with 2575 in Germany, 2067 in Italy, and 10,173 in the Netherlands
(ECB 2017).

The international financial crisis of 2007–2008 had relatively little
effect on the Finnish banking system or indeed the Finnish national economy. However, the crisis did impact on the Finnish banking system when
the Icelandic banks collapsed. During the years preceding the onset of the
financial crisis, the Icelandic banks had grown rapidly and expanded their
operations in several countries, including Finland.

The collapse of the Icelandic Kaupthing Bank h.f. also triggered the
failure of its Finnish branch. As a result, the branch's depositors were
unable to make immediate withdrawals or might have lost part of their
deposits. Fearing a broader loss of confidence among Finnish depositors in
general, the main Finnish banks offered to compensate depositors in full.
The three banks involved—Nordea Bank Finland plc, OP-Pohjola Group
Central Cooperative, and Sampo Bank plc—along with a special-purpose
vehicle took over the credit claims and other assets of Kaupthing Bank h.f.
and settled all the deposit claims in Finland.[8] In 2009, the Finnish state

---

[7] At the end of 2011, S-Bank had around 2.5 million customers. In 2014, S-Bank and
LocalTapiola Bank were merged to create the new S-Bank.

[8] The Finnish branch of Kaupthing Bank was closed in January 2009, marking the end of
Icelandic banking operations in Finland. The bank paid back a loan arranged by Finnish

was authorized by the European Commission to provide a guarantee to the participants, to cover the legal risks, that is, the potential economic losses suffered due to recovery claims or equivalent insolvency claims.[9]

In 2008, banks faced increased demand for corporate financing thanks to the government aid which was intended to secure their lending capabilities (Finland Finance 2008). In November 2008, Finland introduced a guarantee scheme, designed to stabilize the financial markets by ensuring financial institutions' access to financing. The state guarantee was intended to cover, against remuneration, the issuance of new short- and medium-term non-subordinated debt with a maturity period of between 90 days and 3 years and mortgage-backed bonds with a maturity period of up to 5 years. The scheme's overall budget was capped at € 50 billion. The scheme was originally scheduled to expire at the end of April 2009[10] but was initially extended until 31 December 2009[11] and then further until 30 June 2010.[12] An additional measure was put in place by the Finnish government during 2009: the state subscription of three-year non-cumulative and unsecured subordinated debt instruments, issued by eligible banks. The state budget was capped at € 4 billion.[13] Only solvent banks were permitted to take part either in the latter scheme or in the state guarantee scheme.

2   THE ROLE OF CBs WITHIN THE BANKING SECTOR

The two existing co-operative groups in Finland jointly account for over 1.9 million members as at the end of 2017, of which about 1.8 million belong to the OP Financial Group and 87,200 to the POP Bank Group (Table 4.1).

---

banks, which was used to pay its customers' deposits. Icelandic banking activities also ended in Sweden, and Bank of Åland bought Kaupthing Bank Sweden (Federation of Finnish Financial Services 2009).

[9] See the decision of the European Commission published in IP/09/82.

[10] See the decision of the European Commission published in IP/08/1705.

[11] Besides the prolongation of the scheme, some changes to the eligible instruments were made as the material scope of the scheme was broadened, so that guarantees could cover instruments with a maturity of up to five years. Previously, the maximum maturity was three years (except for covered bonds. See the decision of the Commission published in IP/09/681).

[12] See the decision of the European Commission published in MEX/09/1217.

[13] See the decision of the European Commission published in IP/09/1303.

Table 4.1 Members, customers, and governance ratios of the OP Financial Group and the POP Bank Group

	OP Financial Group			POP Bank Group		
	Members	Customers	Governance ratio (%)	Members	Customers	Governance ratio (%)
2004	1,105,000	3,100,000	35.64	n.a	n.a	n.a
2006	1,160,000	4,000,000	29.00	n.a	n.a	n.a
2008	1,230,000	4,143,000	29.69	n.a	n.a	n.a
2010	1,300,000	4,133,000	31.45	n.a	n.a	n.a
2012	1,371,347	4,210,355	32.57	n.a	n.a	n.a
2014	1,434,000	4,284,000	33.47	84,500[a]	241,300[a]	35.02[a]
2016	1,747,000	4,357,000	40.10	86,100	249,900	34.45
2017	1,833,000	4,395,000	41.71	87,200	250,000	34.88

Source: Own calculation on EACB data and the POP Financial Group's financial statement for the years 2015–2017

[a]Year-end data for 2015

Overall the two networks were able to steadily increase their membership and customer bases. For the OP Financial Group, the growth in membership between 2004 and 2017 equaled 65.88% while the second co-operative group, POP Bank, increased its membership by 3.21% between 2015 and 2017. The largest co-operative network in the country has shown itself to be increasingly attractive to new members, especially in the wake of the international financial crisis. This growth has been accompanied by a parallel rise in the governance participation of members: year-end figures for 2017 show that members make up 41.71% of the entire end-users of services channeled through the OP Financial Group (up from 35.64% in 2004) and around 34.88% of the entire end-users for the POP Bank Group. It is interesting to note that OP's increase in the number of members greatly outpaces that of customers in the same period (41.77%), indicating the attractiveness of membership of the financial services provider.

The evolution of the governance ratios reported in Table 4.1 indicates that members have assumed increased national relevance as the primary target customers of the banking services provided by Finnish CBs. However, this phenomenon turns out to be much less pronounced in Finland than, for instance, in Austria and Germany (where the corresponding figure was, respectively, almost 50% and 60% in 2017).

Table 4.2 Domestic market shares of Finnish co-operative networks

Year	Loans (%)		Deposits (%)	
	OP Financial Group	POP Bank Group[a]	OP Financial Group	POP Bank Group[a]
2004	30.50	n.a.	32.30	n.a.
2006	31.10	n.a.	32.70	n.a.
2008	32.00	n.a.	33.80	n.a.
2010	33.00	2.00	32.50	3.10
2012	33.40	1.90	34.10	3.10
2014	32.80	1.80	34.00	3.10
2016	35.40	1.50	38.50	2.40
2017	35.50	1.50	37.00	2.30

Source: EACB and Finance Finland. Own calculations of the governance ratio

[a]Data collected from Finance Finland

In Finland, CBs enjoy high market shares. At the end of 2017, according to data published by the European Association of Co-operative Banks (EACB) and Finance Finland, the two networks together hold 37% of the domestic market share of loans, with OP consistently growing and holding the largest share (Table 4.2). The domestic market share of deposits which they collectively hold is slightly higher: 39.30% (40.90% in 2016), with OP alone holding 37%. OP's market share is even higher in the mortgage sector, equaling 39.30%, while in corporate lending it reports a share of 38.70% (EACB 2017). By contrast, the POP Bank Group plays a relatively marginal role (Table 4.2).

Cumulatively the two co-operative groups managed total assets of € 137.976 million in 2016, which further increased to 141.518 million in 2017.[14] OP controlled almost 97% of the total co-operative banking assets in both years and is growing at a rate of more than 2.61% versus POP Bank's 1.11%.

Additional differences can be found relating to the degree of credit intermediation performed by the two networks (Table 4.3). A measurement of the lending activity using the ratio of bank loans (excluding loans to banks) to total assets shows that the volume of loans has been decreasing for the OP Financial Group since 2006, reflecting an increased degree of asset diversification (almost 60% at the end of 2017). A diverging trend can be observed in the smaller POP Bank, whose focus on lending is

---

[14] Data collected from the Finnish Financial Supervisory Authority.

Table 4.3 Credit intermediation orientation of Finnish co-operative networks

Year	Loans to customers to assets (%) (A)		Deposits from customers to assets (%) (B)		Loans to deposits from customers (%) (A/B)	
	OP Financial Group	POP Bank Group[a]	OP Financial Group	POP Bank Group[a]	OP Financial Group	POP Bank Group[a]
2004	81.89		59.60		137.40	
2006	66.55		43.36		153.48	
2008	68.26		48.96		139.42	
2010	67.68		46.69		145.96	
2012	65.31		49.76		131.25	
2014	63.99	75.85	44.17	84.17	144.87	90.12
2016	58.77	75.39	44.92	82.87	130.83	90.97
2017	59.92	77.77	47.76	83.13	125.46	93.55

Source: Own calculations on data reported by EACB

[a]Data reported for the POP Bank Group are own calculations on data extracted from SNL

higher than that of the largest co-operative banking group and growing slightly (about 78% in 2017). The values recorded in 2016 and 2017 for the foremost Finnish co-operative network, OP, are found to be in line with the corresponding indicator for the German co-operative banking network (61.28% at the end of 2017). In terms of the relationship between deposits and total assets, the relative ratio turns out to be substantially higher for POP Bank (83.13% in 2017) than for OP (47.46%), indicating their significantly differing ability to diversify their funding sources. For both banks this ratio decreased until 2016, though the decrease is more marked in the case of OP.

Table 4.3 shows the ratio of loans to deposits (in %) which represents a proxy of the so-called funding gap broadly measuring the dependence of banks on market-based funding. As a result of OP's lower dependency on traditional deposits from customers, its "funding gap" is notably high, on average being well above 100% (although this decreased from 2016 to 2017). The increase in the funding gap ratio is mainly driven by the larger decrease in the share of deposits compared to that of loans to total assets. This ratio stands in contrast to the corresponding levels at POP Bank and their German counterparts (95.11% at the end of 2017). Between the two co-operative groups, POP Bank appears to be more insulated from the risks arising from substantial reliance on market funding (i.e. via bonds and wholesale funding), thanks to its ability to attract and mobilize the savings of customers and members.

The two networks occupy quite different positions in the territory. In 2017, OP had 407 branches (down from 442 in 2016) while POP Bank had 85 banking outlets (the same number as in 2016). Following a common trend in European countries, the co-operative branch system has gone through a process of rationalization, particularly since 2008. The combination of a persistent low interest rate environment, the increasing digitalization of banking services, and growing competition from new non-banking entrants has prompted the implementation of cost-oriented efficiency measures, which continue to feature in the strategic plans of the networks. For instance, in 2004 OP's branch network consisted of 677 outlets (EACB 2004), but has now decreased by almost 40%.

The concentration of CB ownership within the bank branch network is high in Finland with CBs holding 49.57% of the total branches as of the end of 2016. The OP Financial Group holds 41.58% of total branches (including foreign outlets), while POP Bank has 7.99%.[15]

3   Co-operative Banking: Historical Development in Finland

The creation and spread of CBs in Finland dates back to the beginning of the twentieth century, inspired, as in other European countries, by the ideas of the German ideologist Raiffeisen (Prinz 2002). In Finland, as elsewhere, the development of co-operative banking took place in response to the difficulties faced by the population in rural areas in accessing credit from commercial and savings banks. It was the work of the academician Hannes Gebhard (1864–1933) that first instigated Finnish rural co-operation, with his establishment in 1899 of the constitution of a national Confederation of Agricultural Co-operatives, Pellervo, which went on to become an active participant in the drafting of the Law on Co-operatives of 1901 (Kuisma et al. 2000). In the years in which the co-operative movement was being formed, Finland was under the dominion of the Russian Empire, while still benefiting from a certain political autonomy. The spread of these entrepreneurial entities was tolerated by the Russian authorities, which thus did not hinder their development (Kalmi 2016). This appears to have been vigorous, thanks also to the regulation of the

---

[15] Data collected from Finance Finland.

sector and to national political support. As with the French agricultural credit unions, the Finnish state provided an important financial impetus to the formation of CBs. It was through the state provision of financial aids to guarantee the loans granted to the rural economy that co-operatives were able to develop. A further peculiarity of the Finnish co-operative credit sector was its development of a top-down approach that indicates the state's driving role. In 1902, the central body of the CBs, the Osuuskassojen Keskuslainarahasto (OKO), was established as the Central Lending Fund of the Co-operative Credit Societies Limited Company. State funding in the following year allowed the lending activity of credit co-operatives to be launched on Finnish soil. Therefore, as Kalmi (2016) points out, "first the central unit was established and only afterwards the individual credit unions were formed". The capital of the central bank of the Finnish co-operatives had been provided by wealthy private investors, supporters of the Raiffeisen model. Subsequently, this was relocated to become the property of the co-operatives themselves.

In 1915, OKO's lending function to credit co-operatives was coupled with the financing of every co-operative company and other entities, including municipalities and parishes. OKO's expansion of credit activity produced a greater need for funding that was met through an initial bond issue, and then followed by further issues at the international level. Also, in 1920, local banks were allowed to collect deposits from depositors other than members, including legal persons. The rupture of the exclusivity of the member-customer relationship was a necessary step to support the growing credit intermediation activity carried out by the local banks but did not call into question the solidity and common principles on which these banks were founded. Between 1920 and 1930 the number of CBs more than doubled, reaching 1400 in 1929 (Kuustera 1994). Not all of them were able to survive the increasingly competitive arena in rural areas, with savings and commercial banks competing primarily on the deposit side and later also on the lending side. The liberalization of savings banks' activities decreed in 1918 by the Savings Bank Act (Kuustera 1994) strengthened its competitive potential. If, up to that point, they had operated simply as collectors of savings with a view to financing public utility investments, the Savings Banks Act cleared the way for the short-term financing of local entrepreneurship. Competition between different banking models and between local banks, both co-operative and savings, in rural areas had become particularly fierce, as Kuustera recalls (1994).

The growth in credit co-operation, which brought with it the need to protect its principles and functions, led to the introduction of new organizational mechanisms that in fact contributed to increasing the level of integration in the network. In order to strengthen local credit co-operatives, the Central Association for Credit Co-operatives (Osuuskassojen keskusliitto, OKL) was established in 1928. While OKO continued to act as the sectoral central bank, OKL was responsible for the supervision of credit co-operatives, data gathering, the provision of advisory services, the promotion of the movement, and the management of its external relations. In 1933, to safeguard the financial viability of the Finnish co-operative banking movement, a guarantee fund was established, with mandatory contributions from co-operatives.[16] In the years that followed the Second World War and up until the mid-1980s, CBs became one of three banking business models that, along with savings banks and commercial banking, controlled an equal share of the domestic banking market. While different in governance and mission terms, the three types of banks were very similar in terms of their operations.[17] In 1941, the co-operative banking sector was allowed to grant mortgage loans which in turn permitted them to actively participate in the financing of the rural-urban migration of the early 1950s.[18] With the progress of urbanization, the focus of the co-operative credit societies' operations shifted toward urban areas and the arrangement of home lending. The Finnish banking system had an essential role in the mobilization of national savings, mainly because of a system of tax exemption on interest levied on bank deposits that remained in force until the 1980s. All banks benefited from this tax exemption but some more than others, among them CBs, because they were perceived as less risky. The first regulation of credit co-operatives was enacted in 1970, recognizing them as banks subject to banking legislation. However, they had already, de facto, been operating as banks for a long time (Kalmi 2016).

Up until the late 1980s, Finland was a relatively closed economy with several monopolies, a price regulation regime, cartels, and significant bilateral trade with the Soviet Union. At that time, foreigners were prohibited from buying land in Finland or stocks in Finnish companies traded on the

---

[16] See OP Financial Group's website.

[17] For instance, the employees of CBs were no longer volunteers but professionals, and irregular opening hours were replaced by regular hours (Kalmi 2016).

[18] In 1932, CBs were allowed to offer checking accounts (Kalmi 2016).

Helsinki Stock Exchange (OECD 2003). Restraints on direct competition between banks stimulated them to increase their market shares by building up extensive branch networks and investments in technologies, which ultimately resulted in excess banking capacity and low levels of efficiency (Nyberg and Vihriälä 1994). In Finland, lending rates were constrained by ceilings, and deposit rates were required to be linked to the central bank's base rate in order for depositors' interest income to be exempt from tax (Englund and Vihriälä 2009). In the early 1980s, the banking market underwent a period of deregulation. Banks were allowed to borrow freely on foreign money markets; foreign banks were established (as subsidiaries) in the Finnish market, resulting in more intense competition in the market for foreign exchange; interest rate deregulation made it possible for banks to freely determine the level of interest rates on new loans. The deregulation led to a massive credit expansion largely based on foreign debt. At its peak in 1988, total lending by deposit banks grew by almost 25% (Koskenkylä and Vesala 1994).

Increased competition for market shares inevitably led to lower credit standards in most banks. Soaring stock and real estate prices further boosted speculative activity by banks whose supervision at that time was somewhat lax. As pointed out by Nyberg and Vihriälä (1994) in their reconstruction of the Finnish financial crisis of the early 1990s, "deregulation was accompanied by strong public and political pressures stressing the blessings of unregulated, private choice. Banking regulation focused on judicial compliance, rather than risk evaluation. Furthermore, decisions by the supervisory authorities could be—and were—challenged in court, which probably raised the threshold for introducing stricter supervisory practices and lax controls that led to an unhealthy expansion, especially in lending".

Before the crisis erupted, the co-operative network undertook several steps toward modernizing its offer (e.g. in 1987 it established its fund management company) and in 1989, the central bank, OKO, went public with an initial public offering and listing of its shares on the Helsinki Stock Exchange. With this listing, new shareholders other than CBs owned the capital of OKO Bank with a public limited-liability legal form (plc). Its shares were divided into Series A and K. Series A shares were intended for the general public and quoted on the Helsinki Stock Exchange, whereas the ownership of Series K shares was restricted to companies and entities that were part of the network. The share series also differed in other respects. At a general meeting of shareholders, Series A shares entitled their holders to one vote per share while Series K shares carried five votes each. Furthermore, Series A shares entitled their holders to an annual dividend that was at least one percentage point higher than the dividend paid on Series K shares.[19] The control of the bank was thus firmly in the hands of CBs.

Toward the end of 1989 monetary conditions tightened, mainly due to market effects. Higher interest rates and weaker cashflows gave rise to downward pressure on asset prices. Decreased world demand led to a contraction in exports in 1991, which in the case of Finland was aggravated by the collapse of the Soviet Union. As a result, corporate bankruptcies doubled between 1990 and 1992. Bank earnings were squeezed by nonperforming assets as well as by declining fee income from new lending and trading activity. Falling collateral values increased the costs of bankruptcies to the lending banks (Englund and Vihriälä 2009). All banks were hit by the crisis, but savings banks were a prominent victim along with their mutually owned central institution SKOP (*Säästöpankkien keskusosakepankki*). The latter's former rapid expansion in lending and entry into the new business arena had been a deliberate strategic choice by the Finnish savings banks' central organization, with the aim of improving profitability in light of the low cost efficiency (Koskenkylä and Vesala 1994). The deep crisis at SKOP prompted the Bank of Finland to assume control of it, buying the majority of its shares. Additionally, as a further measure to restore financial stability in the banking sector, the government funded Finnish banks in 1992 and set up a special state-funded Government Guarantee Fund (*Valtion vakuusrahasto*) to support the savings banks, many of which were first merged. The resulting Savings Bank of Finland (SBF) was broken up in 1994, with the sound parts being sold to commercial and co-operative banks, and the defaulted or non-performing assets being transferred to a bad bank, Arsenal (Drees and Pazarbasioglu 1995).

In 1995, the two largest commercial banks in Finland, Suomen Yhdyspankki (Union Bank of Finland—UBF) and the Kansallis-Osake-Pankki (KOP), merged to create Merita Bank. This merger was soon followed by a cross-border merger with the Swedish Nordbanken, followed by successive amalgamations with smaller Danish and Norwegian banks, finally forming the Nordic banking group, Nordea (Kjellman et al. 2004). The state-owned postal savings bank Postipankki survived the crisis but was privatized soon afterward and acquired by the insurance group Sampo.

---

[19] See OKO Bank's Annual Report for the year 2006.

In November 2006, Sampo announced a business deal that stands out in Finnish economic history to this day on account of its enormity. The group sold its banking operations to Denmark's Danske Bank[20] and acquired shares in Nordea, the biggest bank in the Nordic countries, becoming its largest shareholder.

Finnish CBs were also affected by the crisis. As stated by Kalmi (2016), around 15% of CBs suffered significant losses during the crisis, and would not have survived the crisis without the support of other member banks. The larger city-based CBs, which had ventured into risky corporate financing, in particular had to be rescued by other CBs and between 1990 and 1995 many CBs merged into larger or more solid co-operative banks (Kjellman et al. 2004). Nevertheless, CBs overcame the crisis without any explicit subsidy from the government and emerged among the strongest banks (Kalmi 2016).

The crisis unearthed many old grievances within the OP Group that emerged particularly when the CBs opened up a discussion about the existing internal devices to strengthen their resilience. It emerged that not only was their mutual insurance fund not sufficiently capitalized to cope with the financial distress of several CBs but also OKO's and OKL's powers to issue instructions were inadequate. As a result, the network decided to adopt an explicit joint-liability scheme as well as to reinforce OKL's powers of advice and intervention in member banks (Kalmi 2016). While most of the banks decided to increase their co-operation, a number of mostly small and solid rural banks decided to leave the group. These banks went on to form in 1997 a loose network of local CBs, which would be called the POP Bank Group. The POP Bank Group has remained significantly smaller than the OKO Bank Group.

During the 2000s, the OKO network undertook several important developments thanks to favorable conditions in the Finnish economy. It diversified into the non-life insurance sector by acquiring Pohjola Group plc in 2005, thus gaining a leading position in bancassurance in Finland. In 2007 it changed its name to the OP-Pohjola Group, and OKO Bank was renamed Pohjola Bank plc. In February 2014, the OP-Pohjola Group announced a tender offer for all Pohjola Bank plc shares. It also announced and implemented the delisting of Pohjola shares to again become a financial services group fully owned by customers in terms of its ownership structure.

---

[20] See Sampo's website for the history of the insurance group.

4   FINNISH CO-OPERATIVE BANKING NETWORKS: MAIN CHARACTERISTICS

Membership of a Finnish CB is acquired through the purchase of at least one co-operative share. Typically, a member share costs € 100 (Kalmi 2016). CBs may issue profit shares. While co-operative shares entitle the holder to take part in the bank's decision-making, profit shares confer no voting rights. Co-operative shares do not pay any interest to their holders, while profit shares do. The interest paid on profit shares is considered as a profit distribution and is deducted from the annual profits accounted.

The remuneration of members with co-operative shares takes the form of bonuses or rebates which are received by members every time they make transactions in banking, non-life insurance, and wealth management. Members accumulating bonuses may then spend them by, for example, paying insurance premiums or bills relating to one of the three defined areas of transaction.[21] The usage of bonuses is expensed in the income statement while accrued bonuses are recognized as accrued liabilities in the balance sheet.[22] Natural and legal persons can become members of CBs. The large majority of CB members are individuals (including bank employees) whereas it is rare for organizations to be members, although corporations and foundations may become members with limited rights (with no right to bonuses and no voice in elections) (Kalmi 2016). There are no territorial requirements to become a member of a CB.

Redemption of shares is subject to the approval of the issuing bank and is required to be within the limits set by the authorities. The issuing CB has an absolute right to refuse to refund the capital and the remuneration of shares. The redemption is made at the nominal value of the shares within 12 months of the end of the financial year and may be divided over a period of 5 years should the issuing bank be unable to repay the full amount of the shares. Leaving members are not liable for any obligation of the CB of which they have been members.[23]

---

[21] In OP Financial Group, the weight of bonuses on total expenses (including personnel costs, other costs, impairment losses, and bonuses) is on average 11% for the last three available years. The large part of bonuses earned by member-customers refers to banking transactions.

[22] See OP Financial Group's Annual Report for the year 2017.

[23] For further details, see EACB (2012), The Process for the Redemption of Shares in CBs in different EU Member States: A Comparative Analysis, Brussels, 6 November.

The two co-operative banking networks in Finland are highly integrated, as required by the criteria set out in Art. 10 of the Capital Requirements Regulation (CRR). OP formally adopted an integrated strategic network model in 2011, while the POP Bank Group followed suit in 2015, their member banks being more reluctant to adopt this organizational framework. For instance, it was only in 2015 that the POP Bank Group introduced a joint-liability scheme for its members' debts and commitments, whereas the OP Financial Group adopted this in 1997. Both co-operative banking networks are regulated under the provisions of the Act on the Amalgamation[24] of Deposit Banks.[25] Pursuant to this act, the central institution of a co-operative banking network must be a registered entity that is authorized to act as the central institution of the amalgamation. It has legal co-operative status and is responsible for the control and supervision of its member credit institutions and the management and control on a consolidated basis of the minimum capital and liquidity requirements. In view of these responsibilities, the apex entity is entitled to issue instructions to member entities on risk management, good corporate governance, and internal control to ensure the fulfillment of regulatory requirements, as well as instructions on compliance with standardized accounting policies in the preparation of the consolidated financial statements.[26] The central institution prepares consolidated financial statements based also on the accounts of its member credit institutions. Member credit institutions are required to provide the central institution with the information necessary for the consolidation of accounts.[27]

The central co-operative is responsible for overseeing the members of the Group to ensure their compliance with the laws, decrees, and regulations issued by the relevant authorities governing financial markets, and with their own by-laws or articles of associations and the instructions

---

[24] Pursuant to Section 2 of the Act, an amalgamation comprises a central institution, companies belonging to the central institution's consolidation group, member credit institutions, companies belonging to the member credit institutions' consolidation groups, financial institutions and service companies in which the above-mentioned institutions jointly hold more than half of the voting rights.

[25] Act on the Amalgamation of Deposit Banks, 24 June 2010/599 and its subsequent amendments.

[26] See Chap. 5 of the Act on the Amalgamation of Deposit Banks, 24 June 2010/599 and its subsequent amendments.

[27] See Chap. 1, Section 9, of the Act on the Amalgamation of Deposit Banks, 24 June 2010/599 and its subsequent amendments.

issued by the central co-operative. Only OP Financial Group is a significant entity under the meaning of the European Single Supervisory Mechanism. As it is a significant banking group, the central co-operative and the amalgamation of the CBs are supervised by the European Central Bank (ECB). By contrast, the amalgamation of the POP Bank Group is solely under the supervision of the national Financial Supervisory Authority.

Other than supervisory tasks, as already stated, the apex is fully liable for its member credit institutions' debts. A joint-liability scheme between member banks is in place requiring them to participate in any necessary support measures aimed at preventing another member credit institution from going into liquidation. The members of the apex accept unlimited refinancing liability in the event of the central institution's liquidation or bankruptcy. Each member credit institution's liability for the amount the central institution has paid to the creditor on behalf of one member credit institutions is divided between the member credit institutions in proportion to their last adopted balance sheets.[28]

Membership of CBs is subject to the new member's adoption of by-laws or articles of association which recognize the apex's powers of intervention. The admission of new CBs is subject to the approval of the supervisory board of the central institution. Analogously, the supervisory board may take the decision to expel a member due to severe lack of compliance with the instructions issued by the central CB in a way that significantly endangers liquidity or capital adequacy management, the respect of the operating principles of the group, or the rules related to the preparation of financial statements. Withdrawal of CBs is also permitted provided that the aggregate capital resources of the companies belonging to the amalgamation are maintained at the level required by the Act on the Amalgamation of Deposit Banks. Withdrawal or expulsion of member banks does not exempt them from payment of their liabilities vis-à-vis the amalgamation if less than five years from the end of their calendar year have passed since their withdrawal or expulsion from the central co-operative institution. The Financial Supervisory Authority shall be promptly informed by the central institution of the grounds for expulsion

---

[28] See Chap. 5 of the Act on the Amalgamation of Deposit Banks, 24 June 2010/599 and its subsequent amendments.

and of the meeting of the co-operative's body convened to make a decision on the expulsion.[29]

Member CBs which are part of the two amalgamations are legally independent entities, which are involved in retail banking and SME (small and medium enterprise) financing and enjoy some operational independence. For instance, member CBs must comply with the business risk thresholds that have been established for the member institutions to ensure that the risks taken by an individual member institution are within acceptable limits. Their governance and that of the central institution relies on the general meeting of members, which elects a supervisory board for each CB. The latter in turn elects the executive board.

In between the primary banks and their apex institution there are intermediate organizations, local federations of CBs, that have regional coverage and aim to guarantee co-operation and interaction between local banks on specific projects (e.g. corporate social responsibility) as well as providing training to members of the member banks' governing bodies.[30] Federations also nominate their region's candidates for the supervisory board of the central institution.

Another significant difference between the two co-operative networks lies in the degree to which they make use of outsourcing, which clearly reflects their differences in size. Due to its small size, the POP Bank Group relies on several co-operation agreements with third parties that are designed to complete its financial offer with, for example, asset management and non-life insurance products.

5   The OP Financial Group

At the end of 2017, the OP Financial Group consisted of 167 member CBs (173 in 2016 and decreasing over time) and their central institution, OP Central Co-operative, with its subsidiaries and affiliates. Group member CBs are local, independent deposit banks engaged in retail banking, serving households, SMEs, agricultural and forestry customers, and public-sector entities. Over time OKL has increased its strategic and

---

[29] See Chap. 1, Sections 6, 7, and 8, of the Act on the Amalgamation of Deposit Banks, 24 June 2010/599 and its subsequent amendments.

[30] Member CBs of OP Financial Group are grouped into 16 federations whose boundaries essentially mimic those of provinces.

supervisory powers over member co-operatives which in turn own it fully. During the course of several restructurings of the group, OKL was renamed Central Co-operative, a co-operative entity fully owned by the primary banks. In 2011 the Central Co-operative was split into two entities: OP Central Co-operative acts as the central institution and has responsibility for the steering and supervision of the Group's business as well as its risk management and finance functions, while OP-Services Ltd is a service company tasked with the development and production of shared services for the OP Financial Group and its member CBs (Fig. 4.1). The co-operative group has a hybrid nature as it is made up of co-operative companies holding plc entities active in several areas of financial intermediation.

In 2016, the former Pohjola Bank plc (previously OKO Bank) became OP Corporate Bank, a conventional public limited company (PLC). It is fully owned by the Central Co-operative. As the old central bank of the network, OP Corporate Bank retains the treasury function for the whole group and the liquidity and funding management of member credit institutions and the Central Co-operative. It is also responsible for the Group's wholesale funding together with OP Mortgage Bank and is active in derivatives and bonds markets. OP Corporate Bank offers corporate and investment banking services and controls insurance subsidiaries dealing with

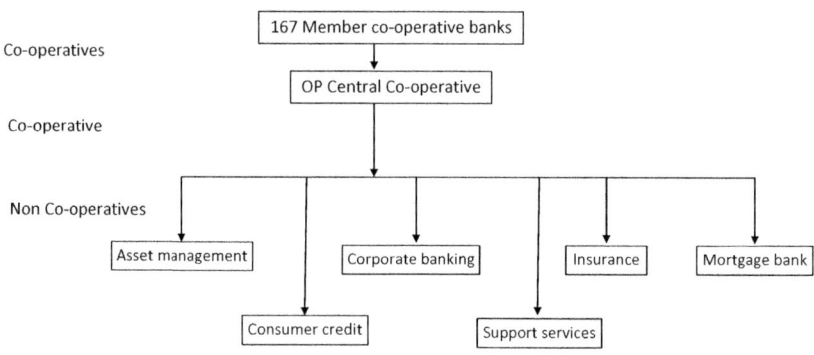

Fig. 4.1 The structure of the OP Financial Group. Source: Adapted from OP Financial Group's website

non-life insurance products for corporate and private customers.[31] Within the Group, OP Mortgage Bank is a special-purpose bank operating with the sole purpose of raising funds for OP member CBs by issuing covered bonds with mortgage collateral. It is wholly owned by the Central Co-operative (Fig. 4.1).

The group is active in three main businesses: banking, non-life insurance, and wealth management. The OP Financial Group also constitutes a financial and insurance conglomerate under the terms of the Finnish Act on the Supervision of Financial and Insurance Conglomerates. Banking provides the major share of earnings before tax (EBT), about 60% in 2017, while the remaining earnings are divided almost equally between its other activities. The Group serves 4,395,000 customers, of which 3,950,000 were private customers and 445,000 were corporate clients at the end of 2017. OP is notable for its technology investments, having launched several initiatives concerning the digitalization and automation of services as well as a crowdfunding platform. Additionally, in 2013 the Group entered the health and well-being services sector, setting up OP hospitals which, according to the management announcements, will create OP's fourth business line in the future, complementing its non-life insurance business.[32] Further investments have been made in the car sharing business and electric car rentals as well as in real estate brokerage services.

The co-operative banking group has a strong domestic focus but also offers banking services through branches located in neighboring countries: Estonia, Latvia, and Lithuania. It has established international partnerships to support the internationalization of its Finnish customers and in 2017 opened a representative office in Shanghai.

The governance of the OP Central Co-operative rests with two main bodies: the supervisory board and the executive board. The former is made up of a minimum of 32 and a maximum of 36 members, of which at least 16 represent the Finnish regional OP federations, with the remainder representing the member CBs. Board members are elected for a term of three years but must be under the age of 68 to be eligible for election. The main tasks of the Supervisory Board are the supervision of the Central Co-operative's management, in line with the provisions of the Co-operatives Act and in the best interests of the Central Co-operative and OP Financial

---

[31] It is intended that the latter subsidiaries will be transferred from OP Corporate Bank plc to OP Central Co-Operative's direct ownership in the future.
[32] See OP Financial Group's investor presentation for the year-end 2017.

Group, as well as the appointment and discharge of the executive board, and the confirmation of the Group's strategies, operational targets, and principles. The tasks of the supervisory board are performed through special committees, covering strategy, auditing, risk management, remuneration policies, and the nomination of the Central Co-operative's top management.

Alongside the co-operative principle of autonomy, the Group makes use of earnings retentions to guarantee the appropriate level of equity to finance its business growth, and to mitigate any economic burden on members should the co-operative group experience losses. In the context of the equity of the OP Financial Group, which stood at € 11.121 million at the end of 2017 (€ 10.237 in 2016), the total retained earnings account for a significant share, 50.11% (46.97% in 2016). Co-operative capital, made up of co-operative and profit shares, amounted to € 3.097 million at the 2017 year-end (€ 2.901 million in 2016) or 27.84% of the total equity (28.34% in 2016) with the without voting rights-profit shares accounting for 93.88% of the co-operative capital (93.72% in 2016). This proportion has increased over time, indicating its importance to the Group and its investors.[33] In fact, only about 6% of the co-operative capital can be used for administrative rights, representing a high level of concentration of decisional powers over the bank's total equity. Holders of co-operative shares receive rebates (or bonuses) through transactions relating to the Group's three main areas of business. It is interesting to note that these owner-customers shared 17% of earnings in 2017, up from 15.46% in the previous year, and that bonuses are equal to 1.15 times the amount of the co-operative shares held by owner-customers (1.14 in 2016), thus providing evidence of the economic benefits returned to the members of OP CBs.

Calculating the ratio between the annual value of rebates and the number of owner-customers, it turns out that in 2017 every member received € 120.02 (€ 119.06 in 2016), with this figure increasing over time. According to Jones, Jussila, and Kalmi's calculations (2016) the average annual bonus paid to members was € 37.38 in 2006, € 62.27 in 2007, € 94.40 in 2008, and € 98.38 in 2009. In their empirical study of the role of monetary incentives in fostering membership in OP member CBs over the period 2001–2009, the authors found evidence that supports the view that monetary incentives (by means of rebates) attract members to co-operatives and that rising monetary remuneration rates increase mem-

---

[33] For the year 2017, interest payable on profit shares issued within the OP Financial group equaled 3.25%. The same coupon was paid for the year 2016.

bership growth, especially in co-operatives that are located in more populous areas. While this result may imply that increasing monetary incentives can reduce the role of the common bond, the authors also show that membership (proxied by the member per population ratio) is important in smaller localities and negatively related to local competition.

6   THE STRUCTURE OF POP BANK GROUP

At the end of 2017, the POP Bank Group was the ninth largest financial group in Finland in terms of its share of the loans and deposits markets,[34] holding shares of 1.5% and 2.3%, respectively (Finance Finland 2018). Formed in 1997 as a network of dissentient banks from across the whole Finnish co-operative banking sector, it initially comprised 44 CBs (Kalmi 2016). Due to mergers, the number of co-operatives decreased, falling to 26 member CBs in 2017. These were amalgamated into the one group in December 2015. In a parallel fashion to OP Financial Group, the network has its own central credit institution, the POP Bank Alliance Co-operative, which remains under the control of the member CBs (Fig. 4.2).

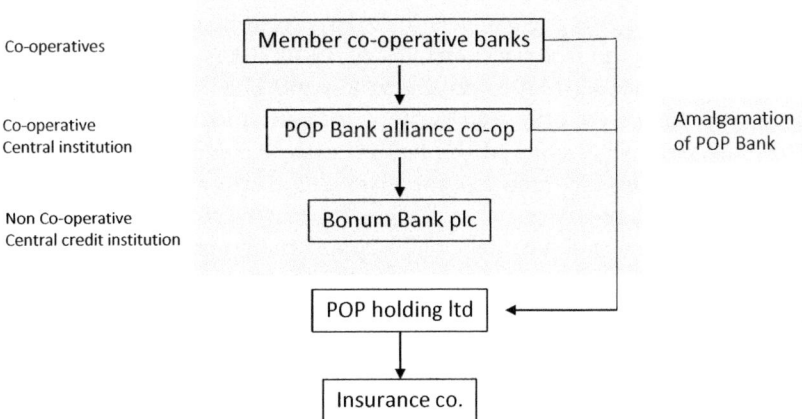

Fig. 4.2   The structure of the POP Bank Group. Source: Adapted from POP Bank Group's Annual Report for the year 2017

[34] Loans are only considered to customers other than Monetary Financial Institutions (MFIs) and deposits only accepted from customers other than MFIs.

The central institution is responsible for the steering of the group and its supervision in accordance with the Act on the Amalgamation of Deposit Banks. A joint-liability scheme is in force between the member CBs, the central institution, and Bonum Bank, taking the legal form of a plc.[35] This is a subsidiary under the control of the central institution and the member CBs. Bonum Bank acts as the central bank of the Group by providing clearing, settlement, and treasury services for POP Banks. It provides funding for the whole Group by issuing certificates of deposits and bonds on the financial markets, and other liabilities vis-à-vis the interbank markets and the ECB. Since 2017 it has also managed the liquidity coverage requirements of the network.

The group also includes a property & casualty (P&C) insurance company, known as POP Insurance, which is held by POP Holding Ltd but which is not included in the scope of the joint liability.

The POP Banks are focused on retail banking, mainly residential real estate lending, but they also engage in SMEs and agricultural lending and services through branches located mainly in Finland's less urban regions. They are co-operatives in terms of their structure and are autonomous. Member CBs of the POP Bank Group use the common marketing name POP Bank to offer retail banking services to private customers (who made up 84.4% of their total customers in 2016), corporates (4.4% in 2016), and agricultural and forestry companies (4.3% in 2016), as well as offering non-life insurance services to private customers. Their customer base has been increasing over time, especially in the insurance business, as since 2011 the Group has enjoyed the highest customer satisfaction rating in Nordic countries according to the Extended Performance Satisfaction Index (EPSI) Rating.[36]

The annual general meeting of CBs adopts the reports on the consolidated basis of the Group, decides on the POP Bank Group's strategy, and elects the members of the supervisory board and the auditor. Additionally, the supervisory board is responsible for ratifying the general operating principles of the POP Bank Group and the principles of bank-specific management. Each member CB has its own representative on the supervisory board, which is made up of a minimum of 3 and a maximum of 34 members elected by the general meeting of the co-operative. The current

---

[35] In order to prevent the liquidation of one CB, each member CB is required to contribute annually up to a maximum of 0.5% of the last confirmed balance sheet. See POP Bank Group's Financial Statements for the year 2015.

[36] See POP Bank Group's Investor presentation, April 2018.

number of members on the supervisory board is 26. As a subsidiary of the Alliance, Bonum Bank plc has no voting rights in co-operative meetings. The board of directors of POP Bank Alliance Co-operative is elected from the supervisory board and consists of a minimum of five and a maximum of seven members so that at least one member is elected from each co-operative region as required by the regulations. These also stipulate that a majority of the Board members must be employed by a member CB[37] and that their term of office shall be three years.

Looking at the equity of the POP Bank Group, this amounted to € 485.65 million at the end of 2017 (€ 463.02 million in 2016) with retained earnings accounting for a significant share at 54.49% (55.05% in 2016), larger than that relating to OP Financial Group in 2017 (50.11%). Co-operative capital comprises co-operative and POP shares (analogous to the OP profit shares paying a coupon) and amounted to € 62.79 million at the 2017 year-end (€ 52.56 million in 2016) or 12.94% of the total equity (11.36% in 2016), with the without voting rights-profit shares accounting for 85.31% of co-operative capital (82.76% in 2016) and increasing over time. POP shares display a trend similar to that recorded by the OP Financial Group despite a lower incidence on total co-operative capital. POP shares were first issued in 2015, most of them resulting from the conversion of supplementary shares since these are not acknowledged as equity instruments by the EU's CRR.[38] The CB issuing POP shares has an unconditional right to refuse both the payment of interest and the redemption of capital.[39] POP shares do not confer voting rights or any other rights on the member. The interest paid on these investments is approved by the co-operative meeting according to proposals submitted by the board of directors. Consequently, the coupon rate can change annually.[40]

---

[37] See POP Bank Group's Annual Report for the year-end 2016.

[38] Finnish CBs used to issue supplementary shares which do pay interest to the holders and are classified as liabilities within the IFRS-compliant financial statements. This is because CBs do not have an unconditional right to refuse a member. As reported in the POP Bank Group's financial statements for the year 2015, the supplementary contribution is refunded within six months of the end of the financial year based on which the refund can be made for the first time. If the refund cannot be made in full, the refund may take place subsequently if it becomes possible, based on the next three financial statements. The conversion of supplementary shares into POP shares allows the latter to be classified as equity instruments.

[39] Refund is made at the subscription price.

[40] The targeted interest rate on POP shares was indicated at 2.25% or 2.5% in the Group's annual report for the year 2015.

7   THE PERFORMANCES OF THE FINNISH CO-OPERATIVE
VERSUS NON-CO-OPERATIVE BANKING GROUPS OVER
THE PERIOD 2005–2017

The Finnish co-operative banking sector plays a pivotal role in Finland, with the OP Financial Group occupying a dominant position. The OP Financial Group is the largest Finnish banking group by market share (see Table 4.2), followed by the shareholder-oriented banking group of Nordea (with market shares of 26.4% and 26% of loans and deposits, respectively).[41] The third largest commercial joint-stock bank historically, Danske Bank Finland, was converted into a foreign branch of Danske Bank in late 2017, amid the wave of restructuring processes that involved the main European banking groups and their cross-border activities. Its market shares of loans and deposits were 9.5% (slightly lower than the growing lender, Municipality Finance, with 9.6% in 2017) and 14.3%, respectively, at the end of 2017 (Finance Finland 2018).

Together these three entities hold a total of 71.4% (72.2% in 2016) of the non-MFIs loans and 77.3% (77.7% in 2016) (Finance Finland 2017) of non-MFIs deposits in Finland. In terms of size, even before the restructuring Nordea was the largest bank in Finland with total assets of approximately € 239 billion (in 2016) as opposed to OP Financial Group's approximate € 134 billion, while Danske, prior to its conversion into a branch, was the smallest with total assets of just under € 29 billion. All three groups have grown considerably over time. From 2005 to 2016, the assets of the Finnish subsidiaries of Danske, Nordea, and the largest co-operative group increased overall by 25%, 93%, and 154%, respectively. However, if we look at the annual growth dynamics (not reported for the sake of brevity), it is only OP that has a stable record of positive growth rates, both before and after the global financial crisis (GFC). The sustained growth of Nordea in the years between 2007 and 2011 was followed by an equally robust period of downsizing that, to a lesser extent, also affected Danske. Although the co-operative DNA was probably strengthened by

---

[41] In 2016, the Nordea annual general meeting approved the plan to merge its Nordic subsidiaries into the Swedish parent bank, turning them into branches. The merger was carried out in 2017. Since then, Nordea has operated as a branch in Finland. In 2018, Nordea moved its headquarters from Sweden to Finland, making it Finland's largest bank in terms of its balance sheet. The process also involved the founding of Nordea Mortgage Bank plc, active in the issuance of mortgage-backed covered bonds.

the decision to delist the bank, in substance the OP Group has a hybrid nature, as in other European countries. As already noted, many of the subsidiaries are joint-stock companies active in, for example, corporate banking, asset management, and payments. In the insurance sector, for example, the OP Group has a leading position in the non-life segment, while it is second in the life sector, after Nordea. As in other sister companies in Europe, the hybridization of the group goes hand in hand with a search for operational diversification and specialization in certain sectors of financial intermediation. These phenomena are insignificant in the country's second co-operative group, POP Bank, whose competitor, S-Bank (indirectly owned by the members of Finnish consumer co-operatives), is recording more sustained rates of growth.

Both the Finnish co-operative banking groups belong to so-called strategic networks, which are fully compliant with the provisions of Art. 10 of the CRR. This enables the central institutions, both of which are co-operative in nature and firmly controlled by member CBs, to take actions regarding the management of local independent CBs. With this high degree of strategic and managerial integration, we can also hypothesize that there is more convergence between the two banking business models, the one oriented toward shareholders and the other toward stakeholders. In fact, competition, on the one hand, and the harmonization of the supervisory rules, on the other, seem to push increasingly toward a leveling of operational choices and consequently of performances. For this reason, as in previous chapters we assess the effects of this ongoing hybridization. In other words, have the mitigation of the principles of mutuality pursued by CBs and the growing complementarity with markets as places of investment and funding meant that the results achieved by CBs have become more similar to those of commercial joint-stock banks? Which areas record analogies and differences in results? Can a convergence in performance be observed over time? To answer these important questions, we have identified a series of indicators in the form of ratios proxying bank performances. The set of indicators used to run the comparisons concerns the capitalization of banks; their activities in lending and investing in securities, including those held for trading on the financial markets; their reliance on customer deposits; the role they play over time in the interbank market; the riskiness deriving from their lending; and, finally, their banking profitability and efficiency.

The data used in this first phase of analysis are consolidated and are therefore representative of the results achieved by the commercial and co-operative groups, including the latter's networks of CBs and their various non-co-operative subsidiaries. Year-end figures are used. In order to verify if, where, and when there have been phenomena of convergence between co-operative and non-co-operative banking groups, one or more national shareholder-oriented banking groups have been identified with which the following comparative analysis is carried out. The analysis covers the period 2005–2017 and is particularly helpful since it allows the results obtained by the two groups of banks to be taken before and after the onset of the GFC. Data for the non-co-operative banking groups are extracted from the SNL, BankScope Bureau van Dijk, and Orbis Bank Focus databases in order to minimize the potential for missing data. Data for POP Bank are hand collected. The results of the two co-operative banking groups in the different areas under investigation are compared with those obtained by the two leading commercial banks, Nordea and Danske Bank, up until 2016 only, due to the restructurings which occurred in 2017 which affect the availability and comparability of the data for the year-end 2017. We provide means and standard deviations of the selected indicators in different sub-periods, covering respectively, the pre-crisis period, 2005–2007; the main GFC period, 2008–2010; the period from 2011 to 2013 during which the sovereign debt crisis severely affected various countries[42] and important regulatory and monetary policy measures were put in place to restore bank financial stability; and the implementation of Basel 3 and initiation of the European Banking Union with the implementation of the Single Supervisory Mechanism (SSM) and the Single Resolution Mechanism (SRM), 2014–2017.

In Table 4.4, we report the first set of indicators under investigation. Selected capital ratios comprise a regulatory proxy for the appraisal of the capital adequacy of the banking groups, the Tier 1 (%) ratio, and an accounting ratio represented by equity over assets (%). The first one represents a measure of capital adequacy under the Basel rules to address credit risk. Broadly speaking, the Tier 1 ratio is calculated as the shareholder funds plus perpetual non-cumulative preference shares as a percentage of risk-weighted assets and some off-balance sheet items. The higher the Tier 1 value, the more capitalized the bank is, which improves

---

[42] In 2012, Greece was granted a new financial aid package while its debt was cancelled resulting in a severe haircut for private investors. Spain entered a difficult period, amidst doubts about the strength of its banking system, the deterioration of its public finances, record unemployment, and deepening recession. These concerns led risk premiums on sovereign debt to climb considerably, triggering bailouts for Greece, Ireland, and Portugal. Italy was not spared, with yields on its debt rising as well, despite the reforms undertaken by the government in charge at the time, led by Mario Monti.

Table 4.4   Comparison of Finnish co-operative vs. non-co-operative banking groups: capital ratios

	OP Financial Group		POP Bank		Nordea Bank[a]		Danske Bank[b]	
	Mean	SD	Mean	SD	Mean	SD	Mean	SD
Tier 1 (%)								
2005–2007	12.79	0.26	–	–	15.44	2.12	9.60	2.85
2008–2010	12.66	0.09	–	–	13.68	0.30	13.61	1.02
2011–2013	15.34	1.75	–	–	15.61	2.64	15.81	1.37
2014–2017	19.49	2.87	20.63	0.78	23.33[c]	4.78	17.58[c]	2.80
Equity/total assets (%)								
2005–2007	8.73	0.24	–	–	9.15	1.59	5.21	1.34
2008–2010	7.53	0.58	–	–	4.67	0.66	7.76	0.80
2011–2013	7.29	0.31	–	–	2.93	0.19	8.23	0.73
2014–2017	7.43	0.66	10.76	0.52	3.88[c]	1.01	8.60[c]	0.41

Source: Author's calculations

This table reports descriptive statistics (means and standard deviations [SDs]) of Finnish co-operative and non-co-operative banking groups. Tier 1 (%) is the ratio between primary regulatory capital and risk-weighted assets; equity/total assets (%) is the ratio between total equity and total assets. Our calculations are based on data extracted from SNL. Data for POP Bank are hand collected

[a]We consider only Nordea Bank Finland plc until 2016 as it was merged with its Swedish parent company in early 2017 and became a Finnish branch. Nordea decided to move its headquarters to Helsinki in 2018
[b]In late 2017, Danske Bank Finland plc became a branch of the Danish parent company, Danske Bank
[c]Only 2014–2016

its ability to face the risks arising from lending to and financing borrowers. Under the Basel 3 rules introduced in Europe in 2014 (with EU Directive 2013/36 and the EU Regulation 575/2013—CRR) the minimum level of Tier 1 permitted is 6% plus the capital conservation buffer of 2.5%.[43] The ratio of equity to total assets (%) proxies the capital cushion against banking risks. The higher this figure the better the bank is able to cope with potential losses arising from its activity.

The Tier 1 ratio has, on average, been increasing over time in all the sub-periods under investigation both for OP Financial Group and for the shareholder-oriented banking groups. Throughout the periods of observation, the co-operative group's Tier 1 values have generally remained lower than those of the two main commercial banks. During 2014–2017, the gap

---

[43] Prior to Basel 3 coming into force, the minimum value of the Tier 1 ratio was 4%.

between OP and Nordea has increased significantly, mainly due to the capital release effects of the asset downsizing undertaken by Nordea. The Tier 1 ratio of OP has increased, reaching an average value of 19.49% (18.56% if recalculated till 2016), which is one of the highest in the sample of European countries under investigation. This value is higher than that of Danske Bank (17.58%) but lower than the average value of Nordea (23.33%). The average level of regulatory capital held by POP Bank is also robust, standing at 20.63% in 2014–2017. Analysis of the ratio of equity to total assets reveals a trend that diverges from that already seen for the Tier 1 ratio (Table 4.4). Only in the case of Danske Bank is an increase in the capital held recorded over time. Both OP and Nordea experienced a decrease in the ratio from 2005 to 2013 and a recovery in the last of the periods examined. Of the two, however, the OP Group recorded the more contained reduction in capital levels. The average value for OP in 2014–2017 stands at 7.43% (7.21% if recalculated up to 2016), almost double that of Nordea (3.88%) but lower than the values for the small cooperative group POP (10.76% and 10.55% if recalculated up to 2016) and Danske Bank (8.60%).

The second set of indicators concerns the asset side of the banking groups and aims to shed light on its composition. In this regard, we employ three types of ratios: the ratio of net customer loans to total assets (%) which measures the degree of dedication to the traditional lending activity; the ratio of the total securities held to total assets (%) which provides an assessment of banks' integration with financial markets in investment terms; and finally the ratio of securities held for trading to total assets (%), which shows the degree of banks' active participation in the financial markets through financial instruments (i.e. bonds, derivatives, and stocks) and allows for an assessment of speculative activities within the financial markets.

The focus on lending activity is different for each of the groups under consideration but follows a declining trend in all cases. OP and the smaller of the two commercial joint-stock banks, Danske Bank, largely focus on providing credit to non-banking sectors of the economy. In the last of the analyzed sub-periods, these two intermediaries recorded rather similar values for the ratio of net customer loans to total assets (%), respectively, equaling 60.70% (60.95% if recalculated until 2016) and 66.64%. POP Bank is decidedly more credit-oriented with 75.75% in the same time period: a figure that clearly shows CBs' typical dedication to direct financing and lower levels of asset diversification. The values of OP and, to a lesser extent, POP Bank are in line with average values recorded in other countries, for example, in Germany, with around 60% in 2014–2017 (see Table 6.6). On the other hand, the disparity with the commercial bank Nordea is evident, with Nordea showing, over time, the lowest percentage incidence of loans on total assets (31.18% in 2014–2016). In Finland, as in other European countries under investigation, there is also a clear specialization in the activity of financing the economy, with co-operative banks playing a prominent role in the lending activity.

CBs' investment in securities, though lower in comparative terms than that of joint-stock banks, nevertheless, shows increasing trends. In parallel with the reduction in the percentage of loans to total assets, OP Financial Group recorded a change in the percentage of the portfolio held in securities, which went from an average value of 10.07% in the three-year period 2008–2010 to 17.30% in 2014–2017 (16.91% if recalculated up to 2016), slightly above that of POP Bank (15.22%). The figures for OP are higher than those recorded by the smaller Danske Bank, reflecting both organizations' growing interest in diversifying banking assets as their size increases. The role of investment in securities is fundamentally different for the largest Nordea commercial bank, which invested approximately 42% of its assets in securities over the period 2014–2016, more than double OP's investment share.

It is interesting to note, despite the limited data available, the different levels of securities held for trading purposes between the co-operative groups and Danske Bank (Table 4.5). After the outbreak of the GFC, OP reduced its share of securities used for trading on the financial markets, increasing it to 5.52% only in the most recent period. Danske's attitude was rather different, doubling its securities held for trading purposes compared to the previous period (13.56% in the 2014–2016 period). The incidence of trading for the POP group was marginal at only 0.06% in the last of the sub-periods under consideration. If we calculate the impact of the assets held for trading on the total securities held, we find that the co-operative banking group reports average values of 31.91% in 2014–2017 while the corresponding figure for Danske Bank is about 90% over the same period, thus providing evidence of commercial joint-stock banks' strong strategic position for trading and their more marked orientation toward a market-based banking.

The third set of selected indicators concerns the percentage of traditional funding through customer deposits and interbank activity (Table 4.6). There is once again substantial divergence between the two

Table 4.5 Comparison of Finnish co-operative vs. non-co-operative banking groups: lending and securities holdings ratios

	OP Financial Group		POP Bank		Nordea Bank[a]		Danske Bank[b]	
	Mean	SD	Mean	SD	Mean	SD	Mean	SD
Net customer loans/total assets (%)								
2005–2007	66.84	1.16	–	–	39.50	1.92	77.34	3.71
2008–2010	67.28	1.24	–	–	28.83	2.77	75.56	3.63
2011–2013	66.09	1.30	–	–	30.56	6.30	71.59	5.63
2014–2017	60.70	2.28	75.75	1.57	31.18[c]	3.59	66.64[c]	2.82
Securities/total assets (%)								
2005–2007	10.07	0.31	–	–	24.25	2.42	9.31	1.96
2008–2010	10.33	1.25	–	–	41.63	3.20	6.47	2.73
2011–2013	11.83	0.76	–	–	46.02	7.66	8.15	1.92
2014–2017	17.30	3.73	15.22	3.35	41.85[c]	2.68	15.26[c]	0.39
Total assets held for trading/total assets (%)								
2005–2007	5.49	1.79	–	–	–	–	5.77	1.02
2008–2010	3.94	1.83	–	–	–	–	6.23	2.74
2011–2013	3.65	0.38	–	–	–	–	6.37	1.35
2014–2017	5.52	0.82	0.06	0.03	–	–	13.56[c]	0.61

Source: Author's calculations

This table reports descriptive statistics (means and standard deviations [SDs]) of Finnish co-operative and non-co-operative banking groups. Net customer loans/total assets (%) is the ratio between net loans and total year-end assets; securities/total assets (%) is the ratio between total securities held and total assets; assets held for trading/total assets (%) is the ratio between total assets held for trading and total assets. Our calculations are based on data extracted from SNL. Data for POP Bank are hand collected

[a]We consider only Nordea Bank Finland plc until 2016 as it was merged with its Swedish parent company in early 2017 and became a Finnish branch. Nordea decided to move its headquarters to Helsinki in 2018
[b]In late 2017, Danske Bank Finland plc became a branch of the Danish parent company, Danske Bank
[c]Only 2014–2016

largest groups, each adopting different business models in terms of their dependence on customer deposits. On average, the co-operative group OP records figures which are almost double those of Nordea, demonstrating a typical feature of co-operative banking across the European countries investigated: the importance of funding from depositors, which persists over time.

This dependency is even more pronounced in the case of the smallest of the co-operative groups, POP Bank, which in 2014–2017 recorded an average value of the ratio of customer deposits to total assets (%) of 83.06%.

Table 4.6   Comparison of Finnish co-operative vs. non-co-operative banking groups: funding and interbank ratios

	OP Financial Group		POP Bank		Nordea Bank[a]		Danske Bank[b]	
	Mean	SD	Mean	SD	Mean	SD	Mean	SD
Customer deposits/total assets (%)								
2005–2007	48.06	1.83	–	–	27.95	0.68	47.47	2.02
2008–2010	47.47	1.29	–	–	19.99	0.60	51.96	7.20
2011–2013	49.76	0.06	–	–	21.39	4.78	55.89	4.30
2014–2017	46.38	1.16	83.06	0.87	22.00[c]	1.30	56.73[c]	3.44
Interbank ratio (%)								
2005–2007	31.51	1.43	–	–	172.76	13.45	248.32	320.72
2008–2010	97.07	34.30	–	–	123.61	10.79	141.96	15.37
2011–2013	62.28	19.71	–	–	66.25	33.11	204.02	15.01
2014–2017	20.26	14.65	441.37[d]	285.89	41.21[c]	0.65	125.41[c]	56.80

Source: Author's calculations

This table reports descriptive statistics (means and standard deviations [SDs]) of Finnish co-operative and non-co-operative banking groups. Customer deposits/total assets (%) is the ratio between customer deposits and total assets; interbank ratio (%) is the ratio between loans to banks and deposits from banks. Our calculations are based on data extracted from SNL. Data for POP Bank are hand collected

[a]We consider only Nordea Bank Finland plc until 2016 as it was merged with its Swedish parent company in early 2017 and became a Finnish branch. Nordea has decided to move its headquarters to Helsinki in 2018

[b]In late 2017, Danske Bank Finland plc became a branch of the Danish parent company, Danske Bank

[c]Only 2014–2016

[d]Excluding 2014

The comparison between OP Financial Group and Danske Bank results in less marked differences. In fact, Danske commercial bank holds a higher ratio of deposits to total assets than OP, and it is increasing over time, in contrast to the slight reduction recorded for the country's main co-operative banking group.

Compared with other European co-operative groups, OP's funding appears more diversified. The funding of the German co-operative group BVR is equal to an average of 60%, while the percentages of deposits on the total assets of the French co-operative groups are more similar to those of the Finnish OP.

As regards participation in the interbank markets, measured by the interbank ratio, the data displayed in Table 4.6 show enormous variability in the recorded values of the interbank ratio. For example, the OP Group increased its interbank position during the 2008–2010 period, making it a weightier provider of funds during the most acute phase of the GFC, and then, in the following periods, recording constantly decreasing average values, falling to 20.26% in 2014–2017. This is a lower value than those recorded in the same period by the two foreign banks, Nordea and Danske. Both recorded a significant decrease in the interbank ratio, particularly in the case of Nordea, while the subsidiary of the Danish banking group of the same name maintained its role as a net gatherer of funds on the interbank market. This phenomenon is often found for the subsidiaries of major banking groups with cross-border presence. POP Bank Group's interbank position is very high, with it investing on average four times the value of funds raised through the same channel.

Table 4.7 shows risk indicators that assumed particular importance during the GFC, prompting regulators to dictate more stringent prudential rules regarding banks' exposure to liquidity and credit risk. The table contains a proxy for exposure to liquidity risk, often used in the empirical literature, and two proxies for credit risk. The use of the ratio of liquid assets to total liabilities (excluding equity) was preferred to the prudential ratios relating to liquidity risk since the latter would have been available only for the last of the periods under investigation. The ratio used examines the amount of liquid assets available to cover all the liabilities held by banks. The higher this percentage is, the more liquid and generally able to redeem its own debts a bank is, and the less vulnerable it is to a classic run on the bank.

The data on liquidity reported in Table 4.7 show a diverging trend for co-operative and non-co-operative banks: the averages of the former decrease over time, being significantly lower than that of commercial banks. By contrast, the liquidity levels of the two commercial banks record higher values in all the periods under investigation, in line with both their more significant investment in highly marketable securities and their more active role in the interbank market as providers of funds. For both the OP and POP Groups, the holding of liquidity reserves is at low levels, slightly lower than, for example, those recorded for the network of German co-operative banks, BVR (on average around 10% as opposed to 7% and 6% for the Finnish POP and OP groups). In the case of Finland, as, for instance, in Germany and France, commercial banks follow operational strategies that lead them to hold far higher degrees of liquidity than CBs. On the one hand, this different degree of liquidity observed in CBs typically originates from their greater involvement in traditional lending activ-

Table 4.7 Comparison of Finnish co-operative vs. non-co-operative banking groups: liquidity and credit risk ratios

	OP Financial Group		POP Bank		Nordea Bank[a]		Danske Bank[b]	
	Mean	SD	Mean	SD	Mean	SD	Mean	SD
Liquid assets/total liabilities (%)								
2005–2007	7.69	2.72	–	–	41.29	3.55	14.14	2.57
2008–2010	8.17	3.70	–	–	30.84	5.73	15.32	8.25
2011–2013	5.64	2.08	–	–	29.56	3.09	24.95	6.00
2014–2017	6.39	4.53	7.15	4.09	50.31[c]	12.78	34.29[c]	2.41
Impaired loans/gross loans and advances (%)								
2005–2007	0.64	0.08	–	–	1.12[d]	0.16	–	–
2008–2010	0.69	0.14	–	–	2.20	0.69	1.92	0.84
2011–2013	0.76	0.03	–	–	1.83	0.09	2.30	0.15
2014–2017	0.79	0.03	0.97	0.10	1.93	0.44	3.24[c]	0.49
LLR/gross customer loans (%)								
2005–2007	51.09	12.17	–	–	55.87[d]	4.62	–	–
2008–2010	51.85	17.82	–	–	43.43	2.72	70.73	4.40
2011–2013	83.20	0.82	–	–	41.86	1.08	66.43	5.41
2014–2017	80.94	3.79	41.50	27.47	49.20	11.90	37.97[c]	9.39

Source: Author's calculations

This table reports descriptive statistics (means and standard deviations [SDs]) of Finnish co-operative and non-co-operative banking groups. Liquid assets/total liabilities (%) is the ratio between liquid assets and total liabilities; impaired loans/gross customer loans and advances (%) is the ratio between impaired loans and gross customer loans and advances; LLR/impaired loans (%) is the ratio between loan loss reserves and impaired loans. Our calculations are based on data extracted from BankScope and Orbis Bank Focus solely for the year-ends 2016–2017. Data for Danske Bank and POP Bank are hand collected for the calculation of the ratio of liquid assets/total liabilities (%)

[a]We consider only Nordea Bank Finland plc until 2016 as it was merged with its Swedish parent company in early 2017 and became a Finnish branch. Nordea has decided to move its headquarters to Helsinki in 2018

[b]In late 2017, Danske Bank Finland plc became a branch of the Danish parent company, Danske Bank

[c]Only 2014–2016

[d]Only 2006–2007

ity which usually absorbs the largest part of banking assets to the detriment of other investments, as, for example, highly marketable securities. On the other hand, the exploitation of more favorable trends in funding through customer deposits seems to allow CBs to hold fewer liquid assets to face unexpected requests from both depositors and borrowers.

Table 4.7 reports two proxies: the ratio of impaired loans to gross loans and advances (%) and the ratio of loan loss reserves to impaired loans (%). The first one shows impaired or non-performing loans as a percentage of the bank's gross customer loans and advances (%). It indicates the weakness of the loan portfolio which increases as the percentage rises. The riskiness of both OP's and POP's credit portfolios, proxied by the first credit risk indicator, follows an increasing trend but turns out to be the lowest among all the business models taken into account. In the period 2014–2017, their average values are lower than 1%, at 0.79% and 0.97%, respectively. shareholder-oriented banks also recorded a growing level of risk, as well as showed more volatility in their results. The quality of Nordea's portfolio appears better over time than that of Danske Bank, but we cannot ignore the fact that the credit portfolio of the former is less than half that of the latter in percentage terms (see Table 4.5). The higher quality of the loan portfolios of the Finnish CBs reflects their better ability to assume and manage credit risk despite a sustained credit commitment. The increase in the levels of risk observed for all the banks shown in Table 4.7 seems to result from the credit expansion that Finland has recorded even after the outbreak of the GFC thanks to the positive dynamics of the real economy. The exposure of the Finnish banking system is among the lowest in Europe (Finance Finland 2018). CBs have the lowest in the sample of countries examined in this book.

The second of the ratios used relates loan loss reserves to impaired loans or non-performing loans. Higher values of this ratio, also known as the "coverage ratio", indicate that the bank is better equipped to face losses on loans. On the other hand, out of all accounting considerations, higher levels of the coverage rate are generally indicative of a poorer quality loan portfolio. The OP Financial Group holds the highest levels of coverage over time. In 2014–2017, its credit loss provisions covered over 80% of non-performing loans in comparison to values of around 40% for commercial banks, and indeed POP. The available reserves increased mainly after the GFC event, highlighting a particularly cautious attitude on the part of the country's second banking group. With regard to the ratio between loss reserves and impaired loans, there are similarities between OP's loans loss reserves percentage values and those of the French Crédit Agricole, which has the highest coverage ratio over time, at slightly over 80% since 2008 (see Table 5.7).

The last battery of indicators that we examine involves variables that are representative of bank profitability and efficiency, widely employed in the empirical literature. With regard to the profitability analysis, three indicators are taken into consideration: the net interest margin (%); the return on average assets (ROAA) (%); and the return on average equity (ROAE) (%). To evaluate the operational efficiency achieved by the bank management, we use a widespread indicator: the cost-to-income ratio (%) (Table 4.8).

Table 4.8   Comparison of Finnish co-operative vs. non-co-operative banking groups: profitability and efficiency ratios

	OP Financial Group		POP Bank		Nordea Bank[a]		Danske Bank[b]	
	Mean	SD	Mean	SD	Mean	SD	Mean	SD
Net interest margin (%)								
2005–2007	2.05[c]	0.08	–	–	1.12[c]	0.00	1.50[c]	0.06
2008–2010	1.67	0.35	–	–	0.69	0.29	1.57	0.24
2011–2013	1.25	0.16	–	–	0.38	0.03	1.21	0.10
2014–2017	1.03	0.13	1.61	0.06	0.35[d]	0.02	1.05[d]	0.07
ROAA (%)								
2005–2007	1.12[c]	0.08	–	–	0.99[c]	0.02	1.83[c]	0.03
2008–2010	0.42	0.11	–	–	0.51	0.20	0.33	0.23
2011–2013	0.55	0.10	–	–	0.30	0.04	0.43	0.06
2014–2017	0.66	0.07	0.26	0.08	0.32[d]	0.04	0.58[d]	0.02
ROAE (%)								
2005–2007	12.91[c]	1.14	–	–	10.61[c]	0.90	24.76[e]	–
2008–2010	5.61	1.43	–	–	9.60	2.25	4.46	3.14
2011–2013	7.60	1.39	–	–	9.94	1.28	5.34	0.66
2014–2017	9.14	0.98	2.44	0.61	9.06[d]	0.82	6.73[d]	0.18
Cost to income (%)								
2005–2007	58.29	3.01	–	–	40.12	7.54	58.82	2.53
2008–2010	69.88	5.25	–	–	38.34	4.36	67.22	3.97
2011–2013	69.72	1.50	–	–	42.09	5.11	67.59	1.97
2014–2017	60.57	2.34	80.80	2.44	43.43[d]	3.18	61.86[d]	0.56

Source: Author's calculations

This table shows descriptive statistics (means and standard deviations [SDs]) of Finnish co-operative and non-co-operative banking groups. Net interest margin (%) is the ratio between net interest income and total earning assets; ROAA (%) is the return on average assets; ROAE (%) is the return on average equity; cost to income (%) is the ratio between operating expenses and intermediation margin. Our calculations are based on data extracted from SNL

[a]We consider only Nordea Bank Finland plc until 2016 as it was merged with its Swedish parent company in early 2017 and became a Finnish branch. Nordea decided to move its headquarters to Helsinki in 2018
[b]In late 2017, Danske Bank Finland plc became a branch of the Danish parent company, Danske Bank
[c]Only 2006–2007
[d]Only 2014–2016
[e]Only 2006

The net interest margin (%) represents the profitability arising from the bank's credit intermediation activity. It is expressed as the percentage of net interest income to earning assets. Less diversified banks generally enjoy higher net interest margins. Higher values of the ratio may be indicative of cost advantages in the funding or may derive from the exploitation of strong market power positions. In the periods analyzed, the ratio is constantly higher for the co-operative banking networks, which is also consistent with their stronger focus on traditional banking activities. The net interest margins of OP and Danske Bank are very similar, while Nordea records the lowest results. Over time all the banks experience a considerable drop in their margins in light of the prolonged low interest rate environment which seems to have hit the traditional source of banking profitability. The ROAA (%) of the co-operative model followed by OP is also on average higher than that of the non-co-operative banks and has been recovering since 2011. This also remains partially true when focusing on ROAE (%). In this regard, it can be seen that only Nordea was able to obtain better results during the most acute phase of the GFC and the following period, 2011–2013. In the last period of observation, OP is the most profitable with an average ROAE of 9.14% versus POP's 2.44%, Nordea's 9.06%, and Danske Bank's 6.73%. In Finland as in Germany, but unlike in France, the co-operative banking sector obtains better profitability results, approximated by the ROAE, than the commercial joint-stock banks.

The last indicator taken into account is the cost-to-income ratio (%), commonly used to analyze and compare the managerial efficiency of banks. Traditionally, CBs exhibit lower levels of efficiency which the literature attributes to the governance model of these banks being insulated from the *stimuli* of market discipline. Data on the levels and trends of the cost-to-income ratio (%) shown in Table 4.8 do not allow us to refute this theoretical view. Commercial banks generally fare better, with Nordea having the lowest ratios, at around 40% on average, POP with the highest (80.80%) during 2014–2017, and OP and Danske Bank with very similar values (about 60%) in the last period.

In order to verify whether there are significant differences between the two banking business models, the non-parametric Wilcoxon-Mann-Whitney (WMW) (1947) test[44] is used. This is suitable for small sample sizes and for testing whether observations in one population tend to be larger than observations in the other as it tests the equality of central tendency of two

---

[44] This test is also known as Wilcoxon ranksum test or Mann-Whitney U test.

distributions (Fay and Proschan 2010). The selected indicators are subjected to the test during the period 2008–2017 only. It was decided to concentrate the analysis on this ten-year period, because we want to check whether and, if so, how the manifestation of the episodes of crisis and the start of the Banking Union in 2014 have affected the performance of the two business models, and whether this makes them more similar or not. The results of the test with the relative *p*-values are reported in Table 4.9.

The table offers a double comparison with the OP Financial Group being compared with the largest bank, Nordea, and with the smaller Danske Bank. We exclude POP Bank from this analysis due to the few data available on it and the large dimensional gap with the remaining groups.

Table 4.9 Wilcoxon-Mann-Whitney test (2008–2017)

	OP Financial Group vs Nordea Bank		OP Financial Group vs Danske Bank	
	Median	*P-value*	*Median*	*P-value*
Capital ratios				
Tier 1 (%)	15.13–16.01	0.51	15.13–14.50	0.87
Equity/total assets (%)	7.55–3.92	0.00	7.55–8.29	0.01
Lending, securities holdings ratios				
Net customer loans/total assets (%)	65.34–29.72	0.00	65.34–71.59	0.01
Securities/total assets (%)	12.24–42.45	0.00	12.24–9.57	0.12
Total assets held for trading/total assets (%)	–	–	4.47–7.71	0.01
Funding and interbank ratios				
Customer deposits/total assets (%)	47.26–20.59	0.00	47.26–55.50	0.00
Interbank ratio (%)	59.33–49.32	0.29	59.33–158.94	0.00
Liquidity and credit risk ratios				
Liquid assets/total liabilities (%)	6.84–33.42	0.00	6.84–27.59	0.00
Impaired loans/gross customer loans and advances (%)	0.78–1.90	0.00	0.78–2.41	0.00
LLR/gross customer loans (%)	79.45–42.91	0.00	79.45–65.82	0.02
Profitability and efficiency ratios				
Net interest margin (%)	1.22–0.38	0.00	1.22–1.22	0.87
ROAA (%)	0.55–0.33	0.02	0.55–0.47	0.12
ROAE (%)	7.55–9.43	0.03	7.55–6.10	0.03
Cost to income (%)	66.87–41.30	0.00	66.87–65.36	0.93

Source: Author's calculations

The results of the separate tests are in some cases diverging. When compared with Nordea, the co-operative group OP turns out to be significantly more capitalized (but not in regulatory terms), more concentrated on lending to customers, and more dependent on funding via deposits from customers. Significantly lower is the exposure to credit risk of OP, as proxied by the two indicators selected, while being less liquid than the largest Nordea. In the observed decade, the profitability of the co-operative banking group is significantly higher, both in terms of net interest margin (%) and in terms of ROAA (%). Conversely, the median return on average equity offered by Nordea to its shareholders is superior to that of OP, as well as higher is the former's operational efficiency, as proxied by the cost-to-income ratio (%). Over a decade, the comparison between the two most important banking groups of the country shows persistent divergences in the operations, ability to face risks, and profitability of the two business models which have been widely documented empirically. However, when the performances of OP are confronted with those of a smaller commercial bank, but one of the three most important of Finland, the degree of differentiation diminishes. For example, the focus of OP on lending in favor of customers and on the collection of deposits is less accentuated than that of Danske, which seems to imply a more intense asset and liability diversification as size increases. On the other hand, the profitability and operational efficiency of the two business models are not found statistically different during the period of observation, as indicated by the p-values above 0.10. Regarding the ability to face risks, co-operative banking turns out to be significantly less capitalized than Danske but less exposed to credit risk and less propense to hold securities for trading purposes. Hence, even from this latter comparison, it emerges that co-operative banking shows statistically significant divergencies that are persistent over time, despite the growing hybridization of the sector and the potential pressures exerted by the prudential regulatory framework for a higher degree of convergence among business models.[45]

8   The Performance of the Finnish Co-operative Banking Network of OP Financial Group and Its Central Institution

To what degree do the performances of the central institutions of co-operative banking networks and the networks of CBs themselves differ? To answer this question, we examine some of the performance indicators ana-

---

[45] Divergences would have increased if POP Bank was to be added in the test.

lyzed in the previous paragraph, comparing the results achieved by central institutions with those of their networks of CBs, as in Ory and Lemzeri (2012). To this end, the consolidated data referring to the OP's central institution were extracted from the databases previously mentioned; the same data were collected for the networks of CBs alone from the Finnish Financial Authority's statistics. We were not able to fully replicate the same analysis for POP Bank but we report the average values for the network of CBs belonging to the amalgamation of POP Bank. We computed average annual values and standard deviations of the selected indicators for the network of CBs alone. Data on the two networks of Finnish CBs refer to individual banks, usually in unconsolidated form. The data obtained do cover all the CBs included in the networks over time as reported in the statistics on banks published by the Finnish Financial Authority (FIN-FSA). To minimize the effect of missing data on our analysis, especially before 2008, we chose to limit our analysis to the period 2008–2017 and to restrict the scrutiny to some of the indicators previously examined. These are the equity to total assets (%); the net customer loans to total assets (%); the impaired loans to gross customer loans (%); the customer deposits to total assets (%); the ROAA (%); and the cost-to-income ratio (%). For each of these we replicate the analysis reported in the previous paragraph by calculating averages of results over sub-periods 2008–2010, 2011–2013, and 2014–2017. Figures are reported in Table 4.10.

Most of the local CBs in the two networks have total assets of less than € 100 million at the end of 2017. As regards the first indicator, the ratio between equity and total assets (%), the data in Table 4.10 show that the OP's network is much better capitalized than its apex, with capital holdings and sample volatility increasing over time. In comparative terms, the networks of CBs of OP and POP have similar values over 2008–2013 while in the last sub-period examined the CBs belonging to OP show a much higher average level of capital than POP (respectively, 13.05% versus 11.41%). At the end of 2017, the gap between the capital held by the central institution of OP and its CBs increased, analogously to what we have detected in other European countries, such as France and Germany.

It is reasonable to assume that networks are more involved in lending activity, in keeping with the specialization of activities common in well-integrated, strategic networks (Table 4.10). In the Finnish case, this is particularly evident for the CBs which are part of OP Financial Group. Their commitment to credit decreased over time (75.38% in the last four years), as did that of the central institution which displays quite consistent

Table 4.10   Comparison of the OP co-operative central institution and the two networks of CBs belonging to the OP Financial Group and the POP Bank Group in terms of capital, lending, funding, and credit risk exposure

	OP central institution		OP network CBs		POP network CBs	
	Mean	SD	Mean	SD	Mean	SD
Equity/total assets (%)						
2008–2010	6.19[a]	1.39	11.77	3.73	12.07	4.02
2011–2013	6.88[b]	0.45	11.93	3.78	11.87	4.69
2014–2017	7.15	0.66	13.05	0.93	11.41	4.61
Net customer loans/total assets (%)						
2008–2010	44.79[a]	2.35	79.99	11.82	75.73	8.66
2011–2013	44.64[b]	0.52	80.80	9.79	76.77	7.12
2014–2017	38.68	2.40	75.38	9.51	74.51	6.35
Customer deposits/total assets (%)						
2008–2010	15.15[a]	1.02	78.83	7.15	82.60	3.82
2011–2013	22.02[b]	0.29	77.62	7.57	82.84	5.03
2014–2017	22.15	1.78	71.72	8.20	82.08	5.28
	Impaired loans/gross loans and advances (%)		*Non-performing assets (%)*			
2008–2010	0.69[a]	0.49	0.47	0.41	0.70	0.54
2011–2013	1.04[b]	0.02	0.55	0.51	0.68	0.49
2014–2017	1.82	1.32	2.48	1.80	1.08	0.87

Source: Author's calculations

This table reports descriptive statistics (means and standard deviations [SDs]) of Finnish co-operative banking networks and their central institutions. Equity/total assets (%) is the ratio between total equity and total assets; net customer loans/total assets (%) is the ratio between net loans and total year-end assets; customer deposits/total assets (%) is the ratio between customer deposits and total assets; impaired loans/ gross customer loans and advances (%) is the ratio between impaired loans and gross customer loans and advances. Non-performing assets as reported in the statistics provided by the Finnish Supervisory Authority (FIN-FSA). Our calculations for the OP central institution are based on data extracted from BankScope and Orbis Bank Focus. Our calculations for the OP and POP networks of CBs are based on publicly available data on the amalgamation of the OP and POP networks. Data available at the Finnish Financial Supervisory Authority (FIN-FSA)'s website

[a]Only 2008–2009
[b]Only 2012–2013

ratios which are half those relating to the network of CBs. This clearly shows the different role of CBs and their apex, with the former highly engaged in lending and the latter involved in providing more specialized functions, that is, treasury and liquidity management. On the other hand, the differences between the two networks become more limited (both having values close to 75%) but differences remain with regard to their volatility. OP's network exhibits higher although decreasing volatility, thus showing a greater degree of convergence. The average lending values of the Finnish networks aligned with those of the French Crédit Agricole's network (see Table 5.10) and were consistently higher than those of the Austrian and German CBs (see Tables 3.11 and 6.11).

Similar to our findings with regard to lending activity, we observe that over time the two networks of CBs are highly concentrated in traditional funding in the form of deposits (Table 4.10), with POP's CBs having higher values in comparative terms. In 2014–2017, the network of CBs belonging to the POP Bank Group funded their activity with an average value of deposits from customers to total assets of 82.08%, as opposed to 71.72% of co-operative members of the OP Financial Group, resulting from a decreasing trend. The central institution of the latter records a percentage of deposits of only 22.02% in the last sub-period of analysis. Findings for the two networks of Finnish CBs are in line with those found for the sample of German CBs: about 75% of customer deposits to total assets (%) (see Table 6.11). Combining this data with that on net lending to total assets, we find

Table 4.11 Comparison of the OP co-operative central institution and the two networks of CBs belonging to the OP Financial Group and the POP Bank Group in terms of profitability and operational efficiency

	OP central institution		OP network CBs		POP network CBs	
	Mean	SD	Mean	SD	Mean	SD
ROAA (%)						
2008–2010	0.14[a]	0.29	0.92	0.45	1.06	0.60
2011–2013	0.75[b]	0.12	0.56	0.30	0.68	0.39
2014–2017	0.80	0.10	0.65	0.24	0.46	0.35
Cost to income (%)						
2008–2010	81.09[a]	16.52	65.24	11.18	65.46	14.78
2011–2013	64.11[b]	5.41	73.15	10.37	72.26	12.74
2014–2017	53.59	3.79	57.61	9.18	68.34	13.04

Source: Author's calculations

This table reports descriptive statistics (means and standard deviations [SDs]) of Finnish co-operative banking networks and their central institutions. ROAA (%) is the return on average assets; ROAE (%) is the return on average equity; cost to income (%) is the ratio between operating expenses and intermediation margin. Our calculations for the OP central institution are based on data extracted from BankScope and Orbis Bank Focus. Our calculations for the OP network are based on publicly available data on the amalgamation of OP co-operative banks. Data available at the Finnish Financial Supervisory Authority (FIN-FSA)'s website

[a]Only 2008–2009
[b]Only 2012–2013

that the funding gaps of the two networks are dissimilar over the whole period, ranging from the highest value of about 105% for OP's network in 2014–2017 to around 91% for the CB members of POP Bank. Due to their higher share of customer deposits over time, individual CBs belonging to POP Bank appear to be more insulated than their competitors from the risks arising from a substantial reliance on market funding.

The comparative analysis of the levels and trends of credit risk is approximated by the ratio of impaired loans to gross loans to customers (%) for the apex of the OP Financial Group and the non-performing assets (%) of the two networks as published in the statistics on individual banks provided by the FIN-FSA (Table 4.10). Comparisons between the central institution and the network of OP should be viewed with caution as no details are publicly available on the way the non-performing asset ratio of individual CBs is calculated.

However, for the two networks at least, we observe a rising trend for credit risk exposure, which is more pronounced for OP. During 2014–2017, the latter reports an average non-performing assets ratio of 2.48% while the smaller POP network has a percentage of 1.08%. An increasing trend for the percentage of impaired loans to gross loans and advances is also detected for the apex of OP Financial Group. It is conceivable that the prolonged period of credit expansion in Finland was accompanied by a gradual reduction in the quality of the process of selecting debtors, resulting in increased levels of credit risk being assumed by the CBs.

The last two indicators examined concern the profitability and efficiency of the organizations under investigation. For these purposes, ROAA (%) and cost-to-income ratio (%) were selected and are reported in Table 4.11. The values of the first show that on average the central institution is more profitable than its network but only after 2011. During the crisis, analogously to what we found for other countries under investigation in this book, the apex is more severely affected by the effects of the GFC, partly due to its greater orientation toward market-based banking and also due to its assets and liabilities mix being more subject to market trends. Of the two networks of CBs, OP's is the most profitable but only in the last four years. The worst results of the OP network should be read in combination with the increase in credit risk to which the network is exposed (as reported in Table 4.10).

Finally, the cost-to-income figures displayed in Table 4.11 show the benefits of the reorganization and rationalization of the Finnish co-operative banking sector, especially after 2013. We report, on average, a general trend of decreasing cost to income, which is enjoyed by both the apex of OP and the two networks but to a greater extent by OP. In 2014–2017, the average value of OP's network was 57.61%, which is very similar to that of the French Crédit Agricole (as displayed in Table 5.11) and much better than the mean value recorded for the sample of German CBs (about 76% in the same period). The operational efficiency of POP Bank's network is lower, at 68.34% in the last sub-period of our analysis.

In summary, following a period of substantial transformation, the profitability and operational efficiency of the OP network of CBs exceeds that of the smaller POP Bank. The assets and liabilities allocation strategies pursued by the two networks show similar trends, but the smaller POP Bank concentrates to a greater degree on traditional banking intermediation activity (measured by the percentages of net loans to customers to total assets and that of customer deposits to total assets) resulting in it being less risky as proxied by the percentage of non-performing assets held. In themselves, therefore, the results observed in comparative terms indicate that higher levels of credit activity do not automatically determine an increasing exposure to risks associated with small-sized banks that can less easily exploit a broad diversification of their loan portfolio. However, size appears to be important in terms of being better able to exploit and benefit from economies of scale.

9   Conclusion

Like the banking sectors in many European countries, the Finnish banking system moved during the 1980s from a heavily regulated banking environment to a deregulated one, although banks, especially those co-operative in nature, still play a key role. The international financial crisis of 2007–2008 had relatively little effect on the Finnish banking system or indeed the Finnish national economy. Two co-operative networks are present in the Finnish banking system, very different from each other in terms of size and operations. The largest is represented by the OP Financial Group, while the POP Bank Group is the smallest amalgamation of CBs. In Finland, CBs enjoy high market shares. At the end of 2017, the two networks together held 37% of the domestic market share of loans, with OP consistently growing and holding the largest share. The domestic market share of deposits which they collectively hold is slightly higher: 39.30% with OP alone holding 37%.

The two co-operative banking networks in Finland are highly integrated, as required by the criteria set out in Art. 10 of the CRR. OP formally adopted an integrated strategic network model in 2011, while the POP Bank Group followed suit in 2015, their member banks being more reluctant to adopt this organizational framework. The group OP is active in three main businesses: banking, non-life insurance, and wealth management. It also constitutes a financial and insurance conglomerate under the terms of the Finnish Act on the Supervision of Financial and Insurance Conglomerates. The co-operative banking group has a strong domestic focus but also offers banking services through branches located in neighboring countries. At the end of 2017, the POP Bank Group was the ninth largest financial group in Finland in terms of its share of the loans and deposits markets, holding shares of 1.5% and 2.3%, respectively. Formed in 1997 as a network of dissentient CBs from across the whole Finnish co-operative banking sector, it underwent an intense aggregation process and became an amalgamation in 2015.

In addition to analyzing the role and organization of co-operative networks in Finland, the chapter offers two empirical investigations, respectively, aimed at verifying empirically the effects of the ongoing hybridization in co-operative banking and at assessing to what degree the performances of the central institutions of co-operative banking networks and the networks of CBs themselves differ. Regarding the first of the two areas of analysis, the data show that overall, in the period 2008–2017, the co-operative model is different from shareholder-oriented banking. From the comparison between the OP Financial Group and the two main commercial joint-stock banks in Finland, more pronounced differences emerge only when the comparison is with the largest of the two selected non-co-operative groups, Nordea. POP Bank was excluded from this analysis due to the few data available on it and the large dimensional gap with the remaining groups.

When compared with Nordea, the co-operative group OP turns out to be significantly more capitalized, more concentrated on lending to customers, and more dependent on funding via deposits from customers. Significantly lower is the exposure to credit risk of OP. In the observed decade, 2008–2017, the profitability of the major co-operative banking network is significantly higher, both in terms of net interest margin (%) and in terms of ROAA (%). Conversely, the median return on average equity offered by Nordea to its shareholders is superior to that of OP, as well as higher is the former's operational efficiency, as proxied by the cost-to-income ratio (%). However, when the performances of OP are compared with those of the smaller peer commercial bank, Danske Bank, the degree of differentiation diminishes.

With reference to the second area of investigation, reported figures show that overall the OP's network of individual CBs is much better capitalized than its apex, with capital holdings increasing over time. In comparative terms, the networks of CBs of OP and POP have similar values over 2008–2013 while during 2014–2017 the CBs belonging to OP show a much higher average level of capital than POP. At the end of 2017, the gap between the capital held by the central institution of OP and its CBs increased, analogously to what we have detected in other European countries, such as France and Germany. The assets and liabilities allocation strategies pursued by the two networks show similar trends, but the smaller POP Bank concentrates to a greater degree on traditional banking intermediation activity, resulting in it being less risky as proxied by the percentage of non-performing assets held. However, for the two networks of individual CBs at least, we observe a rising trend for credit risk exposure, which is more pronounced for OP. On average the central institution of OP is more profitable than its network but only after 2011. During the crisis, analogously to what we found for other countries under investigation in this book, the apex is more severely affected by the effects of the GFC, partly due to its greater orientation toward market-based banking and also due to its assets and liabilities mix being more subject to market trends. Of the two networks of CBs, OP's is the most profitable but only in the last four years. In terms of operational efficiency, reported figures show a general trend of decreasing cost to income, which is enjoyed by both the apex of OP and the two networks but to a greater extent by OP. This result seems to confirm the benefits deriving from the reorganization and rationalization of the Finnish co-operative banking sector, especially after 2013.

References

Drees, B., & Pazarbasioglu, C. (1995). *The Nordic Banking Crises: Pitfalls in Financial Liberalization?* IMF Working papers, No. 61.

Englund, P., & Vihriälä, V. (2009). Financial Crises in Developed Economies. The Cases of Finland and Sweden. In L. Jonung, J. Kiander, & P. Vartia (Eds.), *The Great Crises in the North. Macroeconomic Performance and Economic Policies in Finland and Sweden in the 1990s.* Edward Elgar Publishing, Inc.

European Association of Co-operative Banks (EACB). *Key Statistics*, Various Years.

European Central Bank (ECB). (2017, October). Report on Financial Structures.

Fay, M. P., & Proschan, M. A. (2010). Wilcoxon-Mann-Whitney or T-Test? On Assumptions for Hypothesis Tests and Multiple Interpretations of Decision Rules. *Statistics Surveys, 4,* 1.

Finance Finland. (several years). *Finnish Banking. Financial Overview of Finnish Banks.*

Jones, D. C., Jussila, I., & Kalmi, P. (2016). The Determinants of Membership in Cooperative Banks: Common Bond Versus Private Gain. *Annals of Public and Cooperative Economics, 87*(3), 411–432.

Kalmi, P. (2016). Co-operative Banks in Finland. In S. Karafolas (Ed.), *Credit Cooperative Institutions in European Countries* (1st 2016 ed.). Cham: Springer Verlag.

Kjellman, A., Björkroth, T., Lindholm, C., & Ranki, S. (2004). *Excellence in Banking: Lessons from Banking in Finland* (Turku ed.).

Koskenkylä, H., & Vesala, J. (1994). *Finnish Deposit Banks 1980–1993: Years of Rapid Growth and Crisis.* Bank of Finland Discussion Papers, 1994.

Kuisma, M., Henttinen, A., Karhu, S., & Pohls, M. (2000). *The Pellervo Story: A Century of Finnish Co-operation, 1899–1999.* Helsinki: Kirjayhtyma.

Kuustera, A. (1994). The Finnish Banking System in Broad Outline from the 1860s to the Mid 1980s. In M. Pohl (Ed.), *Handbook on the History of European Banks* (pp. 135–184). Elgar.

Mann, H. B., & Whitney, D. R. (1947). On a Test of Whether One of Two Random Variables Is Stochastically Larger than the Other. *Annals of Mathematical Statistics, 18*(1), 50–60.

Nyberg, P., & Vihriälä, V. (1994). *The Finnish Banking Crisis and Its Handling (an Update of Developments Through 1993).* Bank of Finland Discussion Papers, 1994.

OECD. (2003). *Regulatory Reforms in Finland. Enhancing Market Openness Through Regulatory Reforms.* Paris.

Ory, J., & And Lemzeri, Y. (2012). Efficiency and Hybridization in Cooperative Banking: The French Case. *Annals of Public and Cooperative Economics, 83*(2), 215–250.

Prinz, M. (2002, July). *German Rural Cooperatives, Friedrich Wilhelm Raiffeisen and the Organization of Trust.* 8th International Economic History Association Congress, Buenos Aires.

CHAPTER 5

Co-operative Banking in France

1   BRIEF OVERVIEW OF THE FRENCH BANKING SYSTEM

Since the 1990s, the French banking system has undergone a substantial restructuring process. This was caused by several factors in common with other European countries, such as the deregulation of the banking markets, financial and technological innovations, and the phenomenon of globalization (Marchetti and Sabetta 2010). Despite the existence of these drivers for changes, which in many European countries were a contributing factor in the erosion of the banks' central role at the national level, the banking system in France still enjoys an enviable position. Howarth (2013) describes France as "an equity-dependent but still largely bank-based financial system" in which the French government has played a pivotal role in encouraging specific forms of financial innovation. At the end of 2016, the ratio of Monetary Financial Institutions' (MFIs) total assets to national GDP stood at 3.7 (compared with 2.6 in Germany, 2.3 in Austria and Italy, and 2.4 in Spain),[1] while the percentage of assets held by MFIs as a proportion of the total assets of the financial sector equaled 63.5% (61.1% in Germany, 63.8% in Italy, and 67.2% in Spain) (ECB 2017).[2] Domestic credit institutions held a 92% share of total banking assets in 2016, which places France among the European countries where domestic intermediaries

---

[1] Excluding the data of the European System of Central Banks (ESCB).
[2] These two indicators were 3.6% and 70.2% respectively in 2008 (ECB 2017).

© The Author(s) 2019   193
F. Poli, *Co-operative Banking Networks in Europe*, Palgrave
Macmillan Studies in Banking and Financial Institutions,
https://doi.org/10.1007/978-3-030-21699-3_5

have succeeded in retaining and indeed permeating the banking system, having increased their share by 3% since 2009 (ECB 2017). Only Spain reported a similar trend with domestic banks holding 92% of total assets at the end of 2016. The remaining shares of banking assets belong principally to foreign subsidiaries and branches from other European countries (6.3% in 2016), while non-European intermediaries play a marginal role (ECB 2017). As reported by the ECB (2017), among the leading economies of the European Union, France was the only one to increase its total banking assets between 2015 and 2016 by 4% (1.9% in Germany) and to maintain a growing trend following the financial crisis in 2008.[3] In fact, together with Germany, France remains the largest banking sector in the Eurozone, with total asset values slightly above € 7 trillion in both cases. The Spanish and Italian banking systems are much smaller (€ 3.6 trillion and € 2.7 trillion respectively in 2016) (ECB 2017).

The domestic banking sector is essential for the financing of non-financial companies (NFCs) which rely heavily on domestic banks. Between 2014 and 2016, French banks expanded their lending to non-financial companies by 10.9%, while keeping their share of total domestic financing to the productive sector largely unchanged (69.4% in 2016). However, competition from other intermediaries, such as insurance companies, pension funds, and finance companies, is much fiercer in France than in other leading European countries where banks still record higher shares: 88.7% in Austria, 79.4% in Italy, 75.9% in Germany, 70.3% in the Netherlands, and 73.9% in Finland.[4]

The modernization of the French banking system started in the mid-1980s with the enactment of a new Banking Law in 1984 and the start of an extensive divesture program of state-owned banks which culminated in 2002 with the divestiture of Credit Lyonnais' shares (Marchetti and Sabetta 2010). The aim of the new banking regulation was to promote competition within the financial system which had been largely influenced by government interventions and several restrictions to banking activity since the Second World War. Throughout the 1990s and the following decade, the

---

[3] Despite the increasing capabilities of the French banking system, as in other continental countries, the proportion of banking assets to the total assets of the financial sector has continually decreased in the aftermath of the international financial crisis, falling from 70% in 2008 to 63.5% in 2016, thus evidencing the ongoing disintermediation process which characterizes many developed bank-oriented financial systems.

[4] Our calculations for 2016 on the ECB's data contained in the Report on Financial Structures (ECB 2017).

banking system continued to evolve, becoming more concentrated as a result of aggregations and substantial restructurings (Ory and Lemzeri 2012). Co-operative banks (CBs) have been leading protagonists in these vicissitudes, acquiring the ability to form large co-operative banking groups which now dominate the national banking system. Currently, three co-operative banking networks co-exist: Crédit Agricole, Banque Populaire-Caisses d'Epargne (BPCE), and Crédit Mutuel. These compete with conventional joint-stock companies like BNP Paribas and Société Générale.

The French banking system is one of the most concentrated in the European Union. At the end of 2016, the five biggest credit institutions held a 46% share of total assets (down from 51% in 2008), as compared with 31% in Germany and 43% in Italy (ECB 2017). In 2017, the banking sector comprised 18 domestic banking groups and stand-alone banks and five foreign-controlled (both EU and non-EU) subsidiaries and branches (Statistical Data Warehouse ECB). Despite the ongoing rationalization of branch networks and significant investments in the digitalization of banking, the presence of banks throughout the country is one of the highest in Europe. Looking at the population density per bank branch, France recorded 1794 inhabitants per bank at the end of 2016, as opposed to 2575 in Germany, 2067 in Italy, and 10,173 in the Netherlands (ECB 2017).

All French banks adopt a universal banking model, operating across a broad range of retail, corporate, and investment banking activity. The entry of French banks into investment banking was a consequence of the liberalization of banking activities and the increase in competition faced by banks from financing offered by non-financial firms (Morin 2000; Hardie and Howarth 2009). The reduction in profits triggered by fiercer market rivalry similarly prompted French banks to expand their activities abroad, specifically in the retail banking sector. This wave of internationalization has involved the co-operative groups, as well as joint-stock commercial banks like BNP Paribas and Société Générale. For instance, in 2006, Crédit Agricole took over major retail banks in Italy and Greece, considering them domestic markets. The strong retail component of the French banks' internationalization contrasts markedly with that of the German banks, whose international activities was almost entirely in corporate lending and investment banking (Hardie and Howarth 2009). Following the initial outbreak of the international financial crisis in 2007, the French government, like other European governments, intervened in 2008 and 2009 to recapitalize and finance all the largest national banks, effectively forcing them to accept capital and to commit to increasing domestic lending. Banks were also required to implement other measures, such as curbs on dividend payments and bans on executive bonuses for 2008 (Hardie and Howarth 2009; Barsan 2010; Woll 2014).[5] The French state regained power over its national banks, but this was purely a necessary step to avoid a credit crunch in domestic lending, and to further encourage bank consolidation. Among the 2009 state aids, one was in fact intended to reinforce the equity of the new entity resulting from the merger of the central bodies of the Caisses d'Epargne and Banque Populaire, giving rise to a new national champion, the BPCE network.[6]

---

[5] Following discussions with the European Commission, the French authorities officially notified the Commission of the scheme to inject capital into certain banks on 3 December 2008. The scheme was intended for "fundamentally sound" banks which were under pressure to increase their capital owing to the financial crisis. The French authorities intervened via the creation of the *Société de prise de participation de l'État* (SPPE), a state-owned investment company, whose mission was to invest in securities issued by the beneficiary banks. The securities took the form of hybrid capital instruments (subordinated debt securities classified as non-core Tier 1 capital) to be remunerated at a fixed rate for the first five years and at a variable rate thereafter. Under the scheme, the intervention of the French authorities was capped at € 21 billion. The French authorities announced that their intervention was initially limited to € 10.5 billion. In 2009, the government agreed to expand recapitalization to an additional € 10.25 billion. Two commercial joint-stock banks, BNP Paribas and Société Générale, and four co-operative banks, Crédit Agricole, Banque Populaire, Caisses d'Epargne, and Crédit Mutuel, received capital injections in 2008. In 2009 Crédit Agricole and Crédit Mutuel decided not to participate in the second phase of SPPE intervention, although other banks did (Woll 2014). The scheme included obligations for the beneficiary banks to finance the real economy. These obligations were to be monitored both locally and nationally (European Commission IP/08/1900, IP/09/158 and IP/09/461). The SPPE recapitalization support was available until the end of August 2009 (Woll 2014).

One further measure taken by the French authorities on 16 October 2008 was the legal authorization to set up a refinancing scheme to stabilize the financial markets. The French authorities decided to make use of a structure set up for this purpose, the *société de refinancement des activités des établissements de crédit* (SRAEC—refinancing company for the activities of credit institutions), which was the only institution to enjoy a state guarantee. SRAEC had the right to issue securities guaranteed by the state with a view to making loans to credit institutions against collateral up to an amount not exceeding € 265 billion. The credit institutions had to pay a premium over and above the normal market price and to make commitments regarding their conduct (IP/08/1609 and IP/09/750). SRAEC's activities were limited to five years. The SRAEC was jointly owned by the six big banks and the government, which held 66% and 34% respectively. Access to the state-backed mechanism was requested by other financial institutions which signed an agreement with the SRAEC. It ended its issuing activity in late 2009 and remained in place merely to manage the reimbursement of existing securities that had not reached their maturity. (Woll 2014).

[6] See European Commission IP/09/722. As reported by Hardie and Howarth (2009), the role of the government was fundamental in driving the merger between Caisse d'Epargne and Banque Populaire, as without its ultimatum and aid, the banks would likely have failed to agree on the merger.

2   THE ROLE OF CBs WITHIN THE BANKING SECTOR

With a combined total of 26.6 million members at the end of 2017 (26 million in 2016), France rates as the most co-operative bank-oriented system in Europe. It is followed by Germany with 18.5 million,[7] Austria with 2.4 million, and the Netherlands with 1.9 million (EACB 2017). Of the three co-operative networks, Crédit Agricole has the largest membership: 9.7 million, with constant growth since 2004 (Table 5.1). BPCE has a membership of 9.1 million, of which 4.3 million pertain to the Banque Populaire network and 4.8 million to Caisses d'Epargne (2017),[8] while Crédit Mutuel has a total membership of 7.8 million, having experienced the slowest growth rate of the three networks since 2012. The membership dynamics displayed in Table 5.1 indicate that from 2012 onward French CBs have represented an attractive investment vehicle for members. Since 2012, there has been an overall increase of over 18% across all the networks: a level higher than that seen in other countries. For instance, the corresponding growth rate in Germany is 6.9%.

Over the period 2004–2017, the appeal of CBs as providers of banking and financial services has grown significantly, more than doubling in the case of Crédit Agricole and Crédit Mutuel (Table 5.1). Since the onset of the financial crisis, there has been a particularly evident acceleration in the capability of these banks to attract new customers who were looking for alternative banking partners, who display an intrinsic inclination to exclusively support their local communities. However, unlike the consistent increase in membership highlighted above, the progress of the customer base between 2012 and 2017 has been negative overall, (declining by around 2%). This is entirely attributable to the decrease experienced by the unified BPCE over the period 2014–2017.

The evolution of the governance ratios reported in Table 5.1 indicates that members have substantially lost their relevance as the primary targeted customers for French CBs' banking services, recently representing percentages ranging from about 18% in the case of Crédit Agricole[9] to

---

[7] For the sake of full disclosure, we report the number of members of UK building societies, which totaled 23 million members at the end of 2017 (EACB 2017), although this is beyond our field of analysis.

[8] See BPCE's Annual Report for the year-end 2017.

[9] The total number of domestic and international customers served by Crédit Agricole is 52 million. The governance ratio increases to 46.19%, if we compute it as the ratio of co-operative members to total individual customers of the 39 regional co-operative banks holding the apex of Crédit Agricole.

Table 5.1 Members, customers, and governance ratios of French CBs

	Crédit Agricole			Crédit Mutuel			BPCE[a]		
	Members	Customers	Governance ratio	Members	Customers	Governance ratio	Members	Customers	Governance ratio
2004	5,700,000	21,000,000	27.14%	6,500,000	13,800,000	47.10%	2,800,000	6,600,000	42.42%
2006	5,700,000	31,000,000	18.39%	6,900,000	14,500,000	47.59%	3,200,000	7,000,000	45.71%
2008	6,200,000	58,000,000	10.69%	7,200,000	18,700,000	38.50%	3,300,000	7,800,000	42.31%
2010	6,500,000	54,000,000	12.04%	7,200,000	29,200,000	24.66%	n.a.	n.a.	n.a.
2012	7,000,000	51,000,000	13.73%	7,400,000	30,100,000	24.58%	8,100,000	36,000,000	22.50%
2014	8,171,555	50,000,000	16.34%	7,600,000	30,100,000	25.25%	8,900,000	36,000,000	24.72%
2016	9,300,000	52,000,000	17.88%	7,700,000	30,700,000	25.08%	9,000,000	31,200,000	28.85%
2017	9,700,000	52,000,000	18.65%	7,800,000	31,600,000	24.68%	9,100,000	31,200,000	29.40%

Source: Author's calculations on data reported EACB and BPCE Group for 2017

[a]Data after 2009 refer to the new network created by the merger between Banque Populaire and Caisses d'Epargne. Before 2009, data refers solely to Banque Populaire

29% for BPCE. This phenomenon turns out to be much more pronounced in France than for instance in Austria and Germany (where figures for the Raiffeisen banks stood at around 58% and 60% respectively in 2017), indicating a much greater dilution of the unique missions of these banks among a sizeable and growing number of stakeholders, a phenomenon that may undermine their original values in the long run.

In spite of this concern, co-operative banking in France plays a key role which has been consolidated over time. Of all the European countries where this business model took root in the nineteenth century and went on to grow, France is the one where CBs enjoy the highest market shares. At the end of 2017, according to our calculations on data collected by EACB, the three networks jointly held 62.6% of the domestic market share of deposits (Table 5.2). The collective share of the domestic loan market was slightly lower at 59.8% in 2017. In terms of the mortgage sector, the market shares are even higher: in 2017 for instance, the joint share of mortgage loans was 76.4% (EACB 2017).

Among the three networks, Crédit Agricole is the leader although its market power has been weakened over time by competition, despite maintaining its position in the aftermath of the financial crisis (Table 5.2). The BPCE network that resulted from the state-supported merger between Banque Populaire and Caisses d'Epargne in 2009 is the second largest co-operative network. The difference in the market shares of the two networks is negligible in terms of the proportion of loans held, with each enjoying around 21% of the domestic market. For instance, in 2017,

Table 5.2 Domestic market shares of French co-operative networks

	Loans (%)			Deposits (%)		
	Crédit Agricole	Crédit Mutuel	BPCE[a]	Crédit Agricole	Crédit Mutuel	BPCE[a]
2004	30.00	15.50	8.20	28.00	15.80	6.40
2006	20.90	16.80	8.20	25.00	12.40	6.20
2008	22.00	16.90	7.60	24.00	12.00	6.70
2010	n.a.	17.00	n.a.	n.a.	14.20	n.a.
2012	20.60	15.00	n.a.	23.40	17.10	n.a.
2014	21.00	17.00	21.00	24.80	15.00	22.00
2016	21.40	17.10	20.70	24.40	15.50	21.50
2017	21.70	17.00	21.10	24.40	15.50	22.70

Source: EACB

[a]Data refers solely to Banque Populaire in 2004, 2006 and 2008

BPCE was the leading lender for the small-medium enterprise (SME) sector and local public authorities.[10]

Crédit Agricole's dominance in the deposits market is more pronounced (24.4% versus BPCE's 22.7%). Crédit Mutuel, the third co-operative network, holds market shares not dissimilar to those held by the first two, especially on the lending side, thus indicating quite balanced domestic competition among the co-operative networks in spite of their different sizes.[11]

Collectively, the three networks managed assets totaling € 3.835 billion at the end of 2017 (€ 3.752 in 2016), of which about 46% was attributable to Crédit Agricole, the most internationally diversified, almost 33% to BPCE, and the remaining 21% to Crédit Mutuel. There are additional differences in the degree of credit intermediation performed by the three networks (Table 5.3). Using the ratio of bank loans to total assets, the measurement of lending activity shows that loans account for almost 50.38% of the total assets at the end of 2017 for the three co-operative

Table 5.3   Credit intermediation orientation of French co-operative networks

| | Loans to customers to assets (%) (A) | | | Deposits from customers to assets (%) (B) | | | Customer loans to deposits (%) (A/B) | | |
	Crédit Agricole	Crédit Mutuel	BPCE[a]	Crédit Agricole	Crédit Mutuel	BPCE[a]	Crédit Agricole	Crédit Mutuel	BPCE[a]
2004	44.90	42.50	48.30	41.40	37.23	37.85	108.50	114.12	127.60
2006	39.40	45.60	53.40	31.72	32.28	45.06	124.30	141.21	118.50
2008	44.30	50.80	44.78	41.05	33.97	32.42	108.00	149.56	138.12
2010	51.00	54.60	54.68	46.90	40.35	37.61	108.70	135.39	145.41
2012	43.60	53.20	51.00	40.44	43.08	37.52	107.90	123.48	135.94
2014	40.30	51.60	50.81	35.32	43.21	38.74	114.00	119.46	131.16
2016	44.90	52.30	54.84	40.24	45.15	43.05	111.60	115.85	127.38
2017	46.21	53.49	54.21	41.54	46.01	45.23	111.24	116.26	119.84

Source: Author's calculations on data reported by EACB
[a]Data refer solely to Banque Populaire in 2004 and 2006

[10] Data reported by BPCE's Financial Report for the year-end 2017.

[11] Crédit Agricole is a leader in the agricultural, professional, and business markets, holding shares of 83%, 34%, and 36% respectively. Data refer to different sources reported in Crédit Agricole's Financial Report for the year-end 2016.

networks. The corresponding value for the German co-operative financial network was 61.3% in 2017, decisively higher than the average French one. It is worth noting that the French banks have displayed the highest levels of determination to support the financing needs of the economy after the financial crisis as the pre-crisis ratios are lower than those observed between 2008 and 2010.

All three groups exhibit a common tendency to increase the loan to asset ratio until 2010, followed by a decrease in 2012 and 2014, and a subsequent recovery. Among the group, Crédit Mutuel, which is the most domestically based, holds on average the highest commitment in lending since 2008. For all three networks, the funding gap, proxied by the ratio of loans to customer deposits (%), is significantly high and on average well above 100% but decreasing since 2010, which is in contrast to the corresponding levels in, for example, Germany (95% at the end of 2017). The reduction in the funding gap ratio is mainly driven by the larger increase in the share of deposits compared to that of loans to total assets.

Funding from depositors remains an important source, on average above 40% in 2017. Again, Crédit Mutuel is the network with the highest reliance on deposits from customers, followed by BPCE. These two exhibit an increasing trend over time, while Crédit Agricole's reliance on depositors is lower and more variable, mainly as a result of its greater ability to diversify its funding. All three co-operative banking networks were able to increase the share of deposits to total assets during the most acute phase of the global financial crisis (GFC) (from 2008 to 2010), probably because they were perceived as safe havens for savers.

There is significant variation in the networks' branch presence across the country. Crédit Agricole boasts the largest number of branches with more than 11,000 outlets in 8 countries, of which more than 7000 are in the domestic market (Crédit Agricole 2017); BPCE has 7500 branches (3300 held by Banque Populaire and 4200 by Caisse d'Epargne) (2017), almost entirely in the domestic market; and Crédit Mutuel has 5247 (2017). Following a common trend in European countries, the co-operative branch networks have gone through a process of rationalization, particularly since 2008. The combination of a persistent low interest rate environment, the increasing digitalization of banking services and growing competition from new non-banking entrants has prompted the introduction of cost-oriented efficiency measures, which include, among other things, the closure of hundreds of bank branches, an element which continues to appear in the strategic plans of all three networks. Crédit Agricole and Crédit Mutuel have been the most active in this regard: in 2008, the former had 11,850 branches while the latter had 5619. BPCE's branch network is also decreasing, having stood at around 8000 outlets in 2009, but its level of branch density remains high.[12] It is no coincidence that the French CBs are seen as proximity banks, given that their presence is still widespread across the country.

3   Co-operative Banking: Historical Development in France

The foundation and construction of the legislative architecture of co-operative banking in France was initiated at the end of the nineteenth century. The emergence of co-operative banking, in the form of credit institutions that served the financing and savings needs of sections of the population who had formerly been financially excluded, was motivated by factors which are shared in common with other neighboring European countries. Similarly, the rapid spread of credit institutions enabled rural development and the development of small- and medium-sized manufacturing and trading activities across the country. In the following pages we will briefly examine the history of the three co-operative banking networks.

The modern Crédit Agricole is a financial conglomerate encompassing local retail CBs that co-exist with companies specializing in insurance, asset management, real estate, leasing and factoring, corporate and investment banking, and issuer and investor services. The roots of this (in fact hybrid) co-operative group can be traced back to the end of the nineteenth-century, following the enactment of the Act of 5 November 1894 which permitted the members of farm co-operatives to create a local credit co-operative. The members assumed responsibility for the fledgling banks in line with the co-operative principles in force at the time. These local banks formed the foundation of the institutional "pyramid" created by Crédit Agricole. As in other European countries, it was the difficulties encountered by farmers in meeting their productive investment needs that stimulated the creation of local co-operatives. These were authorized as professional associations of farmers by the Act of 1884 and were soon followed in 1885 by the creation of the Société de Crédit Agricole de

---

[12] BPCE claims that the distance in urban areas from a sales outlet is less than 10 minutes, while in rural areas it is less than 20 minutes. See BPCE's Financial Report for the year-end 2017.

l'arrondissement de Poligny in the Jura region, a local initiative promoted by the Catholic Louis Milcent (1846–1918).

The financial difficulties faced by these fragile credit unions forced the state to intervene via the Banque de France to fund Crédit Agricole with an injection of FRF 40 million and an annual payment of FRF 2 million. The Act of 31 March 1899 set up the mechanisms to distribute the funding. An Agriculture Ministry committee was formed and Crédit Agricole's regional banks were created, with local credit co-operatives being affiliated to them. These banks formed the second level of Crédit Agricole's institutional pyramid. A proliferation of regional and local agricultural co-operative credit associations, which benefited from state financial aid, followed, but shortly before 1920, the need for a central bank which would actively regulate smaller banks and provide central clearing services for regional banks became clear. The Act of 5 August 1920 created the Office National du Crédit Agricole, under the Ministry of Agriculture, which was subsequently renamed Caisse Nationale de Crédit Agricole (CNCA) in 1926.

Growth continued at a local level over the following years, during which Crédit Agricole also received authorization to diversify lending to include customers other than farmers, and in 1935 to set up a joint deposit guarantee fund. In 1945, the Fédération Nationale du Crédit Agricole (FNCA) was set up as an association representing the regional banks vis-à-vis the public authorities and CNCA. The latter also acquired a key role in providing training and advisory services to Crédit Agricole's network. Thanks to the issue of long-term notes, the network managed to channel more stable savings into the reconstruction of the country following the Second World War, becoming financially independent of the state in 1966 when the savings they collected ceased to be transferred to the Treasury. Spurred by the privatization and liberalization of the French banking system, CNCA was privatized in 1988. The central institution was transformed into a public limited company that was acquired by regional banks and listed on the stock exchange in 2001 under the new name Crédit Agricole SA.[13] The intervening years have been characterized by constant growth basically pursued through domestic and foreign acquisitions which have enabled the network to reach a position of leadership in some areas of financial intermediation.

[13] For more details on the history of Crédit Agricole, see Crédit Agricole's website.

Popular banks had two major founding fathers in France: the Capuchin friar Ludovic de Besse (1831–1910) and Charles Rayneri (1858–1940), both of whom were influenced by the German Schulze-Delitzsch's ideas and their spread in neighboring Italy through the work of Luigi Luzzatti (1841–1927) and Francesco Viganò (1807–1891). De Besse created the first popular bank, the Bank of Christian Workers, in 1878 in Angers, which was followed by several other banks in subsequent years. Rayneri also promoted the creation of many popular banks, among them the Banque Populaire de Menton in 1883 which became an organizational model due to the regional federal group structured around it (Albert 1997). Like their German cousins, French popular banks had urban foundations and were created by and for entrepreneurs with a view to pooling funds to enable them to finance their projects. Their co-operative status was established with the Law of 13 March 1917. In keeping with the state's dominant role in the national economy, the law also stated that the French Treasury had to make interest-free loans to popular banks in order to ease their start-up and overcome the operating difficulties encountered by some due to their limited capitalization and inefficiencies (De Angeli 2008). According to the provisions of the law, popular banks were only allowed to grant loans to entrepreneurs, traders, and artisans but could collect deposits without constraint from any type of customer. The founding law was followed by a regulation in 1918 which helped to eliminate some of the uncertainties left by the 1917 Law and to provide legal clarity around the character of popular banks. Specifically, this law stated that the capital of popular banks should be made up of registered shares, which could not be traded without the consent of the administrative board of the issuing bank; at the same time, standard models of by-laws were introduced. These were assigned with the following aims: to specify whether the bank's capital was open or closed-end; to define the extent to which the principle of "one man, one vote" could be derogated, although it was firmly supported; to state the extent and length of time of members' responsibilities for the bank's obligations; and to designate the geographical boundaries of the bank's activities in observance of the principles of territoriality and non-intra-sector competition which French co-operatives followed assiduously and preserved over time at the regional level (De Angeli 2008). All of these provisions still regulate popular banks under current French Banking Law (Code Monétaire et Financier).

The process of centralizing banking activities within the network of popular banks began in 1921 with the founding of the Caisse Centrale des

Banques Populaires, a popular bank which led the way among the French network of popular banks in competing and expanding its business activities from the 1960s and 1970s onward (De Angeli 2008). The coordination and supervision of the banks at the national level was left to the Chambre Syndicale des Banques Populaires, an organization created by law in 1929, which together with the Caisse Centrale formed the apex of the network. In 1999 the central bank was renamed as Banque Féderale des Banques Populaires, emphasizing its federative aims in favor of its shareholders, the affiliated popular banks. Two years later, the new central institution supplanted the activities performed by the now dissolved Chambre Syndicale and was turned into a public limited company. A new form of hybridization had arrived in the co-operative banking sector. The acquisition of Natexis in 1998 provided the Banque Populaire network with a publicly listed vehicle active in corporate and investment banking. Pursuing its development, several regional or specialized banks were affiliated to it in the early 2000s. At the time of the merger with Caisse d'Epargne in 2009, the banking network of Banque Populaire was made up of several regional popular banks, two national specialized popular banks, Casden and Crédit Coopératif, along with Crédit Maritime Mutuel.

The first Caisse d'Epargne was founded in Paris in 1818 by the Protestant businessman Jules Paul Benjamin Delessert (1773–1847) with the aim of promoting, collecting, and managing popular savings. French savings banks were small not-for-profit financial institutions with strong local roots, created in accordance with the original German and British ideas of self-help, encouragement, the mobilization of savings and the promotion of social order. The latter came about as the result of granting access to credit to the poorest in society, thus enabling their inclusion in the emerging capitalist economy (Butzbach 2015). In 1835, the recognition of the nature of Caisses d'Epargne as "private institutions of public utility" offered control of their establishment to the government. At the insistence of the promoters of the Caisses d'Epargne, the management of the savings collected was statutorily transferred to the state-owned specialized financial entity, Caisse des Dépôts et Consignations (CDC), in accordance with the provisions set out in the Law of 31 March 1837. The centralization of deposits was intended to safeguard the deposits collected by Caisses d'Epargne but in fact defined the future of the Caisses d'Epargne for many years. Until after the Second World War, the Caisses d'Epargne basically held the role of collectors of French savings. Funds were initially exclusively channeled into backing the financial needs of the

French state; only in 1895 were Caisses d'Epargne allowed, at their own risk, to make their first local investments in the construction of social housing and public services (such as baths) and in awarding grants to local associations. It was only in 1951, with the enactment of the Minjoz Law, that they became authorized to grant loans to local authorities.

As reported by Butzbach (2015), French savings banks were somehow considered by the state agencies as merely moneyboxes, and were much less autonomous than their counterparts in other European countries (namely, Germany and Italy). They were part of the so-called Treasury circuit, the financing circuit controlled by the French state that helped to transform savings into long-term post-war reconstruction investment (Butzbach 2015). During the 1960s and 1970s, the Caisses d'Epargne were allowed to offer new savings instruments, ranging from house-saving plans, to savings bonds and mutual funds, and to grant personal loans for housing and living costs. The era of bank de-specialization had started and Caisses d'Epargne had to reposition itself to be able to operate in a much more competitive arena. Despite Caisses d'Epargne's increased autonomy and its potential for diversification, they remained under a high level of state control, a position that was facilitated by their peculiar legal status, of being neither publicly nor privately owned (Butzbach 2015). The first reform of their statutory nature was made by the Law of 1 July 1983 that granted the Caisses d'Epargne the status of non-profit credit institutions and thus empowered them to carry out all banking operations. The subsequent Banking Law of 1984 included Caisses d'Epargne along with commercial banks within the broad category of credit institutions, thus further clarifying their nature. However, neither the legislation approved in 1983, nor the Banking Law of the following year clarified their status as either public or private.

During the 1990s a massive wave of consolidation within the sector led to a dramatic reduction in the number of local Caisses d'Epargne, reconfiguring them into a regional model. It was only in 1999, with the Law of 25 June 1999, that Caisses d'Epargne adopted the status of a CB with a universal vocation; despite some political disagreements, this transformation into the new statutory identity was seen as the best fit with the original vocation of savings banks. Ownership under this model is held by members of Local Savings Companies (LSC) which are not authorized to carry out banking activity. However, in accordance with the 1999 Law, the Caisses d'Épargne's capital was opened to customers through share subscription from January 2000 onward. In parallel with the definition of

Caisse d'Epargne's legal status, a new structure was created in 1999, the National Federation of Caisses d'Epargne (FNCE), responsible for representing the interests of the members and Caisses d'Epargne and to define the direction of their co-operative mission. The mutualization of the French Caisses d'Epargne in the 1990s appears somewhat contradictory to the trend toward de-mutualization taking place in other countries, such as Great Britain or Italy. However, as stated by Butzbach (2015), the French case "hides a 'corporatization' of French savings banks consistent with what has happened in other contexts—i.e. a shift from a traditional organizational identity built around the existence of hundreds of small semi-public specialized financial institutions to a new identity embodied by a fully-fledged banking group". Along with the transformation of Caisses d'Epargne into a mutual, their social commitment also changed: while the 1999 Law stated that part of the operating surplus had to be used for the "financing of local and social economy projects" (Projets d'Economie Locale et Sociale, PELS), in 2009, the legislator lifted the legal obligation to finance PELS while reaffirming the social commitment of the Caisses.

The organization of the Caisses d'Epargne's network can be traced back to the Law enacted in 1983 which strengthened the central institution, the Centre National des Caisses d'Epargne et de Prévoyance (CENCEP). This was renamed the Caisse Nationale des Caisses d'Epargne (CNCE) in 1999, which became a public limited company, wholly owned by Caisses d'Epargne and not listed. The relaxation of the ties binding it to the state-owned CDC took place gradually. Only with the Law of 11 July 1991 was it affirmed that funding collected by Caisses d'Epargne could be used by them to finance the local economy.

CNCE undertook three main missions and activities within the Caisses d'Epargne network. As a central body, it represented its affiliated credit institutions to the supervisory authorities and within this framework ensured the application of the laws and regulations specific to these institutions. It was responsible for maintaining the cohesion of the network and ensuring the proper functioning of the affiliated institutions. The CNCE was responsible for taking any measures necessary to maintain the liquidity and solvency of all the affiliated institutions. It also defined the products and services distributed to customers and coordinated commercial policy. As a holding company, CNCE owned and managed its investments through specialized subsidiaries that served the different needs of co-operative banks. With its new mutual status, the Caisses d'Epargne network started a campaign of acquisition, extending its activities with a multi-brand approach. In 1999 the network performed the takeover of Crédit Foncier to further develop its real estate activities; in 2003, with the acquisition of Banque Palatine (formerly Banque San Paolo), the network established closer ties with corporate customers; while in 2004, by purchasing Ixis, the network branched out into investment banking. In 2006, Groupe Banque Populaire and Groupe Caisse d'Epargne took the first step toward a business combination, with the creation of their jointly owned listed subsidiary, Natixis. The CNCE was responsible for centralizing the Caisses d'Epargne's surplus resources and offered banking services to the network's entities. Before the merger with the Banque Populaire network, Caisses d'Epargne's network was comprised of the regional Caisses, the LSCs, the National Federation, and the central institution with its specialized subsidiaries.

The foundation of Crédit Mutuel was strongly inspired by the Raiffeisen model of unlimited responsibility. The first credit co-operative (Caisse) was established in 1882 in Wantzenau near Strasbourg. At the end of the nineteenth century, usury was rife in the region of Alsace-Lorraine. Placed under German control in 1871 (through the Treaty of Frankfurt), Alsace-Lorraine, whose ties with the German economy were very weak, could barely trade as a result of this practice. Faced with the problem of how to finance their production, not even in terms of productive investment but rather through emergency credits, peasants' initial intentions were to compensate for the random nature of the crop harvests and the difficulties of keeping and obtaining a yield from their herds. In these circumstances, the growth of CBs was rapid due to their focus on local communities and their religious beliefs: in 1892 there are already 127 CBs, and by 1914 there were 471. Alsace-Lorraine was a Catholic region where the development of the Raiffeisen banks was most successful, thanks to the investment of parish priests and rural vicars (Moulévrier 2002; Moulévrier and Suaud 2014).

The organization of the co-operative banking network was the result of the work of Louis Durand, a lawyer in Lyon, who brought together the independent local Caisses to form the Union of the French Rural Caisses and Workers in 1893. As a Catholic rigorist, he was particularly interested in Raiffeisen credit co-operatives; he took an active part in their establishment and believed there should be no state interference in the management of the new entities. In fact, when in 1894, the French state introduced measures in favor of the agricultural sector and offered tax and financial benefits to Caisses that agreed to distribute state aid to the rural economy, the Caisses, influenced by the ideas of Durand, refused to participate, anxious to preserve their independence and to keep their purely mutual character. These Caisses gave rise to Crédit Mutuel whose local banks were established as variable-capital companies and in 1901, were assimilated to non-profit associations. In accordance with the Law of 10 September 1947, they were governed by the statute of co-operation.

The Ordinance of 16 October 1958 specified the organization of Crédit Mutuel. The statutes of the Caisses were defined, along with the role of the Confederation, granting it powers of inspection, control, and representation. It also placed Crédit Mutuel under the supervision of the Ministry of Economy and Finance and more specifically under that of a government commissioner. In accordance with the Law of 1947, co-operatives are subject to public administration control, which verifies their functioning in compliance with co-operative legislation. The commissioner, appointed by the Minister, bears the title of government commissioner to the National Confederation of Crédit Mutuel. The commissioner must be present at all general meetings of the group and at the meetings of its Central Committee. The Banking Law of 1984 specified the mission of the government commissioners who represent the state in light of the public interest mission associated with co-operatives. In accordance with a decision made by the Council of State on 2 May 1975, the National Confederation exercises a regulatory power to carry out a public service mission, which translates into a commitment to take all measures necessary to ensure the proper functioning, organization, and development of Crédit Mutuel (Moulévrier and Suaud 2014). During the 1970s, analogously to Banque Populaire and Crédit Agricole, the group diversified into bancassurance, and at the end of the 1990s, Crédit Mutuel took over Crédit Industriel et Commercial (CIC) thereby placing the group among the ranks of the major players in the French banking landscape. In 2010, the group strengthened its co-operation with Banco Popular. This strategic alliance ended in 2017 due to the resolution of the latter. In 2008, the group acquired the German subsidiary of Citibank, lately renamed Targobank, while the acquisition of Cofidis, a specialist in consumer financing in Europe took place in 2009. Further acquisitions were made in Portugal (Banco Banif, a specialist in car financing) and in Spain, with the acquisition of some insurance companies, allowing the group to consolidate its foothold in the neighboring country.

4   French Co-operative Banking Networks: Main Characteristics

The three current co-operative networks, classified by the French Banking Laws of 1941 and 1945 as special intermediaries (De Angeli 2008),[14] still receive special attention under present-day law with dedicated articles specifically regulating their creation, their membership, and the organization and association of local CBs into networks with a central body. The departure of these intermediaries from their commonly imagined position of local and unsophisticated intermediaries, who benefit from fiscal privileges and are delimited by firm barriers that isolate them from intra- and intersectoral competition, started at the end of the 1960s with the termination of the so-called *cloisonnement* (Giannola 1990) or compartmentalization, which had defined the highly specialized and segmented banking system until that time. The reform aimed to disengage the French state from financing channels, expanding banks' capacity for intervention. The resulting initial de-specialization of the banking sector allowed CBs to broaden their scope of activities and expand their clientele (Richez-Battesti and Leseul 2016).

The reforms of the Banking Law in 1984 and again in 1996 strengthened the tentative de-specialization and de-compartmentalization process which had begun in the 1960s with the aim of stimulating the creation of a more competitive arena for financial intermediaries and the parallel construction of a more market-oriented financial system. In view of the emerging European financial integration and harmonization, CBs gained the status of "credit institution", which had formerly only applied to the so-called registered banks (i.e. commercial banks, investment banks, and merchant banks) (Giannola 1990). The CBs' reaction to the new competitive threats and the diversification opportunities contained in the new universal banking framework was to undertake a substantial and innovative restructure. The existing co-operative networks that had historically specialized in retail banking were reorganized into larger entities that were recognized as co-operative groups, offering customers a broad diversified range of products and wide-ranging activity in the financial markets. It was not only CBs (with their central institution and technical subsidiaries) who

---

[14] The Law of 1941 concerned the regulation and organization of banking activity; that of 1945 stated the nationalization of the Bank of France and that of the large private banks, and further regulated the organization of credit intermediation.

were part of the new entities, but also a large range of joint-stock subsidiaries with a national and international focus, specializing in asset management, corporate and investment banking (CIB), insurance, wholesale banking, real estate, and so on. The CBs' access to large accumulated reserves (due to constraints in the distribution of profits), the positive effect of the "solidarity principle" on the funding and capital of the group's entities, and their ability to acquire several subsidiaries at a time when conventional banks were experiencing financial problems have all been identified as factors which facilitated the creation of these groups (Ory and Lemzeri 2012). Since the 1990s, in parallel with their external growth, CBs have also been involved in many merger transactions that have contributed to rationalizing the networks. Of these, the most important has been that of Banque Populaire and Caisse d'Epargne in 2009.

In realizing the hybridization of French co-operative groups, a growing role has been assigned to non-retail activities while contemporaneously a model of governance has been developed whereby internal control is partly allocated to the members (but increasingly transferred to the top of the organizational pyramid), and partly assigned to the stockholders (the new stakeholders resulting from the creation of listed vehicles) (Ory and Lemzeri 2012). The three French co-operatives' networks are organized as "inverted banking groups" with a central body. These groups adopt hybrid structures whereby a group of credit institutions, namely CBs, are affiliated to a central body which is totally or largely under the control of the affiliated banks. The latter are not formally controlled via the central body holding equity stakes, but via affiliation agreements which assure several powers to the central body, ranging from supervision to the management of affiliates. According to EACB (2017), French co-operative groups are integrated co-operative networks under the provisions of Art. 113(6) of the Capital Requirements Regulation (CRR), as transposed into the French Monetary and Financial Code (Art. L. 511-31 and L. 511-32). The central institution[15] is empowered to take all necessary measures to ensure the liquidity and solvency of all affiliated institutions and of the network as a whole on the basis of the consolidated accounts of these institutions.[16] It is authorized to issue instructions to the manage-

---

[15] The three existing central bodies are recognized in Art. L511-30 of the French Monetary and Financial Code.

[16] To this end, no current or foreseen material practical or legal impediment must be in place to allow the prompt transfer of own funds or repayment of liabilities from the central body to the local/regional bank. See Art. 113(6)(e) of the CRR.

ment of the affiliated institutions on managerial and internal control-related issues. For instance, it may decide to prohibit or limit the distribution of dividends to members or the redemption of shares; it may also set limits on the risk exposures of its affiliates. The central body must assure the application of laws and regulations to the institutions within the group and exercise administrative, technical, and financial control over their organization and management. Therefore, it is entitled to carry out on-site controls of the affiliates and their direct or indirect subsidiaries, as well as to sanction any violation of existing regulations and/or internal rules. The central institution has the power to decide on the merger of two or more legal entities which are affiliated to it, the total or partial transfer of their business as well as their dissolution.[17] Any decision of affiliation or withdrawal of affiliation is notified by the central body to the institution or company concerned, and to the French Prudential Supervisory and Resolution Authority.

CBs within the three networks are independent entities whose by-laws regulate several issues relating to the provisions of the French Monetary and Financial Code. By-laws determine the seat, the territorial constituency, and the duration of the bank. They fix the composition of the capital, the proportion in which each member contributes to its constitution, the method of administration of the company, the number of votes available to each shareholder in the general meetings in view of the number of shares held, and, for popular banks, the maximum number of votes members can have irrespective of the number of shares they hold. CBs may accept different members to those historically admitted. The member shares of French CBs earn an annual interest rate that cannot be higher than the average rate of return of corporate bonds, plus two percentage points (Art. 14 of Law 47-1775 modified by Law 2016-1691). The average rate is computed over the three calendar years preceding the date of the members meeting and is regularly published by the Minister of the Economy. The general meeting of members determines the annual interest rate to be paid to members under the conditions set by the articles of association. Redemption of shares is at par subject to approval by the board (ratified by the general assembly of members) with the resulting repayments being made after the board decision or the yearly general assembly (EACB 2012). Additionally, members do not enjoy rights to the

---

[17] Provided prior consultation of the governing bodies of the legal entities involved in the transactions has taken place.

residual assets of the bank in the event of liquidation and remain liable at the time when they leave until the closure of ongoing operations, in the case of Crédit Agricole's members within a maximum of five years[18] (EACB 2012). By-laws determine the conditions for full or partial redemption of member shares. Legal persons remain liable for sums up to the value of the shares subscribed.

Since the 1980s, the capital-related instruments available to CBs have been enriched by new financing tools, offering higher returns than shares (subject to provisions set by the by-laws) but without voting rights. Namely, CBs may issue Parts à Intérêt Prioritaire (shares, introduced in 1992, whose voting rights may be exercised if no dividends have been issued for at least three years), Certificats Coopératif d'Associé—CCAs (co-operative member certificates introduced in 1992) and Certificats Coopératif d'Investissement—CCIs (co-operative investment certificates introduced in 1987). Non-members may subscribe to the former in line with the provisions of the by-laws, and their repayment is at par except in the case of senior holders (those with more than five years of membership) who, like holders of traditional shares, are entitled to a limited distribution of reserves (Art. 18 Law 47-1775 modified by Law 2014-856). CCAs are unlisted securities, which may be traded over-the-counter and may be issued only by co-operative companies. Only members of the issuing bank may subscribe to these. The holders enjoy the right to a share of the residual assets, unlike holders of traditional shares and Parts à Intérêt Prioritaire. CCAs are valued every six months, in line with the results of the issuing CB. CCIs are securities listed on the stock exchange that only co-operative companies may issue. They give their holders rights to a share of the residual assets in the event of bank liquidation. Subscribers to CCIs may be non-members of the issuing CB. The terms of redemption of CCAs and CCIs are stated in the relevant issue prospectuses. The sum of all these financial instruments cannot exceed 50% of the total capital of the issuing CB.

The by-laws establish whether the bank extends the benefit of its operations to those beyond its own membership and set the necessary conditions for the amendment of the statutes and the dissolution of the bank. By-laws may be amended with the approval of the central institution. CBs are allowed to receive deposits from every type of saver, whether they are a natural or legal person.

---

[18] See Art. L 512-26 of the French Monetary and Financial Code.

4.1   The Crédit Agricole Group

Crédit Agricole holds a leading position in Europe in bancassurance, asset management, green financing, and consumer finance. With strong co-operative and mutual foundations, it boasted 9.7 million mutual share-holders in 2017 (9.3 million in 2016) and has a serving capacity of 52 million customers in 49 countries.[19] Alongside the development of the group's activities at national and international levels, a simplification of the group structure was completed in 2016: the stakes held by the apex through CCAs and CCIs, issued by the regional banks, were transferred to a holding company, Sacam, whose capital is totally owned by the 39 regional banks. The listing of the central institution in 2001 was accompanied by the issuance of CCAs and CCIs by regional banks which were underwritten by Crédit Agricole S.A. As a result of this transaction, the apex institution held 25% of the capital of each regional bank, thereby benefiting from their attractive profits but without voting rights. Crédit Agricole was prompted to make this re-organization as regulators and investors look ever less favorably on complex co-operative structures (Fig. 5.1).[20]

The co-operative banking group has a three-tier structure. The previously mentioned 1899 Law grouped primary local banks into regional banks to whom they were and are still affiliated. To operate with a regional bank, a local credit co-operative must first be authorized by the central institution of Crédit Agricole. It must, moreover, be regularly affiliated to a licensed regional co-operative bank and have supplied at least a part of the share capital of the latter.[21] Regional banks have powers over the administration and management of the local co-operatives that are affili-ated to them, similar to those conferred by Art. L. 512-38 to the central body of Crédit Agricole. In the event of the dissolution of a local entity, its assets, including reserves, shall, after payment of the debts and reimburse-ment of the capital actually paid, be allocated to an activity of agricultural interest, by decision of the general assembly approved by the central body of Crédit Agricole.[22] Members of local co-operatives meet at an annual general meeting at which they approve the financial statements of the local

---

[19] Data provided by the Financial Report of Crédit Agricole Group for the year-end 2017.
[20] See the comments of O'Neill (2016) at https://www.euromoney.com/article/b12knyb-s22ybt5/cr%C3%A9dit-agricole-cedes-to-pressure-on-structure?copyrightInfo=true.
[21] See Art. L 512-35 of the French Financial and Monetary Code.
[22] See Art. L. 512-43 of the French Financial and Monetary Code.

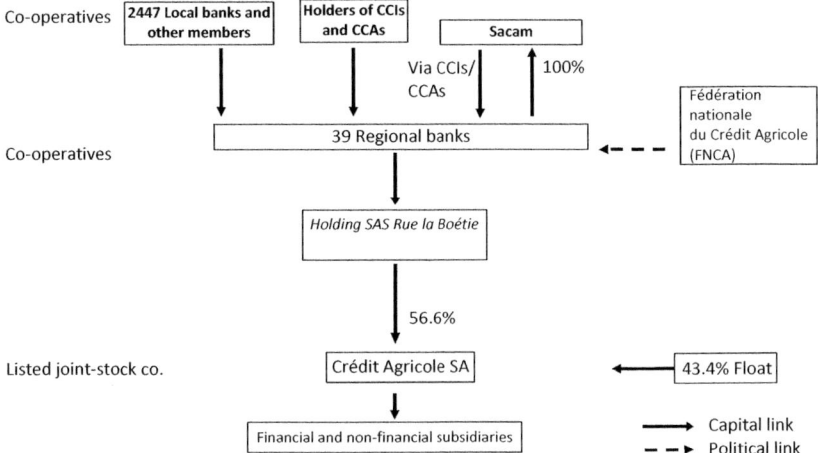

Fig. 5.1 The organizational structure of Crédit Agricole Group. Source: Adapted from Crédit Agricole Group's investor presentations (2017)

banks and elect their directors. The election of their president, vice-presidents, and managing directors must be approved by the regional banks to which local banks are affiliated. Each individual member has one vote at these general meetings, irrespective of the number of shares owned. Local banks may grant loans to their members and collect deposits. However, deposits received by local banks must be forwarded immediately to their own regional bank, which manages them.

The share capital of regional banks is held by 2447 local co-operatives.[23] Holders of member shares receive an annual interest rate which is capped by law; their units are reimbursed at their par value and, as already stated, entail no rights to any proceeds from liquidation. In accordance with Art. L. 512-43 of the French Financial and Monetary Code, in the event of the dissolution of a regional mutual bank, any net remaining assets are placed in deposit, without interest, with the central body, until the amount can be put, as and when the need arises, at the disposal of any regional bank which is constituted to replace the fund dissolved in that constituency. The appointment and dismissal of regional banks' top management is subject to the decision of the network's central body.

[23] See Annual Report of Crédit Agricole Group for the year-end 2017.

The intermediate level of the whole group is represented by 39 regional banks which are independent CBs playing a central role in providing Crédit Agricole with commercial, banking, financial and logistical functions. With 21 million individual customers, in 2017, the regional banks accounted for 23.2% of national household deposits, 34% of SMEs and small businesses, 37% of corporate customers, and 85% of farmers.[24] They provide financial products and services mainly to retail segments via a network of over 7000 branches, about 6000 in-store servicing points installed at small retailers and a full range of remote banking services.[25] The representation of the regional banks' interests within the apex institution's management is assured by their power to elect the majority of the board members of the apex institution.[26]

Within the network, the Fédération Nationale du Crédit Agricole (FNCA) stands as a consultative and representative body, and as a communication forum for the intermediate regional banks. It serves as the political arena where the group's major strategic decisions are taken: as such, it is described as the "Parlement des Caisses régionales".[27]

Like other homologous French co-operative networks, that of Crédit Agricole is highly hybridized, featuring an apex central institution with a joint-stock nature,[28] whose capital is held indirectly by local co-operatives through the shares held by regional banks in a holding company, SAS Rue La Boétie.[29] The majority of the apex institution's equity (56.6% at the

---

[24] See Annual Report of Crédit Agricole Group for the year-end 2017.

[25] See Annual Report of Crédit Agricole Group for the year-end 2017.

[26] As a legacy of the past public nature and role of Crédit Agricole, the Director of the apex is still appointed by joint decree of the Minister of Finance and the Minister of Agriculture thus revealing, despite the privatization of the network, its key role within the French economy.

[27] See the functions of the Fédération Nationale du Crédit Agricole (FNCA) on https://www. creditagricole.info/fnca/dev_7165/la-federation-nationale-du-credit-agricole?dlink=true.

[28] More specifically, Crédit Agricole S.A. is a French Public Limited Company (*Société Anonyme*) and is overseen by the banking supervisory authorities, the French Regulatory and Resolution Supervisory Authority (ACPR), and the European Central Bank, Crédit Agricole S.A. being a significant bank according to Council Regulation (EU) No 1024/2013 of 15 October 2013 which confers specific tasks on the European Central Bank concerning the prudential supervision of credit institutions.

[29] Shares in the holding company SAS Rue La Boétie may not be transferred outside the regional banks' network and any trading of these shares is governed by precise transfer and pricing agreements. The share held by regional banks and the above-mentioned agreement renders Crédit Agricole S.A. immune to takeover bids. The remaining capital of the apex institution is held by institutional investors (30%), individual investors (8.7%), employees (4.6%), and the Treasury (0.1%).

end of 2017) is held by CBs, while the remaining is float capital.[30] The apex has a very important driving role, in terms of centralization processes (data processing and reporting), risk management, and the definition of strategic choices for the whole group (Ory et al. 2013). Additionally, it holds control in financial companies, most of them joint-stock entities, that cover a broad scope of specializations ranging from asset gathering (via asset management, insurance, and private banking companies), retail banking (with national and international subsidiaries), and large customer entities (active in corporate and investment banking and custodian services) to other specialized financial services firms (such as consumer finance, leasing, payment services, real estate).

The apex institution acts as the central body of the network and is responsible for exercising administrative, technical, and financial control over its affiliated institutions according to the provisions of the French Monetary and Financial Code,[31] ensuring compliance with all regulations and legislation governing them. Crédit Agricole S.A. is required to take all essential measures to safeguard the liquidity and solvency of the network as a whole and of each of its affiliated institutions. In this regard, any member of the network (including Crédit Agricole S.A.) potentially facing financial difficulties benefits from the internal financial solidarity mechanism preserved in Art. L. 511-31 of the French Monetary and Financial Code, which applies to the Crédit Agricole network, as defined in Art. R. 512-18 of the same Code. The internal solidarity mechanism is also built on a system of legal guarantees of the obligations of Crédit Agricole S.A. This was granted in 1988 to its third-party creditors by the regional banks on a joint basis, and covers up to the aggregate amount of their own funds.[32] In 2001, at the time of the stock exchange listing, the apex signed an agreement with the regional banks to administer the internal relations within the group. A fund for providing financial assistance to distressed banks was created, the Fund for Bank Liquidity and Solvency Risks (FRBLS) under the administration of the central body.

---

[30] More precisely, the remaining capital of the apex institution in 2016 is held by institutional investors (30%), individual investors (8.7%), employees (4.6%), and by the Treasury (0.1%). See Crédit Agricole's Financial Report at year-end 2016.

[31] See Art. L. 511-31, L. 511-32, and R. 512-18 of the French Monetary and Financial Code.

[32] Under this guarantee, the potential commitment of each regional bank is equal to the sum of its share capital and reserves. Further details may be found in the analysis of the hedging of liquidity and solvency risks provided in Crédit Agricole's Financial Report at the year-end 2017.

As part of the internal guarantee mechanisms, in 2011 a switch mechanism was created according to which certain equity-related assets held by Crédit Agricole S.A. specifically in the insurance sector, would benefit from the regional banks' guarantee, thus providing capital regulatory reliefs to Crédit Agricole in return for the payment of an annual fee. The effectiveness of the mechanism is secured by cash deposits paid by the regional banks to Crédit Agricole S.A. and compensated at a fixed rate based on the prevailing conditions for long-term liquidity.

The historical role of the apex institution as the provider of clearing and liquidity management services to the regional banks is still represented today by the strong centralization of the funding collected by regional banks, despite this having been reviewed over time. Each regional bank holds a current account with Crédit Agricole S.A. where all internal financial transactions are recorded. Funds collected by regional banks in the form of special savings accounts,[33] as well as savings funds (passbook accounts, bonds, warrants, certain term accounts and related accounts, etc.), are collected by the regional banks on behalf of Crédit Agricole S.A. and must be transferred to the latter which recognizes them in its own liabilities. Since 2001, a system of partially re-transferring the funds collected by regional banks in a mirror arrangement (with the same terms and conditions) has allowed them to make use of the savings resources, regional banks being free to use these at their discretion. Currently, the percentage of savings which can be advanced to regional banks is 50%. Monetary deposits such as demand deposits, non-centralized term deposits, and negotiable certificates of deposits may be used by regional banks to finance lending to their customers. However, any available surplus must be transferred to Crédit Agricole S.A. in accordance with Art. L. 512-45 of the Monetary and Financial Code. Analogously, any capital surplus must be invested with Crédit Agricole S.A. in the form of three to ten-year instruments with exactly the same characteristics as any other interbank money market transaction. The financial margins generated by the centralized management of the collected funds (and not transferred back via mirror advances) are shared among all the banks in the network.[34]

The apex institution may use the funds collected by regional banks through the most stable funding instruments to grant loans to the latter,

---

[33] Such as popular savings plans (*Livret d'épargne populaire*), sustainable development passbook accounts (*Livret de développement durable*), home purchase savings plans and accounts, youth passbook accounts, and *Livret A* passbook savings accounts.

[34] For a more detailed description of the internal financial mechanism within the Group, see its Financial Report at year-end 2017.

specifically with the aim of mitigating maturity transformation at the regional level.[35] The control and management of the risks undertaken by regional banks is also performed through a compulsory guarantee system against large exposures borne by the banks via Foncaris, a wholly owned dedicated credit institution of Crédit Agricole S.A. Since intermediate banks are required to ask the group's mutual guarantee company to guarantee their main transactions before agreeing to grant them, Foncaris represents for the central body an effective tool for assessing the risks of regional banks.

In the years following the privatization of the former CNCA, the joint-stock central entity has been the main player in an impressive expansion into new business lines and countries. The acquisition of Banque Indosuez in 1996 enabled Crédit Agricole to diversify into corporate and investment banking, while its entry into consumer credit was realized through the takeovers of Sofinco in 1999 and Finaref in 2003. Following the 2003 merger with Crédit Lyonnais, a re-organization along business lines gave rise to Crédit Agricole Corporate and Investment Bank (CA-CIB) in 2006. Crédit Lyonnais refocused on retail banking and adopted the LCL brand in 2005. The asset management company Amundi was created in 2010 and listed on the stock market in 2015. In 2016 Amundi announced the acquisition of a leading asset management company, Pioneer Investments, from the Italian commercial bank UniCredit, thus further reinforcing its asset management capabilities. Minority and majority stakes in European banks have been acquired over the last two decades, culminating in the acquisition in 2017 of a 95.3% stake in the equity of each of three Italian savings banks in Cesena (Cassa di Risparmio di Cesena SpA), Rimini (Cassa di Risparmio di Rimini SpA), and San Miniato (Cassa di Risparmio di San Miniato SpA). This was undertaken through its Italian subsidiary, Crédit Agricole Cariparma SpA, acquired in 2007. The group has gained a leadership position in financing and insurance in France. It is also the foremost bancassurer in Europe, the leading European asset manager and the world's second largest provider of green financing.[36]

---

[35] For a more detailed description of the internal financing mechanisms of Crédit Agricole, see its Financial Report at year-end 2017.

[36] See Crédit Agricole Group's Financial Report for the year-end 2017.

4.2   The Banque Populaire-Caisse d'Epargne (BPCE) Group

The process of aggregation between Banque Populaire and Caisse d'Epargne began in 2006 with the creation of their joint subsidiary, Natixis,[37] a listed joint-stock company. The transaction has been characterized as an unusual type of restructuring (Ory et al. 2006), given that the two co-operative groups were supposed to remain independent and autonomous while jointly owning most of the subsidiaries of the two groups through the newly formed entity, Natixis. The deal was motivated by the need to make better use of economies of scale and scope, and combined the strengths of the two groups' complementary businesses to form a supra-national company, able to raise capital and compete in international markets. The emergence of the international financial crisis in 2007–2008 prompted the two groups to merge their central institutions, a move that was strongly supported by the Sarkozy government in power at the time. The merger involved the transfer of most of the technical and human resources of their respective central bodies to a common central body. The aggregation was backed by a capital injection from the state aimed to offset the potentially adverse effects on the financing of the economy. In order to put the new central body on a sound financial footing, the French government decided to increase the amount of capital it had already allocated to the networks with these capital injections. In April 2009 the French government formally notified the European Commission of its plan to increase the sum of € 2.55 billion already approved by the Commission in January by a further € 2.45 billion,[38] to be paid to the Caisse d'Epargne and Banque Populaire groups with the second installment of the recapitalization scheme. The two groups had already received € 2.05 billion under the scheme's first installment. The total cost of implementing the plan amounted to € 7.05 billion.[39] The apex company, BPCE is a limited liability company with a two-tier corporate governance structure, and is governed by its articles of association, and the relevant regulations.

---

[37] Natixis derives from the transformation of Natexis (owned by Banque Populaire) and Ixis (owned by Caisse d'Epargne).
[38] See IP/09/158.
[39] See IP/09/722.

4.2.1   The Caisses d'Epargne Network

Granting Caisses d'Epargne the new status of universal CBs would have eased their path to participating in the restructure of European banking, and eventually allowed them to consider a stock flotation which would have been impossible without a clear legal status. Nowadays, regional Caisses d'Epargne are wholly owned by 228 local savings companies (LSCs),[40] co-operative companies with open-ended capital stock, which is wholly owned by co-operative members. Any individual or legal entity that is a customer of a Caisse d'Epargne, as well as any of its employees, may acquire co-operative shares in an LSC, thereby becoming a co-operative member. Lastly, local and regional authorities, and French inter-municipal   co-operation   institutions   (Établissements   Publics   de Coopération Intercommunale) within the local savings company's territorial constituency are also entitled to become co-operative members, but their shareholdings, taken together, may not exceed 20% of the capital of a given local savings company.[41] The LSCs are responsible for the coordination of the co-operative membership base, within the framework of the general objectives defined by the individual Caisse d'Epargne to which they are affiliated. LSCs' members meet annually and cast their vote on a "one man, one vote" basis. LSCs are governed through a two-tier corporate governance structure with a board of directors elected by the annual general shareholders' meeting and a supervisory board. The chairman of the individual LSC represents the local savings company at the annual general shareholders' meeting of the Caisse d'Epargne to which it is affiliated.[42] As is shown in Fig. 5.2, the network of Caisses d'Epargne is organized as a three-tier structure, in contrast with the two-tier structure used by the Banque Populaire network.

4.2.2   The Banque Populaire Network

According to the French Monetary and Financial Code, popular banks are co-operative companies that can undertake business with traders, industrialists, manufacturers, craftsmen, fishermen, trading companies, and members of the liberal professions.[43] They can offer their services to their members and participate in financing operations jointly with a mutual guarantee company. However, their regional growth was facilitated by the

---

[40] See BPCE Group's Financial Report at year-end 2017.
[41] See BPCE Group's Financial Report at year-end 2016 and 2017.
[42] See BPCE Group's Financial Report at year-end 2017.
[43] See Art. L 512-2 of the French Monetary and Financial Code.

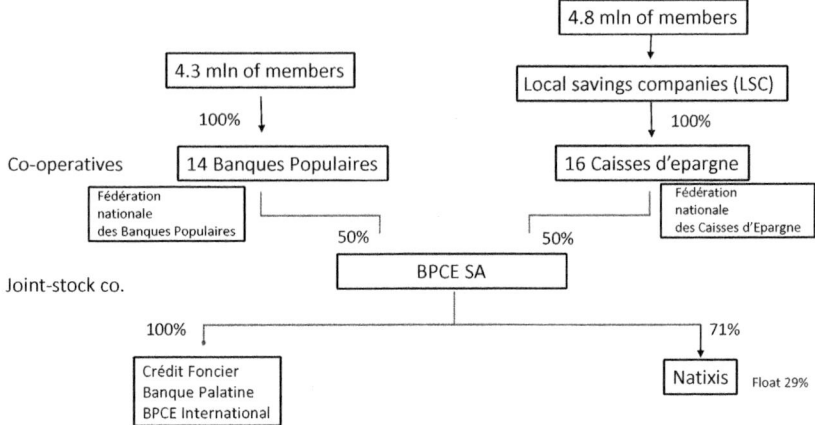

Fig. 5.2   The organizational structure of BPCE's network. Source: Adapted from BPCE Group's website (2018)

decision in 1962 to make their services available to any individual customer irrespective of their activity and status (i.e. whether they were a bank member or not). The ability to extend the banks' activities to customers other than members is defined by the individual banks' by-laws as well as by the limits set for credit facilities, which are determined for the bank by the central body for savings banks and popular banks.

Popular banks are wholly owned by their co-operative members which comprise both individuals and legal entities. Their coordination works at the local and national levels, operating locally through the regional popular banks, while at the national level through the initiatives undertaken by the Fédération Nationale des Banques Populaires. The latter organization retains a key role in providing training activities for the management of popular banks, having also established a Directors' Académie with several digital services in 2014. The statutes of popular banks determine their mode of administration and the rules for the election of the board of directors using a one-tier corporate governance framework. Popular banks may have fixed or variable capital. The admission and termination or expulsion of members in popular banks is subject to the approval of the bank's administrative board. In the event of membership being terminated, the central institution of the network must also give its approval in order to avoid any potential capital shortage across the entire group.

Reimbursement of shares is at nominal value. In cases of the dissolution or liquidation of a popular bank, any surplus assets must be paid into the collective guarantee fund or assigned to other destinations decided by the central body in accordance with the interests of the network. The value of the popular banks' shares as well as their annual compensation are defined by the board of directors and voted on at the annual general meeting under the conditions set out in the bank's articles of association and the relevant regulations.

Following the merger with Caisse d'Epargne, the resulting network has maintained the two brands, its two distribution networks, and its two corresponding federations. The Banque Populaire network had 4.3 million members in 2017 (4.1 in 2016), while that of Caisse d'Epargne numbered 4.8 million members in 2017 (unchanged from 2016).[44] They are represented equally on the supervisory board of the central body. More specifically, the supervisory board is made up of seven representatives of members of Caisse d'Epargne, seven representatives of Banque Populaire, three independent members, and two members representing employees of BPCE. Six members perform an advisory role and do not vote. Among these are the Chairman of the Fédération Nationale des Caisses d'Epargne and the chairman of the Fédération Nationale des Banques Populaires. The remaining non-voting directors are appointed by the members of the two networks.[45] The supervisory board approves the policies and strategic guidelines of the apex and each of the two networks; it also monitors the financial statements of the network.

The joint central body for Caisse d'Epargne and Banque Populaire is an unlisted public limited company, BPCE, which was set up on 31 July 2009.[46] The capital of the apex is owned equally by the two original net-

---

[44] BPCE Group's Financial Report for the year-end 2017.

[45] As stated in BPCE's articles of association and reported in BPCE's Financial Report for the year-end 2017.

[46] The new central body, BPCE, was created by French law n° 2009-715 of 18 June 2009 replacing the two existing central bodies, Banque Fédérale des Banques Populaires (BFBP) and Caisse Nationale des Caisses d'Epargne (CNCE). It was set up via a business transfer by BFBP and CNCE. At the time of the deal, the French state underwrote € 3 billion of preference shares issued by BPCE. The preference shares had no voting rights but gave the French state the right to designate two representatives to the Supervisory Board. Within the state support package, equity warrants were subscribed by the French state allowing it to raise up to a maximum of 20% of the capital and voting rights, provided that BPCE had not previously repurchased the preference shares. See BPCE's press release (2009) http://www.info-financiere.fr/upload/CNS/2009/07/FCCNS021475_20090731.pdf.

works which currently consist of 16 Caisses d'Epargne and 14 Banques Populaires. They own all the shares of the BPCE central institution which is thus totally insulated from takeover bids (Fig. 5.2). BPCE controls banking, capital markets, and financial services subsidiaries.

In accordance with Art. L. 511-31 and Art. L. 512-107 of the French Monetary and Financial Code, the central institution is responsible for the definition of the whole network's strategies, the coordination of sales activities, the set-up of risk management policies on a consolidated basis, and the implementation of effective internal control systems, allowing them to make on-site checks. It undertakes any measure required to manage the liquidity of the network and its solvency. To this end, it may implement internal financing mechanisms and create and run a mutual guarantee fund shared by both networks, for which it determines affiliates' contributions for their initial allocation and reconstitution and the terms and conditions of use, in addition to the guarantee and solidarity funds already set up by the two networks[47] before the merger in 2009. Additionally, in order to strengthen the pervasive power of the central institution, BPCE approves the articles of association of affiliated entities and local savings companies and any changes made to them.[48]

BPCE, the apex, has sole responsibility for taking all measures necessary to guarantee the solvency of the Group and each of its networks, including implementing the appropriate Group internal financing mechanisms. BPCE runs a mutual guarantee fund common to both networks which was established after the merger, in addition to each network's pre-existing fund and defines the contributions made by affiliates for the endowment and reconstitution of mutual guarantee funds. The mutual guarantee funds are booked by BPCE in the form of 10-year term accounts which are indefinitely renewable. The total amount of deposits placed with BPCE may not be less than 0.15% and may not exceed 0.3% of the total risk-weighted assets of the group.[49]

The Banque Populaire network comprises some specialized intermediaries such as Casden, a CB serving all public-sector workers, with more than 1.6 million co-operative shareholders in 2017; Crédit Coopératif, a CB specialized in solidarity-based savings and financial products, with 105,200

---

[47] In accordance with Art. L. 512-12 and L. 512-86-1 of the French Monetary and Financial Code.
[48] See BPCE Group's Financial Report for the year-end 2016.
[49] See BPCE Group's Financial Report for the year-end 2017.

co-operative shareholders in 2017; and Crédit Maritime, specialized in the provision of maritime financial services. The network also includes several mutual guarantee companies that, as in the case of Crédit Agricole, guarantee loans granted by the popular banking networks to different economic agents. Intra-mergers within the two co-operative banking networks have been ongoing over time. In December 2017, two popular banks, Banque Populaire Atlantique and Banque Populaire de l'Ouest, decided to merge with Crédit Maritime Atlantique and Crédit Maritime Bretagne-Normandie to create Banque Populaire Grand Ouest, a regional CB covering the Brittany/Pays de la Loire regions and the Manche and Orne departments in Normandy. Similarly, in April 2017, Caisse d'Epargne Picardie and Caisse d'Epargne Nord France Europe merged, giving rise to Caisse d'Epargne Hauts de France. It is worth mentioning that just one year on from the creation of the BPCE Group, there were 20 popular banks and 17 Caisses d'Epargne. This shows that the wave of mergers has been more pronounced in the popular banking network than in that of the Caisses d'Epargne.

Under the direct control of the apex, BPCE, there are different specialized financial intermediaries, including Natixis, Crédit Foncier, Banque Palatine, and BPCE International. Natixis is an active provider of international financing, asset management, insurance and investment and corporate banking. It is the 15th largest asset manager in the world in terms of assets under management, the 3rd largest bancassurer, and the 3rd largest provider of payment services in France. Crédit Foncier offers real estate loans and services to the domestic market; Banque Palatine provides financial solutions to medium-sized companies through a wide network of financial advisors; while BPCE International targets retail banking services via its subsidiaries operating in Africa, the Indian Ocean region, Vietnam, New Caledonia, and Tahiti as well as holding specialized subsidiaries in structured financing and international development advisory services.

4.3   The Crédit Mutuel Group

The network of Crédit Mutuel is structured as a three-tier co-operative banking organization. The first level is formed by 2092 local CBs[50] which are registered as co-operative associations in certain French departments and variable-capital credit co-operatives in all others.[51] They serve local

---

[50] See Crédit Mutuel Group's Activity Report for the year-end 2017.
[51] See Crédit Mutuel-CM11 Group's Financial Report for the year-end 2017.

communities and are entirely owned by their members. Under the French Monetary and Financial Code, they are co-operative credit institutions whose equity capital is held solely by members, who are at the same time customers (in accordance with the Law of 10 September 1947). Members are entitled to one vote at general meetings. Local co-operatives are legally autonomous, and active in collecting savings, granting loans, and providing a full range of financial services. These primary entities are required to become members of a regional federation (legally being an association of local banks) which fosters cohesiveness between the local co-operatives, contributes to setting the network's strategies, and supervises the federated CBs, representing Crédit Mutuel in each region.[52] There are 19 regional federations. Federations comprise a "Caisse Fédérale", a federal or inter-federal central CB owned by local co-operatives.

The Caisse Fédérale is tasked with financial functions such as liquidity and fund management and provides technical and IT services. The regional federations and federal banks are governed by boards of directors elected by the local CBs. From a regulatory standpoint, Caisse Fédérale holds the collective banking license that covers all affiliated local co-operative banks, in accordance with the French Monetary and Financial Code.[53] As set out in Art. R. 511-3 of the Code, the federal bank is responsible for its mutual banking network's solvency and liquidity as well as its own network's compliance with banking and financial regulations.

These 19 regional networks are further organized into 6 super-regional networks. The regional co-operative banking networks (the second level of the organization) are affiliated into the Confédération Nationale du Crédit Mutuel (CNCM) and its banking arm, the Caisse Centrale du Crédit Mutuel (CCCM) (the third level). A distinctive feature of the Crédit Mutuel Group lies in its central body, the CNCM, which is not a financial intermediary and represents all the member institutions vis-à-vis

---

[52] In accordance with Art. R 512-20 of the French Monetary and Financial Code, local banks must have objectives that comply with the general principles of mutual credit, and in particular have a non-profit character, limit their activity to a territorial division, and establish the responsibility of members. They must respect the statutes, instructions, and decisions of the National Confederation of Crédit Mutuel and the regional federation to which they must adhere in accordance with the provisions of Article L. 512-56.

[53] According to Art. R.515-1, the French supervisory authority may issue a collective license to a local bank for itself and all of its affiliated local banks "when the liquidity and solvency of the local banks are guaranteed through this affiliation". See Crédit Mutuel-CM11 Group's Financial Report for the year-end 2017.

both the domestic and European regulatory and supervisory authorities. In terms of the previously mentioned French banking regulations governing central bodies, CNCM holds administrative, technical, and financial control of the organization and the management of the member CBs and their subsidiaries.

The largest super-regional group is the Crédit Mutuel-CM11 Group comprising 11 federations, 1368 local banks (in 2017), and 1 inter-federal central CB, Caisse Fédérale de Crédit Mutuel (CFCM).[54] The second super-regional network is Crédit Mutuel Arkéa formed by 3 regional networks and 331 local banks in 2017.[55] It is worth noting that both networks are highly hybridized and qualify as diversified bancassurance groups. Their central banks hold controlling stakes in joint-stock companies which are active in corporate and investment banking, insurance, payments, and other financial services. For instance, Banque Fédérative du Crédit Mutuel S.A. (BFCM) is under the control of CFCM and is tasked with refinancing and capital markets activities to the benefit of the CM11 network; additionally, BFCM controls the group Crédit Industriel et Commercial (CIC) whose parent company is the lead bank for the relatively widespread branch network in France and several specialized institutions in France and abroad.[56] Since 2014, Crédit Mutuel Arkéa has been in legal dispute with the Confédération Nationale du Crédit Mutuel, due to potential conflicts of interest concerning the position of the chairman of CNCM who is also the chairman of the CM11 group, a direct competitor of Crédit Mutuel Arkéa, as well as regarding concerns about the strong governance and strategy-setting powers of CNCM which would weaken the independence of regional groups.

Since, according to Crédit Mutuel Arkéa, there are two autonomous and competing banking groups within the network, their proposal was to create two central bodies, but this suggestion was rejected by CNCM in 2016. As a consequence, in 2018 the shareholders' meeting of the inter-federal Crédit Mutuel Arkéa invited the three federations to initiate

---

[54] 88.7% of CFCM's capital is held by local co-operatives across 11 regional federations, while the rest is owned by the captive mutual insurance company of the network, ACM Vie SAM. See Crédit Mutuel, Financial report for the year-end 2016.

[55] See Crédit Mutuel Arkéa Group's Financial Report for the year-end 2017.

[56] CIC was delisted in 2017. The decision was motivated by the need to simplify the Group's structure and eliminate some of the regulatory and administrative constraints associated with the listing of the CIC shares as well as the related costs. See Crédit Mutuel-CM11 Group's Annual Report for the year-end 2017.

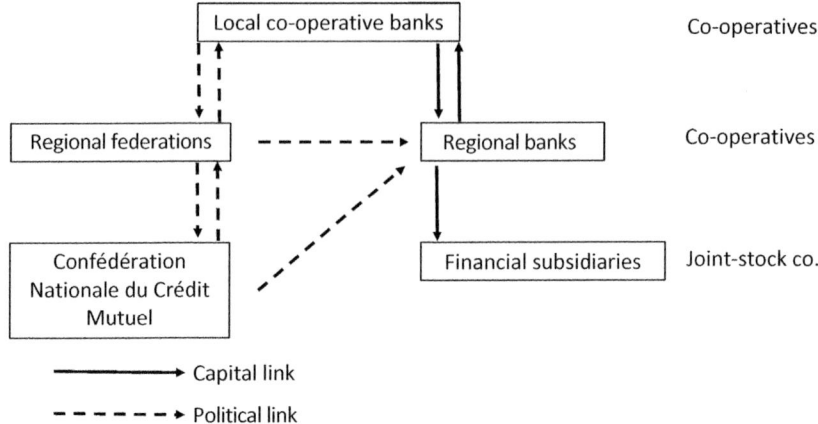

Fig. 5.3 The organizational structure of Crédit Mutuel Group. Source: Author's elaboration

consultations with their local banks on a proposed separation from Crédit Mutuel and the adoption of a name and trademark that do not feature the term "Crédit Mutuel".[57] During the first part of 2018, the majority of local banks opted for independence from CNCM. Arkéa declared that it had started operational procedures to establish its independence from CNCM, but it is currently unclear how this legal dispute will evolve (Fig. 5.3).[58]

From 2015 onward, the central body undertook several governance reforms to comply with national and European supervisory requirements. The modification of the articles of association on 21 March 2016 amended the network's organization: the size of the board of directors was reduced; independent directors were appointed; and specialized committees under a coordination committee[59] were created to advise the administrative

[57] In December 2016, the French Council of State noted that CNCM is the parent company in the union and that "in legal terms, and for as long as Crédit Mutuel Arkéa remains affiliated to the Crédit Mutuel network, there can be no question of any form of independence of this entity with regard to CNCM".

[58] See Crédit Mutuel Arkéa Group's Financial Report for the year-end 2017.

[59] The coordination committee meets monthly or upon request of a member of the general direction of the Confédération Nationale du Crédit Mutuel. It is made up of nine members representing the regional networks and the Confédération. See Crédit Mutuel, Financial report for the year-end 2016.

board. As a central body, CNCM is responsible for the sound functioning of the institutions affiliated to it[60]; for the definition and implementation of the risk guidelines concerning the whole network and its audit; as well as for the set-up of a mutual support mechanism that complies with the mutual principles of subsidiarity and responsibility and with the prudential requirements of coherence and solidity. The mutual support mechanism is a two-tier system, with regional and national levels. The management of the latter is performed by the Caisse Centrale du Crédit Mutuel (CCCM), the national financial body whose share capital is owned by the federal banks. The regional mutual support system is organized around federal banks which, together with their affiliates and shareholders, contribute to a mutual guarantee fund (*Fonds de Solidarité*) on the basis of their respective total assets and net banking income.[61] Financial support provided to local banks may typically cover losses or even insufficient income to remunerate member shares.[62] CNCM prepares the consolidated financial statements at the national level in accordance with International Financial Reporting Standards within the meaning of Article L.511-31 of the French Monetary and Financial Code and the CRR Regulation. Consolidated annual reports are also prepared by the individual super-regional co-operative banking groups.

The corporate governance of local CBs is modeled around a two-tier structure with a supervisory body, the board of directors, made up of volunteer members elected at the shareholders' meeting. At the district level, local CBs elect their representative from the volunteer directors of individual local banks. The chairman of the district becomes a full member of the board of directors of the federation. The chairpersons of the network's central bank, that is, CFCM, are chosen from the directors of the federations.[63] Only the board of directors of the central banks includes independent members. Besides the supervisory board, there is the executive body, whose chief executive officer is appointed by the board of directors. This

---

[60] According to Article L. 511-31 of the French Monetary and Financial Code, CNCM is empowered to take all necessary measures to ensure the liquidity and solvency of each of its affiliated banks and that of the network as a whole. In the event that the management at the level of the regional affiliate proves to be inadequate to deal with the possible difficulties encountered, CNCM has the power to implement adequate solutions.

[61] See Crédit Mutuel-CM11 Group's Financial report for the year-end 2017.

[62] Ibidem.

[63] Volunteer directors are entitled only to the reimbursement of expenses incurred in connection with their duties.

body is further responsible for the approval of the group financial statements and the steering of the group's strategy. In order to limit risk-taking, the networks of the Crédit Mutuel Group follow remuneration policies that largely favor fixed rather than variable remunerations. For instance, managers of Crédit Mutuel Arkéa are not granted options on shares or debt securities and do not receive performance shares, and the Crédit Mutuel Arkéa by-laws do not allow for such grants to be made.

Of the three French co-operative banking groups, Crédit Mutuel is the most focused on the domestic territory, which accounted for around 80% of its banking income in 2017.[64] The two networks, CM11 and Arkéa, hold some investments outside France. The former has significant activities in Germany and, to a lesser extent, in Spain and North Africa. Its subsidiary, CIC, has international branches in London, New York, and Singapore, and representative offices in several other countries. It is active in corporate banking, capital markets activities, private banking, and private equity. However, these international activities typically account for only a small proportion of the group's overall net banking income. The CM11 group also has a presence in the insurance business through Groupe des Assurances du Crédit Mutuel (GACM) which offers life insurance, personal insurance, and property and liability insurance, mostly through the Crédit Mutuel group's banking networks. Due to the role of the insurance sector within the CM11 Group, the latter is itself a financial conglomerate.

The Arkéa group holds subsidiaries in Belgium, Luxembourg, Switzerland, and to a limited extent in Germany and the United Kingdom through Keytrade Bank and ProCapital. The former was acquired in 2016 and is active in online banking. Together with Fortuneo Bank, the French online banking subsidiary, Keytrade Bank strengthens the presence of the Arkéa group in the provision of online services. ProCapital is a securities services provider for institutional investors. The group also has a significant role in electronic payment transactions through its subsidiary, Monext, which handled more than 30% of e-commerce transactions in France in 2017 and offers its services in some European countries, namely the United Kingdom, Germany, Spain, and Luxembourg.[65] Like the CM11 group, its investments in the insurance sector are significant as is its activity in asset and wealth management. It is also regulated and supervised

---

[64] See Crédit Mutuel-CM11 Group's Financial Report for the year-end 2017.
[65] See Crédit Mutuel Arkéa Group's Annual Report for the year-end 2017.

as a financial conglomerate. For both groups their focus on retail banking can be clearly seen by the share of their total net banking income that this represents: in 2017, this stood at 68% for CM11 and 75% for Arkéa respectively.[66]

5   THE PERFORMANCES OF FRENCH CO-OPERATIVE VERSUS NON-CO-OPERATIVE BANKING GROUPS OVER THE PERIOD 2005–2017

Since the nineties, the process of hybridization which took place in France, as in other European countries investigated in this book, has raised a series of issues. A first question concerns the effects of the ongoing hybridization. In other words, have the mitigation of the principles of mutuality pursued by CBs and the growing complementarity with markets as places of investment and funding meant that the results achieved by CBs have become more similar to those of commercial joint-stock banks? Which areas record analogies and differences in results? Can a convergence in performance be observed over time? To answer these important questions, we have identified a series of indicators in the form of ratios proxying bank performances. The set of indicators used to run the comparisons concerns the capitalization of banks; their activities in lending and investing in securities, including those held for trading on the financial markets; their reliance on deposits from customers; the role they play over time in the interbank market; the riskiness deriving from their lending; and, finally, banking profitability and efficiency.

The data used in this first phase of analysis are consolidated, therefore, representative of the results achieved by the commercial and co-operative groups, including the latter's networks of CBs and their various non-co-operative subsidiaries. Year-end figures are used. In order to verify if, where, and when there have been phenomena of convergence between co-operative and non-co-operative banking groups, one or more national shareholder-oriented banking groups have been identified with which the following comparative analysis is carried out. The analysis covers the period 2005–2017 and is particularly helpful, since it allows the results obtained by the two groups of banks to be taken before and after the outbreak of the global financial crisis (GFC). Data are collected from three databases SNL,

---

[66] See Crédit Mutuel CM11 and Arkéa Groups' Annual Reports for the year-end 2017.

BankScope Bureau van Dijk, and Orbis Bank Focus in order to minimize the potential for missing data. The three French co-operative banking groups are compared, on a consolidated basis, with the two major non-co-operative banking groups, namely BNP Paribas and Société Générale, both listed. The former has total assets amounting to € 1960 billion at the end of 2017, while those of Société Générale equal € 1275 billion. In the same period, the groups of Crédit Agricole, BPCE, and Crédit Mutuel have total assets respectively equal to € 1763 billion, € 1260 and € 813 billion as recorded in the SNL database.

We provide means and standard deviations of the selected indicators in different sub-periods, covering respectively: the pre-crisis period, 2005–2007; the main GFC period, 2008–2010; the period from 2011 to 2013 during which the sovereign debt crisis severely affected various countries,[67] and important regulatory and monetary policy measures were put in place to restore bank financial stability; and the implementation of Basle 3 and initiation of the European Banking Union with the implementation of the Single Supervisory Mechanism (SSM) and the Single Resolution Mechanism (SRM), 2014–2017.

In Table 5.4, we report the first set of indicators under investigation. The capital ratios employed consist of a regulatory proxy for the appraisal of the capital adequacy of the banking groups, the Tier 1 (%) ratio, and an accounting ratio represented by equity over assets (%). The first one stands for a measure of capital adequacy under the Basel rules to address credit risk. Broadly speaking, the Tier 1 ratio is calculated as the shareholder funds plus perpetual non-cumulative preference shares as a percentage of risk-weighted assets and some off-balance sheet items. The higher the Tier 1 value, the more capitalized the bank is, which improves its ability to face the risks arising from lending to and financing borrowers. Under the Basel 3 rules introduced in Europe in 2014 (with EU Directive 2013/36 and the EU Regulation 575/2013—CRR) the minimum level of Tier 1 permitted is 6% plus the capital conservation buffer of 2.5%. The ratio of equity to total assets (%) proxies the cushion against banking risks. The higher this figure, the better the bank is able to cope with potential losses

---

[67] In 2012, Greece was granted a new financial aid package, while its debt was cancelled resulting in a severe haircut for private investors. Spain entered a difficult period, amidst doubts about the strength of its banking system, the deterioration of its public finances, record unemployment, and deepening recession. These concerns led risk premiums on sovereign debt to climb considerably, triggering bailouts for Greece, Ireland, and Portugal. Italy was not spared, with yields on its debt rising as well, despite the reforms undertaken by the government in charge at the time, led by Mario Monti.

Table 5.4 Comparison of French co-operative groups vs. non-co-operative banking groups: capital ratios

	Crédit Agricole		BPCE		Crédit Mutuel		BNP Paribas		Société Générale	
	Mean	SD	Mean	SD	Mean	SD	Mean	SD	Mean	SD
Tier 1 (%)										
2005–2007	7.66	0.25	–	–	9.82	0.46	7.44	0.19	7.34	0.63
2008–2010	10.84	0.83	9.71[a]	0.81	13.82	1.11	9.82	1.77	10.01	1.07
2011–2013	12.62	0.64	11.87	1.16	14.06	0.78	12.68	1.04	12.21	1.37
2014–2017	15.58	0.67	13.98	1.19	16.66	0.83	12.43	0.77	14.05	0.57
Equity to total assets (%)										
2005–2007	4.60	0.11	–	–	4.89	0.14	3.66	0.15	3.22	0.29
2008–2010	4.25	0.33	4.77[a]	0.18	5.08	0.70	3.64	0.71	3.96	0.53
2011–2013	4.22	0.51	4.74	0.45	5.96	0.29	4.76	0.44	3.93	0.30
2014–2017	5.76	0.40	5.49	0.25	6.42	0.09	4.90	0.36	3.89	0.04

Source: Author's calculations

This table reports descriptive statistics (means and standard deviations—SD) of French co-operative and non-co-operative banking groups. Tier 1 (%) is the ratio between primary regulatory capital and risk-weighted assets; Equity/total assets (%) is the ratio between total equity and total assets. Our calculations are based on data extracted from SNL

[a]Only 2009 and 2010

arising from its activity. The Tier 1 ratio has, on average, been increasing over time in all the sub-periods under investigation, for both co-operative and non-co-operative banking groups. However, before the crisis (2005–2007) and during the period of recovery (2014–2017), co-operative groups perform on average better than their peers, resulting in them being better equipped to face the risks arising from the intermediation activity. By contrast, during the peak of the GFC (2008–2010) and the following period (2011–2013), the values of the Tier 1 ratio are very close between the two clusters of bank business models. Crédit Mutuel, however, displays the highest levels of Tier 1. Of the three co-operative banking groups, it is the smallest and unlisted Crédit Mutuel that exhibits the highest ratios and lowest standard deviation over time, followed by the largest one, Crédit Agricole. Analysis of the ratio of equity on total assets reveals a similar trend to that already seen for the Tier 1 ratio (Table 5.4). However, what emerges clearly from the reported data is the lower level of capital held by shareholder-oriented banking groups before the crisis and in the most recent period under examination. Crédit Mutuel holds an outstanding position in this regard. Of the three co-operative banking groups, BPCE has the lowest ratio over the period 2014–2017.

The second set of indicators concerns the asset side of the banking groups and aims to shed light on its composition. In this regard, we employ three types of ratios: the ratio of net customer loans to total assets (%) which measures the degree of dedication to the traditional lending activity; the ratio of the total securities held to total assets (%) which provides an assessment of the integration of banks with financial markets in investment terms; and finally, the ratio of securities held for trading to total assets (%), which shows the degree of banks' active participation in the financial markets through financial instruments (i.e. bonds, derivatives, and stocks) which allows for an assessment of speculative activities within the financial markets.

The data shown in Table 5.5 clearly indicate some idiosyncrasies of French CBs, which mostly persist over time. First of all, their propensity to finance the economy through credit is, over the entire period of observation, significantly higher than that of shareholder-oriented banking groups. In the last period of analysis, the average levels of net customer loans to total assets range from 43.79% for Crédit Agricole to over 50% for Crédit Mutuel and BPCE group, as opposed to values of between 32% and 35% for the commercial groups. It is interesting to note that almost all groups have essentially continued to provide credit to the economy during the times of crisis. Similarly, co-operative groups' stronger focus on the more traditional credit activity stands in contrast to their constant lower commitment to investing in securities. Not only do the commercial joint-stock banks show a greater degree of integration with financial markets in terms of their use of financial instruments, but they are also the intermediaries that have most reduced their securities holdings throughout the period (Table 5.5). For the most part, this decreasing trend is also true for CBs. The divergence between their positions is quite evident. While Crédit Agricole holds values of over 40%, the remaining two co-operative groups hold very different average values: 24.98% for the BPCE group and 30.04% for the Crédit Mutuel group respectively over the period 2014–2017. The investment space that co-operative groups devote to financial instruments held for trading purposes is equally distinctive. Here the differences with the non-co-operative banking groups are evident and substantial. For the latter, the volume of financial assets held for trading purposes has significantly decreased over time and is confirmed in the last period (2014–2017) at average values of approximately 30%. There is also a substantial disinvestment from financial

Table 5.5 Comparison of French co-operative groups vs. non-co-operative banking groups: lending and securities holdings ratios

	Crédit Agricole		BPCE		Crédit Mutuel		BNP Paribas		Société Générale	
	Mean	SD	Mean	SD	Mean	SD	Mean	SD	Mean	SD
Net customer loans/total assets (%)										
2005–2007	39.91	1.09	–	–	47.31	3.58	25.90	1.75	30.35	0.58
2008–2010	41.90	2.39	52.99[a]	2.40	53.73	1.75	30.46	5.76	35.27	1.29
2011–2013	40.24	3.17	51.47	0.77	54.88	1.53	33.78	0.60	31.05	2.27
2014–2017	43.79	2.57	53.81	2.17	52.40	0.79	34.37	2.26	31.96	2.79
Securities/total assets (%)										
2005–2007	45.63	0.97	–	–	35.22	0.90	62.05	2.52	55.97	1.51
2008–2010	42.98	2.22	24.43[a]	2.07	29.27	0.55	56.74	6.92	50.26	1.25
2011–2013	44.30	3.88	27.64	1.05	28.03	1.25	51.41	1.49	49.93	1.88
2014–2017	42.84	1.88	24.98	2.25	30.04	1.22	48.06	4.10	48.56	4.13
Total assets held for trading/total assets (%)										
2005–2007	27.80	0.57	–	–	10.19	0.14	50.75	2.43	43.63	1.05
2008–2010	24.85	5.09	13.83[a]	1.92	4.01	0.81	44.15	9.80	38.08	2.50
2011–2013	22.39	5.53	11.52	1.70	2.74	0.09	36.39	2.15	34.89	1.71
2014–2017	14.81	2.29	9.40	1.46	1.85	0.33	29.95	4.21	32.78	4.74

Source: Author's calculations

This table reports descriptive statistics (means and standard deviations—SD) of French co-operative and non-co-operative banking groups. Net customer loans/total assets (%) is the ratio between net loans and assets; Securities/total assets (%) is the ratio between total securities held and total assets; Assets held for trading/total assets (%) is the ratio between total assets held for trading and total assets. Our calculations are based on data extracted from SNL

[a]Only 2009 and 2010

assets destined for trading among co-operative groups. The allocative choices are, however, very different. In the last observation period, the average values range from less than 2% for the Crédit Mutuel Group to a maximum of 14.81% for Crédit Agricole. The reduction in the volume of the securities for both banking business models follows the heavy losses that both suffered between 2007 and 2010. As reported by Howarth (2013), citing Reuters sources (2011), the losses of the top five French banks reached a value of $ 72.4 billion.[68] These losses mainly resulted from CDO/MBS

---

[68] The losses suffered by the French banks were however lower than those of the United States, the United Kingdom, Germany, and other European countries, including the

exposures, exposures to mono-line insurance specializing in the provision of guarantees on securities mostly coming from securitization transactions, and from the default of Lehman Brothers, Iceland and Washington Mutual, as well as from trading activity. Alongside the banks that suffered the greatest losses, the two co-operative groups BPCE and Crédit Agricole were also victims, both through the investment activities carried out by their two companies specializing in market-based activities, Natixis and Calyon (subsequently renamed Crédit Agricole CIB in 2010). Although their losses were lower than those recorded by the two largest commercial banking groups, BNP Paribas and Société Générale, the losses suffered by the two major co-operative groups were surprising. This led Howarth (2013) to affirm that the operational change that had been developing in the co-operative sector in the decade before the GFC, had risen to the surface. Our data show, however, that in the last of the periods examined, the co-operative banks have considerably reduced trading activity, to a greater extent than that observed for shareholder-oriented banks. This seems to mark, at least at first sight, a return to less speculative activity.

If we calculate the impact of the assets held for trading on the total securities held, we find, for example, that the commercial joint-stock banking groups report average values of 62.29% for BNP Paribas (whose average value was 81.80% in 2005–2007) and 67.50% for Société Générale (77.95% in 2005–2007), proving their strong strategic vocation for trading and more marked speculative behavior, in spite of this decreasing. By contrast, for the co-operative groups Crédit Agricole and BPCE, the incidence of assets held for trading is decidedly more contained, respectively, equaling 34.57% (60.9% in 2005–2007) and 37.63% in the period 2014–2017. The corresponding average value recorded by Crédit Mutuel is significantly lower at 6.16%. This is the co-operative group that proves to have maintained over time its focus on traditional lending, while preserving its original vocation for financing local communities, mostly in a retail context.

A third set of selected indicators concerns the incidence of traditional funding activity through customer deposits and the role of interbank activity of French banking groups (Table 5.6). The difference between the two business models in terms of the dependence on funding in the form

Netherlands. In the reconstruction of the loss rates reported by Howarth (2013) the incidence of securities write-downs on total bank assets was 2.6% for the United States, 2% in Germany, 1.8% for the Netherlands, 0.52% for the United Kingdom, and 0.38% in France.

Table 5.6   Comparison of French co-operative groups vs. non-co-operative banking groups: funding and interbank ratios

	Crédit Agricole		BPCE		Crédit Mutuel		BNP Paribas		Société Générale	
	Mean	SD	Mean	SD	Mean	SD	Mean	SD	Mean	SD
Customer deposit/total assets (%)										
2005–2007	32.42	1.37	–	–	32.52	1.34	20.29	0.55	26.62	1.35
2008–2010	33.24	3.30	36.78ᵃ	1.18	37.76	3.36	26.14	5.37	28.03	2.64
2011–2013	35.09	3.10	37.79	2.88	43.64	1.32	29.03	1.72	27.89	0.92
2014–2017	39.36	2.73	42.47	2.71	44.71	1.18	35.50	3.49	29.62	2.48
Interbank ratio (%)										
2005–2007	65.35	7.44	–	–	71.28	12.02	45.17	8.22	50.37	4.06
2008–2010	71.09	16.43	130.95ᵃ	5.72	78.92	15.44	37.96	1.24	73.10	14.64
2011–2013	92.77	12.92	116.02	8.13	119.20	28.26	42.48	14.31	76.22	13.81
2014–2017	101.98	9.75	114.44	11.23	97.88	31.39	54.58	7.15	71.63	8.65

Source: Author's calculations

This table reports descriptive statistics (means and standard deviations—SD) of French co-operative and non-co-operative banking groups. Customer deposit/total assets (%) is the ratio between customer deposits and total assets; interbank ratio (%) is the ratio between loans to banks and deposits from banks. Our calculations are based on data extracted from SNL

ᵃOnly 2009 and 2010

of deposits is once again substantial. All co-operative groups consistently increase the volume of deposits on average terms, demonstrating that they are able to retain high levels of trust among depositors even in times of crisis. Tendentially increasing values are also recorded for the commercial groups. BNP Paribas, for example, experienced significant growth rates, raising its average values from just over 20% in the period 2005–2007 to 35.50% in the period 2014–2017. However, if the percentage of deposits for commercial groups ranges between 30% and 35%, the corresponding values for the co-operative groups are between almost 40% (Crédit Agricole) and around 45% (Crédit Mutuel). Once again, it is the smallest of the three French co-operative groups that stands out for its greater dependence on the most typical bank funding: bank deposits. This bond appears to loosen as banking groups become larger.

As regards participation in the interbank markets, measured by the interbank ratio, the data displayed in Table 5.6 show a mostly increasing trend for both banking business models and clearly indicate the different roles of co-operative and commercial banks in interbank markets: the former are more strongly positioned as fund-givers with ratio values that are close to or even exceed 100% mainly in the most recent periods, while the commercial groups are mostly users of the interbank markets, lending an average of 54.58% (BNP Paribas) and 71.63% (Société Générale) of the interbank funding during 2014–2017. Following the 2008–2010 crisis period, the interbank ratio values of CBs are significantly higher than during the period leading up to the GFC. These values do also account for intra-group transactions, as is typical in co-operative banking.

Table 5.7 presents risk indicators that have assumed particular importance during the GFC, prompting regulators to dictate more stringent prudential rules toward banks' exposure to liquidity risk and credit risk.

Table 5.7 Comparison of French co-operative groups vs. non-co-operative banking groups: liquidity and credit risk ratios

	Crédit Agricole		BPCE		Crédit Mutuel		BNP Paribas		Société Générale	
	Mean	SD	Mean	SD	Mean	SD	Mean	SD	Mean	SD
Liquid assets/total liabilities (%)										
2005–2007	32.31	6.80	–	–	–	–	47.53	1.09	42.44	4.26
2008–2010	14.39	2.70	28.18	0.40	–	–	33.27	2.73	29.92	4.85
2011–2013	18.69	0.60	30.39	2.97	19.77[a]	–	28.05	2.94	35.29	6.08
2014–2017	18.29	3.20	30.86	2.50	20.85	1.44	29.21	1.51	38.16	0.85
Impaired loans/gross loans and advances (%)										
2005–2007	2.86	0.23	–	–	–	–	4.02[b]	–	3.81	0.35
2008–2010	3.49	0.63	3.27	0.71	–	–	5.15	1.25	5.54	1.53
2011–2013	4.00	0.44	3.84	0.20	4.43[a]	–	6.54	0.27	7.26	0.34
2014–2017	3.43	0.25	3.67	0.16	3.92	0.54	5.70	1.27	5.72	0.92
LLR/impaired loans (%)										
2005–2007	101.00	3.30	–	–	–	–	67.90[b]	–	67.40	2.48
2008–2010	85.52	4.56	62.24	9.28	–	–	68.25	6.25	57.88	4.90
2011–2013	81.97	3.00	53.63	1.68	66.06[a]	1.03	61.53	3.04	59.99	1.00
2014–2017	80.77	1.85	52.68	1.00	62.56	1.96	63.90	1.80	62.16	1.02

Source: Author's calculations

This table reports descriptive statistics (means and standard deviations—SD) of French co-operative and non-co-operative banking groups. Liquid assets/total liabilities (%) is the ratio between liquid assets and total liabilities; Impaired loans/gross loans and advances (%) is the ratio between impaired loans and gross customer loans and advances; LLR/impaired loans (%) is the ratio between loan loss reserves and impaired loans. Our calculation on data extracted from BankScope and Orbis Bank Focus for the sole year-ends 2016–2017

[a]Only 2013

[b]Only 2007

The table contains a proxy for exposure to liquidity risk, often used in the empirical literature, and two proxies for credit risk. The use of the ratio of liquid assets to total liabilities (excluding equity) was preferred to the prudential ratios relating to liquidity risk since the latter would have been available only for the last of the periods under investigation. The ratio used looks at the amount of liquid assets available to cover all the liabilities held by banks. The higher this percentage is, the more liquid the bank is and the less vulnerable it is to a classic run on the bank or the more able it is to redeem its own debts.

The data in Table 5.7 show a common trend for co-operative and commercial banks: their average degree of liquidity decreases during the most acute phase of the GFC and then returns to growth. Crédit Agricole and Crédit Mutuel record the lowest ratios throughout the last two subperiods, from 18% to 21%, while BPCE and the two commercial banks tend to have closer values (around 30%), with Société Générale being the most liquid within the group (above 38% during 2014–2017). This is not the case for the ratio of impaired loans to total gross customer loans and advances (%). Table 5.7 reports two proxies: the ratio of impaired loans to gross loans and advances (%) and the ratio of loan loss reserves to impaired loans (%). The first one shows impaired or non-performing loans as a percentage of the bank's gross customer loans and advances (%). It indicates the weakness of the loan portfolio which increases as the percentage rises. The second of the ratios used relates loan loss reserves to non-performing or impaired loans. Higher values of this ratio, also known as the "coverage ratio", indicate that the bank is better equipped to face losses on loans. On the other hand, out of all accounting considerations, higher levels of the coverage rate are generally indicative of a poorer quality loan portfolio. The riskiness of joint-stock banks' credit portfolios grows more rapidly after 2008 and is constantly at values that are on average higher than those of CBs. The latter present an average risk of between 3.4% and 3.9% during 2014–2017 (decreasing from the 2011–2013 period), while for commercial banks the corresponding values stand at around 5.7% in the most recent period (but having substantially decreased since the period from 2011 to 2013). The differences recorded between the two banking business models indicate that although CBs are more exposed to lending (Table 5.5), they are able to activate better debtor selection processes that allow them to contain the riskiness. With regard to the ratio between loss reserves and impaired loans, there are similarities between Crédit Mutuel and the two commercial groups (on average around 60% from 2008 to

2017). Crédit Agricole has the highest coverage ratio over time, at slightly above 80% since 2008, while the BPCE Group has the lowest (an average value of about 53% from 2014 to 2017).

The last battery of indicators that we examine involves variables that are representative of bank profitability and efficiency, widely employed in the empirical literature. With regard to the profitability analysis, three indicators are taken into consideration: the net interest margin (%); the return on average assets (ROAA) (%); and the return on average equity (ROAE) (%). To evaluate the operational efficiency achieved by the bank management, we use a widespread indicator: the cost-to-income ratio (%) (Table 5.8).

Table 5.8 Comparison of French co-operative groups vs. non-co-operative banking groups: profitability and efficiency ratios

	Crédit Agricole		BPCE		Crédit Mutuel		BNP Paribas		Société Générale	
	Mean	SD	Mean	SD	Mean	SD	Mean	SD	Mean	SD
Net interest margin (%)										
2005–2007	1.20	0.24	–	–	0.65	0.16	0.70	0.04	0.32	0.07
2008–2010	1.30	0.11	1.18	0.24	1.19	0.40	1.04	0.26	1.03	0.21
2011–2013	1.30	0.10	1.10	0.12	1.24	0.15	1.14	0.12	0.80	0.21
2014–2017	1.20	0.03	0.98	0.07	1.00	0.08	0.81	0.02	0.47	0.05
ROAA (%)										
2005–2007	0.52	0.10	–	–	0.60	0.08	0.55	0.03	0.40	0.34
2008–2010	0.20	0.03	0.05	0.32	0.31	0.22	0.32	0.14	0.25	0.15
2011–2013	0.05	0.24	0.25	0.04	0.38	0.04	0.32	0.05	0.18	0.07
2014–2017	0.34	0.05	0.32	0.04	0.42	0.03	0.28	0.28	0.22	0.08
ROAE (%)										
2005–2007	11.28	2.11	–	–	12.10	1.72	15.02	0.66	12.02	9.99
2008–2010	4.63	0.65	0.10	7.90	5.97	3.94	8.72	2.65	6.34	3.35
2011–2013	1.22	5.90	5.32	0.71	6.47	0.37	7.06	1.19	4.46	2.16
2014–2017	6.16	0.75	5.88	0.66	6.57	0.48	6.04	5.91	5.66	2.63
Cost to income (%)										
2005–2007	61.39	2.38	–	–	60.58	1.95	59.57	0.21	62.76	1.97
2008–2010	66.62	3.29	86.16	18.38	65.28	7.61	60.26	3.74	67.48	1.80
2011–2013	61.19	5.29	68.93	2.14	64.72	1.81	64.84	1.42	70.86	4.21
2014–2017	63.73	2.58	68.93	1.66	63.65	0.42	67.36	7.12	71.45	8.44

Source: Author's calculations

This table shows descriptive statistics (means and standard deviations—SD) of French co-operative and non-co-operative banking groups. Net interest margin (%) is the ratio between net interest income and total earning assets; ROAA (%) is the return on average assets; ROAE (%) is the return on average equity; Cost to income (%) is the ratio between operating expenses and intermediation margin. Our calculation on data extracted from BankScope and Orbis Bank Focus for the sole year-ends 2016–2017

The net interest margin (%) represents the profitability arising from the bank's credit intermediation activity. It is expressed as the percentage of net interest income to earning assets. Less diversified banks generally enjoy higher net interest margins. Higher values of the ratio may be indicative of cost advantages in the funding or may derive from the exploitation of strong market power positions. In the periods analyzed, especially from 2005 to 2017, it is generally higher among co-operative banking groups, consistent with their stronger focus on traditional banking activity. In the last period, the results achieved decrease uniformly, also due to the prolonged effect of the low interest rate regime. It seems to produce similar levels of performance in the long run. The group that has performed best is Crédit Agricole, with the sole exception being during the period 2014–2017. The ROAA (%) of the co-operative model is generally higher than that of the commercial banks but only in the pre-crisis period and during 2014–2017. In the intermediate years (2008–2013), shareholder-oriented banks fare slightly better than CBs. However, Crédit Mutuel achieves superior results to the remaining co-operative and non-co-operative groups. Crédit Agricole, despite having positive results, performed worse than the other co-operative and non-co-operative groups over the period 2011–2013. In 2012, the group adopted structuring measures which led to the disposal of non-core businesses (as e.g. the Greek subsidiary Emporiki and their stake in the Italian bank IntesaSanpaolo) and the consequent recognition of loan losses (including those related to the disposal of some investment portfolios held by the corporate and investment banking arm).[69]

If, however, attention is focused on ROAE (%), it can be seen that joint-stock banks are able to obtain better results over time, at least up until the last period analyzed. These banks operate, however, with a lower level of capitalization than those of co-operative banks, as reported in Table 5.4. During the period 2014–2017, the results of the various groups are mostly homogeneous and positively close to average values of 6%. Once again, it is worth mentioning the good performance of Crédit Mutuel which records the highest and most consistent values among the co-operative groups over time.

It is often argued in the literature that the co-operative model is less efficient because the governance of these banks is immune to the *stimuli* of market discipline. However, observation of the cost-to-income ratio

---

[69] See the Annual Report of Crédit Agricole Group for the year-end 2012.

(%) shown in Table 5.8 does not allow us to support this above hypothesis at first sight. Excluding the BPCE group, which was emerging from a complex merger operation in 2009 and probably facing problems with rationalizing the two networks that form it, we find instead that on average the co-operative groups achieve slightly better efficiency levels than those of the commercial banks.

In order to verify whether there are significant differences between the two banking business models, the non-parametric Wilcoxon-Mann-Whitney (WMW) (1947) test[70] is used. This is suitable for small sample sizes and for testing whether observations in one population tend to be larger than observations in the other as it tests the equality of central tendency of two distributions (Fay and Proschan 2010). The selected indicators are subjected to the test for the period 2008–2017 only. It was decided to concentrate the analysis on this ten-year period, because we want to check whether, and if so, how the manifestation of the episodes of crisis and the start of the Banking Union in 2014, have affected the performance of the two business models, and whether this makes them more similar or not. The result of the test with the relative *p*-values are reported in Table 5.9.

The two business models show significant differences in the results they have achieved, as evidenced by the *p*-values obtained. The capitalization of the co-operative groups is significantly higher, and their asset and funding mix is significantly different. They devote more attention to credit to the real economy and, as a result, are less active on financial markets, including through their central institutions. Funding is more oriented toward deposits from customers and this seems to imply these banks' sound ability to establish relationships of trust with savers (both thanks to the guarantee mechanisms they have been using for many years, and to their natural inclination toward relationship banking). Also, in terms of the role they play in interbank banking, the CBs' clear and significantly different position is evident. They are active givers on the interbank and this puts them in a position of extreme importance for the banking system as a whole. As regards exposure to risks, co-operative groups result less liquid but with substantial lower credit risk, as proxied by the ratio of impaired loans to gross customer loans and advances (%). This seems to somehow support CBs' greater ability to achieve lower levels of risk, although their credit commitment is more sustained. In terms of both profitability and efficiency, significant differences between the two business models are found only with regard to the net interest margin (%).

---

[70] This test is also known as Wilcoxon ranksum test or Mann-Whitney U test.

Table 5.9   Wilcoxon-Mann-Whitney test (2008–2017)

Co-operative vs. non-co-operative banks

	Median	P-value
Capital ratios		
Tier 1 (%)	13.33–12.35	0.02
Equity/total assets (%)	5.29–4.08	0.00
Lending, securities holdings ratios		
Net customer loans/total assets (%)	51.63–33.74	0.00
Securities/total assets (%)	29.43–51.00	0.00
Total assets held for trading/total assets (%)	10.65–35.86	0.00
Funding and interbank ratios		
Customer deposit/total assets (%)	39.46–29.12	0.00
Interbank ratio (%)	100.23–60.48	0.00
Liquidity and credit risk ratios		
Liquid assets/total liabilities (%)	19.01–31.67	0.00
Impaired loans/gross customer loans and advances (%)	3.70–6.17	0.00
LLR/impaired loans (%)	64.16–62.58	0.40
Profitability and efficiency ratios		
Net interest margin (%)	1.17–0.83	0.00
ROAA (%)	0.31–0.27	0.25
ROAE (%)	6.07–6.45	0.37
Cost to income (%)	64.39–66.48	0.31

Source: Author's calculations

6   THE PERFORMANCES OF FRENCH CO-OPERATIVE BANKING NETWORKS AND THEIR CENTRAL INSTITUTIONS

To what degree do the performances of the central institutions of co-operative banking networks and the networks of CBs themselves differ? To answer this question, we examine some of the performance indicators analyzed in the previous paragraph, comparing the results achieved by central institutions with those of their networks of CBs, as in Ory and Lemzeri (2012). To this end, the consolidated data relating to each central institution and its subsidiaries were extracted from the databases previously mentioned; similar data were calculated for the networks of CBs alone. We calculated average values of the selected indicators for the network formed by CBs. Data on the networks of CBs refer to regional banks in consolidated form. The data obtained cover a large proportion of the CBs included in each of the French co-operative banking groups.[71] To minimize the effect of missing data on our analysis, especially before 2008, we chose to limit our analysis to the period 2008–2017 and to restrict our scrutiny to some of the indicators previously examined. These are: the equity to total assets (%); the net customer loans to total assets (%); the impaired loans to gross customer loans and advances (%; the customer deposits to total assets [%]); the ROAA (%); and the cost to income ratio (%). For each of these, we replicate the analysis reported in the previous paragraph by calculating averages of results over the sub-periods 2008–2010, 2011–2013, and 2014–2017. Figures are reported in Table 5.10.

As regards the first indicator, the ratio between equity and total assets (%), the data in Table 5.10 show that the two largest networks of CBs, those of Crédit Agricole and BPCE, are better capitalized than their

---

[71] The sample of CBs from the Crédit Agricole Group comprises: Crédit Agricole Alsace Vosges, Crédit Agricole Alpes Provence, Crédit Agricole de l'Anjou et du Maine, Crédit Agricole d'Aquitaine, Crédit Agricole Atlantique Vendée, Crédit Agricole Brie Picardie, Crédit Agricole Centre France, Crédit Agricole Centre Loire, Crédit Agricole Centre-Est, Crédit Agricole Champagne-Bourgogne, Crédit Agricole de Charente Maritime Deux-Sèvres, Crédit Agricole de Normandie, Crédit Agricole des Savoie, Crédit Agricole du Finistère, Crédit Agricole de Franche-Comté, Crédit Agricole d'Ille-et-Vilaine, Crédit Agricole du Languedoc, Crédit Agricole de Loire Haute-Loire, Crédit Agricole de Lorraine, Crédit Agricole du Morbihan, Crédit Agricole Nord de France, Crédit Agricole Nord Est, Crédit Agricole Nord Midi-Pyrénées, Crédit Agricole Normandie-Seine, Crédit Agricole de Paris et d'Ile-de-France, Crédit Agricole Provence Côte d'Azur, Crédit Agricole de Pyrénées Gascogne, Crédit Agricole Sud Rhône Alpes, Crédit Agricole Toulouse 31, Crédit Agricole Touraine Poitou.

The sample of CBs from the BPCE Group comprises Banque Populaire Alsace Lorraine Champagne, Banque Populaire Auvergne Rhône Alpes, Banque Populaire Bourgogne Franche-Comté, Banque Populaire du Sud, Banque Populaire Grand Ouest, Banque Populaire Occitane, Banque Populaire Rives de Paris, Banque Populaire Val de France, BRED, Casden Banque Populaire, Crédit Coopératif, Caisse d'Epargne et de Prévoyance Aquitaine Poitou-Charentes, Caisse d'Epargne et de Prévoyance de Bourgogne Franche-Comté, Caisse d'Epargne et de Prévoyance Hauts de France, Caisse d'Epargne et de Prévoyance Loire Drôme Ardèche, Caisse d'Epargne et de Prévoyance Bretagne Pays de Loire, Caisse d'Epargne et de Prévoyance Côte d'Azur, Caisse d'Épargne et de Prévoyance de Midi-Pyrénées, Caisse d'Épargne et de Prévoyance de Rhône Alpes, Caisse d'Epargne et de Prévoyance du Languedoc-Roussillon, Caisse d'Epargne et de Prévoyance Grand Est Europe, Caisse d'Epargne et de Prévoyance Ile-de-France, Caisse d'Épargne et de Prévoyance Loire-Centre, Caisse d'Epargne et de Prévoyance Provence-Alpes-Corse.

The sample of CBs from the Crédit Mutuel Group comprises: Caisse Fédérale de Crédit Mutuel, Caisse Fédérale du Crédit Mutuel de Maine-Anjou et Basse-Normandie, Caisse Fédérale du Crédit Mutuel Nord Europe, Caisse Fédérale du Crédit Mutuel Océan, Crédit Mutuel Arkéa.

Table 5.10 Comparison of French co-operative central institutions and their networks of CBs in terms of capital, lending, funding and credit risk exposure

	Crédit Agricole–Central institution		Crédit Agricole–Network CBs		BPCE–Central institution		BPCE–Network CBs		Crédit Mutuel–Central institution		Crédit Mutuel–Network CBs	
	Mean	SD	Mean	SD	Mean	SD	Mean	SD	Mean	SD	Mean	SD
Equity/total assets (%)												
2008–2010	3.16	0.26	11.28	1.60	4.45	0.37	8.78	2.07	3.74	1.75	7.46	3.36
2011–2013	2.81	0.33	12.11	1.69	3.75	0.26	9.02	2.48	7.79	0.74	7.88	3.48
2014–2017	3.95	0.31	13.57	1.57	3.60	0.16	9.34	1.77	11.12	1.31	8.58	3.82
Net customer loans/total assets (%)												
2008–2010	22.86	1.49	81.23	4.03	27.93	11.20	57.10	14.69	0.10	0.02	53.43	12.14
2011–2013	20.25	2.70	77.00	4.59	30.59	0.64	61.75	12.38	0.05	0.05	54.76	12.85
2014–2017	21.89	1.55	75.79	2.41	31.92	1.62	66.35	10.30	0.00	0.00	53.90	13.94
Customer deposits/total assets (%)												
2008–2010	28.92	3.08	23.99	4.54	10.03	0.61	56.90	8.49	0.14	0.08	42.94	12.37
2011–2013	29.43	2.80	26.88	5.18	9.38	1.73	60.06	7.56	0.38	0.05	46.51	10.31
2014–2017	33.54	2.51	28.63	4.13	12.58	2.33	65.85	6.89	0.34	0.07	48.75	10.67
Impaired loans/gross loans and advances (%)												
2008–2010	–	–	2.02	1.60	4.46[a]	1.49	3.16	2.01	–	–	3.10	0.93
2011–2013	5.64	0.88	2.93	1.25	4.62	0.63	3.82	2.07	–	–	3.47	1.42
2014–2017	4.58	0.30	2.94	1.26	4.51	0.14	3.82	1.86	–	–	3.61	1.38

This table reports descriptive statistics (means and standard deviations—SD) of French co-operative banking networks and their central institutions. Equity/total assets (%) is the ratio between total equity and total assets; Net customer loans/total assets (%) is the ratio between net loans and total year-end assets; Customer deposits/total assets (%) is the ratio between customer deposits and total assets; Impaired loans/gross loans and advances (%) is the ratio between impaired loans and gross customer loans and advances. Our calculations of the ratios Equity/total assets (%), Net customer loans/total assets (%) and Customer deposits/total assets (%) are based on data extracted from SNL. Our calculations of the ratio Impaired Loans/Gross Customer Loans are based on data extracted from BankScope and Orbis Bank Focus solely for the year-ends 2016–2017

[a]Only 2009–2010

respective apexes. In 2014–2017, Crédit Agricole's network registered the highest average value of the indicator at 13.57%, compared to 3.95% for its apex. This differential has increased over time. In the case of the BPCE group, the network holds an average value of 9.34% for the same period, while the apex records 3.60%, consequently being slightly less capitalized than the central institution of Crédit Agricole. For BPCE, the differential between the values recorded by the network and the apex has also increased over time, in favor of the former. However, the difference is more contained, being about half that recorded for Crédit Agricole. For the Crédit Mutuel group, we observe values close to 8.60% from 2014 to 2017 for the network of CBs, while its financial hub, CCCM, is better capitalized. It is worth pointing out that, as already explained in the pages dedicated to the Crédit Mutuel group, the latter has the Confédération Nationale du Crédit Mutuel as its central body, while its financial arm is CCCM. The values shown in Table 5.10 refer to the Caisse Centrale which, unlike the other central institutions, does not wield any administrative power over the network as a whole. As we will see, the different role of the financial apex of the Crédit Mutuel group brings with it a series of elements which differentiate it from the other apexes: it is not active in granting lending to customers and does not collect deposits from customers.

As is reasonable to expect, networks are more involved in lending activity, in keeping with the specialization of activities common in well-integrated, strategic networks (Table 5.10). Crédit Agricole's network is the most focused on lending to customers. Over the last period, about 76% of the assets held are allocated to net loans to customers. BPCE and Crédit Mutuel rank respectively second and third, with almost 66% and 54%. Of the three networks, only that of BPCE follows a growing trend over time. The lending of the central institutions of Crédit Agricole and BPCE is much less intense (respectively, almost 22% and 32% over the period 2014–2017). Since these are central institutions that control and consolidate companies operating in specialized credit segments (e.g. corporate banking, leasing), it is not unusual for lending to have some impact on their assets. However, it is clear that a large part of the financial investments made by the central institutions is invested in securities. The CBs therefore delegate to the apex the role of carrying out the diversification of the overall resources of the groups, albeit to a lesser extent than that found in the non-co-operative banking groups. Specialization also becomes evident when looking at the funding mix of the apex and its network of CBs and, in particular, at the impact of customer deposits on total assets (%)

(Table 5.10). The BPCE networks and, to a lesser extent Crédit Mutuel, finance their lending to customers, especially through deposits, demonstrating a customer deposits to total assets ratio of close to 66% and 49%, respectively. The case of Crédit Agricole is different. The average percentage value of customer deposits collected by the network is very close to that of the apex (nearly 30%), especially between 2011 and 2013. In the remaining period 2009–2011, the apex and its subsidiaries (which include foreign banks) succeed in achieving higher ratios than regional banks (about 34% and 29% respectively, in the most recent sub-period).[72]

From a comparative analysis of the levels and trends of credit risk, approximated by the ratio between impaired loans to gross loans to customers and advances (%) (Table 5.10), two phenomena emerge. In the first instance, apexes turn out to be consistently riskier than their networks of CBs. The differentials have been significantly decreasing over time for Crédit Agricole, partly due to the disposal of loss-making foreign assets. Reductions have also been observed in the BPCE group, but the differentials are on average smaller between the apex and its network than in the case of Crédit Agricole. Since 2014, the exposure to credit risk of the Crédit Agricole and BPCE apexes has been decreasing, but it is the former that records the highest average value at 4.58%, against 4.51% in 2014–2017. The variations in riskiness exhibited by the networks compared to their apexes are more pronounced. Among the three co-operative groups, the networks of Crédit Agricole and Crédit Mutuel show the lowest levels of volatility, proxied by their standard deviations.

Crédit Agricole's network of CBs, with the highest net loans to assets ratio (%), achieves the lowest levels of risk with an average of 2.94% in the last sub-period, and over the whole period 2008–2017. This indicates that a high credit exposure, such as that recorded by the Crédit Agricole network, should not be immediately associated with higher levels of risk. Close proximity with the debtors and the territories served favor more effective screening and monitoring of the risks assumed. The last two indicators examined concern the profitability and efficiency of the organizations under investigation. For these purposes, ROAA (%) and cost to income ratio (%) were selected. The values of the first, shown in Table 5.11, provide evidence once again of the superior ability of the networks to

---

[72] It is worth mentioning that regional banks' customer deposits account for about 56% of the total group's due to customers at the end of 2017. Own calculations on data reported in the Crédit Agricole's Financial Report for the year-end 2017.

Table 5.11 Comparison of French co-operative central institutions and their networks of CBs in terms of profitability and operational efficiency

	Crédit Agricole– Central institution		Crédit Agricole– Network CBs		BPCE– Central institution		BPCE– Network CBs		Crédit Mutuel– Central institution		Crédit Mutuel– Network CBs	
	Mean	SD	Mean	SD	Mean	SD	Mean	SD	Mean	SD	Mean	SD
ROAA (%)												
2008–2010	0.09	0.01	0.78	0.17	−0.05	0.34	0.37	0.17	0.19	0.12	0.28	0.21
2011–2013	−0.31	0.45	0.67	0.25	0.18	0.10	0.32	0.16	0.35	0.05	0.40	0.12
2014–2017	1.13	1.07	0.72	0.15	0.20	0.06	0.43	0.11	0.81	1.14	0.48	0.17
Cost to income (%)												
2008–2010	67.39	4.37	55.02	5.55	71.97	9.04	70.37	9.99	24.91	6.52	70.47	9.97
2011–2013	62.88	9.13	55.40	5.49	68.15	3.76	66.94	8.03	25.03	9.16	66.68	6.43
2014–2017	65.38	3.39	56.54	4.51	73.18	1.66	64.53	5.69	25.78	5.02	64.28	5.93

This table reports descriptive statistics (means and standard deviations—SD) of French co-operative banking networks and their central institutions. ROAA (%) is the return on average assets; ROAE (%) is the return on average equity; Cost to income (%) is the ratio between operating expenses and intermediation margin. Our calculations are based on data extracted from SNL

generate an average profitability that is higher than that of their apexes, except in the last sub-period. This result is indicative of the value of networks of CBs within their reference groups, especially in difficult times. Furthermore, once again it is worth noting that the higher profitability of the networks is associated with the significantly lower volatility of the results obtained, at least for Crédit Agricole and Crédit Mutuel.

Finally, the cost to income figures shown in Table 5.11, offer us further interesting insights. Both in the case of Crédit Agricole and BPCE, the networks are on average more efficient than their apexes throughout the period of analysis. This seems to indicate that the outsourcing of the complementary and peripheral functions of the CBs to the apex determines, in the two cases in question, organizational costs that are transferred to the apex. This does not apply to the Crédit Mutuel group because the central institution in this case is purely financial in nature, and does not carry out other activities. In fact, its cost to income ratio is on average significantly lower than the corresponding value for the network. Of all the networks, Crédit Agricole is the most efficient (almost 57% in 2017), followed by Crédit Mutuel and BPCE with similar values (64.28% and 64.53% respectively in 2014–2017).

Overall, it seems therefore possible to affirm from the significant results obtained that the networks of the French CBs assume a strategic value that persists over time. The expansion of the delegation of powers to central entities with strategic, coordination, and control functions appears to have a positive effect on their performance over time. And this allows them to continue to propose themselves as an essential channel of financial and social inclusion, as well as an engine for economic development. The complexity and diversification of the French co-operative groups also testifies to the vocation of CBs to test out organizational solutions that enhance their ability to serve their communities, reconciling their social vision of the economy with the contingencies created by the dominance of the market economy paradigm.

7   Conclusion

The modernization of the French banking system started in the mid-1980s with the enactment of a new Banking Law and the start of an extensive divesture program of state-owned banks which culminated in 2002 with the divestiture of Credit Lyonnais' shares. Currently, three co-operative banking networks co-exist: Crédit Agricole, Banque Populaire-Caisse d'Epargne (BPCE), and Crédit Mutuel. These compete with conventional joint-stock companies like BNP Paribas and Société Générale. With a combined total of 26.6 million members at the end of 2017, France rates as the most co-operative bank-oriented system in Europe. In spite of this concern, co-operative banking in France plays a key role which has been consolidated over time. Of all the European countries where this business model took root in the nineteenth century and went on to grow, France is the one where CBs enjoy the highest market shares. At the end of 2017, the three networks jointly held 62.6% of the domestic market share of deposits and 59.8% of customer loans. Among the three networks, Crédit Agricole is the leader, although its market power has been weakened over time by competition, despite maintaining its position in the aftermath of the financial crisis. The BPCE network that resulted from the state-supported merger between Banque Populaire and Caisse d'Epargne in 2009 is the second largest co-operative network. Crédit Mutuel, the third co-operative network, holds market shares not dissimilar to those held by the first two, especially on the lending side, thus indicating quite balanced domestic competition among the co-operative networks in spite of their different sizes.

The three French co-operatives' networks are organized as "inverted banking groups" with a central body. These groups adopt hybrid structures whereby a network of credit institutions, namely CBs, are affiliated to a central body which is totally or largely under the control of the affiliated banks. The latter are not formally controlled via the central body holding equity stakes, but via affiliation agreements which assure several powers to the central body, ranging from supervision to the management of affiliates. French co-operative groups are integrated co-operative networks under the provisions of Art. 113(6) of the CRR, as transposed into the French Monetary and Financial Code. The central institution is empowered to take all necessary measures to ensure the liquidity and solvency of all affiliated institutions and of the network as a whole on the basis of the consolidated accounts of these institutions. It is authorized to issue instructions to the management of the affiliated institutions on managerial and internal control-related issues.

In addition to analyzing the role and organization of co-operative networks in France, the chapter offers two empirical investigations, respectively aimed to verify empirically the effects of the ongoing hybridization in co-operative banking, and to assess to what degree the performances of the central institutions of co-operative banking networks and the networks of CBs themselves differ. Regarding the first of the two areas of analysis, the data show that overall, in the period 2008–2017, the two business models exhibit significant differences in the results they have achieved. The capitalization of the co-operative strategic networks is significantly higher, and their asset and funding mix is significantly different from that of shareholder-oriented banking groups. They devote more attention to credit to the real economy and, as a result, are less active on financial markets, including through their central institutions. Funding is more oriented toward deposits from customers and this seems to imply these banks' sound ability to establish relationships of trust with savers and to their natural inclination toward relationship banking. As regards exposure to risks, co-operative groups result less liquid but with substantial lower credit risk, as proxied by the ratio of impaired loans to gross customer loans and advances (%). In terms of both profitability and efficiency, significant differences between the two business models are found only with regard to the net interest margin (%).

With reference to the second area of investigation, the average values of the individual CBs that are part of the networks show values of capitalization higher than those of its central institutions. There is high specialization in the activity of credit intermediation, with a large share of assets and liabilities respectively occupied by loans to customers and deposits. In the first instance, apexes turn out to be consistently riskier than their networks of CBs. The differentials have been significantly decreasing over time for Crédit Agricole, partly due to the disposal of loss-making foreign assets.

As regards the indicators of profitability and operating efficiency, the data provide evidence once again of the superior ability of the networks to generate an average profitability that is higher than that of their apexes, except in the last sub-period. Both in the case of Crédit Agricole and BPCE, the networks are on average more efficient than their apexes throughout the period of analysis. This seems to indicate that the outsourcing of the complementary and peripheral functions of the CBs to the apex determines, in the two cases in question, organizational costs that are transferred to the apex. Overall, it seems therefore possible to affirm from the significant results obtained that the networks of the French CBs assume a strategic value that persists over time.

References

Albert, E. (1997). *Les Banques Populaires en France (1917–1973)*. Paris: Ed. Economica.

Barsan, I. M. (2010). French Authorities' Reactions in the Wake of the Crisis. *European Business Organization Law Review, 11*(4, December), 549–574.

Butzbach, O. (2015). From Thrifts to Universal Banks: The Sources of Organisational Change in French Savings Banks (1945–2000). *Business History, 57*(8), 1155–1191.

Crédit Agricole. (2017). *Annual Report for the Year-End 2017*.

De Angeli, S. (2008). Francia. In S. De Angeli (Ed.), *Il credito cooperativo in alcune significative realtà straniere*. Milano: Vita e Pensiero.

European Association of Co-operative Banks (EACB). (2012). *The Process for the Redemption of Shares in Co-operative Banks in Different EU Member States. A Comparative Overview*. Brussels.

European Association of Co-operative Banks (EACB). *Key Statistics*, Various Years.

European Central Bank (ECB). (2017, October). *Report on Financial Structures*.

Fay, M. P., & Proschan, M. A. (2010). Wilcoxon-Mann-Whitney or T-Test? On Assumptions for Hypothesis Tests and Multiple Interpretations of Decision Rules. *Statistics Surveys, 4*, 1.

Giannola, A. (1990). *Le grandi banche in Europa*. Napoli: Guida Editori.

Hardie, I., & Howarth, D. (2009). Die Krise but Not La Crise? The Financial Crisis and the Transformation of German and French Banking Systems. *Journal of Common Market Studies, 47*(5), 1017–1039.

Howarth, D. (2013). State Intervention and Market-Based Banking in France. In J. Hardie & D. Howarth (Eds.), *Market-Based Banking and the International Financial Crisis*. Oxford University Press.

Mann, H. B., & Whitney, D. R. (1947). On a Test of Whether One of Two Random Variables Is Stochastically Larger than the Other. *Annals of Mathematical Statistics, 18*(1), 50–60.

Marchetti, P., & Sabetta, A. (2010). The Cooperative Banking System in France. In V. Boscia, A. Carretta, & P. Schwizer (Eds.), *Cooperative Banking in Europe. Case Studies*. Palgrave Macmillan.

Morin, F. (2000). A Transformation in the French Model of Shareholding and Management. *Economy and Society, 29*(1), 36–53.

Moulévrier, P. (2002). *Le mutualisme bancaire. Le Crédit mutuel, de l'Église au marché*. Presses universitaires de Rennes.

Moulévrier, P., & Suaud, C. (2014). The Crédit Mutuel and Its Institutionalised and Strategic Uses of Its Past. *Sociologies Pratiques, 29*(2), 73–82.

Ory, J., & And Lemzeri, Y. (2012). Efficiency and Hybridization in Cooperative Banking: The French Case. *Annals of Public and Cooperative Economics, 83*(2), 215–250.

Ory, J., Gurtner, E., & Jaeger, M. (2006, July). *The Challenges of Recent Changes in French Cooperative Banking Groups*. RECMA—Revue Internationale de l'Économie Sociale, 301.

Ory, J., De Serres, A., & Jaeger, M. (2013). Comment resister à l'effet de normalization: le défi des banques cooperatives. *La Revue des Sciences de Gestion, 258*, 69–82.

Richez-Battesti, N., & Leseul, G. (2016). Cooperative Banks in France: Emergence, Mutations and Issues. In S. Karafolas (Ed.), *Credit Cooperative Institutions in European Countries*. Springer.

Woll, C. (2014). *The Power of Inaction: Bank Bailouts in Comparison*. Cornell University Press.

CHAPTER 6

Co-operative Banking in Germany

1 Brief Overview of the German Banking System

The German banking sector has historically been structured around the so-called three pillars. The first is formed by the commercial banking sector and foreign banks which collectively hold a market share of 40%[1]: the main players are commercial, listed banks such as the two German banks, Deutsche Bank and Commerzbank, and the foreign banks, Unicredit, ING, and Santander.[2] Each holds an individual market share of less than 10%. CBs form part of the second pillar. These are privately owned banks, which make up the Volksbanken/Raiffeisen Banks Financial Network (Bundesverband der Deutschen Volksbanken und Raiffeisenbanken— BVR), which at the end of 2017 consisted of a central institution (the former Deutsche Zentral-genossenschaftskasse, now known as DZ Bank and its Group) and 915 local CBs (972 in 2016).[3] BVR is one of the three largest groups in Germany, along with Deutsche Bank, and the savings banks which comprise it share the common characteristic of being decentralized in nature. CBs' market share amounted to 25% of private households' deposits as at the 2017 year-end (24% in 2016). Its business is

---

[1] Market share according to the deposits of private households as reported in DZ Bank's corporate presentation for the year 2017.
[2] Ibidem.
[3] Ibidem.

© The Author(s) 2019
F. Poli, *Co-operative Banking Networks in Europe*, Palgrave Macmillan Studies in Banking and Financial Institutions,
https://doi.org/10.1007/978-3-030-21699-3_6

predominantly focused on the domestic retail, and small- and medium-sized enterprises (SMEs) banking markets, with selected niche activities abroad through its central bank and specialized product providers. Germany's CBs are legally independent and spread across the entire country. They have also established strong market positions in non-bank financial services through specialized sector entities. The various services offered by DZ Bank's subsidiaries comprise insurance, home savings plans, consumer loans, residential and commercial real estate finance, public-sector financing, private banking, mutual funds, and leasing. The third pillar has a public mandate and in 2017 encompassed six Landesbanks groups,[4]

[4] Landesbanks are primarily owned by Germany's Federal States and by savings banks based in their respective federal states. The first Landesbanks were established in the mid-nineteenth century in various federal states. They primarily acted as central banks for the savings banks of a given region and soon became an important provider of local government financing. They are particularly active in the municipal loan and mortgage lending business, which they refinance through Pfandbriefe (covered bonds) or via municipal bonds. They engage mostly in wholesale activities and are active both in Germany and abroad. Landesbanks have retained their regional roots and operate as service providers for savings banks in more complex product areas. There is co-operation between Landesbanks and savings banks in the joint lending to medium-large sized companies and in real estate financing. Landesbanks did not undertake retail banking in the past, but this is now offered by many Landesbanks, partly through subsidiaries. Former savings banks were founded by citizens in the eighteenth century, a set-up reminiscent of private foundations. Later, they were predominantly founded as municipal entities. This legal structure was replaced in the 1930s, with savings banks becoming incorporated under public law—that is, becoming legally and economically independent institutions, eliminating third party interests. Savings banks act as independent and decentralized banks and serve a clearly identified administrative region of the municipality or district in which they were founded. The regional principle is laid down by law and is aimed to incentivize savings banks to operate very close to the market, balancing risks carefully and taking a long-term perspective with their clients and the community as a whole. Savings banks and Landesbanks are part of the Savings Banks Finance Group which is Germany's biggest banking group. The network also comprises specialized entities in real estate financing, public-sector insurance companies, leasing, factoring, capital investment, and consulting companies, and service enterprises, for example, in the fields of IT, securities settlement, and payment transactions. Documentation on the structure and mission of the Savings Banks Finance Group can be found at https://www.dsgv.de/en/savings-banks-finance-group/index.html.

DekaBank,[5] and 390 independent local savings banks[6] (393 in 2016)[7] forming the Savings Banks Finance Group (Deutscher Sparkassen-und Giroverband—DSGV). Its collective market share stands at 36% of the deposits from private households, making it Germany's biggest banking network.

Within the national financial system, German banks play a substantial, although decreasing, role. At the end of 2016, the ratio of Monetary Financial Institutions' (MFIs) total assets to national GDP stood at 2.6 (3.2 in the Netherlands, 3.7 in France, 2.3 in Italy, and 2.4 in Spain) as compared to 3.9 in 2008; while the percentage of assets held by MFIs as a proportion of the total assets of the financial sector equaled 61.1% (22.2% in the Netherlands, 63.5% in France, 63.8% in Italy and 67.2% in Spain) (ECB 2017).[8] Germany embraces a universal banking system, with a huge number of banks and a variety of business models. Domestic banks dominate the industry with a virtually unchanging 86% share (in 2016) of total banking assets; 11.9% are held by foreign subsidiaries and branches, mostly from other European countries (ECB 2017), while the remainder is attributable to the rest of the world. Foreign bank intermediation in Germany is following a growing trend which is largely explained by the attractiveness of the German economy which performed comparatively well following the onset of the international financial crisis. It is noteworthy that in 2008 EU foreign subsidiaries accounted for just 2.2% of total banking assets as compared to 7.9% at the end of 2016.

The domestic banking sector has an important but slightly declining role in the financing of non-financial companies (NFCs) which rely heavily on domestic banks. At the end of 2016, the total financing provided by

[5] DekaBank originated from the merger of Deutsche Kapitalanlagegesellschaft (formerly active in investment advisory services and fund-based asset management) and Deutsche Girozentrale, DGZ (German Savings Banks Clearinghouse, founded in 1918) in 1999. Its capital is totally owned by savings banks. It acts as the reference bank for investment banking, asset management services and financing for savings banks, Landesbanks, and customers not belonging to the Savings Banks Finance Group. See DekaBank history at https://www.deka.de/deka-group/about-us/history.

[6] Local savings banks are affiliated with the public bodies governing the local area in which they operate and to which they are by law also restricted in their activity. As reported by Behr and Schmidt (2015), local authorities are not the owners in a legal sense but rather owner-like supporting institutions with certain property rights and obligations. The profits of savings banks are for the most part allocated as reserves or used for various public welfare projects. Local savings banks are independent legal entities.

[7] Data reported in DZ Bank's corporate presentation for the year 2017.

[8] These two indicators were equal to 3.6 and 70.2% respectively in 2008 (ECB 2017).

the domestic financial sector amounted to € 1069.3 billion, almost 76% of which was granted by MFIs, mainly banks. The corresponding value in 2014 was 79% with Other Financial Intermediaries (OFIs) (excluding insurance companies and pension funds) gaining market share over time (19% in 2016 versus 16.5% in 2014). In parallel, financing granted by MFIs to NFCs in other countries of the Eurozone totaled € 144.2 billion in 2016, following an increasing trend (€ 126.6 billion in 2014) with lending to foreign NFCs representing 15.1% of the total financing to NFCs (an increase from 13.8% in 2014).

The German banking sector is currently undergoing a process of consolidation. Over the course of 2017, the overall number of credit institutions fell to 1653, continuing the unambiguous downward trend that has prevailed since 2000 (Table 6.1). By 2017 this corresponded to a total decline of 40%. A parallel decline can be seen in the number of branches across the country. After an increase in branches between 2000 and 2004, the numbers since have been constantly dropping, totaling 30,072 units at the end of 2017. Competitive pressures arising from existing and new competitors (e.g. fintech) and customers' growing use of remote banking services have been the forces driving the rationalization of the branch network which comprises a variety of bank business models. Among these, co-operative banking holds the largest share: 55.5% of the total number of banks in 2017, having shrunk from 64.9% in 2000. In 2016, the number of institutions in the co-operative banking sector dropped below 1000 for the first time and, at the end of 2017, stood at 918.[9] Most of the decrease in the number of CBs across the country is due to mergers within the sector. Savings and commercial banks have experienced less significant reductions.

In terms of branches, CBs hold 31.4% of the total, which is similar in percentage terms to that of the savings banks (32.6%) and slightly higher than that of the commercial banks (29.9%). It appears that over time the three types of business models on which the German banking industry is built continue to be well-balanced in terms of their territorial presence.

The ongoing contraction of bank branches has led to an increase in the population density per bank branch: in 2016 this stood at 2595 inhabitants per branch, a figure that is higher than the corresponding figures in other European countries such as France, Italy, and Spain (respectively, 1794, 2067, and 1613). In these countries, branch numbers are declining at a slower pace, with the exception of Spain (ECB 2017).

[9] The number of CBs in 2017 reported by BVR is slightly lower: 915 CBs.

Table 6.1 Number of banks and branches[a] in Germany

Year	Commercial banks		Savings banks		Landesbanken		Regional institutions of credit co-operatives[b]		Credit co-operatives		Mortgage banks		Building and loan associations		Special purpose banks		Total[c]	
	Banks	Branches	Banks	Branches	Banks	Branches	Banks	Branches	Banks	Branches	Banks	Branches	Banks	Branches	Banks	Branches	Banks	Branches
2000	314	6520	562	16,892	13	638	3	25	1795	15,332	31	192	31	3677	15	18	2764	43,294
2004	357	14,750	477	14,292	12	549	2	11	1338	12,967	25	59	27	2784	18	31	2256	45,443
2008	283	11,277	438	13,457	10	482	2	12	1199	12,344	19	56	25	1872	19	31	1995	39,531
2012	294	9610	423	12,643	9	451	2	11	1104	11,778	17	49	22	1668	20	29	1891	36,239
2016	281	9407	403	10,555	9	384			975	10,156	15	36	20	1400	21	36	1724	31,974
2017	284	9004	390	9818	8	356			918	9442	13	38	20	1385	20	29	1653	30,072

Source: Deutsche Bundesbank (2017)

[a]Branches of banks headquartered in Germany

[b]From 2016, Deutsche Zentral-Genossenschaftsbank (DZ Bank) is included in the category Special Purpose Banks

[c]Investment companies are no longer classified as credit institutions and are therefore no longer included in these statistics

Banking concentration in Germany remains very low by international standards even though the share of total assets of the five largest credit institutions has shown an upward trend in the last decade and now equals 31% (46% in France, 62% in Spain and 43% in Italy in 2016) (ECB 2017). Since the 1980s, almost all German banks have expanded into the neighboring countries of Central and Eastern Europe.

The global financial crisis (GFC) inflicted heavy blows on some large private German banks. Deutsche Bank and Commerzbank, Hypo Real Estate (HRE), and Industrie-Kreditbank (IKB) experienced large losses due to sizeable investments in toxic assets and increasing dependence from wholesale market-based funding in the pre-crisis period (Hardie and Howarth 2013). HRE, IKB, and Commerzbank had to be rescued with substantial government interventions, which in the case of HRE constituted a full nationalization. Four Landesbanken (HSH Nordbank, BayernLB, SachsenLB, and WestLB) suffered greatly, indirectly also causing losses to other institutions in the savings banks' network (Behr and Schmidt 2015). Some Landesbanken were merged with stronger ones, others went through liquidations, while others embraced a process of realigning their business models. By contrast, the local savings and CBs overcame the crisis and were even profitable during the crisis period (Hardie and Howarth 2013; Behr and Schmidt 2015).

2   The Role of CBs Within the German Banking Sector

At the end of 2017, the German co-operative financial network managed assets totaling € 1243 billion, corresponding to 16% (15.51% in 2016) of the entire banking assets in Germany. This amount relates to the network as a consolidated entity, consisting of independent co-operative banks, the central institution and its group, DZ Bank Group, and Münchener Hypothekenbank.[10] Local independent co-operatives alone hold

---

[10] Münchener Hypothekenbank eG is the partner organization for the German co-operative banks (Volksbanken and Raiffeisenbanken), providing the full spectrum of residential and commercial property financing services.

The Bank was founded as a co-operative bank in 1896 with the support of the Bavarian government. Over the years, the Bank has evolved from its original agrarian orientation to become a modern mortgage bank that is active in both national and international markets. Furthermore, Münchener Hypothekenbank has retained the same legal status as a registered co-operative since it was founded and is one of the few remaining independent mortgage banks in Germany today. https://www.muenchenerhyp.de/en/company/aboutUs/index.html.

Table 6.2 Members, customers, and governance ratios of the co-operative financial network

Year	Members	Customers[a]	Governance ratio (%)
2004	15,506,866	30,000,000	51.69
2006	15,921,502	30,000,000	53.07
2008	16,200,000	30,000,000	54.00
2010	16,689,214	30,000,000	55.63
2012	17,300,000	30,000,000	57.67
2014	18,024,983	30,000,000	60.08
2016	18,435,585	30,000,000	61.45
2017	18,514,854	30,000,000	61.72

Source: EACB and BVR. Author's calculations of the governance ratio

[a]Estimates

€ 891 billion or 71% of the entire network's assets. The group relies on a vast and constantly growing membership base: rising from 15,506,866 in 2004 (EACB 2004) to 18,514,854 in 2017,[11] which represents a total growth of 19.4% (Table 6.2). Currently, German co-operative banking retains the second largest number of members in Europe, after France which had 26,600,000 members in 2017. It also exhibits the highest levels of governance ratio, which testify to the success of this business model in its homeland.

BVR has remained true to its original mission of traditional banking intermediation despite growing competition and the pull of wider diversification opportunities which have arisen through the deregulation of the European banking industry. The ability to attract and retain deposits as well as mobilize them toward lending opportunities, especially in favor of households and small-medium sized companies, is confirmed by their expanding market shares (Table 6.3). The last available data reported by EACB shows that almost 21% of loans and deposits in Germany are ascribable to CBs. It is worth noting that in the past co-operatives' share of the lending market has been lower than its share of the deposits market due to their likely lower capacity to be competitive. This gap has effectively been bridged in the space of a decade.

From 2004 to 2017, the percentages of customer loans and deposits to total assets have reached values above 60%, showing a more strongly held aptitude to collect and channel funds to the real economy (Table 6.4).

[11] Data collected from BVR's website.

Table 6.3 Domestic market shares of the co-operative financial network

Year	Loans (%)	Deposits (%)
2004	11.60	18.50
2006	11.80	15.80
2008	16.00	18.60
2010	16.90	19.40
2012	18.30	19.80
2014	20.10	20.90
2016	21.10	21.40
2017	21.70	21.50

Source: EACB

Table 6.4 Credit intermediation orientation of the co-operative financial network

Year	Loans to customers to assets (%) (A)	Deposits from customers to assets (%) (B)	Funding gap (A/B) (%)
2004	55.80	60.47	92.28
2006	51.78	57.32	90.33
2008	53.46	55.37	96.56
2010	57.17	60.76	94.09
2012	58.00	60.98	95.13
2014	59.05	62.82	94.00
2016	60.30	63.69	94.69
2017	61.28	64.43	95.11

Source: Author's calculations on data reported by EACB and BVR for 2017 only

When comparing these figures with those of French co-operative banking groups, it is clear that the German network favors asset and liability diversification strategies to a lesser extent than others, instead being more and more focused on lending and deposit collection from customers. In France in 2017, for instance, the ratio of loans to assets amounted to 46%, while the ratio of deposits collected from customers to assets equaled almost 42%; both ratios have followed a concave trend over the period under investigation. The ratio of bank loans to deposits from customers (%) also diverges from others (Table 6.4). The German "funding gap" indicator is constantly below 100% despite increasing since 2014 and is lower than the corresponding values recorded for, for example, French CBs and German commercial and savings banks (Hardie and Howarth 2013). The German

CBs' more conservative attitude toward the values of the funding gap measure seems to reflect a distinct strategy that was intended to lower German CBs' exposure to funding and interest rate risks which could arise from a bank's excessive dependence on wholesale and market-based funding.

3 CO-OPERATIVE BANKING: HISTORICAL DEVELOPMENT IN GERMANY

Co-operative banking in Germany and its spread across other European countries is mainly due to the ideas of Hermann Schulze-Delitzsch (1808–1883), who established the first urban co-operatives (e.g. a shoemakers' co-operative but also savings and credit co-operatives), and Friedrich Wilhelm Raiffeisen (1818–1888), who founded agricultural co-operatives and rural savings and credit co-operatives in the second half of the nineteenth century. As a liberal, Schulze-Delitzsch firmly rejected all forms of state support. For him co-operatives represented self-help facilities that enabled people to respond to the effects of the process of industrialization that affected large sections of the German population.

The growing industrialization of the German economy in the nineteenth century produced profound structural changes. Completely new industries emerged and grew quickly, attracting workers to the rapidly expanding cities. However, innovations and technical and economic changes came at the cost of a profound social crisis: broad swathes of the population became impoverished. The rural population was hit by several famines and various groups of craftsmen faced increasing competition from industrial production both at home and abroad. The idea of market-based co-operatives can be interpreted as an answer to the social question that had emerged. Hermann Schulze-Delitzsch, a Prussian lawyer and state administrator, inspired the initial founding of "raw material associations" for carpenters and shoemakers in 1849. These first co-operatives procured significant price advantages for their members by pooling the large quantities of raw materials they purchased. In 1850, Schulze-Delitzsch, together with other citizens of his hometown of Delitzsch, founded a credit association, the precursor to the Volksbank or People's/Popular bank. Schulze-Delitzsch's ideas spread rapidly to neighboring communities. In 1855, he published the book, "Credit Association and People's Banks", containing the business principles of credit co-operatives and practical instructions on how to establish them. Credit co-operatives, together with trade co-operatives, were for Schulze-Delitzsch bottom-up organizations which offered capital, savings incentives, goods and education to their members, in order to enable small-scale entrepreneurs to gain a competitive edge and more generally to foster social inclusion. The General Association of self-help-based German labor and economic co-operatives was created in 1864.

In 1862, Friedrich Wilhelm Raiffeisen, the devout Christian mayor of several rural villages in Westerwald, founded the first rural credit co-operative, having been involved for several years in the promotion and creation of agricultural co-operatives. This prototype of a CB was designed to promote mutual help while offering relief from usury (and ultimately starvation) to farmers unable to afford to purchase the goods they required for production. In contrast to Schulze-Delitzsch's organization, which was more widespread in the cities and among artisans, the Raiffeisen co-operative movement spread in rural areas, promoted by mayors, teachers, clergy, and landowners. Raiffeisen successfully campaigned for the founding of co-operatives, the basic principles of which were set out in 1866 in a book entitled "The credit-banks as a means to fight the misery of the rural population as well as the urban artisans and workers" (Guinnane 2001, 2011).

Two of the most important features distinguishing Raiffeisen's from Schulze-Delitzsch's ideas—besides the restriction of the co-operative's activity to its local parish—were, on one hand, the unlimited liability of its members in the event of bankruptcy, a principle genuinely championed by Raiffeisen, and on the other hand, the exclusive destination of profits generated by the business to a "undividable fund" that was earmarked for charitable purposes: schools and education, poor relief, and support of the elderly (Prinz 2002).

The legality of co-operatives was established by the introduction of the Co-operative Act in Prussia and in the North German Confederation in 1867–1868, which was soon extended to apply nationwide in the following years. It did not include a licensing stipulation (Faust 1977), but it gave a legal status to co-operatives that up to that point had had to be realized through the joint liability and guarantees of individuals.

The association of Raiffeisen banks was set up in 1877 in Neuwied. In the same year in which Raiffeisen founded his first rural credit co-operative, the General Association of German co-operatives decided to establish the first central bank of Volksbanks in Berlin: the co-operative bank Soergel and Parisius & Co.[12] Until then, credit co-operatives had worked with merchants, private bankers, savings banks or other banks. However, raising cash and investment was often associated with increased risks or bad conditions. The management of liquidity between credit co-operatives only took place rarely as the early co-operatives had little knowledge of each other and a cashless payment system did not yet exist. Through branches in Berlin and from 1871 in Frankfurt am Main, the newly established central bank of Volksbanks organized liquidity management services and a cashless payment system which operated between credit unions. The first central bank for Raiffeisen banks was created in 1872 in Neuwied, followed by other regional central banks. In 1876, one of the central institutions, the Rhenish Agricultural Co-operative Bank was converted into a public limited company, which in 1923 was renamed Deutsche Raiffeisenbank AG. The new bank operated nationwide. Branches were set up to establish business relationships with the credit co-operatives, and regional central banks were dissolved.

In addition to the efforts of Schulze-Delitzsch and Raiffeisen, in 1872, another promoter of the co-operative system, Wilhelm Haas (1839–1913), set up a consumer co-operative society for farmers in Friedberg in the state of Hesse. His goal was to secure price advantages for members purchasing agricultural inputs and was soon followed by the creation of credit co-operatives.[13] Like the Raiffeisen banks and Volksbanks, the organizations promoted by Haas created their own central bank in Darmstadt in 1883, the origin of DZ Bank, whose shareholders were the savings and loan banks of the state of Hesse (Guinnane et al. 2013).

The amendment of the Co-operatives Act in 1889 allowed the establishment of limited-liability co-operatives and made their auditing compulsory (Guinnane, 2001). The new legal framework and the provision of cheap lending favored a wave of start-ups in the co-operative sector. Between 1895 and 1900 the number of CBs in Prussia more than doubled (Guinnane et al. 2013). To tackle the crisis faced by the German agricultural sector, which was suffering through falling prices, in 1895, the Prussian Council of State founded a central co-operative bank to provide

---

[12] Soergel and Parisius were two bankers involved in the co-operative movement from the very start.

[13] Despite the importance Haas' co-operatives attained during the second half of the nineteenth century, Wilhelm Haas is barely known among the general public, as his activities and ideas have been eclipsed by Raiffeisen. In fact, one may call Haas the pragmatic heir of Raiffeisen (Prinz 2002).

cheap loans to rural and craft co-operatives. A multi-tier solidarity system was set up to collateralize the loans made by the new Prussian Central Bank—also known as the Preußenkasse.

A fourth and lesser founding father of co-operative banking in Germany was the painter Karl Korthaus, who supported the creation of craftsmen's co-operatives and related credit associations, thereby extending access to cheap loans. He was the initiator of the central association of German commercial co-operatives in Osnabruck in 1901 and, unlike Schulze-Delitzsch, did not reject the idea of receiving the state support extended by the Preußenkasse. The growth of the co-operative movement was now unstoppable—despite the fact that it was divided into a large number of increasingly fragmented entities: by 1903, there were more than 12,000 local CBs with around three million members (Guinnane et al. 2013).

Before the Second World War, the four co-operative associations underwent a process of merging which culminated in 1971 with the creation of a joint umbrella organization for all commercial and rural co-operatives: the German Co-operative and Raiffeisen Confederation (Deutscher Genossenschafts- und Raiffeisenverband—DGRV), initially headquartered in Bonn and later moved to Berlin.

The development of credit co-operatives after the Second World War and during the period of Germany's partition was very different. In East Germany, credit co-operatives were part of the planned economy and were no longer informed by the principles of individual responsibility and self-governance introduced by their founding fathers. By contrast, Volksbanks and the Raiffeisen banks in the Federal Republic of Germany benefited from the economic miracle that unfolded under the conditions of the social market economy. The CBs expanded their market shares, and there was a gradual increase in competition both within the co-operative banking sector and between the different bank business models.

Within the DGRV, the BVR grouped together all rural and urban credit co-operatives which were given a common national association for the first time.

Until 2000, the co-operative financial network had a two-tier structure in Northern, Eastern, and Southern Germany and a three-tier structure in Western and South-western Germany. The process of rationalizing the central CBs started in the last century and ended in 2016 with the merger of DZ Bank based in Frankfurt am Main (Deutsche Zentral-Genossenschaftsbank) with Westdeutsche Genossenschafts-Zentralbank (WGZ Bank) headquartered in Düsseldorf.

The DZ Bank is a joint stock company which is the financial apex of the co-operative banking network, which ranked in 2017 as the second largest German banking group.[14] DZ Bank acts as a central institution with a statutory mandate to support the work of local CBs and to boost their competitiveness. At the end of 2017, 94.4% of the capital of DZ Bank was held, either directly or indirectly, by local co-operative banks, while the remaining 5.6% was held by other co-operative entities and enterprises.[15] In regulatory terms, the DZ Bank Group is a financial conglomerate, including insurance activities performed by a controlled company, R+V, one of the leading insurers in Germany.[16]

4   GERMAN CO-OPERATIVE BANKING NETWORK: MAIN CHARACTERISTICS

BVR acts as an umbrella association for the co-operative banking sector, whose members are all registered CBs—Volksbanken, Raiffeisenbanken, Sparda banks,[17] PSD banks,[18] church banks, and co-operative specialized

---

[14] See the Investors' presentation of DZ Bank for 2018. https://www.dzbank.com/content/dam/dzbank_com/en/home/profile/investor_relations/DZ-BANK-Presentation/Kundenversion_InternetE.pdf.

[15] See DZ Bank Corporate Presentation at https://www.dzbank.com/content/dzbank_com/en/home/DZ_BANK/profile/dz_bank_ag.html.

[16] See DZ Bank Group's Annual Report for the year-end 2017.

[17] The first Sparda Bank was created in 1896 in Karlsruhe as the savings and loans association of railroad employees (Spar- und Vorschuss-Verein der Badischen Eisenbahnbeamten). In common with the history of other German CBs, Sparda banks represented the affordable way through which a given section of the population could afford to invest money on attractive terms and borrow on non-usury terms. During the 1970s, the membership base was opened to all private individuals, rather than only railroad employees, but the ties with retail banking customers remain at the heart of the strategic thinking and actions of these banks. Currently, Sparda banks form a group of 12 regional CBs spread across more than 400 branches. They serve almost 3.6 million members in Germany with roughly 6000 employees. For additional data and information, see http://www.sparda-verband.de/en/history.php.

[18] PSD banks are retail CBs which originated their name from the Post-Spar- und Darlehnsverein (postal savings and loan association). These CBs were originally created as savings and loan associations for the employees of the postal service. The first PSD bank started to operate in 1872 under the Prussian Empire and acquired a legal status in 1879 when Kaiser Wilhelm granted the association the rights of a legal entity. PSD banks form a non-formal banking group made up of 14 regional independent CBs spread across the German territory and with their own Association. In recent decades, the PSD banks have strategically focused on direct banking, strengthening their operations in on-line and mobile banking. According to the latest figures available, 1.2 million customers are served by PSD banks, which employ a total of 2136 employees. The branch network consists of 57 local

institutions—as well as the central bank, DZ Bank, financial companies in the Cooperative Financial Network and co-operative audit associations.[19] Every member of the association has one voting right irrespective of its size.

From an economic point of view, the wide range of specialized financial entities active within the network allows the primary banks to act as universal banks despite their local nature and size. Primary banks become members of the Association by means of a written declaration of intent to join and an admission resolution adopted by the management board of BVR. All associated banks must be audited by an auditing association.[20] Termination of membership is possible only with two years' written notice. Members' expulsion from the Association occurs in the event of gross violations of members' duties with regard to the Association as well as total breaches of the Association's interests and objectives.[21] The associated banks are entitled to join the BVR-ISG protection scheme, which we will examine in the following pages. Membership of BVR is subject to the payment of annual contributions determined by the Association's council as well as contributions to a nationwide advertising fund, which is operated by BVR. BVR has responsibility for the performance of marketing campaigns for the "Volksbanken Raiffeisenbanken" brand and for the development of marketing concepts and advertising tools for local, regional, and national use.

The Association's governing bodies are made up of the Association council, the management board, the administrative board, and the members' general meeting. The council consists of up to 53 members who are elected for a three-year period by the members' general meeting of the Association. Its composition allows for a high level of representation of all members of the association: up to 30 members are chosen from the members of the management boards of the local banks within the Association; up to 10 management board members are chosen from the auditing associations and the national association of co-operatives (DGRV); the council

branches. For additional information and data, see https://www.psd-bank.de/PSD-Banken/Die-PSD-Bankengruppe/Wer-wir-sind/c163.html.

[19] BVR's website information. https://www.bvr.de/About_us/Cooperative_Financial_Network.

[20] It is not mandatory for individual CBs to be members of the association in order to be entitled to use the denomination of Volksbank or Raiffeisen bank and to start to operate. However, they are restricted from using the credit co-operatives' logo belonging to the federal association (Biasin 2016).

[21] See BVR's by-laws revised in 2015.

also includes one management board member or managing director of the central institution, DZ Bank, and of the specialized banks and financial companies, as well as the chairman of the German Association of Raiffeisen co-operatives.[22] The Association council is responsible for the definition of the general guidelines for the Association's activities; for advising the management board on matters of fundamental importance; deciding on the strategic alignment of the group; and defining the annual contributions of all associated entities, including those related to the Institutional Protection Scheme managed by the Association. Twelve components of the Council are elected onto the administrative board, in accordance with the principle of representing all Association members, and are automatically appointed to the corresponding board of the Institutional Protection Scheme. Conforming to a model of dual governance common in Germany, the administrative board appoints and removes the management board, and exercises a supervisory and advisory function with regard to the activities of the management board. It may also submit recommendations to the Association council. The board of managing directors consists of at least three members whose term of office is five years and who have responsibility for the management of the protection scheme. The internal organization of the Association features defined special committees with an advisory role in markets, products, IT, payment transactions, human resources, banking regulation, and a steering committee. Their presence enables the uniform strategy followed by the co-operative financial network to be strengthened.

The by-laws of the German BVR clearly state that the co-operative financial network is made up of legally and economically independent banks at local levels who do not intend to become a corporate group in the formal sense in the future. In the preamble to the by-laws, it is expressly stated that the autonomy of local banks is complemented by their specific responsibility to tap the market and revenue potential in their respective market areas and to pass on to the financial network the ability to enter the market of the local bank, in the event of the latter not exploiting it adequately.[23] The power of the Association to monitor and influence members is set out in its specific rights to attend members' general meetings and to order the audits of local banks and other Association members by auditing firms or associations. These are authorized and obliged to audit

---

[22] Members of the Council are elected for a period of three years.
[23] See BVR's Bylaws revised in 2015.

the extent to which members comply with their duty of care under company law as well as the extent to which they conform to the provisions of the Statute of the Protection Scheme including the procedural rules, and to comment on this compliance in the audit reports.[24] Auditing is mandatory for local banks and performed by co-operative auditing associations which are thus able to verify the correctness of financial statements and also of managerial actions. Members are obliged to notify BVR and the relevant auditing association without delay whenever their ability to cover risks incurred through their activity is deeply compromised.

BVR and the auditing association also have the power to put in place preventive measures with regard to members, and specifically for our purposes local banks, if their operating policy contravenes the duties of care established. The different governing bodies of banks may be, in the first instance, notified about any inconsistency in their conduct with respect to the principles set out by the Association or be asked to prepare a restructuring plan, potentially supported by the relevant auditing association, and/or be forced to implement personnel and/or material changes.[25]

The role of BVR within the financial network is valuable both in strategic and operational terms. It is responsible for the coordination and development of the CBs' common strategy as well as for the promotion of the interests of the network at national and international levels. Operationally, BVR provides advice and support to its members on legal, tax, and business matters and runs the Cooperative Financial Network's protection scheme—the oldest bank protection scheme in Germany set up in 1934—along with the newly institutional protection scheme set up under the German Deposit Guarantee Act in 2015, the BVR Institutssicherung GmbH (BVR-ISG). At the regional level, local banks are also supported by regional associations which act as consultants for the Volksbanks Raiffeisen banks, dealing with tax, legal, and training issues; they represent the economic and political interests of the local banks, and are responsible for the auditing of member co-operatives. Services provided to the affili-

---

[24] The duties of care under which members must operate are established in section 6 of the statute of the Protection Scheme. In brief, members must hold adequate human and technical resources and organization to conduct their business and to comply with the relevant applicable guidelines and recommendations that have been adopted by the BVR Association council, that is, as far as concerns risk-taking due to business developments.

[25] In line with the requirements defined by article 113(7) sentence 1 of Regulation (EU) no. 575/2013 of the European Parliament for the recognition of institutional protection schemes.

ated primary banks are partly free or are charged at competitive rates, their costs being cross-subsidized by the audit services and membership fees invoiced (Biasin 2016). On the one hand, these cost advantages incentivize banks to prefer and exploit the services offered by the regional and national association, thus improving their managerial competences, while, on the other hand, the strategic and operational alignment of the whole network is eased.

4.1   The German Co-operative Financial Network

In organizational terms, the German co-operative banking system is currently a two-tier quasi-strategic network encompassing a large number of local primary banks and specialized banks, and both financial and non-financial companies at the national level (Fig. 6.1).[26] Local banks are, in regulatory and operational terms, universal banks *in toto*, which compete with commercial and savings banks but are constrained in their ability to compete with neighboring associated CBs. In line with the so-called *Regionalprinzip*, largely followed at the network level, CBs are required to limit their activities to a specific geographic area (Biasin 2016).

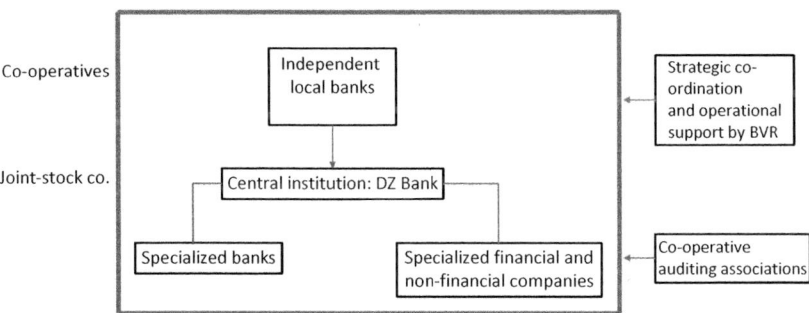

Fig. 6.1   The organization of the German co-operative banking network. Source: Author's elaboration

[26] As examined in the previous paragraph, the German co-operative banking sector was historically organized more in line with a three-tier system, with regional central institutions and associations which underwent a substantial consolidation and rationalization process over the passage of time.

Primary banks are responsible for exploiting the market potential of the community they serve, building and holding customer relationships; their local nature allows them to have a detailed understanding of customers' needs, and to evaluate the risks associated with borrowers through their superior ability to collect and process soft information. In "marketing terms", primary banks are a local market developer, whose capability is supported by the presence of top-level specialized entities within the DZ Bank Group which provide a full array of financial services covering savings, investments, payments, and retail and corporate lending both at the local and international level. As in other co-operative financial networks, the central institution develops and runs liquidity management services and offers advice for the benefit of its main shareholders. Consulting services are free and encompass several administrative issues faced by local banks, including regulatory ones and their strategic implications in managerial terms.[27] The central institution's group acts as a product provider primarily for CBs, whose interests and individual features are carefully taken into account. Indeed DZ Bank Group's alignment toward the co-operative financial network represents its primary function.[28] This mission provides a strong incentive for the DZ Bank Group as a whole to constantly target the needs of primary banks which are not only its shareholders but also its main customers and the distributors of the specialized financial services produced by the central institution's group. The clear objective of their strategic focus being centered on the local co-operative banks and their customers is to consolidate the positioning of the co-operative financial network as one of the leading financial services providers in Germany.[29]

In order to strengthen the outsourcing of local banks' business activities in favor of the DZ Bank Group, the latter is incentivized to keep its production competitive in terms of both market and price levels. Local banks are, in fact, not obliged to outsource any part of their activity in specialized areas to the DZ Bank Group, in line with the principle of the independence of primary banks. Different mechanisms are in place to align the incentives of both parties to favor intra-network transactions. The first relates to the process of the development and distribution of products and services by the DZ Bank Group. At the national and regional levels, DZ Bank is a member of committees whose function is to identify

---

[27] See DZ Bank Group's Investor Presentation for the year 2018.
[28] See DZ Bank Group's Annual Report for the year-end 2017.
[29] See DZ Bank Group's Annual Report for the year-end 2017.

key future-related issues so as to safeguard the competitiveness of the co-operative financial network, and to support local banks with consultancy and other services which are designed to strengthen the strategic relationship with partner banks and their ability to deliver the financial group's products and services. A second type of tool concerns the pricing mechanisms in place for the brokerage of financial products "manufactured" by specialized entities that belong to the top central institution and/or for the purchase of various facilities by primary banks. Basically, DZ Bank Group's products are priced according to a cost-approach pricing policy, which agrees to pass on cost synergies created within the network. Additionally, performance attribution gears are in place to reward/incentivize local banks acting as brokers, via commissions/bonuses (Biasin 2016). The third mechanism relates to the governance of the central institution, DZ Bank. The involvement of the association in the appointment of top members of the boards of DZ Bank facilitates the design and implementation of group strategies where the interests and needs of local banks may be represented. As an additional instrument, more recently, DZ Bank announced the creation of a central advisory committee in 2018, primarily to facilitate the banks' co-operation in and influence over the strategic decisions of the central institution.[30] Despite not being a group in legal terms, the co-operative financial network has become an integrated economic group of companies, producing consolidated financial statements since 2003, which are voluntarily divulged by BVR, and which result in the leading rating agencies providing them with a single rating.

In accordance with the principle of solidarity on which the German co-operative movement has been built, the financial co-operative network established an institutional protection scheme (IPS) in 1934: BVR Sicherungseinrichtung, BVR-SE, whose specific aim even now remains to avert or remedy imminent or existing financial difficulties at its member institutions ("bank protection") and thereby ensure comprehensive protection for customers' deposits.[31] The vital importance of the IPS is clearly stated in the preamble of the co-operative financial network's statute. Its fundamental function is to maintain the credit rating of protected institutions even though this may give rise to conflicts with the principles of self-responsibility and self-management which inspire the conduct of primary banks. In fact, due to the existence of the protection scheme, banks may

---

[30] See DZ Bank Group's Investor Presentation for the year 2018.
[31] See BVR's Statute of the Protection Scheme revised in 2015.

be tempted to engage in riskier activities that endanger their own stability and ultimately the confidence of depositors, members, and other stakeholders in their solvency. On the other hand, thanks to the creation of the IPS, CBs may survive and remain independent while continuing to operate across the whole German territory, being a reference intermediary for large numbers of retail customers and SMEs.

The institutional protection schemes of BVR, as well as that of German Savings Banks and Giro Association (Deutsche Sparkassen-und Giroverband—DSGV) pursuant to Article 113(7) of the CRR, are associations of multiple banks which have entered into a liability arrangement aimed to offer institutional protection to member institutions by preventing, for instance, their bankruptcy. Within the meaning of the 1994 EU Deposit Guarantee Scheme Directive 94/19, these IPSs have been viewed up to now as "alternative" systems whose members were exempted from belonging to any statutory depositor compensation scheme. Their "alternative" nature stems from the original idea of protecting depositors indirectly through a "bank protection" protection scheme[32] (Deutsche Bundesbank 2015). In performing its institutional function, the protection scheme mainly implements preventive measures aimed at averting adverse trends at the affiliated institutions (such as the imposition of personnel and preparation of restructuring plans) and, if necessary, takes measures to restructure the institutions concerned with funding measures which are linked to changes in personnel and/or material conditions.[33]

According to the new EU Directive 49/2014 on Deposit Insurance and the new national deposit insurance legislation, the Deposit Guarantee Act (*Einlagensicherungsgesetz*), which came into effect on 3 July 2015, those institutions previously exempted from membership of a statutory depositor compensation scheme are subject to a statutory obligation to compensate depositors. All banks are required to adhere to statutory compensation schemes which repay depositors only if a bank has been declared insolvent but which may be also involved in the resolution of members and the set-up of measures aimed to prevent bank failures (Deutsche Bundesbank 2015).[34]

---

[32] German private banks hold their own private deposit protection fund which currently voluntarily insures the deposits of each individual customer up to 20% of that bank's own regulatory funds. As of 1 January 2012, the Federal Association of German Banks decided to gradually reduce the limit for its voluntary deposit insurance to 8.75% of its liable capital by 2025. Besides this supplementary protection of deposits, private banks enjoy a statutory protection provided by the Compensation Scheme of German Banks (*Entschädigungseinrichtung deutscher Banken GmbH*, or EdB) (Bundesbank 2015).

[33] See BVR's Statute of the Protection Scheme revised in 2015.

[34] See Article 11(1) and (2) of the Deposit Guarantee Scheme Directive 2014/49.

Therefore, the BVR protection scheme has been complemented by BVR Institutssicherung GmbH (BVR-ISG), which is recognized as a statutory deposit guarantee system whose sole shareholder is BVR. This provides protection to customers' deposits (mainly consisting of savings deposits, savings certificates, time deposits, and sight deposits) and bearer bonds issued by affiliated institutions and held by customers in line with the requirements set out by European regulations on deposit insurance. The two protection schemes are however mutually complementary.

The institutional protection scheme of CBs is based on the set-up of a guarantee fund and a guarantee network. The first of these is created through annual contributions made by depository and non-depository institutions which are members of BVR. The contribution is based on an *ex-ante* asset-based risk-adjusted system of premiums that is designed to reward institutions which enjoy a high rating by offering them a lower premium.[35] The funds collected are administered separately by BVR's own funds and are not legally claimable by affiliated institutions or creditors, in accordance with Section 36 of the IPS' statute. In addition to the guarantee fund, a system of bond guarantees is in place to cover guarantee or indemnity obligations that BVR assumes on behalf of affiliates. According to the rules specified in Section 5 of the statute, members of the IPS have to provide BVR with guarantee bonds which are a multiple of the levy rates paid by affiliates as their annual contribution to the guarantee fund. The guarantee bonds provided by the affiliated institutions define the guarantee volume in the guarantee network.

Member banks are required to make annual contributions to both schemes, but funds may be transferred from one scheme to the other: BVR is empowered to transfer resources from the protection scheme's guarantee fund to the BVR-ISG protection scheme to fulfill the banks' contribution obligations (annual contributions, special contributions, and special payments) with regard to the BVR-ISG. Furthermore, in order to avoid a double burden being placed on the banks by their contribution obligations *vis-à-vis* the protection scheme and the BVR-ISG protection scheme, BVR may suspend or temporarily reduce the banks' contributions to the guarantee fund as stated in Section 4a of the statute. The management board of BVR is responsible for the management of the protection scheme while the administrative board of the same BVR is tasked with monitoring the management protection scheme, auditing the protection

---

[35] See BVR's Statute of the Protection Scheme revised in 2015.

scheme's annual financial statement, and reporting on the protection scheme's activities and financial position.

The central committee, made up of ten members representing respectively local co-operatives, auditing associations, DZ Bank, and BVR, constitutes a further governing body of the national IPS. The committee exists in both the statutory (BVR-ISG) and the pre-existing bank protection scheme (BVR-SE), with both being chaired by BVR. The central committee monitors the financial performance of the IPS, performs advisory functions on several managerial related issues (annual levies, investment of IPS' funds, restructuring plans of members, rating methodology of members, etc.), and consents to the admission and expulsion of members.[36] At a regional level, restructuring committees are in place, representing both the BVR-SE and BVR-ISG. Committees are strictly linked to and supported by local auditing associations and are responsible for formulating opinions and proposals for funding measures for local distressed co-operatives up to a value of € 25 million, and for receiving information on restructuring decisions taken by BVR.

The BVR protection scheme is regulated and monitored by the German Federal Financial Supervisory Authority (BaFin). This organization also has the right to obtain information from and audit the protection scheme in accordance with section 44(1) of the Banking Act (Kreditwesengesetz—KWG) (Bundesbank 2015). In light of its aims, the measurement and monitoring of risks of all its members are complemented by its competence to propose and agree to preventive and restructuring management activities for member banks in difficulty, in order to ensure the viability of their business and the common interests of all the members of the co-operative financial network.

5   The Performances of the German Co-operative Versus Non-Co-operative Banking Groups over the Period 2005–2017

The German financial co-operative network represents the second largest private group in Germany (after the commercial joint-stock Deutsche Bank), with total assets of € 1243 billion at the end of 2017 (€ 1475 for Deutsche Bank). Unlike Deutsche Bank, BVR has grown consistently since 2007,

---

[36] See BVR's Statute of the Protection Scheme revised in 2015.

according to the consolidated data publicly available. Overall, its assets grew by 22.8%, whereas the top private commercial banking group suffered a reduction in its total assets of 23.3%. The German Savings Banks Finance Group (for brevity Savings Banks) occupies a commanding position with € 2129.5 billion at the end of 2017 representing the first banking group in the country but operating with a public mandate (Savings Banks Finance Group 2016).

The German co-operative banking group has assumed a hybrid character which has allowed it to be a competitive player over time, focusing its attention strongly on its members and customers. Its Allfinanz model embeds a diversified range of specialized activities that are offered via its financial apex, DZ Bank, and its controlled subsidiaries, without taking the legal form of a co-operative but being firmly in the hands of local CBs. The existence of a recognized IPS which can take some actions regarding local CBs' risk management, but leaves each individual institution and its independent board of managing directors and its supervisory board to make business decisions, places the German network among what we have defined as quasi-strategic networks. With this lesser degree of strategic and managerial integration, we can also hypothesize that there is less convergence between the two banking business models: the one being oriented toward shareholders and the other toward stakeholders. For this purpose, as in the previous chapters, we assess the effects of the ongoing hybridization. In other words, have the mitigation of the principles of mutuality pursued by CBs and the growing complementarity with markets as places of investment and funding meant that the results achieved by CBs have become more similar to those of commercial joint-stock banks? Which areas record analogies and differences in results? Can a convergence in performance be observed over time? To answer these important questions, we have identified a series of indicators in the form of ratios proxying bank performances. The set of indicators used to run the comparisons concerns the capitalization of banks; their activities in lending and investing in securities, including those held for trading on the financial markets; their reliance on customer deposits; the role they play over time in the interbank market; the riskiness deriving from their lending; and, finally, their banking profitability and efficiency.

The data used in this first phase of analysis are consolidated, therefore, representative of the results achieved by the commercial and co-operative groups, including the latter's networks of CBs and their various non-co-operative subsidiaries. Year-end figures are used. In order to verify if, where and when there have been phenomena of convergence between co-operative and non-co-operative banking groups, one or more national commercial banking groups have been identified with which the following comparative analysis is carried out. The analysis covers the period 2005–2017 and is particularly helpful, since it allows the results obtained by the two groups of banks to be taken before and after the onset of the GFC. Data for the financial co-operative network have been collected manually from BVR's annual public financial statements. Data are available from 2007 and are consolidated. Data for commercial banking groups are extracted from the databases SNL, BankScope Bureau van Dijk, and Orbis Bank Focus in order to minimize the potential for missing data. BVR's results in the different areas under investigation are compared with those obtained by the two leading German commercial banks, Deutsche Bank and Commerzbank, and with the German savings banks finance group, which, like BVR, is organized as an integrated network of affiliated institutions (Behr and Schmidt 2015).

We provide means and standard deviations of the selected indicators in different sub-periods, covering respectively: the pre-crisis period, 2005–2007; the main GFC period, 2008–2010; the period from 2011 to 2013 during which the sovereign debt crisis severely affected various countries[37] and important regulatory and monetary policy measures were put in place to restore bank financial stability; and the implementation of Basel 3 and initiation of the European Banking Union with the implementation of the Single Supervisory Mechanism (SSM) and the Single Resolution Mechanism (SRM), 2014–2017.

In Table 6.5, we report the first set of indicators under investigation. Selected capital ratios comprise a regulatory proxy for the appraisal of the capital adequacy of the banking groups, the Tier 1 (%) ratio, and an accounting ratio represented by equity over assets (%). The first one represents a measure of capital adequacy under the Basel rules to address credit risk. Broadly speaking, the Tier 1 ratio is calculated as the shareholder funds plus perpetual non-cumulative preference shares as a percentage of risk-weighted assets and some off-balance sheet items. The

---

[37] In 2012, Greece was granted a new financial aid package while its debt was cancelled resulting in a severe haircut for private investors. Spain entered a difficult period, amidst doubts about the strength of its banking system, the deterioration of its public finances, record unemployment, and deepening recession. These concerns led risk premiums on sovereign debt to climb considerably, triggering bailouts for Greece, Ireland, and Portugal. Italy was not spared, with yields on its debt rising as well, despite the reforms undertaken by the government in charge at the time, led by Mario Monti.

Table 6.5 Comparison of German co-operative vs. non-co-operative banking groups: capital ratios

	BVR		Deutsche Bank		Commerzbank		Savings Banks	
	Mean	SD	Mean	SD	Mean	SD	Mean	SD
Tier 1 (%)								
2005–2007	7.90[a]	–	8.55	–0.07	7.20	0.70	–	–
2008–2010	8.33	0.55	11.67	1.37	10.83	0.95	–	–
2011–2013	10.20	1.15	14.97	2.00	12.57	1.29	–	–
2014–2017	13.65	2.00	14.83	1.28	12.98	1.16	15.40	0.73
Equity/total assets (%)								
2005–2007	5.36[a]	–	1.94	0.20	2.74	0.39	–	–
2008–2010	5.66	0.45	2.21	0.65	3.42	0.39	–	–
2011–2013	6.72	0.59	2.88	0.49	4.25	0.58	–	–
2014–2017	8.03	0.72	4.28	0.24	5.58	0.72	7.19	0.43

Source: Author's calculations

This table reports descriptive statistics (means and standard deviations—SD) of German co-operative and non-co-operative banking groups. Tier 1 (%) is the ratio between primary regulatory capital and risk-weighted assets; Equity/total assets (%) is the ratio between total equity and total assets. Our calculations are based on data extracted from SNL for Deutsche Bank and Commerzbank; calculations for BVR and Savings Banks are based on data hand-collected from consolidated Annual Reports available at the respective websites

[a]Only 2007

higher the Tier 1 value, the more capitalized the bank is, which improves its ability to face the risks arising from lending to and financing borrowers. Under the Basel 3 rules introduced in Europe in 2014 (with EU Directive 2013/36 and the EU Regulation 575/2013—CRR) the minimum level of Tier 1 permitted is 6% plus the capital conservation buffer of 2.5%.[38] The ratio of equity to total assets (%) proxies the cushion against banking risks. The higher this figure, the better the bank is able to cope with potential losses arising from its activity.

The Tier 1 ratio has, on average, been increasing over time in all the sub-periods under investigation for both BVR and the commercial banking groups. Throughout the periods of observation, the co-operative network's Tier 1 values have remained lower compared to those of the main private bank, Deutsche Bank. However, during 2014–2017, the gap between BVR and the two major commercial banks has been significantly

---

[38] Prior to Basel 3 coming into force, the minimum value of the Tier 1 ratio was 4%.

reduced. The Tier 1 ratio of BVR has significantly increased, reaching an average value of 13.65%. This value is higher than that of Commerzbank but lower than the average value of the savings banks group (15.40%). Analysis of the ratio of equity to total assets reveals a similar increasing trend to that already seen for the Tier 1 ratio (Table 6.5). However, what emerges clearly from the reported data is the lower level of capital held by shareholder-oriented banking groups before the crisis and in the most recent period under examination. Over the period 2014–2017, BVR and Savings Banks were both better capitalized than the commercial joint-stock banking groups, with BVR more capitalized than the Savings Banks Group (with a ratio of 8.03% compared to Savings Banks's 7.19%).

The second set of indicators concerns the asset side of the banking groups and aims to shed light on its composition. In this regard, we employ three types of ratios: the ratio of net customer loans to total assets (%) which measures the degree of dedication to the traditional lending activity; the ratio of the total securities held to total assets (%) which provides an assessment of banks' integration with financial markets in investment terms; and finally, the ratio of securities held for trading to total assets (%), which shows the degree of banks' active participation in the financial markets through financial instruments (i.e. bonds, derivatives, and stocks) and allows for an assessment of speculative activities within the financial markets. The data shown in Table 6.6 clearly indicate some idiosyncrasies of the German co-operative banking group, which mostly persist over time. First of all, its propensity to finance the economy through credit is, over the entire period of observation, significantly higher than that of the two commercial banking groups. BVR's average levels of net loans to total assets (%) range from 50.51% in 2008–2010 to 59.57% in 2014–2017 against average values of 21% and 44% respectively for Deutsche Bank and Commerzbank over the whole period. It is interesting to note that in the last sub-period, BVR's average value is higher than that of Savings Banks (55.49%). The co-operative group's greater business focus on more traditional credit activity stands in contrast to its consistently lower commitment to investing in securities. Commercial joint-stock banks show a greater degree of integration with financial markets in terms of their allocation in financial instruments, although this has decreased over time (Table 6.6). Deutsche Bank, for instance, has reduced its ratio of securities to total assets (%) from almost 71% in the first period of analysis to 54% in the last phase. This decreasing trend is also shared by

Table 6.6 Comparison of German co-operative vs. non-co-operative banking groups: lending and securities holdings ratios

	BVR		Deutsche Bank		Commerzbank		Savings Banks	
	Mean	SD	Mean	SD	Mean	SD	Mean	SD
Net customer loans/total assets (%)								
2005–2007	50.51[a]	–	16.62	0.22	42.18	7.65	–	–
2008–2010	54.10	1.93	19.23	4.50	43.58	3.92	–	–
2011–2013	57.56	1.42	21.87	1.99	44.46	0.57	–	–
2014–2017	59.57	0.98	26.42	1.43	44.02	5.55	55.49	1.99
Securities/total assets (%)								
2005–2007	35.58[a]	–	70.80	1.20	39.69	2.93	–	–
2008–2010	32.24	1.63	67.69	6.96	40.47	2.00	–	–
2011–2013	28.59	1.04	61.86	1.90	36.91	2.18	–	–
2014–2017	25.30	2.00	53.95	5.40	34.53	6.02	21.17	1.15
Total assets held for trading/total assets (%)								
2005–2007	13.68[a]	–	51.86	5.77	17.48	4.47	–	–
2008–2010	9.25	2.28	56.99	9.15	22.37	3.48	–	–
2011–2013	6.33	0.89	48.49	3.68	21.68	2.49	–	–
2014–2017	4.26	0.98	42.56	4.72	19.37	4.06	–	–

Source: Author's calculations

This table reports descriptive statistics (means and standard deviations—SD) of German co-operative and non-co-operative banking groups. Net customer loans/total assets (%) is the ratio between net loans and total year-end assets; Securities/total assets (%) is the ratio between total securities held and total assets; Assets held for trading/total assets (%) is the ratio between total assets held for trading and total assets. Our calculations are based on data extracted from SNL for Deutsche Bank and Commerzbank; calculations for BVR and Savings Banks are based on data hand-collected from Annual Reports available at the respective websites. With respect to BVR data, total assets held for trading stands for financial assets held for trading. Securities of Savings Banks are calculated as the sum of debt securities and other fixed-income securities with equities and other non-fixed-income securities

[a]Only 2007

German CBs, whose values dropped from 35.58% to 25.30%. Their mean value in 2014–2017 was above that of Savings Banks (21%).

The importance that the co-operative network assigns to financial instruments held for trading purposes is similarly individual. In this, differences with the commercial banking groups are evident and substantial. For the latter, the financial assets held for trading purposes have significantly decreased over time and are confirmed in the last period (2014–2017) at average values of approximately 42.56% and 19.37% respectively for Deutsche Bank and Commerzbank. For BVR, there has also been a substantial disinvestment from financial assets held for trading. Its allocative choices are, however, very different from those of commercial banks. In the last observation period, 2014–2017, the average value is equal to 4.26%, around one-third of the value recorded in 2008–2010. If we calculate the impact of the assets held for trading on the total securities held, we find that the co-operative banking group reports average values of 17% in 2014–2017, while the corresponding figure is about 79% for Deutsche Bank and 56% for Commerzbank, thus providing evidence of the strong strategic vocation of commercial joint-stock banks to trading and more marked speculative behavior, in spite of this decreasing over time.

The third set of selected indicators concerns the percentage of traditional funding through customer deposits and the interbank activity (Table 6.7). The difference between the two business models in terms of their dependence on customer deposits is once again substantial. On average, the co-operative group is consistently increasing its percentage of deposits, demonstrating its ability to maintain high levels of trust among

Table 6.7 Comparison of German co-operative vs. non-co-operative banking groups: funding and interbank ratios

	BVR		Deutsche Bank		Commerzbank		Savings Banks	
	Mean	SD	Mean	SD	Mean	SD	Mean	SD
Customer deposits/total assets (%)								
2005–2007	53.55[a]	–	24.99[b]	1.70	24.05	1.53	–	–
2008–2010	57.99	2.70	22.97	5.04	29.64	2.63	–	–
2011–2013	62.07	1.80	29.70	2.67	37.44	3.50		
2014–2017	63.62	0.65	34.99	3.36	48.77	6.53	55.65	5.10
Interbank ratio (%)								
2005–2007	69.29[a]	–	13.52[b]	2.88	61.79	3.97	–	–
2008–2010	43.02	10.18	161.58	66.36	88.86	2.72	–	–
2011–2013	38.12	4.87	258.71	17.86	93.89	16.92	–	–
2014–2017	38.85	5.07	239.34[c]	108.22	83.41	18.11	72.84	1.46

Source: Author's calculations

This table reports descriptive statistics (means and standard deviations—SD) of German co-operative and non-co-operative banking groups. Customer deposit/total assets (%) is the ratio between customer deposits and total assets; Interbank ratio (%) is the ratio between loans to banks and deposits from banks. Our calculations are based on data extracted from BankScope and Orbis Bank Focus for Deutsche Bank and Commerzbank; calculations for BVR and Savings Banks are based on data hand-collected from Annual Reports

[a]Only 2007

[b]Only 2006–2007

[c]2017 not available

depositors over time. In the two most recent sub-periods, BVR's ratio is above 60% and higher than that of Savings Banks (55.65%). The low volatility of BVR's ratios, compared to the other groups, is also noteworthy. Increasing values are also recorded for the commercial groups. Deutsche Bank, for example, after a drop during the most acute phase of the GFC (from an average value of 24.99% to 22.97%), returns to growth in the following years. By contrast, BVR and Commerzbank show a constant increase in their average values over time, with Commerzbank achieving a substantial uplift. In the case of both Deutsche Bank and Commerzbank, the increase in the ratio of deposits from customers to total assets is almost entirely driven by the asset reduction that the two commercial banks experienced especially after 2011.

As regards participation in the interbank markets, measured by the interbank ratio, the data displayed in Table 6.7 show that BVR has decreased its ratios, while Commerzbank and Deutsche Bank follow the opposite trend up to 2013. The differences between the co-operative banking network and the other groups are substantial. BVR almost halved its interbank exposure over the time analyzed, arriving at a rate of 38.85% in 2014–2017. In the same period, Deutsche Bank was a net placer of interbank funds with an average value was 239.04%, while Commerzbank and Savings Banks recorded respectively 83.41%, and 72.84%. Unlike for example, the French network, especially after 2008, when there was a long period of declining interest rates, the German co-operative network has become a growing user of funds provided by other banks, including the central bank. During 2014–2017, the interbank ratios displayed by the two networks diverge substantially, with Savings Banks's average ratio value standing at twice that of BVR.

Table 6.8 presents risk indicators that have assumed particular importance during the GFC, prompting regulators to dictate more stringent prudential rules relative to banks' exposure to liquidity and credit risk. The table contains a proxy for exposure to liquidity risk, often used in the empirical literature, and two proxies for credit risk. The use of the ratio of liquid assets to total liabilities (excluding equity) was preferred to the prudential ratios relating to liquidity risk since the latter would have been available only for the last of the periods under investigation. The ratio used examines the amount of liquid assets available to cover all the liabilities held by banks. The higher this percentage is, the more liquid a bank is and the more generally able it is to redeem its own debts, and the less vulnerable it is to a classic run on the bank.

Table 6.8   Comparison of German co-operative vs. non-co-operative banking groups: liquidity and credit risk ratios

	BVR		Deutsche Bank		Commerzbank		Savings Banks	
	Mean	SD	Mean	SD	Mean	SD	Mean	SD
Liquid assets[a]/total liabilities (%)								
2005–2007	21.75[b]	–	32.89[c]	1.82	22.48	5.96	–	–
2008–2010	16.20	3.19	29.08	5.90	21.62	5.68	–	–
2011–2013	12.35	1.57	32.51	1.82	28.60	3.96	–	–
2014–2017	10.50	0.42	31.62	4.70	29.14	1.50	16.94[d]	1.04
Impaired loans/gross loans and advances (%)								
2005–2007	–	–	1.41	0.12	4.20	0.69	–	–
2008–2010	–	–	1.96	0.72	5.95	1.42	–	–
2011–2013	–	–	2.63	0.14	7.17	0.29	–	–
2014–2017	–	–	1.86	0.32	3.70	1.26	–	–
LLR/gross customer loans (%)								
2005–2007	2.53[b]	–	0.88[c]	0.04	2.64	0.66	–	–
2008–2010	2.11	0.22	1.00	0.28	2.52	0.58	–	–
2011–2013	1.52	0.08	1.21	0.23	2.95	0.10	–	–
2014–2017	1.09	0.13	1.12	0.13	1.91	0.52	–	–

Source: Author's calculations

This table reports descriptive statistics (means and standard deviations—SD) of German co-operative and non-co-operative banking groups. Liquid assets/total liabilities (%) is the ratio between liquid assets and total liabilities; Impaired loans/gross customer loans and advances (%) is the ratio between impaired loans and gross customer loans and advances; LLR/gross customer loans (%) is the ratio between loan loss reserves and gross customer loans. Our calculations for BVR and Savings Banks are based on data hand-collected from Annual Reports; calculations for Deutsche Bank and Commerzbank are based on data extracted from BankScope and Orbis Bank Focus solely for the year-ends 2016–2017

[a]With respect to BVR data, Liquid Assets are proxied by the sum of the following accounting items: cash and cash equivalent, loans and advances to banks, financial assets held for trading

[b]Only 2007

[c]Only 2006–2007

[d]With respect to Savings banks' data, Liquid Assets are proxied by the sum of the following accounting items: cash reserves and loans and advances to banks

There is not sufficient publicly available data to calculate the ratio of impaired loans to gross loans (%) of BVR and Savings Banks. Analogously, we are not able to calculate the ratio of loan loss reserves (LLR) to impaired loans (%) due to the data not being publicly available. Consequently, in order to be able to compare the riskiness of the business models we have introduced the ratio of loan loss reserves to gross customer loans (%).

The data on liquidity reported in Table 6.8 show a diverging trend for co-operative and commercial banks: the averages of the former decrease over time, being significantly lower than that of commercial banks after 2008. By contrast, the liquidity level of commercial banks follows an increasing trend and takes on very similar values in the period 2011–2017, at around 30%. The ratio of BVR in the last of the examined periods has an average value equivalent to one-third of that of the two commercial groups. In the case of Germany, as for instance, in France, commercial banks follow operational strategies that lead them to hold far higher degrees of liquidity than those of CBs. On one hand, this different degree of liquidity observed in CBs typically originates from their greater involvement in traditional lending activity which usually absorbs the largest part of banking assets to the detriment of other investments, as, for example, highly marketable securities. On the other hand, the exploitation of more favorable trends in funding through customer deposits seems to allow CBs to hold fewer liquid assets to face unexpected requests from both depositors and borrowers. For BVR, the riskiness of the credit portfolio, proxied by the ratio of loan loss reserves to gross loans (%), follows a declining trend. In the period 2014–2017, its average value (1.09%) is the lowest among the German groups under investigation but close to that of Deutsche Bank (1.12%). Commercial banks also recorded favorable reductions in risk with Deutsche Bank in a better position than Commerzbank. The reduction in BVR's ratio by more than a half during the period under observation, alongside its steady increase in the volume of lending seems to indicate that the processes for selecting and monitoring debtors have become more effective. This could also be caused by the revision of BVR's IPS in order to obtain recognition by the ECB pursuant to art. 113(7) of the CRR. Greater integration in risk monitoring processes and the ability of the IPS to formulate intervention proposals for the network CBs may have decisively contributed to reducing the risk of the network.

The last battery of indicators that we examine involves variables that are representative of bank profitability and efficiency, widely employed in the empirical literature. With regard to the profitability analysis, three indicators are taken into consideration: the net interest margin (%), the return on average assets (ROAA) (%), and the return on average equity (ROAE) (%). To evaluate the operational efficiency achieved by the bank management, we use a widespread indicator: the cost-to-income ratio (%) (Table 6.9).

Table 6.9 Comparison of German co-operative vs. non-co-operative banking groups: profitability and efficiency ratios

	BVR		Deutsche Bank		Commerzbank		Savings Banks	
	Mean	*SD*	*Mean*	*SD*	*Mean*	*SD*	*Mean*	*SD*
Net interest margin (%)								
2005–2007	1.60[a]	–	0.55[b]	0.06	0.74	0.05	–	–
2008–2010	1.75	0.15	0.81	0.19	0.90	0.11	–	–
2011–2013	1.88	0.23	0.90	0.06	1.04	0.06	–	–
2014–2017	1.68	0.14	1.05	0.07	1.08	0.05	1.54	0.06
ROAA (%)								
2005–2007	0.30[a]	–	0.40[b]	0.01	0.31	0.03	–	–
2008–2010	0.36	0.30	0.07	0.24	−0.14	0.42	–	–
2011–2013	0.56	0.12	0.09	0.10	0.05	0.05	–	–
2014–2017	0.57	0.10	−0.11	0.21	0.10	0.08	0.09	0.05
ROAE (%)								
2005–2007	5.61[a]	–	18.87[b]	0.60	11.63	1.15	–	–
2008–2010	6.06	5.23	2.84	12.74	−4.75	13.42	–	–
2011–2013	8.32	1.38	3.36	4.24	1.22	1.38	–	–
2014–2017	7.08	1.70	−2.53	5.14	1.90	1.49	4.35	0.61
Cost to income (%)								
2005–2007	73.00[a]	–	68.96[b]	0.69	68.18	3.91	–	–
2008–2010	72.27	15.61	98.55	43.48	76.96	6.84	–	–
2011–2013	64.63	5.69	83.85	4.63	70.87	2.95	–	–
2014–2017	64.15	2.69	92.98	4.89	80.33	7.11	69.43	1.40

Source: Author's calculations

This table shows descriptive statistics (means and standard deviations—SD) of German co-operative and non-co-operative banking groups. Net interest margin (%) is the ratio between net interest income and total earning assets; ROAA (%) is the return on average assets; ROAE (%) is the return on average equity; Cost to income (%) is the ratio between operating expenses and intermediation margin. Our calculations for BVR and Savings Banks are based on data hand-collected from Annual Reports; calculations for Deutsche Bank and Commerzbank are based on data extracted from BankScope and Orbis Bank Focus solely for the year-ends 2016–2017

[a]Only 2007

[b]Only 2006–2007

The net interest margin (%) represents the profitability stemming from the bank's credit intermediation activity. It is expressed as the percentage of net interest income to earning assets. Less diversified banks generally enjoy higher net interest margins. Higher values of the ratio may be indicative of cost advantages in the funding or may derive from the exploitation of strong market power positions. In the periods analyzed, especially from

2007 to 2017, the ratio is constantly higher for the co-operative banking network, which is also consistent with its stronger focus on traditional banking activities. Only during 2014–2017 does BVR record a drop in the average value of its net interest margin. The prolonged low interest rates environment seems to have hit the profitability of German co-operative banking, which remains, nonetheless, the best performer within the national banking system. The ROAA (%) of the co-operative model is also on average higher than that of the commercial banks and shows less volatility over time. This also remains true when focusing on ROAE (%). In this regard, it can be seen that commercial banks were only able to obtain better results before the outbreak of the financial crisis. In more turbulent times, CBs perform better and in a more stable way. In Germany, unlike France, the co-operative banking sector obtains better profitability results, approximated by the ROAE, than the commercial banks.

It is often argued in the literature that the co-operative model is less efficient because the governance of these banks is immune to the *stimuli* of market discipline. However, observation of the cost-to-income ratio (%) shown in Table 6.9 does not allow us to support this hypothesis at first sight. Commercial banks only fare better in the period before the GFC: Deutsche Bank and Commerzbank have ratios of 68.96% and 68.18% respectively versus BVR's 73%. However, from 2008 onward, the opposite becomes true and BVR is able to significantly improve its operating efficiency, reaching an average value of 64.15% over the period 2014–2017.

In order to verify whether there are significant differences between the two banking business models, the non-parametric Wilcoxon-Mann-Whitney (WMW) (1947) test[39] is used. This is suitable for small sample sizes and for testing whether observations in one population tend to be larger than observations in the other, as it tests the equality of central tendency of two distributions (Fay and Proschan 2010). The selected indicators are subjected to the test during the period 2008–2017 only. It was decided to concentrate the analysis on this ten-year period, because we want to check whether, and if so, how the manifestation of the episodes of crisis and the start of the Banking Union in 2014, have affected the performance of the two business models, and whether this makes them more similar or not. The Savings Banks Finance Group was excluded from the test due to insufficient data. The results of the test with the relative *p*-values are reported in Table 6.10.

---

[39] This test is also known as Wilcoxon ranksum test or Mann-Whitney U test.

Table 6.10   Wilcoxon-Mann-Whitney test (2008–2017)

	Co-operative vs. non-co-operative banks	
	Median	*P-value*
Capital ratios		
Tier 1 (%)	10.75–13.00	0.03
Equity/total assets (%)	6.98–3.94	0.00
Lending, securities holdings ratios		
Net customer loans/total assets (%)	57.70–34.52	0.00
Securities/total assets (%)	28.19–44.85	0.00
Total assets held for trading/total assets (%)	6.00–31.46	0.00
Funding and interbank ratios		
Customer deposit/total assets (%)	61.96–33.53	0.00
Interbank ratio (%)	37.71–94.72	0.00
Liquidity and credit risk ratios		
Liquid assets/total liabilities (%)	11.78–29.86	0.00
Impaired loans/gross customer loans and advances (%)	–	–
LLR/gross customer loans (%)	1.49–1.42	0.69
Profitability and efficiency ratios		
Net interest margin (%)	1.79–1.01	0.00
ROAA (%)	0.54–0.05	0.00
ROAE (%)	7.77–1.05	0.00
Cost to income (%)	63.45–78.85	0.00

Source: Author's calculations

The two business models display several statistically significant differences in the results they have achieved, as evidenced by the *p*-values obtained. BVR's capitalization is significantly higher, and its asset and funding mix significantly different. It is more focused on lending to the real economy and, as a result, is less active on financial markets. Funding is more oriented toward deposits from customers and this seems to imply the sound ability of the entire BVR to build and maintain savers' confidence over time. In terms of its role in interbank banking, BVR's clear and significantly different position is also evident. In contrast to commercial groups, the network is much more a net receiver on the interbank market. As regards exposure to risks and economic performances, the differences between the two groups of banks remain substantial. Significant differences in values are found, in terms of both profitability and efficiency. With regard to the risks, no significant differences are found between the LLR/gross loan values of the two business models. Significant differences are found however for the liquid assets to total liabilities (%), with BVR being less liquid than the two commercial groups. Overall, the co-operative banking network has shown that it is able to develop higher performances than those of the first two German commercial groups, recording economic and patrimonial results, and distinct operational characteristics over time.

6   THE PERFORMANCES OF THE GERMAN CO-OPERATIVE BANKING NETWORK AND ITS CENTRAL INSTITUTION

To what degree do the performances of the central institutions of co-operative banking networks and the networks of CBs themselves differ? To answer this question, we examine some of the performance indicators analyzed in the previous paragraph, comparing the results achieved by central institutions with those of its network of CBs, as in Ory and Lemzeri (2012). To this end, the consolidated data relating to each central institution and its subsidiaries were extracted from the databases previously mentioned; similar data were calculated for the networks of CBs alone. We calculated average annual values and standard deviations of the selected indicators for the network of CBs. Data on the network of German CBs refer to individual banks in unconsolidated form. Data obtained do not cover all the CBs included in BVR due to missing data in the databases we employed.[40] To minimize the effect of these missing data on our analysis, especially before 2008, we chose to limit our analysis to the period 2008–2017 and to restrict our scrutiny to some of the indicators previously examined. These are the equity to total assets (%); the net customer loans to total assets (%); the impaired loans to gross customer loans (%); the customer deposits to total assets (%); the ROAA (%); and the cost-to-income ratio (%). For each of these, we replicate the analysis reported in the previous paragraph by calculating averages of results over sub-periods 2008–2010, 2011–2013, and 2014–2017. Figures are reported in Table 6.11.

As regards the first indicator, the ratio between equity and total assets (%), the data in Table 6.11 show that the network of German CBs is much better capitalized than its respective apex, DZ Bank. At the end of 2017, the average value of the indicator for the sample of CBs forming the net-

---

[40] The data extracted from BankScope refer to a sample of 926 CBs, having excluded banks with just one observation in the entire period of analysis (2008–2015). The data extracted from Orbis Bank Focus cover the period 2016–2017 only and refer to a sample of 635 CBs.

Table 6.11 Comparison of the German co-operative central institution and its network of CBs in terms of capital, lending, funding, and credit risk exposure

	DZ–Central institution		BVR–Network CBs	
	Mean	SD	Mean	SD
Equity/total assets (%)				
2008–2010	2.47	0.44	6.97	1.81
2011–2013	3.14	0.50	8.31	2.03
2014–2017	4.62	0.16	9.60	1.89
Net customer loans/total assets (%)				
2008–2010	29.68	1.32	56.39	12.06
2011–2013	30.57	1.10	57.24	12.75
2014–2017	32.73	2.50	59.74	13.14
Customer deposits/total assets (%)				
2008–2010	23.46	0.75	75.09	7.54
2011–2013	24.08	1.44	75.47	7.50
2014–2017	24.44	0.61	75.99	7.60
Impaired loans/gross loans and advances (%)				
2008–2010	3.98	0.32	–	–
2011–2013	3.72	0.34	4.38	4.22
2014–2017	3.18	0.54	2.77	2.39

Source: Author's calculations

This table reports descriptive statistics (means and standard deviations—SD) of German co-operative banking networks and their central institutions. Equity/total assets (%) is the ratio between total equity and total assets; Net customer loans/total assets (%) is the ratio between net loans and total year-end assets; Customer deposits/total assets (%) is the ratio between customer deposits and total assets; Impaired loans/gross customer loans and advances (%) is the ratio between impaired loans and gross customer loans and advances. Our calculations are based on data extracted from BankScope and Orbis Bank Focus

work is 9.60%, compared to 4.62% for its apex. The gap between the capital held by the central institution and the sample of CBs has decreased over time but remains substantial, in keeping with what we detected in other European countries, such as France.

As is reasonable to expect, the network of CBs is more involved in lending activity in accordance with the specialization of activities common in quasi-strategic networks (Table 6.11). Over the entire period of analysis, German CBs hold a constantly increasing average ratio of net customers to total assets (%), recorded at close to 60% in the last sub-period of observation. The variability registered, proxied by the standard deviations, is however quite high within the sample (at about 12–13%), but similar to the corresponding ones recorded for the networks of BPCE and Crédit

Mutuel in France (the standard deviations reported for the network of CBs of Crédit Agricole are much lower, while its ratios are higher and above 70%). The lending commitment of German CBs is consistently almost double that of their apex which is active in financing through its specialized subsidiaries in real estate financing, consumer finance, lending to SMEs, corporate finance, and so on. DZ Bank is the second largest commercial bank in Germany after Deutsche Bank with € 506 billion of consolidated assets at the end of 2017, compared with Deutsche Bank's € 1475. However, it is clear that a large part of the financial investments made by the central institution is invested in securities. CBs therefore delegate to the apex the diversification of the groups' overall resources, albeit to a lesser extent than in the commercial banking groups. Specialization is also found by looking at the funding mix of the apex and its network of CBs and, in particular, the impact of customer deposits on total assets (%) (Table 6.11). CBs hold on average about 75% of customer deposits to total assets (%) over the entire period of analysis which places the German network far above the French ones. Combining this data with that on net lending to total assets, we find that the funding gap of the network is on average below 80% over the whole period. Due to the high and mostly stable share of customer deposits over time, German CBs appear to be more insulated from the risks arising from a substantial reliance on market funding. At the same time, their ability to attract and mobilize the savings of customers and members is a distinctive and strategic element of the whole BVR. The apex's reliance on customer deposits is about one-third of the corresponding values recorded for the network of CBs. Over time, the ratio has increased slightly but permanently rests at just under 25%.

From a comparative analysis of the levels and trends of credit risk, approximated by the ratio between impaired loans to gross loans to customers (%) (Table 6.11), two phenomena emerge. In the first instance, a decreasing trend is recorded for both the apex and the network of CBs. Secondly, we identify a change in the riskiness ratios between the apex and the CBs. If in the period 2011–2013, the network of CBs is more risky than the apex (4.38% versus 3.72%), in the following period there is a significant reversal that positions the network at less risky levels (2.77%) than the central institution (3.18%). A similar phenomenon is also found in the French case. And once again we find that the significantly higher financing commitment of CBs, compared to their central institutions, does not correspond to a higher degree of credit risk. Proximity to the debtors and the territories assisted enable more effective screening and monitoring of the risks assumed.

The last two indicators examined concern the profitability and efficiency of the organizations under investigation. For these purposes, ROAA (%) and cost-to-income ratio (%) were selected and reported in Table 6.12. The values of the first provide evidence once again of the superior ability of the networks to generate an average profitability that is higher than that of their apexes, except in the last sub-period. This result, analogously to what was recorded in the French case, is indicative of the value of networks of CBs within their reference groups, especially in unfavorable times.

Finally, the cost-to-income figures displayed in Table 6.12 show that only in the period 2008–2010 were the individual CBs in our sample more efficient than their apex. The worst result recorded by the apex during 2008–2010 is entirely due to the effects of the GFC on the operating income of DZ Bank Group, especially in 2008, when impairment losses in the securities portfolio peaked (at € 1757 million, of which € 1095 million was accounted for by the sole holding DZ Bank).[41] In the periods following the most acute phase of the GFC, the central institution undertook efficiency measures that allowed it to achieve an average cost-to-

Table 6.12 Comparison of the German co-operative central institution and its network of CBs in terms of profitability and operational efficiency

	DZ–Central institution		BVR–Network CBs	
	Mean	SD	Mean	SD
ROAA (%)				
2008–2010	0.03	0.28	0.30	0.19
2011–2013	0.25	0.11	0.35	0.24
2014–2017	0.39	0.14	0.29	0.17
Cost to income (%)				
2008–2010	75.12	38.84	71.15	9.43
2011–2013	60.61	11.03	68.36	8.92
2014–2017	55.04	4.32	76.45	12.39

Source: Author's calculations

This table reports descriptive statistics (means and standard deviations—SD) of French co-operative banking networks and their central institutions. ROAA (%) is the return on average assets; Cost to income (%) is the ratio between operating expenses and intermediation margin. Our calculations are based on data extracted from BankScope and Orbis Bank Focus. The data extracted from BankScope refers to a sample made of 926 CBs after having dropped banks with just one observation in the entire period of analysis (2008–2015)

[41] See the Annual Report of DZ Bank Group for the year-end 2008.

income ratio of 55.04% by 2014–2017. By contrast, the network's level of operational efficiency worsened in the last of the periods examined, reaching an average level of 76.45%, but with a considerable increase in the variability (proxied by the standard deviation) in the sample. The worsening of the efficiency of the network together with that of the decrease in ROAA (%) seems to motivate and support the aggregation processes occurring within the sector (see Table 6.1).

Overall, we may conclude that the network of the German CBs has a strategic value that persists over time. They are noteworthy for their constant commitment to the traditional intermediation function over time, their ability to face increasing risks, thanks to the growing levels of capital held, and the improvement in the credit quality of their loan portfolios, due in part although not exclusively, to more integrated and incisive risk management practices. In terms of profitability and efficiency in the last period, there has been a worsening of the results achieved by the network, which indicate, for instance, a substantial departure from the more favorable performances enjoyed by the French CBs' networks (see Table 5.11). This stimulates a desire for continuous improvements in the levels of economic performance achieved (through aggregations, redefinitions of functions and processes, rationalization of branch networks, etc.) which represent a necessary but not sufficient condition for the exercise of banking activity according to co-operative principles.

7   CONCLUSION

The German banking sector has historically been structured around the so-called three pillars. The first is formed by the shareholder-oriented banking sector and foreign banks which collectively hold a market share of 40%. CBs form part of the second pillar. These are privately owned banks, which make up the Volksbanken/Raiffeisen Banks Financial Network (Bundesverband der Deutschen Volksbanken und Raiffeisenbanken—BVR), which at the end of 2017 consisted of a central institution (the former Deutsche Zentral-genossenschaftskasse, now known as DZ Bank and its Group) and 915 local CBs. The third pillar has a public mandate and, in 2017, encompassed six Landesbanks groups, DekaBank, and 390 independent local savings banks forming the Savings Banks Finance Group. BVR acts as an umbrella association for the co-operative banking sector, whose members are all registered CBs— Volksbanken, Raiffeisenbanken, Sparda banks, PSD banks, church banks, and co-operative specialized institutions—as well as the central bank, DZ Bank, financial companies in the Cooperative Financial Network and co-operative audit associations. The network of CBs relies on a vast and constantly growing membership base: around 18.5 million in 2017. The last available data shows that almost 21% of loans and deposits in Germany are ascribable to CBs. The member CBs of the BVR are entitled to join the network's protection scheme. BVR has responsibility for the performance of marketing campaigns for the "Volksbanken Raiffeisenbanken" brand and for the development of marketing concepts and advertising tools for local, regional, and national use. The power of the Association to monitor and influence members is set out in its specific rights to attend members' general meetings and to order the audits of local banks and other Association members by auditing firms or associations. Auditing is mandatory for local banks and performed by co-operative auditing associations which are thus able to verify the correctness of financial statements and also of managerial actions.

The role of BVR within the financial network is valuable, in both strategic and operational terms. It is responsible for the coordination and development of the CBs' common strategy as well as for the promotion of the interests of the network at national and international levels. Operationally, BVR provides advice and support to its members on legal, tax, and business matters and runs the Cooperative Financial Network's protection scheme— the oldest bank protection scheme in Germany set up in 1934—along with the newly institutional protection scheme set up under the German Deposit Guarantee Act in 2015, the BVR Institutssicherung GmbH (BVR-ISG). In organizational terms, the German co-operative banking system is currently a two-tier quasi-strategic network encompassing a large number of local primary banks and specialized banks, and both financial and non-financial companies at the national level. The central institution's group acts as a product provider primarily for CBs, whose interests and individual features are carefully taken into account. Indeed DZ Bank Group's alignment toward the co-operative financial network represents its primary function. The German co-operative banking group has assumed a hybrid character.

In addition to analyzing the role and organization of co-operative networks in Germany, the chapter offers two empirical investigations, respectively aimed to verify empirically the effects of the ongoing hybridization in co-operative banking, and to assess to what degree do the performances of the central institutions of co-operative banking networks and the networks of CBs themselves differ. Regarding the first of the two areas of analysis, the comparison of the performances of the two business models displays several statistically significant differences in the results they have achieved. BVR's capitalization is significantly higher, and its asset and funding mix significantly different. It is more focused on lending to the real economy and, as a result, is less active on financial markets. Funding is more oriented toward deposits from customers. As regards exposure to risks and economic performances, the differences between the two groups of banking models remain substantial. Significant differences in values are found, in terms of both profitability and efficiency. With regard to the risks, no significant differences are found between the LLR/gross loan values of the two business models. Overall, the co-operative banking network has shown that it is able to develop higher performances than those of the first two German commercial groups, recording distinct characteristics over time.

With reference to the second area of investigation, the average values of the individual CBs that are part of the network show values of capitalization that are higher than those of the central institution. CBs are more specialized in the lending activity. Specialization is also found by looking at the funding mix of the apex and its network of CBs and, in particular, the impact of customer deposits on total assets. As regards the exposure to credit risk, there is a marked improvement in the average risk of CBs compared to that of the apex, perhaps as a consequence of the implementation of the IPS and of the more careful control of the risks at the local level that resulted from it. In terms of profitability and operational efficiency in the last period, there has been a worsening of the results achieved by the network of CBs. Overall, we may conclude that the network of the German CBs has a strategic value that persists over time. They are noteworthy for their constant commitment to the traditional intermediation function over time, their ability to face increasing risks, thanks to the growing levels of capital held, and the improvement in the credit quality of their loan portfolios, due in part although not exclusively, to more integrated and incisive risk management practices.

REFERENCES

Behr, P., & Schmidt, R. H. (2015). *The German Banking System: Characteristics and Challenges*. White Paper No. 32, SAFE.

Biasin, M. (2016). The German Cooperative Banks: An Economic Overview. In S. Karafolas (Ed.), *Credit Cooperative Institutions in European Countries* (1st 2016 ed.). Cham: Springer Verlag.

Bundesverband der Deutschen Volksbanken und Raiffeisenbanken (BVR). (2015a). *Statute of the Protection Scheme,* May 6.

Bundesverband der Deutschen Volksbanken und Raiffeisenbanken (BVR). (2015b). *By-Laws,* May 6.

Deutsche Bundesbank. (2015). *Deposit Protection in Germany.* Monthly Report December 48.

Deutsche Bundesbank. (2017, November). *Banking Statistics, Statistical Supplement to the Monthly Report.*

Deutscher Sparkassen und Giroverband (SGV). (2016). *Inside the Savings Banks Finance Group.* Berlin.

DZ Bank. *Annual Report,* Various Years.

European Association of Co-operative Banks (EACB). *Key Statistics,* Various Years.

European Central Bank (ECB). (2017, October). *Report on Financial Structures.*

Faust, H. (1977). *Geschichte der Genossenschaftsbewegung* (3rd ed.). Frankfurt a.M.

Fay, M. P., & Proschan, M. A. (2010). Wilcoxon-Mann-Whitney or T-Test? On Assumptions for Hypothesis Tests and Multiple Interpretations of Decision Rules. *Statistics Surveys, 4,* 1.

Guinnane, T. W. (2001). Cooperatives as Information Machines: German Rural Credit Cooperatives, 1883–1914. *The Journal of Economic History, 61*(2), 366–389.

Guinnane, T. W. (2011). The Early German Credit Cooperatives and Microfinance Organizations Today: Similarities and Differences. In B. Armendàriz & M. Labie (Eds.), *The Handbook of Microfinance.* World Scientific.

Guinnane, T. W., Bormann, P., Scholtyseck, J., Wixforth, H., Paul, S., Theurl, T., & Rudolph, B. (2013). Die Geschichte der DZ-BANK: Das genossenschaftliche Zentralbankwesen vom 19. Jahrhundert bis heute. CH Beck.

Hardie, I., & Howarth, D. (2013). A Peculiar Kind of Devastation: German Market-Based Banking. In I. Hardie & D. Howarth (Eds.), *Market-Based Banking and the International Financial Crisis.* Oxford University Press.

Mann, H. B., & Whitney, D. R. (1947). On a Test of Whether One of Two Random Variables Is Stochastically Larger than the Other. *Annals of Mathematical Statistics, 18*(1), 50–60.

Ory, J., & And Lemzeri, Y. (2012). Efficiency and Hybridization in Cooperative Banking: The French Case. *Annals of Public and Cooperative Economics, 83*(2), 215–250.

Prinz, M. (2002). *German Rural Co-operatives, Friedrich Wilhelm Raiffeisen and the Organization of Trust.* Manuscript, University of Bielefeld.

Savings Banks Finance Group. (2016). Annual Report for the Year-End 2016.

CHAPTER 7

Co-operative Banking in Italy

1   Brief Overview of the Italian Banking System

Italy is one of the European countries where banks still have a prominent role in mobilizing savings mainly due to the slow development of alternative financial channels. Monetary Financial Institutions (MFIs) play an important role in this context: the ratio of their total assets to national GDP stood at 2.3 at the end of 2016, which is lower than the corresponding values recorded in Germany (2.6) and France (3.7)[1] and somewhat lower than that in 2012 (2.5). However, looking at the percentage of assets held by MFIs as a percentage of the total assets of the financial sector, Italy records the highest values: 63.8% in 2016 as compared with 61.1% in Germany and 63.5% in France (ECB 2017).[2]

The banking industry is mainly composed of domestic banks which held an 87% share of total banking assets in 2016, a figure that has remained almost unchanged since 2008 (88%); foreign subsidiaries and branches, mostly from other European countries, held 12.9% of national banking assets in 2009 versus 12.1% at the end of 2016 (ECB 2017). In a country largely populated by SMEs, the banking sector has a fundamental role in the financing of non-financial companies (NFCs) which rely heavily on banks. At the end of 2016, the total financing provided by the

---

[1] Excluding the data of the European System of Central Banks (ESCB).
[2] These two indicators were 3.6 and 70.2% respectively in 2008 (ECB 2017).

© The Author(s) 2019   295
F. Poli, *Co-operative Banking Networks in Europe*, Palgrave
Macmillan Studies in Banking and Financial Institutions,
https://doi.org/10.1007/978-3-030-21699-3_7

domestic financial sector amounted to € 982.9 billion (€ 1018.1 billion in 2014), almost 85% of which was granted by MFIs, mainly banks, while another 14.3% came from Other Financial Intermediaries (OFIs) (excluding insurance companies and pension funds). In parallel, MFIs' financing to NFCs in other countries of the Eurozone totaled € 76.1 billion, following an increasing trend (€ 59.6 billion in 2014).[3] Like Germany and Spain, Italy has experienced a decline in its entire loan portfolio, in contrast, for instance, with France and the Netherlands (ECB 2017). Among the major European countries, Italy has experienced the largest increase in impaired loans which has hindered credit growth and the economic recovery of the country. Net impaired loans peaked at 10.5% in 2015. At the end of 2017, the incidence of net impaired loans out of the total loans granted by the banking system fell to 7.5% (14.5% in gross terms), following a downward trend (Bank of Italy 2018). The Italian banking system was only affected by the first phase of the global financial crisis (GFC), thanks to its low exposure to the risks of structured finance. Impaired loans increased sharply at the end of 2011 but remained relatively low in relation to total loans. However, their growth resumed following the second recession, during the so-called sovereign debt crisis that hit Italy in 2011–2012. The end of the crisis has not been painless. Four intermediaries were placed in resolution and, in some other cases, proceeded to liquidation. The state has carried out the precautionary recapitalization of a large bank, Monte dei Paschi Siena—MPS, becoming its principal shareholder. In more than one case, savers incurred heavy losses due to the implementation of the new European rules on bank resolution. After the outbreak of the GFC, Italy, like other European countries, put in place several measures to rescue the banking system, ranging from state guarantees on bank liabilities, to liquidity support, to bank recapitalizations[4]

---

[3] ECB's data reported in the Report on Financial Structures (ECB 2017).

[4] On 13 October 2008, the Italian government adopted a decree establishing several measures to stabilize the financial markets. Among other things, this included a state guarantee on new liabilities issued by banks for maturities of between 3 months and 5 years, which was renewed until December 2009. For further details, see IP 08/1706 and IP 09/292. In light of the difficulties faced by Italian banks in 2011 and 2012, state guarantees were temporarily reintroduced in 2012. Guarantees were also in place during 2016 and also comprised large tranches of securitizations of non-performing loans. The latter were temporarily extended in 2017 and 2018 to favor the divestment of banks' non-performing loans. Other measures implemented by the Italian government to cope with the GFC included bank recapitalization measures through the purchase of subordinated debt instruments, to be counted as bank Core Tier 1 capital (IP 08/2059 and IP 09/302) and liquidity support measures to facilitate

(Panetta 2018).[5] The crisis has brought to light the long-debated problems of the governance of Italian CBs. In response to this, two major reforms were enacted in 2015 and 2016. The first found a solution to the inadequacies of the governance model of large popular banks by making their conversion into joint-stock companies mandatory. The second reform, which related to small credit co-operative banks (CCBs), instead set out the conditions for preserving the values of mutuality, overcoming the disadvantages of being small in size by making affiliation to a joint-stock central institution compulsory. The banking system has been gradually overcoming the difficulties of the past few years. Credit to the private sector returned to rise at the end of 2016 (Bank of Italy 2018) although the slow rate of growth that still characterizes its dynamics is largely attributable to low internal demand.

Structural changes to the Italian banking system began in the 1990s, facilitated by new sets of rules which allowed the privatization of state-owned banks and introduced the universal banking model. As in other European member states, these legislative changes gave rise to a process of bank aggregations and regroupings within the country. This nationwide process of consolidation was fundamentally characterized by mergers between small- to medium-sized regional banks, primarily within the group of CBs and joint-stock companies. At the same time, this wave of privatization facilitated the growth of larger Italian banks beyond their national boundaries, particularly in Eastern Europe. Between the middle of the 1990s and the 2000s, major cross-border acquisitions involving the country's then largest banks (Unicredit and IntesaSanpaolo) focused on CESEE countries, enabling the Italian banking system to gain important market shares in some of them. Further restructuring of the banking system occurred in response to the 2011–2012 crisis, which led to significant financial sector distress in Italy, due to strains that emerged mainly at the domestic level.

More recently, the process of consolidating bank branches has gained extra momentum due to the trend toward self-service and online banking which has further speeded up the rationalization of bank outlets. At the end of 2017, there were 27,374 bank branches, as opposed to 31,103 in 2015 and 32,338 in 2006. The restructuring of the banking system has

the liquidation of two failing popular banks during 2017 (IP 17/1791). More details can be found in the EU State Aid Cases Database at http://ec.europa.eu/competition/elojade/isef/index.cfm.

[5] According to Panetta (2018), state funds used to recapitalize or facilitate the liquidation of Italian banks equaled 1.3% of the total GDP, against an average four times larger in the other countries of the European Union.

increased the population density per credit institution (99,218 inhabitants per bank at the end of 2016[6]) (ECB 2017), placing Italy in an intermediate position between countries with low population densities such as Germany (48,462 in 2016) and high density such as France (150,243). The degree of concentration within the banking market has increased over time. The five largest credit institutions in Italy in terms of total assets held a collective market share of 43% in 2016, significantly increased from 31% in 2008 (ECB 2017). The level of concentration is expected to rise further, especially due to the poor performance of small and medium-sized banks, among which there are several CCBs. Currently, commercial banks play the leading role within the banking system, their importance having increased further following the reform of large-scale popular banks.

2   THE ROLE OF CBs WITHIN THE ITALIAN BANKING SECTOR

The process of bank consolidation which has been in progress since the deregulation and privatization of the banking system in the 1990s has led to a significant reduction in the number of Italian banks. There were 841 in 2000, but numbers had fallen to 538 by the end of 2017,[7] with the major decrease registered by CBs. These banks which in 2000 represented 64.6% of the total number of banks, only accounted for 57.9% at the end of 2017. After the reform of the popular banks in 2015, the mandatory conversion of major popular banks into joint-stock companies took place, along with certain aggregations which brought the total number of banks in this category to 23 at the end of 2017. Most of these banks are autonomous (15), while just over a third (8) form part of banking groups. These banks and their groups mostly operate on a regional basis; for the most part, their average size at the end of 2017 stood at less than € 5 billion. In terms of their market share of bank branches, popular banks now have a smaller presence in the territory than CCBs: 6% (1619 branches in absolute terms) of the total number of branches as opposed to the 15% held by co-operative credit banks (4257 branches) at the end of 2017.

CCBs are much more numerous, totaling 289 at the end of 2017, but their number is constantly decreasing as a result of intra-sector aggregations,[8] which are mainly triggered by bailouts in response to financial difficulties.

---

[6] There were 72,423 inhabitants per bank in 2008 (ECB 2017).

[7] Data collected from the statistical database of the Bank of Italy.

[8] At the end of 2018, the number of CCBs decreased to 265 according to data reported on their national federation's website.

The restructuring within the sector has been severe as, for instance, in 1998 there were 559 CCbs, almost double the number of banks existing nowadays. This phenomenon was most intense before 2002 and in the aftermath of the sovereign debt crisis which severely affected Italy. The two co-operative networks currently existing in Italy jointly accounted for just under 1.8 million members at the end of 2017, of which 1.27 million belonged to the CCB sector and about 500,000 to popular banks.[9] The data show that membership of CBs in Italy is a relatively rare phenomenon nowadays. By contrast, consider how in smaller countries than Italy, such as Finland and the Netherlands, where there are fewer co-operative banks, the number of members exceeds 1.9 million members. Equally Austria had more than 2.3 million members at the end of 2017. It is therefore quite evident that during the course of co-operative banking's evolution in Italy, banks have failed to maintain and enhance their links with members. This is particularly true of popular banks which have long lost their original operational link with the principle of mutuality, in law as well as in practice. In fact, the data displayed in Table 7.1 show that during the entire period preceding the reform of the popular

Table 7.1 Members, customers, and governance ratios of popular banks and credit co-operative banks

Year	Popular banks			Credit co-operative banks		
	Members	Customers	Governance ratio (%)	Members	Customers	Governance ratio (%)
2004	1,035,000	8,400,000	12.32	729,462	1,422,189	51.29
2006	1,065,000	8,100,000	13.15	822,893	5,000,000	16.46
2008	1,160,000	9,400,000	12.34	939,667	5,700,000	16.49
2010	1,212,739	9,593,158	12.64	1,010,805	5,700,000	17.73
2012	1,212,739	9,593,158	12.64	1,135,096	6,000,000	18.92
2014	1,370,000	12,350,000	11.09	1,200,485	6,000,000	20.01
2016	1,380,000	12,400,000	11.13	1,250,992	6,000,000	20.85
2017	500,000	6,100,000	8.20	1,275,000	6,000,000	21.25

Source: Author's calculations on EACB data and figures reported by the National Association of Popular Banks (Associazione Nazionale fra le Banche Popolari) for the years 2012–2017

Data for popular banks in 2016 refers to 2015

Data on CCB customers for the period 2012–2017 are estimates reported by EACB

[9] Data reported by the National Association of Popular Banks (Associazione Nazionale fra le Banche Popolari).

banks and the mandatory conversion of the major banks into joint-stock companies during 2016 and 2017, the growth in popular banks' membership was weak in comparison with that of CCBs.

Overall, the network of CCBs was more successful in increasing its membership: between 2004 and 2016, growth equaled 71.60% (74.90% including 2017), while membership of popular banks increased by 33.33% in the same period.[10] Both types of CBs have therefore recorded upward trends in terms of customer numbers. However, during the period 2004–2016, CCBs more than tripled their existing customers, whereas popular banks grew by 47.62%. The CCBs' network has shown itself to be increasingly attractive to both new members and customers, although its growth in customer numbers largely outpaces that of members.

In parallel, this growth has been accompanied by a slower rise in members' participation in governance: year-end figures for 2017 show that members make up 21.25% of the entire end-users of services of CCBs (down from 51.29% in 2004); and around 8.20% of the entire end-users of popular banks. In contrast to CCBs, the governance ratio for popular banks has exhibited a downward trend, thus indicating loose links with their members.

The governance ratios reported in Table 7.1 indicate that membership of domestic CBs is not a significant factor for the primary target customers of the banking services provided by Italian CBs. This phenomenon becomes even more pronounced if we compare it to, for example, the governance ratios in Austria (where the figure was almost 50% in 2017) or Germany (around 60% in 2017). Governance ratios similar to those of Italian CCBs can be found in the Netherlands where the rate was 22.54% in 2017.

In Italy, CBs enjoy relatively modest market shares when compared with those of the CBs in the other countries under investigation in this book. At the end of 2017, according to our calculations reported in Table 7.2, the two networks jointly held a 10.50% share of the domestic loans market, with CCBs managing to increase or broadly maintain their market share at slightly above 7% (Table 7.2). CCBs' market share is even higher in the mortgage sector, at 10.30% (EACB 2017).

Popular banks' market share decreased in 2016 and again in 2017 due to the mandatory conversion of the largest popular banks into joint-stock companies. In 2017, CCBs' market share was double that of popular banks. CBs' collective share of the domestic deposit market was slightly higher at 11.70% in 2017, with CCBs alone holding 7.80%.

---

[10] Observations for the last year have not been taken into account in order to eliminate the effects of the popular banks' reform enacted in 2015.

Table 7.2   Domestic market shares of Italian co-operative networks

Year	Customer loans (%)		Customer deposits (%)	
	Popular banks	Credit co-operative banks	Popular banks	Credit co-operative banks
2004	19.50	6.40	20.80	8.30
2006	20.10	6.60	21.90	8.40
2008	23.10	7.20	25.40	8.90
2010	24.70	7.20	26.90	7.30
2012	24.70	7.10	26.90	7.40
2014	25.90	7.30	25.50	7.90
2016	9.30	7.20	9.30	7.70
2017	3.30	7.20	3.90	7.80

Source: Author's calculations on data reported by the Bank of Italy for popular banks for the years 2012–2017. The remaining data was provided by EACB

Table 7.3   Credit intermediation orientation of Italian co-operative networks

	Loans to customers to assets (%) (A)		Deposits from customers to assets (%) (B)		Customer loans to deposits (%) (A/B)	
	Popular banks	Credit co-operative banks	Popular banks	Credit co-operative banks	Popular banks	Credit co-operative banks
2004	58.37	68.77	42.97	58.28	135.84	117.99
2006	58.33	73.77	40.95	56.39	142.45	130.81
2008	46.38	76.07	32.60	51.27	142.27	148.37
2010	46.93	75.64	37.11	51.84	126.45	145.91
2012	51.31	62.71	39.94	47.74	128.48	131.37
2014	65.19	54.88	51.77	47.77	125.92	114.87
2016	65.75	55.47	70.01	57.44	93.92	96.56
2017	61.23	56.59	67.18	61.23	91.14	92.42

Source: Author's calculations on data collected from the Bank of Italy

There are additional peculiarities relating to the degree of credit intermediation performed by the two networks (Table 7.3). Measurement of lending activity using the ratio of loans to total assets (excluding loans to banks) shows that the importance assigned by CCBs to their lending activity decreased until 2014, only resuming thereafter. At the end of 2017, the incidence of loans to customers equaled 56.59% for CCBs: a value lower than that of the popular banks at 61.23%.

The outbreak of the financial crisis caused a contraction of credit that is evident just for CCBs. The values recorded in 2016 and 2017 for both Italian networks are close to the corresponding indicator for the German co-operative banking network (60.30% and 61.27% respectively at the end of 2016 and 2017) and are higher than the French one (50.38% in 2017). In terms of the relationship between deposits from customers and total assets, the ratio was historically higher for CCBs but it reversed after 2014.

One final observation concerning the recorded values of the "funding gap", proxied by the ratio of bank loans to customers to liabilities from customers: this ratio is notably high for both networks and follows a similar trend for each, increasing until 2008 and then constantly decreasing and falling below 100% during 2016 and 2017. Only in France we find such high values of the ratio in question, which, although decreasing over time, remains above 100%, unlike in Italy. The German values of the funding gap proxy are much more akin to the Italian ones at around 95% in 2017, indicating in both cases a reduced dependence on funding from financial markets.

3   Co-operative Banking: Historical Development in Italy

The first type of CBs active in Italy, popular banks, originated from Schulze-Delitzsch's ideas which were adapted by the economist and Minister of Finance Luigi Luzzatti (1841–1927). A fervent liberal and a strenuous defender of an inclusive economy, he was active in promoting their creation. Since Italian legislation did not contain any legislation on co-operatives, Luzzatti was able to incorporate into these new popular banks elements of the culture and the individualistic spirit of the Latin peoples that were considered important, in order to encourage the success and growth of the banks (Colombo 2012). In Luzzatti's view, popular banks had to be able to distribute a part, however minimal, of the profits generated. Furthermore, the principles of joint and unlimited liability were abandoned by the Italian popular banks. The fundamental element that links Italian popular banks to CBs in the other European countries under investigation in this book is the democratic notion of "governance", based on the "one head, one vote" principle, irrespective of the size of each person's capital contribution. Closely related to this principle are two other characteristics that are present in all CBs: the admission of members, subject to the approval of the bank's administrative body, and a limit on the ownership of co-operative shares. Then, as now, shares were nominative and the capital indeterminate, therefore variable at any time. The value of the shares was commensurate with that of the equity (De Bruyn and Ferri 2005). As in Germany and France, small entrepreneurs and traders in the emerging urban areas were the ideal customers for the popular banks. For them, investment in the shares of a popular bank would have constituted both a means of ensuring their participation in the economic development taking place, and a small financial investment. In the mid-nineteenth century the only external source of financing for small traders, artisans, and farmers was, in fact, usury. The banks in existence at the time, few in number and geographically concentrated in the largest cities, operated almost exclusively with large companies and the public administration. On the other hand, savings banks, established with philanthropic goals a few decades before the popular banks, used to invest almost exclusively in real estate and government bonds until after World War II (Polsi 1993). The system of popular banks should be seen simply as an attempt by the nascent bourgeoisie to establish market capital, to the benefit of local entrepreneurs (De Bruyn and Ferri 2005). Rather than being true CBs, Luzzatti's popular banks represented a compromise between a partnership and a limited liability company, expressed in the form of an anonymous co-operative (Pecorari 2003). The first popular bank was founded in 1864 in Lodi, a small town close to Milan. It was soon followed by popular banks in the cities of Milan, Bologna, and Cremona, and by many other banks which sprang up especially in the north of the country, although not without arousing a degree of distrust and polemic. Originally, they were very modest banks with small capital, few deposits, and limited lending. The latter was limited to the discount of bills and unsecured small short-term loans, while funding mainly took the form of collecting sight and term deposits. In the first years of their existence, the banks granted loans strictly to members only, thus applying the principle of mutuality, and always took care to allocate a substantial part of their earnings to reserves (Salvione 1985).

However, within the co-operative movement, popular banks were viewed with some suspicion as they did not offer rebates, which the co-operative movement considered the way to remunerate work and not capital (Cafaro 2001). In particular, at the end of the nineteenth century, criticisms of popular banks grew, coinciding with the onset of the agrarian crisis. Starting in the agrarian sector, the crisis soon affected the weak Italian manufacturing sector and, finally, the real estate sector. The crisis in the latter constituted a violent attack on the entire banking system that had become excessively and unwisely exposed to the real estate sector. Since popular banks were mostly seen as commercial banks, the resentment against the latter, which were held responsible for the worsening of the country's economic conditions, extended to popular banks (Colombo 2012).

In 1876, a few years after the foundation of the first popular bank, the National Association of Popular Banks was established, at Luzzatti's instigation, with the aim of promoting the spread of popular banks and providing a place where experiences could be shared and debates and representation could take place, as stated in Art. 1 of the Statute of the Association. However, the Association was never to succeed in fostering integration between popular banks as, for instance, in the German case. Popular banks have remained an atomistic sector, albeit one which has become more and more concentrated over time. The need for a financial intermediary like the popular bank was so great that, after just 20 years, popular banks already commanded a fifth of the national banking market. On the eve of the "first great war", the spread of popular banks reached a historical peak with around 800 banks in operation.[11] Subsequently and up until the beginning of the 1950s, the category suffered a dramatic downsizing, almost halving in size, in part due to the severe impact of the financial crises of the 1920s and 1930s, but also due to the increasing importance of the productive sectors which became characterized by large corporations with corresponding increasing financial needs that could be better served by larger commercial banks. Popular banks fell out of favor with the political powers of the time, who were intent on managing a profound industrial reconversion in the aftermath of the First World War, pushing and supporting the process of the country's industrialization and the growth of large companies (Conti et al. 2003). The fascist period corresponded to a period of profound decline: in 1936 the number of popular banks had fallen to 431, while their market share had fallen to 8.7%. The post-war period following the Second World War began with an important legislative provision, the legislative decree n. 105 of 1948, which modified the requirements for popular banks, omitting any

---

[11] As reported by De Bruyn and Ferri (2005) citing data collected from the Italian Ministry of Agriculture, Industry and Commerce on Popular Banks for the year 1893.

reference to the principles of mutuality, and placing them outside the co-operative world, excluding them from any tax and social security benefits. Of the co-operative principles, only the "one head, one vote" remained firm along with the limit on members' share ownership, set at one twentieth of the share capital.[12] Despite this increasing similarity between popular and commercial banks, many popular banks have maintained in their statutes credit facilities dedicated to members (De Bonis et al. 1994). It is also clear that Italian popular banks quickly replaced their principle of mutuality in the strict sense with a social mission to which individual CBs subscribed. This is the prevalent concept of "spurious" or "partial" mutuality adopted by Italian popular banks and incorporated into their statutes (Salvione 1985).

During the 1940s the popular banks reorganized themselves, developing dedicated intermediaries that could help the sector to widen its product range and reap economies of scale in areas such as payment and clearing systems (Central Institute of Italian Popular Banks, created in 1939), long and medium-term credit for small and medium-sized businesses (Centrobanca, set up in 1947) and credit for craft enterprises (Artigiancassa, established in 1947). However, unlike in the case of the French popular banks, neither the establishment of the National Association, nor the subsequently created specialized financial intermediaries led to higher degrees of integration in the sector. Over time, the sector remained highly decentralized, probably because of the non-co-operative influence of the public liability company originally embedded in the Italian popular banks.

The difficulties faced by the sector prompted a process of aggregation among popular banks which started in the 1920s and continued over a period of time. Along with the re-establishment of their competitive power came the continual expansion of their branch network. This was also the result of new branch regulations introduced during the 1980s by the regulatory and supervisory authority, the Bank of Italy, and the progressive liberalization of banking activity, which culminated in the reform of the

---

[12] The decree also established that a fifth of the profits had to be allocated to the reserve until the latter reached half of the share capital. Only when this figure had been reached could the quota allocated to the legal reserve be lowered to a tenth of the annual net profits. Furthermore, according to the same rule, the portion of profits that was not allocated to the legal reserve, to any statutory reserves or extraordinary reserve and that was not distributed to shareholders had to be allocated to bodies of public charity and assistance. With this rule, another main feature of co-operative banking, the retention of earnings, was de facto overcome.

banking law in 1993. At the end of the 1970s, some of the largest popular banks listed their shares on the newly established stock market segment as a means of benefiting their trading and liquidity and attracting new capital (De Bruyn and Ferri 2005). By the end of the 1990s, few popular banks chose to leave the sector, deciding instead to adopt a joint-stock legal form, permitted under the new banking law. Through frequent intra-sector mergers, some popular banks have become part of the major Italian banking groups: in 2009 the 38 popular banks then in existence held a market share of 21.1% of total banking assets (compared to 16.8% recorded ten years previously) and 27.3% of total bank branches (Tarantola 2009). The number of active popular banks has since diminished, but the notable expansion of their branch network has made it possible for popular banks to maintain a high level of competition with other types of banks in their local markets. The wave of mergers that took place during the 1990s and the beginning of the 2000s not only caused an increase in the average size of these intermediaries but also led to greater complexity in their organizational structures, and greater diversification in their banking business and its distribution channels. However, the organizational format used most frequently by the leading popular banks was a poor fit with that of federal groups. Indeed, unlike the latter, there wasn't any actual federation of legally independent banks, as was the case in France. Instead, popular banks acquiring other banks simply tended to preserve the brand of the controlled intermediaries, mainly out of a desire to keep their specific inclination toward "localism" intact.

In 2010, of the five largest banking groups in Italy, two were held by popular banks, Banco Popolare and UBI Banca. Of the 16 banking groups held by popular banks, 7 were listed on the stock exchange. Additionally, in 2010, the average assets of the top five popular banking groups was 25 times the average value of the other popular ones, compared to just 10 times the value in 1999 (Tarantola 2009). The emergence of popular banks with systemic relevance had not been accompanied by a parallel revision of their governance model. In the immediate aftermath of the GFC, the move to reconsider the governance of popular banks regained popularity for several reasons. Tarantola (2011) observed that the expansion of the popular banks' activities, particularly the largest and listed ones, had led to a further decline in the governance ratio, from 5.8% in 2006 to 4.8% in 2011. The corresponding average value for the entire category was higher but decreased over the same period, from 9.4% to 8.4%. Of all the co-operative banking systems under investigation in this book, it has been and clearly continues to be the Italian popular bank system that has strayed furthest from its original focus on members and mutuality.

In the wake of the global financial crisis, the combination of this factor with the low rates of participation in voting,[13] the weak or non-existent discipline exercised by institutional investors (caused by individual banks having the legal option of excluding the latter from any representation on their boards), and the limitations of the voting proxy mechanisms (Tarantola 2011), has resulted in popular banks appearing to be overly exposed to the risks of management's excessive self-reference and of insufficient monitoring of senior management's actions.[14] These weaknesses in the governance model were most evident in the way the global financial and sovereign debt crises progressed between 2011 and 2012. These crises demonstrated very clearly the importance of banks, especially those of systemic significance in the country, being able to cope quickly with additional capital injections, as the subsequent adoption of the regulations introduced by Basel 3 would go on to show shortly thereafter. It was difficult to effect capital increases due to individual limits on bank equity holdings that weakened the active and participatory role of institutional investors. At the start of the European Banking Union in 2014 and the implementation of Basel 3, the Italian popular banks model seemed to manifest signs of tension, especially in the case of the major listed banks: regulators, scholars, and some political parties highlighted the gap that existed between a proprietary structure which was in principle open to both the market and institutional investors and a regulatory framework that, despite being designed to protect participatory democracy, made it difficult to exert control, limited the representation of the various components of the shareholding, and deterred participation in meetings (Gutiérrez 2008).

The lengthy debate on the fragility of the Italian popular banks' governance model was put to rest, for better or worse, with the reform introduced by Decree 3/2015 which was converted into Law 33/2015. Since the secondary provisions, enacted by the Bank of Italy, came into force,

---

[13] On average 9.6% as reported by Tarantola (2011).

[14] An empirical study by Gutiérrez (2008) also showed that Italian CBs enjoyed a significantly higher degree of monopoly power than commercial banks, making it even more urgent to consider this result vis-à-vis the need for regulations in order to ensure a level playing field for all banking institutions.

popular banks with assets exceeding € 8 billion had to comply with mandatory conversion into a joint-stock company within 18 months. The sector's inability to proactively revise a model that had gradually lost all connotations of mutuality, at least in the case of the largest popular banks, led the legislator to intervene by setting out a twin-track reform. This left the banks with the option of reducing their total assets to below the € 8 billion threshold which would trigger their mandatory conversion into a joint-stock company. The supervisory and regulatory authority, the Bank of Italy, welcomed the reform[15] and enacted the criteria for determining the value of assets to comply with the maximum limit of € 8 billion at the individual and consolidated level and the conditions for limiting or postponing in whole or in part the redemption of the shares of withdrawing members, based on the assessment of the financial situation, liquidity, and solvency of the bank and its capital ratios (CET1, Tier 1, and total capital). As we will analyze later, ten popular banks were required to transform into joint-stock companies. Out of these, two popular banks lodged legal appeals against the new regulation and the issue remains unresolved.[16] In

[15] See, for instance, the evidence of the Bank of Italy's general director, Salvatore Rossi, at the Joint Commissions Finance and Production Activities, Trade and Tourism, Italian House of Representatives on 17 February 2015. We report some of the passages and the motivations used to welcome and support the reform: "the Bank of Italy had long hoped for an intervention by the legislator in this matter. A reform was also repeatedly referred to as necessary by the International Monetary Fund and the European Commission". The two motivations offered were the following: "If bank recapitalizations by several European banks became necessary simultaneously, in an increasingly competitive and very selective market in the allocation of capital, it would be essential to present oneself without competitive disadvantages. The co-operative legal form is a competitive disadvantage in this context: if the increase in capital that is required is, due to its size and urgency, only achievable on the capital market, factors such as the "one head, one vote" principle and the limits on share ownership and representation at meetings are very unattractive for institutional investors who wish to influence the management choices of the subjects financed in order to protect their investment". "But there is a second important topic to consider. We operate within one new European regulatory framework on banking crises, the one defined by the directive on the reorganization and resolution of banks and the single resolution mechanism. In the new framework, the capital requirements, if they are not satisfied within a short timeframe, can trigger the conditions for the "resolution" of the bank. Shareholders and other creditors other than depositors would be called upon to participate in the losses (bail-in), without state support. This is, however, configured as one extreme ratio for exceptional cases, notwithstanding the general prohibition of state aid".
[16] Another popular bank, Banco Popolare dell'Alto Adige, adopted the decision to convert to a joint-stock company in 2016 on account of having total consolidated assets over € 8 billion.

October 2018, the Italian State Council, a consultative and judicial body on administrative matters, referred the decision on the legality of the reform of popular banks to the European Court of Justice due to certain inconsistencies between the EU regulation on the reimbursement of shares and the rules enacted by the Italian regulatory authority, the Bank of Italy. However, since the introduction of the popular banks' reform, three of the banks subject to mandatory conversion, Banca Popolare di Vicenza, Veneto Banca (both in 2017), and Banca Popolare dell'Etruria e del Lazio (in 2015), have fallen into a state of serious financial distress, leading the Italian and European supervisors to decree their compulsory administrative liquidation. The outbreak of the GFC and the persistent difficulties in Italy's economic recovery, together with the detection of serious irregularities in the governance and management processes of these banks, have led to their failure. This has contributed to a weakening of public trust in this category of banks, which had previously enjoyed high levels of trust in their territories of reference and consequently had not been subject to high levels of discipline.

The reform of popular banks introduced significant changes in terms of banks' abilities to issue financial instruments with a participatory nature. These instruments can carry administrative and representation rights and may consequently be attractive to popular banks whose total consolidated assets are below € 8 billion. Additionally, the rule specifying that the majority of directors had to be chosen from the co-operative membership has been removed. This eliminated one mechanism that influenced the governance of the popular banks and was considered responsible for boards' excessive self-reference and the limited administrative skills in popular banks.

Only a year after the reform of popular banks, the Renzi government in power at the time decreed a reform of credit co-operative banks, which was then converted into Law 8 April 2016 n. 49. The reform was motivated by the need to protect the financial stability of the sector while preserving CCBs' purpose in terms of their mutuality, their localism, their democratic functioning, and their aversion to speculative conduct. More than a hundred years after their foundation, Italian credit co-operative banks have finally started the process of integration that was lacking until this reform. Of all the countries considered in this study, Italy has displayed the most decentralized and atomized system (Ferri et al. 2013). Italian credit co-operative banks arose simultaneously with the popular banks, thanks to the activism of Leone Wollemborg (1859–1932). The model that inspired

Wollemborg was that of Raiffeisen, in most cases with the Catholic clergy strongly involved in the promotion and management of the first rural banks, named Casse Rurali (CR). Secular CRs were in a minority in the sector. Wollemborg's CR became a formidable aggregation tool, as well as a means of enabling the financial inclusion of the poorest in rural areas. Adapting the Raiffeisen credit co-operatives model to the Italian context involved the widespread practice of not offering an individual rebate on a part of the bank's profits, instead replacing it with a sort of collective rebate in favor of the community served by individual banks. As Cafaro (2001) points out, this was possible due to the perfect overlap between the membership structure of the banks and the reference community. The principle of mutuality was therefore raised higher than the principle of individuality and proved to be the glue that held single banks and local communities together. The first CR was established in 1883 in Loreggia, in the province of Padua, by Leone Wollemborg. In 1890 the young priest Luigi Cerutti founded the first Catholic rural bank in Gambarare, in the province of Venice. In 1892, Pope Leo XIII's encyclical Rerum Novarum endorsed the credit co-operative movement, thus positioning CRs in the mainstream of Catholic activities. In the period between 1883 and 1897 alone, 904 CRs were established, located mostly in the north of Italy (83% in 1897). Only a few banks were located in the center (13%) and the south of the country (4%) (Micheli 1898). CRs became an instrument for countering the economic crisis, flourishing while traditional banks withdrew due to the lack of economic convenience. By contrast, CRs could rely on a contained cost structure, both because the bank's premises were often located in parish buildings, and because the activities carried out were mostly performed on a voluntary basis.

The willingness of CRs to differentiate themselves clearly from the popular banks allowed them to rapidly establish a loosely federated structure. The national federation, Federcasse, was created in 1909. In the early years of the twentieth century, provincial federations were created to support the small local CRs whose activities were often linked to those of the savings banks and major CRs that carried out secondary-level activities. Subsequently the federations should have had the dual function of carrying out inspections, as well as acting as points of connection between the small CRs and the banks to which their liquidity surpluses were diverted. Between 1922 and 1924, many CRs disappeared as a result of the failure of many of the banks to which they had channeled their liquidity, and the lack of coordination between federations. The fascist period presented many difficulties for these banks and their federations. With the reforms introduced in the 1930s, the local CRs became subject to the supervision of savings banks located in their local territories; membership was expanded beyond those active in agriculture and credit to include craftsmen; and stringent limits were set on the distribution of profits to members. During the fascist period, it was precisely the extension of the relationship to small and medium-sized artisan entrepreneurs that allowed the CRs to survive even in areas of the country that were already experiencing industrial development on a larger scale (Locatelli 2011).[17] The reorganization of CRAs (Casse Rurali e Artigiane) and their national federation did not take place until the 1950s. In 1947 the first comprehensive law on co-operation, the Basevi Law, was introduced, while in the following years the national and regional federations were redesigned in terms of their representation (Cafaro 2001) and subsequently their auditing function.[18] However, all proposals aimed at enlarging the federations' functions in strategic and control activities have always given way in the face of individual local banks' strenuous protection of their autonomy. In 1963, the central bank for CRAs (Istituto di Credito delle Casse Rurali Artigiane—ICCREA) was founded with the aim of intensifying the activities of its member banks and making them more effective by facilitating, coordinating, and increasing their involvement in credit functions, banking brokerage, and financial assistance. ICCREA was originally devised as a vehicle which would complete the intra-sector financial circuits and finally make the CRAs independent of other non-CBs. With the new Banking Law of 1993, CRAs were allowed to act as universal banks and to open their membership to all natural or legal persons working or residing in the territory of operation, regardless of their profession. They were also renamed credit co-operative banks (CCB), thus abandoning their original focus on the rural and artisan economies. In the middle of the 1990s, the CCBs' central financial body was reorganized: a holding company, ICCREA Holding, held by CCBs, became operational, controlling subsidiaries active in banking, leasing, asset management, and other financial services. Expanding the spectrum of activities performed by the central financial hub represented a strategic and

---

[17] The extension of their activity to artisans led to a change of name: they were no longer simply rural banks but rural and artisanal banks (Casse Rurali e Artigiane—CRA).

[18] In addition, the creation of a central institute was resumed with financial functions supporting the category. Law n. 707 of 1955 transferred responsibility for the auditing of the credit CBs to the associative bodies, having previously been carried out by auditors appointed by the government.

practical way of strengthening the competitiveness and efficiency of hundreds of small-scale banks. By the end of the 1990s, the network of credit CCBs established its own mandatory guarantee fund for the protection of its associated banks' depositors.[19] In 2004 a voluntary guarantee fund for the banks' bondholders was also established. An additional guarantee mechanism, the institutional guarantee fund, was set up in 2008 with the aim of protecting bank customers, safeguarding the "liquidity and solvency" of the participating banks through corrective actions and support measures, and crisis prevention. In addition to this fund, the system of CCBs added a temporary fund in 2015 with the aim of creating a safety net for the increasing concentration that would result within the sector when the reform of the credit CCBs enacted in 2016 came into force.[20] In fact, from 2015 onward, it became no longer viable for the mandatory national deposit guarantee funds to intervene for the purposes of crisis management. As mandatory deposit guarantee funds had a public mandate, any intervention by them could be interpreted as state aid, in violation of European principles. Therefore, the set-up of a temporary guarantee fund to intervene in cases of individual CCBs' financial distress seemed a necessary short-term solution which could also help to keep members' and customers' confidence in the co-operative banking sector as high as possible.[21]

Until the new regulations were issued, Italian CCBs operated within the framework of a "decentralized co-operative network". The new regulation, set out in the Law of 8 April 2016, n. 49, formally introduced the hybridization of co-operative banking into Italy in keeping with a trend that was already manifesting itself in other European countries. As in France or the Netherlands, the regulation makes it mandatory for small CCBs to become part of a much larger group with a central institution which, in the case of Italy, must be a joint-stock company with a minimum capital of € 1 billion. The apex may act as the holding company for specialized financial and non-financial subsidiaries and direct and supervise the

[19] The deposit guarantee fund of CCBs was established in 1997 pursuant to the EU Directive on deposit guarantee schemes 94/19. It is a private consortium with mandatory membership. However, as early as 1978, CBs voluntarily constituted a central guarantee fund, which was an early form of Institutional Protection Scheme (IPS) designed to protect CBs' depositors and customers. As reported by Dell'Erba (2016), the fund managed several situations of financial distress, with no impact on customers.

[20] As reported in the statute of the temporary guarantee fund available at http://www. fondotemporaneo.bcc.it/template/default.asp?i_menuID=53901.

[21] See the annual report of the Deposit Guarantee Fund of the credit co-operative banks for the year-end 2017.

affiliated CCBs.[22] The choice of the joint-stock company as the mandatory legal form and the level at which the minimum capital endowment was set were motivated by the need to have apex companies whose size facilitates access to capital markets and the achievement of an adequate rating.

To protect the stability of the co-operative banking group and its components, the apex must be able to: perform strategic directions and define operational objectives common to all the banks in the group; influence the composition and professional qualification of administrative bodies; define common credit policies; and carry out incisive, widespread, and independent controls to monitor the criteria for assuming the risks and related limits established in group policies. The apex must have the power to issue instructions to CCBs and implement corrective measures, which may include the removal of the CCBs' management in some specific cases. The reform requires the implementation of a cross-guarantee scheme in compliance with the applicable prudential regulations with the dual purpose of guaranteeing the obligations of any entity belonging to the group against a third party, in relation to a possible default (external guarantee) and ensuring financial support mechanisms for the solvency and liquidity of the members (intra-group financial support mechanism). An important aspect of the reform is also the introduction of investment shares which CCBs may issue to raise their capital (specifically their Core Equity Tier 1—CET1) in specific circumstances of financial distress and which, unlike analogous shares issued, for example, in France or Finland, are intended for certain investors, namely the apex, guarantee funds of CBs and funds dedicated to the promotion and development of the co-operation.

To preserve the mutual and local character of co-operative banking in Italy, the reform and a recent Decree 91/2018 state that at least 60% of the apex's capital must be held by CCBs belonging to that co-operative banking group and that the majority of the members of the apex's board of directors must be appointed by CBs. The new co-operative banking groups' authorization by the supervisory authority is subject to verification of its compliance with European banking rules, and the ability of the groups to be competitive in the market and to guarantee economies of scale and the reduction of costs for individual CCBs. An additional legislative interven-

---

[22] In case of withdrawal or exclusion from a co-operative banking group, the individual CCB, according to the procedures established by banking law, subject to authorization issued by the Bank of Italy may decide to convert into a joint-stock company. Failing this, the CCB must consider liquidation. Surprisingly, the rule leaves no room for conversion into a popular bank.

tion (Law 136/2018) exclusively allowed the CBs of the autonomous provinces of Trento and Bolzano to set up an IPS as an alternative to the forced membership of a co-operative banking group. In response to co-operative banking fears that the governance of co-operative banking groups resulting from the reform may alter the original mutual nature of these banks, the above mentioned law enabled the governmental authority to subject the parent companies of the co-operative banking groups to controls aimed at verifying that the exercise of the role and functions of the parent company is consistent with the mutualistic aims of the CCBs belonging to the groups. In the event of discrepancies, the Bank of Italy, upon notification by the government authority, can take appropriate supervisory measures.

It is quite evident that the two reforms are fundamentally motivated by certain elements which they hold in common, while other elements by contrast reflect the profoundly different systematic outcomes which the legislator pursued. In the case of the latter, different views on the specific mutuality of the two categories are evident, where, in one case, the disappearance of mutuality is in a sense "certified" (Fiordiponti 2015) when a bank's size increases beyond a certain threshold, while, in the other, the organizational solution found serves to strengthen the resilience of CCBs in the market. In both cases, the reluctance shown by both categories of CBs to spontaneously undertake the changes that the supervisory authorities had indicated several times was decisive. In both cases, however, the debate on the value and legitimacy of the reforms is still far from over. As reported by Romano (2017), leaders in the CCB sector argue that their reform will drive the market's evolution toward a more coherent, competitive, and stable form of co-operative banking, in which the central traits of mutuality and localism will remain unchanged and even be increased (Azzi 2016). Others, by contrast, maintain that aggregation into groups, with the consequent removal of decision-making concerning operational strategies from individual banks' spheres of influence, will end up compromising the co-operative essence of CCBs, which will be transformed into mere distributors of the parent company's products (Tonelli 2017).

4   ITALIAN CO-OPERATIVE BANKING NETWORKS: MAIN CHARACTERISTICS

In other European countries, the development of CBs has occurred mainly within legal and institutional frameworks in which the central bodies play a driving role. The development model followed by Italian CBs is characterized by a greater degree of differentiation between CCBs and popular banks and a lower degree of integration, with each type of institution following an autonomous development path. Both models have strengths and weaknesses. On the one hand, elements of close central coordination can compensate for limitations and inefficiencies which arise from the small size of individual CBs. On the other hand, in banking as in other industries, entrepreneurial autonomy fosters competition, the search for innovative solutions, and the ability to adapt to local economic needs. The existence of a heterogeneous group of banks has benefited the Italian banking system and proved invaluable for the economic development of the country over time (Tarantola 2009). CCBs in particular, thanks to the social mission and principles of solidarity inherent in their corporate model, in addition to helping customers potentially at risk of exclusion from the credit market and, therefore, of being forced to accept very high interest rates, have actively supported particular segments of the market, such as small and medium-sized enterprises (SMEs). It is on the basis of these premises that the Italian system has always safeguarded the peculiarities of CBs in their various forms.

4.1   The Popular Banks' Network

Popular banks and CCBs represent the two types of limited liability co-operative banking companies governed by Italian legislation. The former are defined as CBs with limited mutuality, as there is no reference in Italian banking law to their prime banking activity being to the benefit of their members. Any link between the regulations governing popular banks and those of co-operatives (decree No. 1577 of 1947 and subsequent amendments) is expressly excluded by the legislation which thus confirms these organizations' severance with any duties of mutuality. Where these remain at all, they are set out in the statutes of these banks. A popular bank is constituted with a minimum of 200 members and, as in the tradition of CBs, may make use of an approval clause when considering potential members.[23] Each member holds a single voting right, regardless of the number of shares held.[24] Limits are set on the holdings of co-operative shares (set at a maximum of 1% of the bank capital) to enable the establishment of public companies with a large number of members.[25] However, this restriction does not apply to investment funds and bank foundations whose contribution to the bank's capital may ease capital increases, thus overcoming one of the typical weaknesses of CBs: their difficulty in raising large amounts of capital quickly. Their openness to new types of members however, as has also been the case in other European banking contexts, sits ill with maintaining the principle of "one head, one vote" in these institutions. The limits on exercising administrative rights discourage investment from these types of members who come to assume a purely funding role. On the other hand, this opportunistic solution of making the popular banks' capital available to investors other than the typical co-operative members represents a clumsy attempt to prevent the popular banks from becoming infected with the now established historical hybridization with the shareholder-oriented banking model, which is influenced by the logic of how capital markets function. As highlighted earlier, the reform of the popular banks has forced individual intermediaries or banking groups led by a popular bank to be converted into joint-stock companies when their consolidated assets exceed the amount of € 8 billion. The ten banks affected by this provision already held group structures, controlling other popular and non-popular banks, as well as companies active in various areas of financial intermediation and in the insurance business.

Italian popular banks are fully configured as an atomized network, according to the classification provided by Desrochers and Fischer (2005). They share a national association, Associazione Nazionale fra le Banche Popolari (ANBP), which represents its members in issues of common concern. The association performs various functions, at the national, European, and international level, in support of the sector, including in particular: proposing measures useful to the development and protection

---

[23] The Italian banking law regulates popular banks in Articles 29–32. The Bank of Italy has responsibility for issuing the rules of implementation.

[24] By way of derogation from this principle, the reform of popular banks enacted in 2015 states that up to five voting rights may be assigned to legal persons by the bylaws. Furthermore, it is envisaged that the number of voting proxies assigned to a single member may be between a minimum of 10 and a maximum of 20.

[25] The nominal value of the shares cannot be less than € 2.

of popular banks to the regulatory and supervisory authorities; assisting members in economic, financial, legal, tax, technical, and social matters and in all other matters related to the organization and operation of popular banks; and promoting awareness of popular banks through studies, publications, and conferences.

4.2 The Credit Co-operative Banks' Networks

The establishment of CCBs is regulated by Italian banking law,[26] which provides for a form of co-operative society with limited liability for members. In order for access to co-operative partner status to be as broad and democratic as possible, Italian legislation sets the minimum and maximum value of co-operative shares at between € 25 and € 500. In addition, individual shareholdings are limited to a value of € 100,000 and one vote is attributed to each member, regardless of the number of shares they hold. Banks' individual statutes may make the acquisition of shareholder status conditional on the subscription of a given minimum number of shares. The minimum number of members of credit co-operative banks cannot be less than 500. If the number falls below this threshold, the social structure must be reinstated within a year; otherwise, the bank is put into liquidation.[27] The banking law does not specify particular categories of persons who are permitted to acquire member status, but by keeping the banks' historical links with their original communities, it establishes that members must reside, be based or operate on an ongoing basis within the territory of the bank itself. In terms of activity, as in other European countries, the Italian regulations do not restrict bank funding, allowing banks to pursue different types of contracts (e.g. deposits, CDs, bonds, etc.) and counterparties (members and resident and non-resident non-members). However, the law states that the lending activity must be mainly to the benefit of the members, in deference to the banks' original remit of enabling sections of the population to access credit, thereby enabling them to participate in and promote economic development.[28] The Bank of Italy may authorize individual CCBs to undertake particular operations

---

[26] See Articles 33–37 of the Italian banking law.

[27] Members have the right to withdraw from the bank provided the withdrawal does not prejudice the stability of the bank.

[28] Exceptions to this rule can only be granted by the supervisory authority, the Bank of Italy, provided that this is functional to the maintenance or pursuit of the individual bank's financial stability.

for specified time periods in favor of customers other than its shareholders, but only for reasons of stability. The authorization to start up a new bank, as well as for any aggregation between co-operative banks, rests with the supervisory authority. However, as already highlighted above, the recent reform ties the new banks into an affiliation with a co-operative banking group, with the bank becoming a member of its apex. Individual banks can be expelled from a banking group due to serious violations of the law or can withdraw from it under two circumstances: liquidation or conversion into a joint-stock company. There is no option to convert to a popular bank.

Finally, there are restrictions in place on the distribution of profits: at least 70% of the annual net profits must be allocated to the legal reserve. A portion of the annual net profits must be paid into a fund for the promotion and development of co-operative activity, while the remaining portion of profits may be used for the revaluation of shares, assigned to other reserves, distributed to members, or allocated for charitable purposes or to promote the principles of mutuality.

Individual CCBs are part of local federations (15 federations covering one or more Italian region), which in turn are members of Federcasse, the national federation of CCBs. Before the reform, Federcasse had responsibility for representing the sector and offered legal, fiscal, and organizational assistance, providing support in communications and training to the benefit of the entire sector. The local federations are the associative bodies of CCBs (which adhere to them voluntarily) and represent them within their geographic territory. They were involved in the gathering of information and signals coming from the local CCBs and channeling them toward the national bodies, while also distributing information and indications from the latter to the banks. They offered consultancy support and contributed to the development of local-regional strategies. Following the reform, the roles of the regional and national associative bodies are undergoing a process of revision. While the national federation will retain its strategic role in the general representation of the Italian co-operative banking sector as well as certain other tasks, including liaison with trade unions, the role of regional federations is currently less clear. However, their historical roles will certainly be revisited in light of the coordination activities assigned to the central institutions of the new co-operative banking groups.

To date, in addition to ICCREA (historically the central institution which due to the reform of the sector has acquired the apex role of one of the two new co-operative banking groups), another organization, Cassa Centrale Banca that has already been acting as a central institution at a provincial level, has become the apex of the second most important co-operative banking group. A third network of Raiffeisen CBs located in a narrow geographical area of the Trentino-Alto Adige region, having initiated legal disputes and opened a dialogue with the Italian government with the aim of preserving their autonomy, were allowed to form an IPS at the end of 2018.

ICCREA co-operative banking group, with ICCREA Bank as its apex, supports the affiliated CCBs, both directly and indirectly through its subsidiaries, providing products, services, and consultancy to enable local CBs to maximize their market performance. The subsidiaries held by the apex are active across three main business segments: institutional business, covering activities ranging from wholesale trading and market-making for Italian government securities, bonds, and derivatives, as well as structured finance transactions and activities related to the payments system; corporate business, providing financial solutions to small- and medium-sized enterprises and local government entities through dedicated subsidiaries, which offer special corporate finance products, medium/long-term lending and international services, leasing, factoring, rental, and other advanced consulting services; and finally, the retail business segment which consists of companies that offer products and services to the retail customers of CCBs. Products developed include asset management, personal loans, electronic money, and insurance products. The failure of the project to unify the co-operative banking sector is mainly a reflection of the cultural differences that still characterize the sector and the country and that over time, unlike in other European countries examined in this work, for example, France, have prevented the development of self-determined integration projects. Both Cassa Centrale Banca and Cassa Centrale Raiffeisen have already been acting as central institutions, regulating transactions on the payment system, participating in refinancing operations, and offered financial services of various kinds to member banks (including portfolio management for owned securities, the underwriting of derivatives for hedging purposes, portfolio management for customers, and intermediation in currencies). Additionally, they have been active in the issuance of payment cards, in the development of specific financial products (e.g. leasing, factoring, insurance products, consumer credit), and in the provision of advisory services (such as methodological/IT support for the measurement and analysis of risks and for planning as well as the management of anomalous credits/real estate assets and their sale).

Cassa Centrale has been operating for over 40 years as a reference partner for individual CCBs, and, following the decision to reform the co-operative banking system in Italy, was chosen to become the central institution for its existing network and the other CCBs that joined the new co-operative banking group. The group comprises CCBs mostly located in northern and central Italy, along with a smaller number from southern Italy.

The third co-operative banking network is the one formed by the CCBs that maintained the name of their founder in their denomination, Raiffeisen, and whose distinctive feature is its strong local focus. It falls under the category of the so-called provincial co-operative groups introduced by the reform. It comprises CCBs located in the province of Bolzano, an Italian/German-speaking province in the north of Italy close to Austria, which enjoys some economic benefits due to its regional autonomy. Not all CCBs in this province have joined the Raiffeisen network and its related IPS.

According to the publicly available data, 142 CCBs (nearly 54% of the total number of CCBs at the end of 2018) amalgamated with the ICCREA group, 84 joined the Cassa Centrale Group (32%), and 39 the IPS of the Raiffeisen CBs (14%). Both the ICCREA and Cassa Centrale groups are subject to the supervision of the ECB as they hold total assets of over € 30 billion. In January 2019, the extraordinary meeting of ICCREA Banca was held to approve the statutory changes for the set-up of the ICCREA co-operative banking group and a sizeable equity increase. The newly established co-operative banking group ICCREA is the fourth national banking group in terms of assets, with about € 148 billion, and the third in terms of its branch network, with about 2650 branches. The Group, together with the participating CCBs, has a total of 4.2 million customers, of which 750,000 are members. The Group is expected to start its operations during 2019. In January 2019, Cassa Centrale Banca banking group began operations. The group holds 1500 branches, 11,000 employees, € 72 billion in assets, € 45 billion in gross loans and € 6.7 billion in equity. Based on the figures for the end of 2017, the ICCREA and Cassa Centrale Banca groups, which operates nationwide, is respectively the sixth and tenth largest Italian banking groups, measured by market share of loans (5.3% and 2.7% respectively) (Bank of Italy 2018). The provincial co-operative Raiffeisen IPS in the Alto Adige region, with a 0.6% share of the national loan market, is among the major banks in the region of Trentino-Alto Adige (with 22% of loans).[29] The ICCREA and Cassa Centrale groups fall within the provisions of Art. 10 of the CRR and will in all respects be strategic groups according to the taxonomy provided by Desrochers and Fischer (2005), under the supervision of the ECB. The Raiffeisen IPS falls within the provisions of Art. 113(7) of the CRR and may be considered, analogously to the Austrian and German ones, as a quasi-strategic network. The Raiffeisen IPS will come under the joint supervision of the ECB and the Bank of Italy.

5   The Performances of Italian Co-operative Versus Non-Co-operative Banking Groups over the Period 2005–2017

In Italy, as in other European countries under investigation in this book, the process of the hybridization of co-operative banking originated mainly in the 1990s, following the deregulation of the national banking system. In the years preceding the reform, the major popular banks were already acting as de-mutualized companies but with a co-operative governance system; the small, independent CCBs operated within a decentralized network, although they had a central reference institution, a joint-stock bank, essentially intended to act as a financial product factory. The different configuration of the hybridization assumed by the CBs in Italy has, over time, highlighted critical elements that the GFC has amplified, leading to the reforms of the popular banks and the CCBs. A series of issues arise as a consequence of the ongoing hybridization. A first question concerns its effects. In other words, have the mitigation of the principles of mutuality pursued by CBs and the growing complementarity with markets as places of investment and funding meant that the results achieved by CBs have become more similar to those of commercial joint-stock banks? Which areas record analogies and differences in results? Can a convergence in performance be observed over time? To answer these important questions, we have identified a series of indicators in the form of ratios proxying bank performances. The set of indicators used to run the comparisons concerns the capitalization of banks; their activities in lending and investing in

[29] See the Bank of Italy's Annual Report for the year-end 2017.

securities, including those held for trading on the financial markets; their reliance on deposits from customers; the role they play over time in the interbank market; the riskiness deriving from their lending; and, finally, banking profitability and efficiency.

In order to verify if, where and when there have been phenomena of convergence between co-operative and non-co-operative banking groups, one or more national peer shareholder-oriented banking groups have been identified with which the following comparative analysis is carried out. The analysis covers the period 2005–2017 and is particularly helpful since it allows the results obtained by the two groups of banks to be taken before and after the outbreak of the GFC. Data are collected from three databases SNL, BankScope Bureau van Dijk, and Orbis Bank Focus in order to minimize the potential for missing data. In line with the reorganization of the CCBs system, we reconstruct the three groups, made up of the CCBs' networks and their respective top institutions, weighting the data of each group member. The weighting is calculated using the balance sheet assets of the individual components. This procedure was adopted in order to try to provide a view of the performances of these three co-operative entities at a consolidated level. The data available in the databases used make it possible to cover well over 90% of the entities belonging to each group at the end of 2017. Specifically, the sample of CCBs that opted for the establishment of an IPS is fully covered; of the 84 CCBs belonging to the Cassa Centrale group, 82 are present in the databases; while there are 130 out of the 142 CCBs of the ICCREA group. Where mergers and acquisitions have taken place between CBs, the individual entities involved are considered autonomously until the time of the aggregation operation. Following that, data from the new entity is used, where available.

In order to identify peer shareholder-oriented banks, the total year-end assets for 2018 for each of the three co-operative banking groups were used. According to the data publicly available, the total assets of ICCREA were valued at approximately € 150 billion in 2018 with 2650 branches; those of Cassa Centrale were approximately € 75 billion with 1500 branches, while the Raiffeisen banks' network held total assets of about € 19 billion.

The three Italian co-operative banking groups are compared, on a tentative aggregated basis, with three shareholder-oriented banking groups, namely UBI Banca (a former popular bank which converted into a joint-stock company in 2015, with about € 127 billion of consolidated assets at the end of 2017), BNL-BNP Paribas (a joint-stock subsidiary of the

French BNP Paribas group, with around € 79 billion of consolidated assets), and Credito Emiliano (a joint-stock banking group with about € 42 billion of consolidated assets).

The data used in this first phase of analysis are representative of the results achieved by the co-operative and non-co-operative groups, including the latter's networks of CBs and their various non-co-operative subsidiaries. Year-end figures are used. We provide means and standard deviations of the selected indicators in different sub-periods, covering respectively the pre-crisis period, 2005–2007; the main GFC period, 2008–2010; the period 2011–2013 during which the sovereign debt crisis severely affected various countries and important regulatory and monetary policy measures were put in place to restore bank financial stability; and the implementation of Basel 3 rules, the initiation of the European Banking Union with the implementation of the Single Supervisory Mechanism (SSM) and the Single Resolution Mechanism (SRM), 2014–2017.

In Table 7.4, we report the first set of indicators under investigation. The capital ratios employed consist of a regulatory proxy for the appraisal of the capital adequacy of the banking groups, the Tier 1 (%) ratio, and an accounting ratio represented by equity over assets (%). The first one stands for a measure of capital adequacy under the Basel rules to address credit risk. Broadly speaking, the Tier 1 ratio is calculated as the shareholder funds plus perpetual non-cumulative preference shares as a percentage of risk-weighted assets and some off-balance sheet items. The higher the Tier 1 value, the more capitalized the bank is, which improves its ability to face the risks arising from lending to and financing borrowers. Under the Basel 3 rules introduced in Europe in 2014 (with EU Directive 2013/36 and the EU Regulation 575/2013—CRR), the minimum level of Tier 1 permitted is 6% plus the capital conservation buffer of 2.5%. The ratio of equity to total assets (%) proxies the cushion against banking risks. The higher this figure, the better the bank is able to cope with potential losses arising from its activity.

The Tier 1 ratio has, on average, followed a similar trend for the co-operative banking groups: it decreased between 2008 and 2013 and rose in the following period, reaching average values ranging from about 18% to 21%. This result reflects mainly the effects of an asset recomposition of the co-operative networks that has seen average lending decrease and investment in securities increase, with a large part of the securities made up of government bonds. On the other hand, the capital endowments of commercial joint-stock banks, which are much lower than those held by

Table 7.4 Comparison of Italian co-operative vs. non-co-operative banking groups: capital ratios

	ICCREA Group		Cassa Centrale Group		Raiffeisen network		UBI Banca		BNL-BPN Paribas		Credito Emiliano	
	Mean	SD	Mean	SD	Mean	SD	Mean	SD	Mean	SD	Mean	SD
Tier 1 (%)												
2005–2007	16.38	1.59	18.20	0.21	18.98	0.16	7.02	0.43	7.05	0.33	7.88	0.15
2008–2010	15.55	0.62	16.80	0.27	17.47	0.24	7.72	0.24	7.13	0.12	7.96	0.73
2011–2013	15.14	0.15	16.98	0.53	17.16	0.44	11.04	2.08	8.73	1.17	9.35	0.64
2014–2017	17.87	0.75	21.19	3.34	18.87	0.28	11.86	0.41	11.55	0.55	12.89	1.20
Equity to total assets (%)												
2005–2007	10.51	0.23	12.44	0.11	17.88	0.15	8.46	1.87	5.60	0.17	5.94	0.20
2008–2010	10.56	0.11	11.61	0.43	16.87	0.23	9.77	0.54	5.43	0.18	6.28	0.63
2011–2013	8.52	0.53	9.41	0.22	15.29	0.15	8.19	0.73	5.92	0.71	6.20	0.79
2014–2017	7.91	0.21	9.97	0.66	14.59	1.08	8.35	0.50	7.16	0.20	6.52	0.26

Source: Author's calculations

This table reports descriptive statistics (means and standard deviations—SD) of Italian co-operative and non-co-operative banking groups. Tier 1 (%) is the ratio between primary regulatory capital and risk-weighted assets; Equity/total assets (%) is the ratio between total equity and total assets. Our calculations are based on data extracted from BankScope and Orbis Bank Focus solely for the year-ends 2016–2017 for the co-operative banking groups ICCREA and Cassa Centrale, and for the network of Raiffeisen CBs and their apex (Raiffeisen network). Consolidated data for UBI Banca, BNL-BNP Paribas, and Credito Emiliano are extracted from SNL

co-operatives, have followed a consistently increasing trend, reaching similar sectoral average values of about 12% in the period 2014–2017. However, in each sub-period analyzed, the co-operative groups perform on average better than their non-co-operative peers, resulting in them being better equipped to face the risks arising from the intermediation activity. Of the three co-operative networks, Cassa Centrale and, with even greater concentration, the network of the Raiffeisen banks hold the highest regulatory capital endowments.

Analysis of the ratio of equity to total assets reveals once again the co-operative banking groups holding comparatively higher levels of capital (Table 7.4). However, the average percentages of equity held by the co-operative groups have decreased over time, at close to 10% for Cassa Centrale, 14.6% for the Raiffeisen banks, and around 8% for the largest co-operative group, ICCREA, in 2014–2017. These values are largely below those held in the pre-crisis period. Shareholder-oriented banks, by contrast, thanks to their more intensive pursuit of a combination of asset reduction and recapitalization, hold higher average equity to total assets ratios than those recorded before the outbreak of the GFC. Nevertheless, what emerges clearly from the reported data is that the gap in capital endowments that exists between co-operative and non-co-operative banks has been decreasing over time, with the smallest co-operative banking groups showing higher levels of capital. Compared internationally, in the various periods under observation, the capitalization of Italian co-operative banks is higher than that of the German financial co-operative network (see Table 6.5) and of the corresponding French CBs (see Table 5.4).

The second set of indicators concerns the asset side of the banking groups and aims to shed light on its composition. In this regard, we employ three types of ratios: the ratio of net customer loans to total assets (%) which measures the degree of dedication to the traditional lending activity; the ratio of the total securities held to total assets (%) which provides an assessment of banks' integration with financial markets in investment terms; and finally, the ratio of securities held for trading to total assets (%), which shows the degree of banks' active participation in the financial markets through financial instruments (i.e. bonds, derivatives, and stocks) and allows for an assessment of speculative activities within the financial markets.

The data shown in Table 7.5 indicate that, in contrast to what has been found in the other European countries under investigation, the lending activity of the Italian co-operative networks is on average lower than that recorded for shareholder-oriented banks. The average values recorded in

Table 7.5 Comparison of Italian co-operative vs. non-co-operative banking groups: lending and securities holdings ratios

	ICCREA Group		Cassa Centrale Group		Raiffeisen network		UBI Banca		BNL-BPN Paribas		Credito Emiliano	
	Mean	SD	Mean	SD	Mean	SD	Mean	SD	Mean	SD	Mean	SD
Net customer loans/total assets (%)												
2005–2007	57.97	1.31	64.14	2.49	71.51	0.74	72.11	3.94	71.84	2.36	59.87	0.48
2008–2010	62.99	1.74	66.37	1.02	68.29	1.60	79.07	1.05	74.99	4.56	62.51	3.92
2011–2013	50.03	8.05	54.98	6.60	67.20	3.34	72.71	3.60	77.10	3.33	64.80	2.02
2014–2017	43.64	3.45	49.41	2.28	56.96	3.26	71.96	1.12	77.59	0.38	60.79	1.38
Securities/total assets (%)												
2005–2007	–	–	–	–	–	–	–	–	–	–	–	–
2008–2010	–	–	–	–	–	–	8.77	1.79	7.55	0.22	26.42	2.72
2011–2013	34.33	3.72	33.15	5.40	18.56	5.57	15.20	4.63	8.75	0.89	27.09	2.61
2014–2017	35.44	0.91	33.08	1.86	32.43	4.95	16.89	2.83	9.51	1.89	32.61	0.93
Total assets held for trading/total assets (%)												
2005–2007	–	–	–	–	–	–	–	–	–	–	–	–
2008–2010	–	–	–	–	–	–	1.76	0.42	2.59	0.05	7.50	6.54
2011–2013	0.46	0.20	0.51	0.41	3.18	0.61	2.57	0.42	3.40	0.45	1.29	0.87
2014–2017	0.28	0.13	0.18	0.02	1.55	1.23	0.85	0.23	2.72	1.54	0.40	0.10

Source: Author's calculations

This table reports descriptive statistics (means and standard deviations—SD) of Italian co-operative and non-co-operative banking groups. Net customer loans/total assets (%) is the ratio between net loans and assets; Securities/total assets (%) is the ratio between total securities held and total assets; Assets held for trading/total assets (%) is the ratio between total assets held for trading and total assets. Our calculations are based on data extracted from BankScope and Orbis Bank Focus solely for the year-ends 2016–2017 for the co-operative banking groups ICCREA and Cassa Centrale, and for the network of Raiffeisen CBs and their apex (Raiffeisen network). Consolidated data for UBI Banca, BNL-BNP Paribas, and Credito Emiliano are extracted from SNL

the last period are much lower than the pre-crisis values and those observed in 2008–2010, during which time the support given by the majority of the co-operative groups to the Italian real economy was highlighted. The reduction in the impact of lending to customers is around 15 percentage points. According to our calculations, of the three groups, it is the smallest, consisting of the Raiffeisen CBs, that lend most in the period 2014–2017 (56.96%), followed by Cassa Centrale (49.41%) and ICCREA (43.64%). These values are mostly aligned with those of the French co-operative banking groups in 2014–2017, but are significantly lower than those of the German co-operative financial network (59.57%) (see Table 6.6).

Surprisingly, the selected Italian commercial joint-stock banks, especially the largest UBI Banca and BNL-BNP Paribas, are more involved in lending (with percentages above 70%) and, unlike their co-operative counterparts, recorded average values in 2014–2017 that are higher or similar to those prior to the start of the GFC. Over the period 2011–2017, the co-operative banking groups show a greater degree of integration with financial markets in terms of their allocation in financial instruments (Table 7.5). A third of the assets of the new Italian co-operative groups are almost permanently made up of securities, most of which are often government securities. Among the non-co-operative banks, only Credito Emiliano occupies a similar position. The percentage weights of the other commercial banks' securities portfolios are decidedly lower, although they are increasing. For example, UBI Banca allocated 16.89% of its total assets to securities in 2014–2017, while BNL-BNP Paribas placed only 9.51%.

The sustained investment in the co-operative banking groups' securities portfolios, which was accompanied by a reduction in the commitment to loans to customers, reflects the need of these banks to diversify their asset mix and pursue prudent credit policies in light of the deterioration of the Italian macro-economic situation since 2010. The interest in trading is generally lower for CCBs than for non-co-operative ones (see Table 7.5), except in the case of the Raiffeisen network.

If we calculate the impact of the assets held for trading on the total securities held, we find that the two main co-operative banking groups allocated less than 1% of their securities portfolios to financial assets held for trading purposes in the period 2014–2017. Average values of around 5% were held by Raiffeisen and UBI Banca during the same period (a significant decrease from the previous period), while the incidence was about 29% for the BNL-BNP Paribas group and only 1.2% for Credito Emiliano.

These values indicate that for the vast majority of the Italian co-operative banking sector, trading activities are very limited and are substantially below the level of French and German co-operative banking groups.

The third set of selected indicators concerns the percentage of traditional funding through customer deposits and interbank activity (Table 7.6). CBs' reliance on the collection of customer deposits does not appear to be significantly different from that of commercial banks. In the period 2014–2017, average values stood at 50%, with the sole exception of the Raiffeisen network which exhibits an average value of 61.35%. The latter was able to increase its attractiveness for deposits, while for the other two co-operative groups, the values recorded in 2014–2017 are similar to or slightly higher than those of the pre-crisis period. Shareholder-oriented banks have actually increased their dependence on deposits compared to their position in 2005–2007. In comparative terms, the Italian co-operative banks' funding in the form of deposits is based on values that are higher than those of the French co-operative groups (around 40%) but lower than that of the German co-operative financial network (close to 64%) in the last sub-period.

As regards participation in the interbank markets, measured by the interbank ratio, the data displayed in Table 7.6 show that both co-operative banking groups and their shareholder-oriented counterparts have generally decreased their ratios over time. As has been observed in the other European banking systems under investigation, such as in Austria and France, the co-operative groups are more widely involved in the provision of funds on interbank markets than the joint-stock banks.

Table 7.7 presents risk indicators that assumed particular importance during the GFC, prompting regulators to dictate more stringent prudential rules toward banks' exposure to liquidity risk and credit risk. The table contains a proxy for exposure to liquidity risk, often used in the empirical literature, and two proxies for credit risk. The use of the ratio of liquid assets to total liabilities (excluding equity) was preferred to the prudential ratios relating to liquidity risk, since the latter would have been available only for the last of the periods under investigation. The ratio used looks at the amount of liquid assets available to cover all the liabilities held by banks. The higher this percentage is, the more liquid and generally able to redeem its debts the bank is, and the less vulnerable it is to a classic run on the bank.

The data in Table 7.7 show that co-operative groups are on average much more liquid than non-co-operative counterparts. In the period 2011–2017, the distance between the levels of liquidity held by the two

Table 7.6 Comparison of Italian co-operative vs. non-co-operative banking groups: funding and interbank ratios

	ICCREA Group		Cassa Centrale Group		Raiffeisen network		UBI Banca		BNL-BPN Paribas		Credito Emiliano	
	Mean	SD	Mean	SD	Mean	SD	Mean	SD	Mean	SD	Mean	SD
Customer deposit/total assets (%)												
2005–2007	47.22	0.16	50.46	0.60	43.71	0.66	40.51	1.05	40.61	1.45	44.31	1.27
2008–2010	46.76	1.58	48.56	0.54	45.90	2.04	39.32	3.00	37.55	2.60	44.32	4.29
2011–2013	42.33	2.19	40.04	2.18	51.93	5.01	37.07	0.77	40.55	3.92	43.53	0.43
2014–2017	51.82	6.94	50.40	8.12	61.35	1.71	45.84	7.34	52.19	4.77	49.46	4.38
Interbank ratio (%)												
2005–2007	309.93	29.23	320.67	30.45	183.00	44.35	55.90	15.65	81.71	23.27	75.08	6.11
2008–2010	305.61	85.44	321.16	85.48	218.93	51.37	67.41	22.66	37.70	18.52	35.78	20.51
2011–2013	86.88	6.44	74.81	15.07	148.17	61.59	32.83	20.81	23.24	11.02	13.76	0.77
2014–2017	85.61	13.75	78.94	14.61	140.73	38.68	31.02	11.06	19.99	7.23	15.01	9.68

Source: Author's calculations

This table reports descriptive statistics (means and standard deviations—SD) of Italian co-operative and non-co-operative banking groups. Customer deposit/total assets (%) is the ratio between customer deposits and total assets; Interbank ratio (%) is the ratio between loans to banks and deposits from banks. Our calculations are based on data extracted from BankScope and Orbis Bank Focus solely for the year-ends 2016–2017 for the co-operative banking groups ICCREA and Cassa Centrale, and for the network of Raiffeisen CBs and their apex (Raiffeisen network). Consolidated data for UBI Banca, BNL-BNP Paribas, and Credito Emiliano are extracted from SNL

Table 7.7 Comparison of Italian co-operative vs. non-co-operative banking groups: liquidity and credit risk ratios

	ICCREA Group		Cassa Centrale Group		Raiffeisen network		UBI Banca		BNL-BPN Paribas		Credito Emiliano	
	Mean	SD	Mean	SD	Mean	SD	Mean	SD	Mean	SD	Mean	SD
Liquid assets/total liabilities (%)												
2005–2007	24.59[a]	1.40	17.80	2.13	13.03	0.53	10.20	2.97	18.83	3.34	31.80	1.81
2008–2010	18.46	2.66	13.72	1.45	14.70	0.36	4.98	0.31	13.62	5.88	13.25	7.68
2011–2013	21.40	2.02	17.55	1.58	11.96	1.12	7.27	1.17	9.36	3.11	7.49	1.46
2014–2017	21.19	1.47	12.87	2.25	14.78	1.60	5.34	1.70	6.96	2.46	9.19	2.22
Impaired loans/gross loans and advances (%)												
2005–2007	6.19[a]	0.00	5.42[a]	0.15	12.51[a]	1.32	3.35	1.03	6.52	0.34	1.02	0.19
2008–2010	7.90	1.16	6.63	0.86	10.24	0.80	4.79	1.40	7.66	1.50	3.01	0.97
2011–2013	13.22	2.11	10.90	2.82	8.56	0.32	9.64	2.12	12.93	1.97	4.80	0.78
2014–2017	16.98	0.72	16.61	0.68	7.31	1.31	13.81	1.02	17.47	1.57	5.51	0.32
LLR/impaired loans (%)												
2005–2007	42.55[a]	0.25	42.04[a]	0.10	16.00[a]	1.22	48.23	6.58	78.10	3.44	83.45	1.76
2008–2010	41.92	1.25	34.68	1.65	20.33	2.29	49.05	3.49	69.51	6.79	55.96	8.94
2011–2013	39.29	2.33	38.29	3.32	23.69	2.07	38.62	2.95	58.19	4.01	46.69	1.43
2014–2017	51.04	3.77	54.64	5.00	39.29	14.34	36.19	3.73	55.43	1.75	50.96	1.78

Source: Author's calculations

This table reports descriptive statistics (means and standard deviations—SD) of Italian co-operative and non-co-operative banking groups. Liquid assets/total liabilities (%) is the ratio between liquid assets and total liabilities; Impaired loans/gross loans and advances (%) is the ratio between impaired loans and gross customer loans and advances; LLR/impaired loans (%) is the ratio between loan loss reserves and impaired loans. Our calculation on data extracted from BankScope and Orbis Bank Focus for the sole year-ends 2016–2017

[a]Only 2006–2007

business models was accentuated. While CCBs exhibit a fluctuating trend, joint-stock banks constantly and sensibly reduce the liquidity held. This seems to stem on the one hand from the greater attention these banks pay to lending activity, and on the other, from their reduced need to hold liquidity reserves due to the positive effect exerted by the increase in the insurance coverage of bank deposits. The latter, in strengthening depositors' trust in banks, favors the inflow and stability of the deposits themselves.

Although the co-operative banking groups are more able to cope with unexpected requirements for liquidity, their exposure to credit risk has increased over time. Table 7.7 reports two proxies: the ratio of impaired loans to gross loans and advances (%) and the ratio of loan loss reserves to impaired loans (%). The first one shows impaired or non-performing loans as a percentage of the bank's gross customer loans and advances (%). It indicates the weakness of the loan portfolio which increases as the percentage rises. This is true, in particular, for ICCREA and Cassa Centrale (with an average value of around 17% in 2014–2017), while the trend observed for the Raiffeisen network is inverse (7.31% in the last of the analyzed sub-periods). The riskiness of the non-co-operative banks' credit portfolios also worsened, but most noticeably only for the two largest commercial banks in the sample, UBI Banca and BNL-BNP Paribas.

The other ratio reported in Table 7.7 relates loan loss reserves to non-performing or impaired loans. Higher values of this ratio, also known as the "coverage ratio", indicate that the bank is better equipped to face losses on loans. On the other hand, of all accounting considerations, higher levels of the coverage rate are generally indicative of a poorer quality loan portfolio. The deterioration in the quality of the loan portfolios of the banks under examination has had different repercussions in the definition of the provisioning levels to cover the loan losses. In fact, while the co-operative networks have increased the percentages of coverage of the impaired loans as a result of the higher percentage of impaired loans, the commercial banks, who were originally better equipped, have reduced the coverage of the impaired loans. In the context of the European banking systems under analysis here, the Italian system is the most involved in absorbing the negative impacts of the double financial crises on banking intermediation. The co-operative banking system analyzed here has been severely hit, weakening its traditional capacity to support the real economy. Only the smallest network of Raiffeisen CBs has managed to absorb the effects of financial and economic turbulence on the Italian economy more effectively. On one hand, this could be the result of their individual capacity to put in place more effective processes for selecting debtors; on the other hand, the CB network's high degree of geographical and cultural proximity seems to facilitate the emergence of informal forms of coordination that serve to improve the risk management abilities of these banks.

The last battery of indicators that we examine involves variables that are representative of bank profitability and efficiency, widely employed in the empirical literature. With regard to the profitability analysis, three indicators are taken into consideration: the net interest margin (%), the return on average assets (ROAA) (%), and the return on average equity (ROAE) (%). To evaluate the operational efficiency achieved by the bank management, we use a widespread indicator: the cost-to-income ratio (%) (Table 7.8).

The net interest margin (%) represents the profitability stemming from the bank's credit intermediation activity. It is expressed as the percentage of net interest income to earning assets. Less diversified banks generally enjoy higher net interest margins. Higher values of the ratio may be indicative of cost advantages in the funding or may derive from the exploitation of strong market power positions. In the periods analyzed, the ratio is constantly higher for the co-operative banking groups. The average net interest margins of the two largest co-operative banking groups, ICCREA and Cassa Centrale, are very similar. In the last sub-period, the Raiffeisen network enjoys a slightly higher profitability. Over time all the banks experience a considerable drop in their margins in light of both the deterioration in the quality of their loan portfolios, and the effects of a persistent low interest rate environment. Among commercial banks, only the Italian subsidiary of BNP Paribas has shown itself able to almost entirely recover its pre-crisis net interest margin. A common decreasing trend is also recorded for the ROAA (%) and the ROAE (%). However, in relation to both indicators, the performance of the co-operative model turns out to be on average higher than that of the two largest commercial banks in the sample. In this sample, the smallest banks under consideration, that is, the Raiffeisen network and the commercial bank Credito Emiliano, obtain the best income performance, especially after 2010.

The last indicator taken into account is the cost-to-income ratio (%), commonly used to analyze and compare the managerial efficiency of banks. Traditionally, CBs exhibit lower levels of efficiency which the literature attributes to the insulation of the governance model of these banks from the *stimuli* of market discipline. Data on the levels and trends of the

Table 7.8 Comparison of Italian co-operative vs. non-co-operative banking groups: profitability and efficiency ratios

	ICCREA Group		Cassa Centrale Group		Raiffeisen network		UBI Banca		BNL-BPN Paribas		Credito Emiliano	
	Mean	SD	Mean	SD	Mean	SD	Mean	SD	Mean	SD	Mean	SD
Net interest margin (%)												
2005–2007	2.93	0.24	3.06	0.28	2.41	0.21	2.53	0.05	2.48	0.18	2.32	0.49
2008–2010	2.72	0.40	2.68	0.52	2.23	0.36	2.35	0.45	2.25	00.6	2.07	0.18
2011–2013	2.23	0.24	2.17	0.19	2.12	0.14	1.68	0.15	2.19	0.05	1.86	0.02
2014–2017	1.67	0.11	1.75	0.10	1.83	0.26	1.51	0.14	2.20	0.27	1.51	0.23
ROAA (%)												
2005–2007	0.74	0.11	0.98	0.20	0.68	0.22	0.88	0.05	0.17	0.39	1.11	0.14
2008–2010	0.40	0.27	0.53	0.24	0.54	0.19	0.17	0.06	0.17	0.12	0.38	0.15
2011–2013	0.23	0.07	0.31	0.11	0.58	0.13	−0.38	0.91	0.12	0.08	0.36	0.04
2014–2017	0.19	0.08	0.14	0.11	0.49	0.12	−0.15	0.62	0.06	0.15	0.43	0.06
ROAE (%)												
2005–2007	7.32	0.94	8.15	1.76	4.42	1.69	8.46	0.49	2.95	6.86	18.50	1.93
2008–2010	3.76	2.34	4.62	1.98	3.62	1.22	1.71	0.58	3.12	2.19	6.25	2.87
2011–2013	2.87	0.90	3.65	1.18	4.17	1.02	−4.56	10.89	2.23	1.61	5.96	0.62
2014–2017	2.23	1.28	1.52	1.24	3.65	1.00	−1.57	7.43	0.78	2.11	6.54	0.84
Cost to income (%)												
2005–2007	67.40	3.39	64.70	4.53	67.82	5.22	61.59	2.26	68.21	7.15	65.63	3.87
2008–2010	69.46	4.07	69.26	5.37	66.21	2.80	68.37	1.98	64.59	4.77	76.35	4.52
2011–2013	61.14	5.30	59.80	7.14	63.83	3.75	73.02	10.72	60.85	0.80	70.09	1.64
2014–2017	64.09	5.78	61.37	9.04	61.08	4.18	70.04	9.66	65.82	3.49	69.71	2.90

Source: Author's calculations

This table shows descriptive statistics (means and standard deviations—SD) of Italian co-operative and non-co-operative banking groups, the network of popular banks. Net interest margin (%) is the ratio between net interest income and total earning assets; ROAA (%) is the return on average assets; ROAE (%) is the return on average equity; Cost to income (%) is the ratio between operating expenses and intermediation margin. Our calculation on data extracted from BankScope and Orbis bank Focus for the sole year-ends 2016–2017. Consolidated data for UBI Banca, BNL-BNP Paribas, and Credito Emiliano are extracted from SNL

cost-to-income ratio (%) shown in Table 7.8 do not allow us to support this theoretical view. Shareholder-oriented banks fared slightly better from 2005 to 2010. After this period, their operating efficiency significantly worsened, reaching an average value of between 65% and 70%. By contrast, the cost-to-income ratio of the co-operative banking sector is decidedly lower. It seems to have undertaken processes of operational efficiency more rigorously, reaching values close to 60%. Among the co-operative groups, ICCREA records the highest average value in 2014–2017, at 64.09%.

In order to verify whether there are significant differences between the two banking business models, the non-parametric Wilcoxon-Mann-Whitney (WMW) (1947) test[30] is used. This is suitable for small sample sizes and for testing whether observations in one population tend to be larger than observations in the other as it tests the equality of central tendency of two distributions (Fay and Proschan 2010). The selected indicators are subjected to the test during the period 2008–2017 only. It was decided to concentrate the analysis on this ten-year period, because we want to check whether, and if so, how the manifestation of the episodes of crisis and the start of the Banking Union in 2014, have affected the performance of the two business models, and whether this makes them more similar or not. The results of the test with the relative p-values are reported in Table 7.9.

The two business models display significant differences in the results they have achieved, as evidenced by the p-values obtained. CCBs' capitalization is significantly higher over 2008–2017 than that of joint-stock banks. Significant differences have been found also in comparing the asset and funding mix of the two business models. Unlike what has been recorded in other countries investigated in this book, Italian CCBs have median values for lending activity lower than those recorded by shareholder-oriented banks. On the contrary, the asset allocation in securities is significantly higher and has a value twice that of commercial joint-stock banks. These are mostly government bonds of which the Italian CCBs are known to be investors. The sustained investment in this type of financial asset generally reflects the numerous difficulties these banks face in supporting local credit markets, especially after the outbreak of the GFC. The uncertainties on the evolution of the macroeconomic context, on the one hand, and the managerial and technical criticalities in the assumption and management of the risks connected to the lending activity, on the other hand, have facilitated the fall-back to market financial assets that facilitate the management of the related risks,

---

[30] This test is also known as Wilcoxon ranksum test or Mann-Whitney U test.

Table 7.9   Wilcoxon-Mann-Whitney test (2008–2017)

Co-operative vs. non-co-operative banks

	Median	P-value
Capital ratios		
Tier 1 (%)	17.33–9.95	0.00
Equity/total assets (%)	10.61–6.88	0.00
Lending, securities holdings ratios		
Net customer loans/total assets (%)	58.78–72.33	0.00
Securities/total assets (%)	33.67–14.82	0.00
Total assets held for trading/total assets (%)	0.29–2.24	0.00
Funding and interbank ratios		
Customer deposit/total assets (%)	47.87–43.28	0.00
Interbank ratio (%)	103.94–25.38	0.00
Liquidity and credit risk ratios		
Liquid assets/total liabilities (%)	15.34–7.70	0.00
Impaired loans/gross customer loans and advances (%)	9.83–7.44	0.04
LLR/gross customer loans (%)	37.98–51.02	0.00
Profitability and efficiency ratios		
Net interest margin (%)	2.04–1.92	0.13
ROAA (%)	0.34–0.20	0.01
ROAE (%)	3.28–2.56	0.68
Cost to income (%)	65.00–68.16	0.01

Source: Author's calculations

also in terms of prudential regulation. This is clearly amplified in a highly atomistic co-operative banking system, such as the Italian one, which has failed over time to appropriate narrower levels of integration, at least until now. The attitude of the CCBs toward the holding of securities for trading purposes is also particularly prudent. It appears to be more limited than that of the shareholder-oriented banks.

Funding is more oriented toward deposits from customers and this seems to imply the sound ability of the entire credit co-operative banking system to build and maintain savers' confidence over time. In terms of its role in interbank banking, it holds a clear and significantly different position. In contrast to commercial groups, CCBs are much more a net giver on the interbank market. As regards exposure to risks and economic performances, the differences between the two groups of banks remain substantial. Significant differences in values are found, in terms of both profitability and efficiency. The median values of the ROAA are higher for all co-operative banking groups, and better their degree of operational efficiency, approximated by the cost-to-income ratio.

With reference to the risks assumed, two different outcomes are claimed. The CCBs have significantly higher median liquidity levels than those of the three identified non-co-operative banks. This puts the CCBs in a better position to meet the repayment obligations arising from their liabilities. However, the picture changes if we consider the exposure of the CCBs to credit risk, measured by the ratio of impaired loans on gross loans, and the amount of reserves held to cover losses on loans. Under these analysis profiles, Italian CCBs are significantly riskier than joint-stock banks. This seems to confirm the need to introduce more effective and integrated risk governance systems that are not compatible with a decentralized co-operative sector. In this sense, the reform of Italian co-operative banking, both through the formation of strategic groups and through the establishment of quasi-strategic networks, based on an IPS, are, in the opinion of the writer, organizational solutions that seem to ensure superior performances, as recorded by the foreign experiences examined.

6   The Performance of Italian Co-operative Banking Networks and Their Central Institutions

To what degree do the performances of the central institutions of co-operative banking networks and the networks of CBs themselves differ? To answer this question, we examine some of the performance indicators analyzed in the previous paragraph, comparing the results achieved by central institutions with those of their networks of CBs, as in Ory and Lemzeri (2012). To this end, the consolidated data referring to the three networks' central institutions were extracted from the databases previously mentioned; the same data were collected for the individual CBs that form part of the three types of networks that emerged from the reform of the co-operative banking sector. Additionally, we include a sample of 20 popular banks (out of 23) with individual total assets below € 8 billion at the end of 2017. To minimize the effect of missing data on our analysis, especially before 2008, we chose to limit our analysis to the period 2008–2017 and to restrict the scrutiny to some of the indicators previously examined. These are: the equity to total assets (%); the net customer loans to total assets (%); the impaired loans to gross customer loans (%); the customer deposits to total assets (%); the ROAA (%); and the cost-to-income ratio (%). For each of these, we replicate the analysis reported in the previous paragraph by calculating averages of results over sub-periods 2008–2010, 2011–2013, and 2014–2017. Figures are reported in Table 7.10.

Table 7.10 Comparison of Italian co-operative central institutions and their networks of CBs in terms of capital, lending, funding, and credit risk exposure

	Cassa Centrale–Central institution		Cassa Centrale–Network		Raiffeisen–Central institution		Raiffeisen–Network		ICCREA–Central institution		ICCREA–Network		Popular banks	
	Mean	SD	Mean	SD	Mean	SD	Mean	SD	Mean	SD	Mean	SD	Mean	SD
Equity to total assets (%)														
2005–2007	12.39	0.97	12.44	3.61	11.19	0.30	18.87	8.10	4.85	0.32	12.35	6.86	11.33	2.55
2008–2010	9.37	1.37	11.73	3.45	9.67	1.43	18.26	7.10	5.50	1.05	11.91	7.07	11.34	2.89
2011–2013	2.84	0.65	10.44	3.23	8.70	0.19	16.90	4.29	4.12	0.98	10.50	7.11	10.61	3.07
2014–2017	7.68	6.64	10.24	3.15	9.53	0.82	16.01	4.50	3.69	0.48	9.86	3.27	10.17	3.08
Net customer loans/total assets (%)														
2005–2007	36.30	5.55	65.55	13.14	49.78	3.46	74.69	13.48	46.28	1.00	61.78	13.95	64.68	13.18
2008–2010	32.42	4.73	68.21	11.65	52.19	4.68	71.40	12.26	56.45	4.26	64.77	13.55	70.58	11.19
2011–2013	10.20	2.48	61.90	11.44	47.85	5.35	71.93	12.65	30.88	9.39	58.60	12.58	66.73	12.94
2014–2017	9.29	1.76	53.55	10.24	40.31	4.46	61.66	10.02	28.65	7.49	50.74	10.75	57.40	13.36
Customer deposit/total assets (%)														
2005–2007	11.95	1.57	52.36	9.57	25.48	4.70	46.42	9.51	17.18	3.52	56.94	12.27	55.24	11.51
2008–2010	9.85	0.78	50.64	10.50	31.16	4.94	48.74	9.98	16.96	4.22	54.66	13.64	54.19	12.12
2011–2013	4.19	1.02	45.61	9.50	24.20	1.93	58.74	11.51	25.88	11.87	49.04	11.21	53.33	11.08
2014–2017	11.06	6.75	54.46	11.73	28.06	3.73	70.74	9.96	41.52	18.04	56.13	10.39	61.59	11.43
Impaired loans/gross loans and advances (%)														
2005–2007	1.10[a]	0.20	5.61	3.88	5.03[a]	1.20	10.86	3.84	3.68[a]	0.48	6.99	5.12	6.96	3.36
2008–2010	5.60	2.94	6.82	3.49	9.27	4.49	9.25	4.46	7.52	2.73	8.03	4.99	8.98	5.72
2011–2013	9.44	4.80	11.09	5.19	5.45	0.67	7.80	3.69	14.96	1.38	12.47	6.04	12.45	7.32
2014–2017	20.93	2.48	16.19	6.45	6.45	1.48	7.11	3.92	16.51	1.02	17.16	6.74	18.09	7.33

(continued)

Table 7.10 (continued)

Source: Author's calculations

This table reports descriptive statistics (means and standard deviations—SD) of Italian co-operative banking networks, their central institutions and popular banks. Equity/total assets (%) is the ratio between total equity and total assets; Net customer loans/total assets (%) is the ratio between net loans and total year-end assets; Customer deposits/total assets (%) is the ratio between customer deposits and total assets; Impaired loans/gross customer loans and advances (%) is the ratio between impaired loans and gross customer loans and advances. Our calculations are based on data extracted from BankScope and Orbis Bank Focus solely for the year-ends 2016–2017

[a]Only 2006–2007

As regards the first indicator, the ratio between equity and total assets (%), the data in Table 7.10 show that the three co-operative networks of CBs are much better capitalized than their respective apexes, with capital holdings decreasing over time. This remains true also for the sample of popular banks whose mean values closely resemble those exhibited by the networks of Cassa Centrale and ICCREA. The network of Raiffeisen CCBs is found to be much better capitalized in each of the analyzed sub-periods. In comparative terms, the apexes hold less capital than their networks but improved their endowments over the period 2014–2017 in light of the forthcoming implementation of the reform of co-operative banking. The apex of the largest network, ICCREA, displays the lowest average level of capital over assets.

It is reasonable to assume that networks of individual CCBs are more involved in lending activity than their central institutions (Table 7.10). In the Italian case, this is particularly evident for all the networks of CBs. However, their commitment to credit decreased over time, as did that of the central institution which quite consistently records ratios which are different to those referring to the networks. This clearly shows a different role for CBs and their apex, with the former highly engaged in lending and the latter involved in providing more specialized functions, that is, treasury, specialized lending, and liquidity management. However, the differences between the lending activity of the apex and the network become more limited in the case of the Raiffeisen sample. Of the three co-operative networks, the one which is on average most active in lending is Raiffeisen (61.66% in 2014–2017), while ICCREA is the least involved (50.74% in 2014–2017). In all cases there is a high degree of variability, proxied by the standard deviations reported. The sample of popular banks occupies an intermediate position, allocating on average 57.40% of its total assets to loans to customers in the last sub-period. It is interesting to note that almost all the networks increased their lending during the main part of the GFC, with the exception of the Raiffeisen network whose higher percentage of impaired loans during the pre-crisis period may have influenced their lending ability for the following period. The average lending values of the Italian networks were broadly aligned with those of the French and German networks (see Tables 5.10 and 6.11).

Similar to our findings with regard to lending activity, we observe that over time, the networks of CBs are distinctly concentrated in traditional funding in the form of deposits (Table 7.10), with Raiffeisen CBs having higher values in comparative terms only in the last sub-period. For almost all networks, the period between 2008 and 2013 saw a reduction in the impact of customer deposits on total assets, which was accompanied by an increase in the funding gap and associated market risks. In 2014–2017, all networks increased their dependence on deposits, recording noteworthy increases and values on average above 50%. The highest average values are recorded for the Raiffeisen network and the sample of the popular banks, which stand respectively at 70.74% and at 61.59% in 2014–2017. Among the apexes, it is that of the ICCREA group that is mainly dedicated to raising funds through customer deposits, especially in the last period. The average value recorded for ICCREA is, however, affected by the temporary effect of extraordinary transactions. In fact, in 2017, the apex of ICCREA, like the other two, regains a net specialization in the collection of funds from other banks and through the issue of debt securities.

The comparative analysis of the levels and trends of credit risk is approximated by the ratio of impaired loans to gross loans to customers (%) and reported in Table 7.10. Both for the apexes of ICCREA and Cassa Centrale, and for their CBs networks and the sample of popular banks, we observe an increasing deterioration in the quality of loan portfolios. Only the nascent IPS for the Raiffeisen CBs has a single-digit level of risk, especially from 2008 onward. In the other cases, the average values calculated for the period 2014–2017 are between 16% and 20%. In the Italian case, there is no clear distinction between the riskiness of central institutions and that of the CBs network, especially in the last period.

The last two indicators examined concern the profitability and efficiency of the organizations under investigation. For these purposes, ROAA (%) and cost-to-income ratio (%) were selected. The values of the first, shown in Table 7.11, provide evidence of the superior ability of the networks to generate an average profitability that is higher than that of their apexes, with some exceptions in the last sub-period. This result is indicative of the value of networks of CBs within their reference groups, especially in difficult times. Additionally, it is worth noting that the higher profitability of the networks is associated with the significantly higher volatility of the results obtained. For the entire co-operative sector, profitability has decreased over time. Only Raiffeisen banks achieve levels of profitability more than double those obtained by the other components. In the European context, the profitability of Italian co-operative networks and their apexes has average values equal to about half of those in Germany and France.

Table 7.11   Comparison of Italian co-operative central institutions and their networks of CBs in terms of profitability and operational efficiency

	Cassa Centrale–Central institution		Cassa Centrale–Network		Raiffeisen–Central institution		Raiffeisen–Network		ICCREA–Central institution		ICCREA–Network		Popular banks	
	Mean	SD	Mean	SD	Mean	SD	Mean	SD	Mean	SD	Mean	SD	Mean	SD
ROAA (%)														
2005–2007	0.57	0.21	1.00	0.42	0.51	0.21	0.70	0.58	0.27	0.05	0.90	0.53	0.73	0.28
2008–2010	0.68	0.09	0.53	0.48	0.55	0.22	0.54	0.55	0.12	0.11	0.48	0.59	0.46	0.40
2011–2013	0.19	0.03	0.33	0.54	0.51	0.20	0.59	0.32	0.17	0.10	0.26	0.57	0.25	0.52
2014–2017	0.29	0.09	0.13	0.69	0.66	0.12	0.45	0.37	0.06	0.07	0.25	0.50	0.12	0.59
Cost to income (%)														
2005–2007	61.45	3.99	64.82	10.44	59.43	5.58	69.06	9.42	69.21	1.60	66.76	11.49	62.02	8.75
2008–2010	55.46	2.34	70.01	14.22	55.90	13.40	68.13	10.01	61.76	7.16	71.32	19.79	64.81	10.83
2011–2013	44.89	16.11	62.27	10.23	43.03	13.26	69.04	8.52	54.86	5.15	63.93	10.75	63.72	12.49
2014–2017	55.42	22.05	62.21	12.26	37.04	6.16	67.71	10.71	67.21	6.28	62.49	12.49	63.16	13.88

Source: Author's calculations

This table reports descriptive statistics (means and standard deviations—SD) of Italian co-operative banking networks, their central institutions, and popular banks. ROAA (%) is the return on average assets; Cost to income (%) is the ratio between operating expenses and intermediation margin. Our calculation on data extracted from BankScope and Orbis Bank Focus for the sole year-ends 2016–2017

Finally, the cost-to-income figures reported in Table 7.11 offer us further interesting insights. The operational efficiency of the networks tends to be lower than that of the central institutions, but it is precisely the former entities that have intentionally adopted a virtuous approach. On the other hand, the average improvement registered in the case of Raiffeisen banks is more limited. In the period 2014–2017, their average value is close to 68%, while it stands at values close to 62% for the other networks, including the popular banks. These values are slightly better than those of the French groups BPCE and Crédit Mutuel (about 64% in 2014–2017) but much lower than those of the sample of German CBs (around 76%). In the case of the apexes of the two largest co-operative groups, there is a fluctuating trend and a worsening of the average cost-to-income ratio over the last period. Only the central institution of the Raiffeisen CBs reports a noticeable improvement in its operating efficiency (from 59% in the pre-crisis period to 37% in the period 2014–2017). This result is one of the best in the sample of co-operative banking systems under investigation in this book. The average values of the cost-to-income ratio for the other apexes of the Italian co-operative banking groups are similar to those recorded in other analyzed European countries.

Overall, it can be said that the nascent co-operative groups and IPS-based co-operative banking network, even in the face of a long-lasting adverse macro-economic scenario, are well capitalized (including by comparison with their European counterparts) but poorly performing in economic terms. Their ability to attract and mobilize savings, especially after the period of double crises, is also noteworthy. However, the Italian co-operative banking sector, with the sole exception of Raiffeisen banks, has been severely exposed to a deterioration in credit quality. The lack of cohesion and shortcomings in the coordination of strategic risk management would seem to be important factors in explaining the high risk of these banks. The formation of the new strategic groups and of an IPS, along the lines of the Austrian-German model, will enable them to carry out operations for the restructuring of their loan portfolios more easily, as well as to make significant improvements in their risk management and in the offer of products, services, and technologies available to customers.

7   Conclusion

After the outbreak of the GFC, Italy, like other European countries, put in place several measures to restore the stability and efficiency of its banking system. The crisis has brought to light the long-debated problems of the governance of Italian CBs. In response to this, two major reforms were enacted in 2015 and 2016. The first found a solution to the inadequacies of the governance model of large popular banks by making their conversion into joint-stock companies mandatory. The second reform, which related to small CCBs, instead set out the conditions for preserving the values of mutuality, overcoming the disadvantages of being small in size by making affiliation to a joint-stock central institution compulsory. The two co-operative networks currently existing in Italy jointly accounted for just under 1.8 million members at the end of 2017, of which one fourth belonged to the CCB sector and the remaining to popular banks. In Italy, CBs enjoy relatively modest market shares when matched with those of the CBs in the other European countries. At the end of 2017, the two networks jointly held a 10.50% share of the domestic loans market, with CCBs managing to increase or broadly maintain their market share at slightly above 7%. Popular banks' market share decreased due to the mandatory conversion of the largest popular banks into joint-stock companies. CBs' collective share of the domestic deposit market was slightly higher at 11.70% in 2017, with CCBs alone holding 7.80%.

Italian popular banks are fully configured as an atomized network. They share a national association, Associazione Nazionale fra le Banche Popolari (ANBP), that represents its members in issues of common concern. Following the CCBs reform, two strategic and one quasi-strategic networks were created. The ICCREA and Cassa Centrale groups fall within the provisions of Art. 10 of the CRR and will in all respects be strategic networks under the supervision of the ECB. The Raiffeisen IPS falls within the provisions of Art. 113(7) of the CRR and is under the joint supervision of the ECB and the Bank of Italy.

In addition to analyzing the role and organization of the co-operative networks in Italy, the chapter offers two empirical investigations, respectively aimed to verify empirically the effects of the ongoing hybridization in co-operative banking, and to assess to what degree do the performances of the central institutions of co-operative banking networks and the networks of CBs themselves differ. In line with the reorganization of the CCBs system, we reconstruct the three groups, made up of the CCBs' networks and their respective top institutions, weighting the data of each group member. The three Italian co-operative banking groups are compared, on a tentative aggregated basis, with three shareholder-oriented banking groups. The comparison of the performances of the two business models displays several statistically significant differences in the results they have achieved. CBs' capitalization is significantly higher over 2008–2017 than that of the commercial joint-stock banks. Significant differences have been found also in comparing the asset and funding mix of the two business models. Unlike what has been recorded in other countries investigated in this book, Surprisingly, Italian CBs have median values for lending activity lower than those recorded by shareholder-oriented banks. Funding is more oriented toward deposits from customers and this seems to imply the sound ability of the entire credit co-operative banking system to build and maintain savers' confidence over time. Significant differences in values are found, in terms of both profitability and efficiency. The median values of the ROAA are higher for all co-operative banking groups, and better their degree of operational efficiency, approximated by the cost-to-income ratio. With reference to the risks assumed, CCBs have significantly higher median liquidity levels than those of the three identified commercial banks, but their exposure to credit risk is considerably high. This seems to confirm the need to introduce more effective and integrated risk governance systems that are not compatible with a decentralized co-operative sector.

Regarding the second area of investigation, the average values of the individual CCBs that are part of the three newborn networks show values of capitalization higher than those of the central institution. Similarly, to what has been found in other European countries, the networks of individual CCBs are more dedicated to customer lending, and their dependence on the collection of deposits from customers is greater than that of their apex. In the Italian case, there is no clear distinction between the riskiness of central institutions and that of the CCBs network, especially in the last period.

The reported figures provide evidence of the superior ability of the networks of CCBs to generate an average profitability that is higher than that of their apexes, with some exceptions in the last sub-period. On the contrary, instead, the operational efficiency of the networks of individual CCBs tends to be lower than that of the central institutions. Overall, it can be said that the newborn formal networks, even in the face of a long-lasting adverse macro-economic scenario, are well capitalized (including by comparison with their European counterparts), but poorly performing in economic terms, especially over the period 2014–17. The establishment of the new strategic groups and of an IPS is believed to allow them to carry out operations for the restructuring of their loan portfolios more easily, as well as to make significant improvements in their risk management and in the offer of competitive products, services, and technologies.

References

Azzi, V. A. (2016). Introduzione. In P. Verzaro & S. Trombani (Eds.), *Profili giuridici della riforma delle BCC*. Roma: Ecra. Edizioni del Credito Cooperativo.

Bank of Italy. (2018). *Annual Report*. Rome.

Cafaro, P. (2001). *La solidarietà efficiente. Storie e prospettive del credito co-operativo in Italia (1883–2000)*. Laterza: Roma-Bari.

Colombo, E. C. (2012). Radici, consolidamento e crescita del credito cooperativo tra Ottocento e Novecento. In A. Carretta (Ed.), *Il credito cooperativo. Storia, diritto, economia, organizzazione*. Il Mulino Editore.

Conti, G., Ferri, G., & Polsi, A. (2003). Banche cooperative e fascismo: performance e controllo durante le crisi finanziarie negli anni '20 e '30. *Credito Popolare, 1*.

De Bonis, R., Manzone, B., & Trento, S. (1994). La proprietà cooperativa: teoria, storia e il caso delle banche popolari. *Temi di discussione del servizio della Banca d'italia, 238*.

De Bruyn, R., & Ferri, G. (2005). *Le ragioni delle banche Popolari: motivi teorici ed evidenze empiriche*. Disefin.

Dell'Erba, A. (2016). *Hearing of Representatives of Federcasse*, May, 10. http://documenti.camera.it/leg17/resoconti/commissioni/stenografici/html/06/indag/c06_clientela/2016/05/10/indice_stenografico.0006.html.

Desrochers, M., & Fischer, K. P. (2005). The Power of Networks: Integration and Financial Cooperative Performance. *Annals of Public and Cooperative Economics, 76*(3), 307–354.

European Association of Co-operative Banks (EACB). *Key Statistics*, Various Years.

European Central Bank (ECB). (2017, October). *Report on Financial Structures*.

Fay, M. P., & Proschan, M. A. (2010). Wilcoxon-Mann-Whitney or T-Test? On Assumptions for Hypothesis Tests and Multiple Interpretations of Decision Rules. *Statistics Surveys, 4*, 1.

Ferri, G., Kalmi, P., & Kerola, E. (2013). Governance and Performance: Reassessing the Pre-crisis Situation of European Banks. In S. Goglio & Y. Alexopoulos (Eds.), *Financial Cooperatives and Local Development*. Abingdon: Routledge.

Fiordiponti, F. (2015). Lo scopo mutualistico: un'assenza certificata. *Diritto della banca e del mercato finanziario, III*, 417.

Gutierrez, E. (2008). The Reform of Italian Cooperative Banks: Discussion of Proposals. *IMF Working Papers, 8*(74), 1.

Locatelli, A. M. (2011). Lo scollamento fra credito e cooperazione negli anni tra primo dopoguerra e anni Cinquanta. In A. Carretta (Ed.), *Il credito cooperativo. Storia, diritto, economia, organizzazione*. Bologna: Il Mulino.

Mann, H. B., & Whitney, D. R. (1947). On a Test of Whether One of Two Random Variables Is Stochastically Larger than the Other. *Annals of Mathematical Statistics, 18*(1), 50–60.

Micheli, G. (1898). *Le casse rurali italiane. Note storiche, statistiche, con appendice sulle banche cattoliche d'Italia, Parma.*

Ory, J., & Lemzeri, Y. (2012). Efficiency and Hybridization in Cooperative Banking: The French Case. *Annals of Public and Cooperative Economics, 83*(2), 215–250.

Panetta, G. (2018, May 10). *Il sistema bancario italiano nel quadro dell'Unione bancaria europea.* Camera dei Deputati, Seminario di aggiornamento professionale, Rome.

Pecorari, P. (2003). *Luigi Luzzatti. Economista e politico della nuova Italia.* Napoli: Edizioni Scientifiche Italiane.

Polsi, A. (1993). *Alle origini del capitalismo italiano. Stato, banche e banchieri dopo l'unità.* Torino: Einaudi.

Romano, G. (2017). La riforma della cooperazione di credito in Italia. In M. C. Cardarelli (Ed.), *Nuove opportunità e sfide per le banche di credito cooperativo: la riforma 2016.* Atti del Convegno di Lecce, 16–17 dicembre 2016, Giappichelli Editore.

Rossi, S. (2015). *Hearing in the Context of the Legislative Investigation on the Draft Law C. 2844, of Conversion into Law of the Decree n. 3 of 2015, Containing Urgent Measures for the Banking System and Investments.* Joint Commissions Finance and Production Activities, Trade and Tourism, Italian House of Representatives on February 17.

Salvione, M. (1985). *Le banche cooperative.* Dossier di Ricerca e Documentazione, Parlamento Europeo, Segretariato generale, Direzione generale della Ricerca e della Documentazione, Serie economica, 6, n. 10.

Tarantola, A. M. (2009, February 27). *Le banche popolari nel confronto competitivo: vocazione territoriale e profili di governance.* Speech of the Deputy General Director of the Bank of Italy at the Convention of the National Association of Popular Banks and the Central Institute of Popular Banks, Taormina.

Tarantola, A. M. (2011, June 22). *La riforma delle banche popolari.* Hearing of the Deputy General Director of the Bank of Italy at the VI Commission of Finance and Treasury of the Italian Senate.

Tonelli, E. (2017). La riforma delle BCC del 2016: nuove (?) forme di integrazione tra imprese bancarie e vecchi sistemi. In M. C. Cardarelli (Ed.), *Nuove opportunità e sfide per le banche di credito cooperativo: la riforma 2016.* Atti del Convegno di Lecce, 16–17 dicembre 2016, Giappichelli Editore.

CHAPTER 8

Co-operative Banking in the Netherlands

1   Brief Overview of the Dutch Banking System

The outbreak of the international financial crisis led to a reduction in the total size of the Dutch banking sector, especially after 2013. Nonetheless, the sector is large in relation to the size of the country's economy from both a historical and an international perspective. At the end of 2016, the ratio of Monetary Financial Institutions' (Mfis) total assets to national GDP amounted to 3.2 (2.6 in Germany, 2.3 in Austria and Italy, and 2.4 in Spain).[1] The Dutch figure is rather high both in comparison to the equivalent data from other leading European countries, but also from a historical perspective: at the end of the 1970s, the Dutch banking system equated to around 100% of GDP (DNB 2015). The solid growth of the banking sector since the end of the 1990s is largely due to rising mortgage portfolios as well as increasing trading portfolios. The growth in the latter materialized particularly after 2005, with values peaking at the outbreak of the international financial crisis, coinciding with the peak in foreign activities, particularly in Europe and the United States. This expansion was a European phenomenon: the banking sector within the Eurozone (especially the 20 largest banks) grew strongly in the years preceding the crisis, during which its foreign claims roughly tripled (DNB 2015).

---

[1] Excluding the data of the European System of Central Banks (ESCB).

© The Author(s) 2019
F. Poli, *Co-operative Banking Networks in Europe*, Palgrave
Macmillan Studies in Banking and Financial Institutions,
https://doi.org/10.1007/978-3-030-21699-3_8

The shrinkage in the percentage of assets held by MFIs in relation to the total assets of the financial sector following the onset of the crisis has been substantial: from 30.0% in 2008 to 22.2% at the end of 2016 (63.5% in France, 61.1% in Germany, 63.8% in Italy, and 67.2% in Spain) (ECB 2017).[2] Competition from non-bank market participants along with the lack of trust in banks resulting from the crisis contributed to the downsizing of the banking sector. Insurance companies have gained an increasing role in the market for mortgage lending; investment funds or credit unions have set up to finance SMEs; and the proliferation of crowdfunding initiatives have all contributed to reducing the role of banks. For instance, just in the period 2014–2016, the financing provided by MFIs to non-financial companies decreased to € 293.7 billion in 2016 (from € 334.7 bn in 2014), while the financing granted by other financial institutions (OFIs) (i.e. non-monetary investment funds, finance companies, etc.) rose to € 109.3 billion from € 73.9 bn in 2014. Insurance companies and pension funds financed € 15 billion at the end of 2016, increasing from € 13.9 bn in 2014 (ECB 2017).

At the end of 2017, the Dutch banking system comprised 81 domestic and foreign (EU and non-EU) credit institutions with 26 domestic banking groups and stand-alone banks, of which 12 are national banking groups.[3] The industry is dominated by domestic credit institutions, which in 2016 held a 93% share of total banking assets (ECB 2017). This places the Netherlands among the European countries where domestic banks have succeeded in regaining market share soon after the crisis, domestic market power having dropped from 95% to 85% between 2009 and 2010 (ECB 2017). Three domestic banking groups dominate the market: the co-operative Rabobank and the two commercial groups ABN-AMRO and ING. While Rabobank did not need a state bailout, capital injection or guarantees during the 2008–2009 global credit crisis, the other two had to be rescued: ABN-AMRO was nationalized in 2008 and subsequently publicly re-listed through an initial public offering (IPO) in 2015, followed by further placings through which the Dutch state has progressively divested its stakes; ING was indebted to the government to the amount of € 10 billion until 2014 due to bailout operations in 2008.

The remaining shares of banking assets belong principally to foreign branches of other European banks (4.5% in 2016), while non-European

---

[2] These two indicators were respectively 3.6% and 70.2% in 2008 (ECB 2017).
[3] Data collected from ECB's Statistical Data Warehouse.

intermediaries play a marginal role (ECB 2017). The widespread adoption of online and mobile banking in the Netherlands has led to a drastic reduction in the number of bank branches in the country, significantly increasing their population density. Namely, over the period 2008–2016, the number of inhabitants per branch has risen from 4806 in 2008 to 10,173 in 2016, the highest value among the countries under our investigation. The corresponding values for 2016 are 1794 inhabitants in France, 2575 in Germany, and 2067 in Italy (ECB 2017).

Dutch banks adopt a universal banking model, operating across the broad range of retail, corporate, and investment banking activity. Their ambitions with respect to internationalization have been directed at two market segments: investment banking and large corporate clients; and foreign retail markets. All three banking groups previously mentioned have, to a large extent, succeeded in positioning themselves as major players in international markets, mainly through acquisitions. The global financial crisis (GFC) hit the Dutch banking system, as it did the Belgian, because their sizeable international orientation and heavy dependence on cross-border funding made them vulnerable to market conditions. Before the outbreak of the GFC, growth, especially international growth, had become an imperative for Dutch banks, both to be able to withstand internal competitive pressures, and as a means of diversifying banking risks. During the pre-crisis period, major banks were attracted by shadow banking activities which led to the growing importance of originating and trading sophisticated financial instruments (credit derivatives, hedge funds, asset-backed securities, structured finance, etc.) at an international level.

As pointed out by Chang and Jones (2013), Dutch banks had become reliant on securitization and suffered heavily when the market for asset-backed securities contracted. Hardie and Howarth (2013) report that securitization fueled bank lending to a greater extent than in other countries of the European Union. The securitization technique represented the solution to the problem of financing the growth of loans beyond the limits of the growth of domestic funding. However, it encouraged risk taking. Losses originated by securities write-downs in the Netherlands were among the highest among the countries under investigation in this book: 1.8% as against 2% in Germany, 0.086% in Italy (only in 2008–2009), and 0.38% in France (Hardie and Howarth 2013). Among the three major Dutch banks, the co-operative group, Rabobank, despite suffering some losses, managed to remain profitable in 2008–2009, thanks to its more traditional operations (Chang and Jones 2013).

2   The Role of Co-operative Banks Within the Banking Sector

The dynamics of membership in co-operative banking in the Netherlands do not follow a trend similar to that observed in, for instance, France and Germany. As displayed in Table 8.1, the number of members grew up until 2014, rising from 1,456,000 in 2004 to 1,959,000, with an overall 35% increase. Since then, the number of members has been declining progressively. In 2016, 1,927,000 members were recorded, while in 2017 the number dropped to 1,916,000.[4] Two main factors may be the cause of this recent trend: the potential disaffection of local members toward the deep governance restructuring undertaken by the network in 2015 which led to the merger of local independent CBs with their central institution; and the continual dilution of the bank's co-operative identity due to the gradual opening up of its operations to non-members. The reduction in the bank's total customer base (domestic and international) is more pronounced in the years after 2012, with a substantial drop of 1.5 million customers. This reduction is partly due to domestic competition but much more to the effects of the restructuring process that took place both nationally and internationally which since 2012 has led to the divestment of subsidiaries and a substantial reduction in the national branch network.

The evolution of the governance ratios reported in Table 8.1 indicates that members have slightly increased their relevance as the primary targeted

Table 8.1   Members, customers and governance ratios of the Rabobank Group

Year	Members	Customers	Governance ratio
2004	1,456,000	9,000,000	16.18%
2006	1,641,000	9,000,000	18.23%
2008	1,707,000	9,500,000	17.97%
2010	1,801,000	10,000,000	18.01%
2012	1,918,000	10,000,000	19.18%
2014	1,959,000	8,800,000	22.26%
2016	1,927,000	8,700,000	22.15%
2017	1,916,000	8,500,000	22.54%

Source: EACB and Rabobank's Annual Report for the year-end 2017

Own calculations of the governance ratio

[4] Data collected from Rabobank Group's Annual Report for the year-end 2017.

customers of the banking services provided by Dutch co-operative banks, representing a percentage of 22.54% in 2017, although this is due to the more severe drop in the number of customers served. This figure is much more akin to that observed in France (where the ratio ranges from about 18% to 29% in the cases of Crédit Agricole and BPCE respectively) than those recorded in Austria (63% in 2017) and Germany (around 62%). As in the case of France, the low governance ratio in the Netherlands carries the risk of a dilution of the unique missions of these banks which may eventually harm their original values.

Co-operative banking in the Netherlands plays a key role in terms of both loans granted and deposits collected. However, as shown in Table 8.2, the market shares enjoyed by the CBs on the funding side decreased from 2004 (39%) to 2010 (29%) but subsequently changed direction to reach a percentage value of 34% at the end of 2016. Analogous data for 2017 indicates a similar value. Among the European countries under our investigation, the Rabobank group is one of the leading CBs in terms of attracting customer deposits. On the lending side, the bank has been able to capture a substantial gain, as its market share grew from 25% in 2004 to 39% in 2012. Total lending increased mainly before the outbreak of the international financial crisis due to the large number of mortgages taken out in the Netherlands and the increase in overseas lending, as reported by the bank. In 2006 alone, private sector lending increased by 17%, from € 278.1 billion in 2005 to € 324.1 billion in 2006.[5] According to corporate presentations, at the end of 2016 the bank held a 43% share of business

Table 8.2 Domestic market shares of the Rabobank Group

Year	Loans (%)	Deposits (%)
2004	25.0	39.0
2006	25.5	39.0
2008	43.0	30.0
2010	40.0	29.0
2012	39.0	31.0
2014	n.a.	36.0
2016	n.a.	34.0
2017	n.a.	34.0

Source: EACB

[5] See Rabobank's Annual Reports for the years from 2006 to 2008.

lending and 21% of mortgages in the domestic market.[6] It occupied a dominant position in agri-food financing, holding a domestic market share of 84% in 2016 and 86% in 2017.[7]

The Dutch CBs' prominent role in the national economy has been maintained despite an intense asset reduction program which the management explained was necessary to comply with new capital requirements introduced in 2013 in line with the strategic program, Vision 2016, and its subsequent addendum. Whereas total assets decreased from € 752.4 billion in 2012 to € 662.6 billion in 2016, with a further decrease in 2017 to € 603.0 billion, representing a total decrease of almost 20%, the lending activity of the bank has not been similarly disrupted as displayed in Table 8.3. The Group's management set out in its strategic plans that the Group would follow a policy of refocusing domestic lending activity and that some sectors, such as agriculture, food, mineral raw materials, and water, would be closely supported. Indeed, looking at the ratio between total loans and total assets, the corresponding percentage values have

Table 8.3 Credit intermediation orientation of the Rabobank Group

Year	Loans to customers to assets (%) (A)	Deposits from customers to assets (%) (B)	Customer loans to deposits (A/B) (%)
2004	40.44	53.25	75.94
2006	58.25	38.80	150.12
2008	66.75	49.70	134.32
2010	66.86	45.78	146.03
2012	60.88	44.43	137.04
2014	63.19	47.93	131.83
2016	68.34	52.48	130.22
2017	68.15	56.50	120.61

Source: Author's calculations on data reported by EACB

[6] See   https://www.rabobank.com/en/images/02-infographic-rabobank-in-2016-eng.pdf. In 2017, its market share of mortgages rose to 22%. This increase is due to a combination of factors which Rabobank has favorably exploited, such as: the return of the Dutch housing market to almost pre-crisis levels, the broad-based national economic recovery, an ongoing low interest rate environment, and the positive effect of the National Mortgage Guarantee that contributes to the strength of the Dutch residential mortgage market. Data reported by Rabobank indicates that 20.0% of Rabobank's mortgage portfolio benefits from National Mortgage Guarantee. See Rabobank's Investor Presentation for the year 2017.

[7] See Rabobank's Annual Reports for the year-ends 2016 and 2017.

grown since 2012, with lending covering almost 68.15% of assets in 2017, slightly lower than in 2016 (68.34%) (Table 8.3). These figures are far higher than the corresponding values in Germany and France, which respectively equal 61% and almost 50% for the three co-operative French networks in 2017. There has been an increase in customer deposits since 2012, reaching a value of 56.50% in 2017.[8] This improvement reflects the Group's ability to attract deposits from customers. Table 8.3 reports an indicator of the "funding gap" recorded by the Group, proxied by the ratio of bank loans to deposits from customers. In 2017, Rabobank recorded the highest level at 120.61% in comparison to France and Germany, who averaged 115% and 95% respectively.[9]

3   CO-OPERATIVE BANKING: HISTORICAL DEVELOPMENT IN THE NETHERLANDS

Inspired by the ideas of the German Friedrich Wilhelm Raiffeisen, Dutch co-operative agricultural banks were founded from 1895 onward, promoted by farmers and horticulturists. The founding father of Dutch CBs was Gerlacus van den Elsen (1853–1925), the son of a farmer who joined the Abbey of Bern in Heeswijk as a Norbertine. After his ordination, he became increasingly occupied by social issues, spurred on by the fate of the impoverished population that was being severely affected by the agrarian crisis taking place at the time. For Van den Elsen, agricultural co-operative credit associations were more social institutions than financial institutions. He defined them as instruments to "prevent usury, to help the farmer in his need, but also to promote thrift, charity, industriousness and temperance".[10] He was the promoter of the former CBs, Boerenleenbanks, which had a strong Catholic inspiration, and a co-founder of the North Brabant Christian Farmers' Union (NCB) in 1896, as well as of the Coöperatieve Centrale Boerenleenbank (CCB) two years later in 1898. In parallel, Raiffeisen banks, which were secular equivalent organizations, developed in the north of the country.

---

[8] Own calculations on EACB's data.
[9] Ibidem.
[10] See Rabobank's website dedicated to the Rabo Canon. https://www.rabobank.com/rabo-canon/bouwen-aan-een-duurzame-samenleving/pater-van-den-elsen/.

The emergence of agricultural credit co-operatives in the Netherlands is linked with the transformation of the agricultural sector between 1880 and 1914 and with farmers' difficulty in obtaining credit in some regions. As the lack of capital prevented farmers from benefiting from technological improvements in their operations and from adapting their businesses, a government investigation in 1866 concluded that credit co-operatives like Raiffeisen's could offer a solution in funding farmers' credit needs via the mobilization of savings. The members of the newly established credit vehicles were mostly local farmers, horticulturalists, and small, local agricultural co-operatives; these members were eligible for loans but were also required to take on joint unlimited liability for the bank's obligations. As in the Raiffeisen model, bank members were responsible for managing co-operative agricultural banks but without any compensation in return: only bookkeepers were paid.[11] Analogously, profits were added to the annual reserves to compensate for any losses without having to have recourse to the members' unlimited liability. A distinguishing feature of Dutch CBs was that members were not required to buy member shares to capitalize their local bank as its capitalization relied strictly on the full retention of earnings and the firm prohibition on distributing reserves. Additionally, in keeping with the social role of early CBs, part of their earnings had to be devoted to community projects aimed at improving local living conditions. As reported by Groeneveld (2016b), even today Rabobank still redistributes profits for the benefit of society and agricultural co-operation both in the Netherlands, and in developing and emerging economies, with about 3% of net profits being allocated via the Rabobank Foundation and local co-operative funds.

While lending was firmly linked to membership in the first CBs, anyone was allowed to make deposits.

The number of CBs grew considerably, rising from 67 affiliated co-operative agricultural banks in 1900 to 1324 in 1955. Due to their low operating costs, CBs had become an inclusive financial vehicle, able to offer low-cost loans to rural businesses. However, it soon became clear that small-scale banking carried some disadvantages. In 1898, a few years after the set-up of CBs, two umbrella organizations were created: the Coöperatieve Centrale Raiffeisen-Bank (CCRB) in Utrecht and the Coöperatieve Centrale Boerenleenbank (CCB) in Eindhoven. These two

---

[11] See Rabobank's publication "Rabobank through the years" at https://www.rabobank.com/en/images/r652-rabodoordetijd-eng-def.pdf

main bodies, acting as the central bank and facilitator for their member banks, differed in the exact legal forms they required their member banks to take. CCRB accepted banks that had been established according to the Co-operative Associations Act of 1876 as members, while CCB preferred the less expensive form of association set out in the Freedom of Association and Assembly Act of 1855 but accepted both types of credit associations as members. The central co-operative banking entities served as representatives of their members' interests, clearing banks, liquidity management hubs, training centers, and as supervisory bodies, also conducting regular inspections to monitor the member banks' management and administration. Additionally, due to the crisis faced by the entire sector in the 1930s, from 1932 onward the central co-operatives intensified their supervision of local lending and made any form of credit provision subject to the central approval procedure (Groeneveld 2016b). Interestingly, no local CBs have ever gone bankrupt.

These functions were the result of the double co-operative structure and statutory obligations of central bodies.[12] As founders of their respective central banks, local CBs contributed to the capital of their central institution by buying shares in them.

In the early 1950s the Dutch central bank charged both CCRB and CCB with central supervisory tasks over their member banks (so-called delegated supervision) and monitored CCB and CCRB's compliance with these rules on supervision. During the 1950s and 1960s, structural changes in the national economy redefined the relative importance of the agricultural sector to CBs' traditional areas of business. A wave of intra-sector mergers took place, introducing lending diversification in favor of non-agricultural borrowers. The two central organizations also followed a business diversification strategy to benefit their member co-operative banks via the establishment and/or acquisition of specialized subsidiaries in the mortgage loan sector, insurance, and so on. However, the emergence of unproductive intra-sector competition as well as business overlap soon led to a merger between the two co-operative banking organizations. On 1 December 1972, CCRB and CCB officially became the Coöperatieve Centrale Raiffeisen-Boerenleenbank B.A. The new central organization would be known as Rabobank Nederland, Rabo being chosen as incorporating the two initial letters of the two original banks: the secular Raiffeisen

---

[12] See Rabobank's publication "Rabobank through the years" at https://www.rabobank.com/en/images/r652-rabodoordetijd-eng-def.pdf.

banks and the Catholic Boerenleenbanks. As reported by Groeneveld (2016b), the merger of the central co-operatives was also favored by the growing secularization of Dutch society which eliminated the differences that existed between the Catholic Eindhoven organization and the formally neutral Utrecht organization. Furthermore, the emergence of large trading and manufacturing companies required huge amounts of capital that only larger banks could offer. Local CBs kept their role as members in the new central institution and could be remunerated via a dividend. The influence of CBs on the governance of their central institution was secured by the creation of regional and central representative bodies. From an economic and organizational standpoint, the central institution and the local CBs had become one group, even though each local bank had its own banking license and local Board of Directors. Nevertheless, the supervision of the group was conducted on a consolidated basis by the Dutch central bank.

Alongside the necessary restructuring in response to organizational redundancies created by the merger, the network followed an expansionary strategy both domestically and internationally. The co-operative nature of Dutch Rabobanks and their degree of integration developed further during the 1980s and 1990s. As highlighted by Wilson (1986), the Dutch Act on the Supervision of the Credit System, which adopted the EU Directive 77/780 and was enacted in 1978, made it mandatory for any existing or newly established CB to be affiliated with a central institution. The Act permitted the central institution to retain its delegated supervisory role over CBs provided that the central institution had the legal authority to issue enforceable instructions concerning the management of local CBs. The supervision of the CBs was then performed on a consolidated basis, along with the reporting of results to stakeholders. The concept of group mimicking, which was later introduced by European regulators in Art. 10 of the CRR, was born. In 1980 a "cross-guarantee" scheme was also created between all the entities within the network. The scheme safeguarded against the effects of financial difficulties faced by any participating member in meeting its obligations which would have been covered by the other participants. No claim has ever been made on the scheme.[13] To strengthen the solidity of the network further, an own guarantee fund, the Stichting Garantiefonds Rabobanken, was set up in 1985 (Cotugno 2010).

[13] Ibidem.

In parallel, membership requirements were reviewed: private customers were no longer required to become members, while the per-member liability of individual business members was limited to a maximum of 5000 Dutch guilders. During the following decade, the exclusivity of bank membership to certain categories of members became subject to further debate due to both the constant decline of bank members and the dilution of the original co-operative identity. After the so-called Cooperative Discussion (1995–1997), it was agreed that any customer of a local CB could become a member.[14]

It is worth noting that while the distinctive co-operative mission of the former banks was challenged by this relaxation of the historical member-customer pairing, the two former networks had chosen to reinforce the co-operative mission by establishing charitable foundations (which later merged to form the Rabobank Aid Foundation), with the aim of supporting and promoting the co-operative vision both at home and in developing countries. In 2002 the foundation's name was changed to Rabobank Foundation. Through Rabobank Foundation, an independent non-profit organization funded by the Rabobank Group, financial and technical support is provided to small-scale farmers to enable them to become economically self-propelling (Blok et al. 2013).

The Rabobank network has employed a combination of strategies, covering cost reduction and revenue growth. However, the implementation of these strategies has been driven by the co-operative nature of the bank and has therefore been oriented toward the maximization of customer/member value rather than the maximization of profit. The drive to reduce costs has pushed the network toward a process of aggregating very small local banks, restructuring branches into a more functional model, reducing employee numbers, and looking for strategic partnerships in the provision of financial services that may benefit from scale upgrades.

The revenue growth opportunities have been addressed in several ways: investing in tools, such as Customer Relationship Management (CRM), which are designed to increase the selling power of the distribution channels; and undertaking acquisitions and alliances with the aim of strengthening the Allfinance ambitions the group has harbored since the 1990s (i.e. in the insurance sector, online brokerage). At the international level, Rabobank Group has opted for a pragmatic approach in line with Rabobank's co-operative nature and history.

---

[14] See Rabobank's publication "Rabobank through the years". https://www.rabobank.com/en/images/r652-rabothroughtheyears-uk-vdef.pdf.

Rabobank's international activities began in the early 1980s, initially for business clients conducting business around the world. The growth and expansion led to the opening of bank offices in major financial centers. Maintaining Rabobank's historical specialization in the agri-food business niche, from the early 1990s onward the organization undertook targeted acquisitions of small foreign banks with analogous missions worldwide (such as in Australia and United States) (Groeneveld and Wagemakers 2004). The provision of wholesale/corporate banking products for the agri-food sector has been realized mainly through branches, while entry into the retail segment has been pursued via the remote provision of banking and financial services abroad.

An important reorganization of the international business of Rabobank was made in 1996. Foreign activities were grouped into a new entity, "Rabobank International", with its own management and a large degree of autonomy (Groeneveld 2016a) that led to the set-up of an investment banking division in London (Vogelaar 2012), although this has lately been substantially closed down.

In 2002, Rabobank launched its International Direct Banking (IDB) arm in Belgium to also tap into the new opportunities the internet offered for savings and banking services for its new customers outside the Netherlands. In the following years, other internet banks soon opened in Ireland (2005), New Zealand (2006), and Australia (2007). Blending its historical identity with the ability to innovate is a trait that characterizes Rabobank. In fact, Rabobank was an early adopter of the new virtual distribution channels and is the largest internet bank in Europe (Smits and Groeneveld 2001). With operations in 42 countries, the network's international presence has grown from 330 branches in 2006 to 769 in 2013. However, with the outbreak of the international financial crisis, the network has undergone a new wave of restructuring. In spite of Rabobank being the only Dutch bank not to receive any state aid, from 2010 onward, its number of subsidiaries and participating interests in the Netherlands and worldwide has been reduced. Asset management companies Orbay, Robeco, and Sarasin were sold. The Polish Bank BGZ was sold in 2014. In the same year, the Irish subsidiary ACC (Agricultural Credit Corporation) Bank returned its banking license to the Central Bank of Ireland and changed the company name to ACC Loan Management, focusing on debt recovery. By 2016, total subsidiaries and participating interests had been brought down to 382, spread over 40 countries.[15]

At the end of 2012 Rabobank started a restructuring program, called Vision 2016, in response to the trend toward the increasing digitalization of banking services. Consequently, the strengthening of their virtual distribution channels counterbalanced the closure of branches, whose services were supplanted by, for example, desks in retirement homes and buses visiting remote villages in the Netherlands. As in other European banking systems, the branch network of Rabobank on Dutch soil has undergone radical change. Whereas in 2004 the co-operative bank operated 1643 branches, by 2017 the figure had shrunk to 446. As an integral part of the cost rationalization program set out by the bank management, staffing has been cut dramatically in recent years: from 53,912 in 2014 to 43,810 in 2017 with further cuts still being announced.

Furthermore, the Dutch activities of Rabobank International were merged with those of Rabobank Nederland. This step was also seen as a way of mitigating the reputational damage suffered as a result of Rabobank International's involvement in the Libor affair at the end of 2013 and the consequent legal losses borne, which totaled $ 1 billion (Groeneveld 2016a).

The growing competition from non-banks (i.e. crowdfunding platforms, providers of payment services, etc.), the steps taken toward European Banking Union from 2014 onward and the increase in regulatory capital needs, led to the Vision 2016 program being revised. In December 2015, the General Assembly voted for fundamental changes to the governance of Rabobank. Until 2015, the co-operative banking group had consisted of about 100 independent local banks and their co-operative central institution, all operating with individual banking licenses. This structure entailed high maintenance costs, and impeded prompt compliance with complex regulations. As a result of the decisions taken in December 2015, on 1 January 2016, all 106 local Rabobanks existing at the time and the central institution Rabobank Nederland merged into one CB operating under one banking license. The resulting legal entity is Coöperatieve Rabobank U.A. (Rabobank). The decision to merge was preceded by the so-called Great Governance Debate, which commenced

---

[15] See Rabobank's publication "Rabobank through the years". https://www.rabobank.com/en/images/r652-rabothroughtheyears-uk-vdef.pdf.

in March 2014 (Groeneveld 2016a).[16] Internal and external reasons motivated this democratic discussion which ended with the merger of local independent CBs and the revision of the governance structure. From the internal perspective, there was widespread disaffection at the local level with the growing focus on banking technicalities which was obscuring its social mission; parallel to this, in addition to acting as the central bank and supervisor of the legally independent banks, the central institution had centralized many functions (i.e. IT, product development, marketing, etc.), including the external funding for the group that the domestic and international growth of Rabobank had required. From an external standpoint, Rabobank's structure, with its network of just over 100 local CBs, was called into question by the national and European supervisory authorities who wondered whether the central institution's ability to impose the evolving regulatory rules could somehow be weakened by the legal independence of the local CBs. After an intense debate with huge local involvement, the new governance was approved by the member councils of the local CBs in December 2015, followed by the approval of the merger by the General Meeting (Groeneveld 2016b).

4   Dutch Co-operative Banking: Main Characteristics

With the merger and the resulting demise of the independence of local CBs, local members were given direct representation on the co-operative's highest body, the General Members Council. The merger of local CBs does not seem to go against the principle of decentralization which is still followed in the new governance framework and the "bottom-up" governance model which characterized and still fully typifies co-operative banking.

In Rabobank, each local bank, although nowadays formally equivalent to a bank outlet, adopts a two-tier governance structure, with its own supervisory board and board of directors. Member representation is implemented through local members' councils (LMCs), made up of 30 to 50 members. These represent the local member base and are required to monitor and advise the management of the local Rabobanks. LMCs have statutory formal duties and responsibilities, such as the right to advise the

---

[16] A governance committee was nominated in 2014, composed of four chairmen of LSBs, four chairmen of local boards of directors, two executive board members of the central institution, and representatives from relevant staff directorates of the apex institution.

chairman of the local Rabobank's management on members' policy plans. LMCs monitor the financial performance of local Rabobanks and the policies implemented by the local management and supervise the activities of the members of the Local Supervisory Body (LSB). LSB members are appointed by and accountable to their LMCs. Each LSB is comprised of three to seven members. Their functions and those of LMCs are defined in Rabobank's articles of association. The LSBs perform several functions which range from supervising the implementation of the bank strategy at local level, to the appointment of the local management's chairman, to monitoring local banks' conduct and compliance with laws, regulations, and the articles of association. At any time, the authorizations granted to the LSBs and to local bank management can be withdrawn by the executive board of Rabobank, in accordance with an advisory communication to them and the right of appeal being granted by Rabobank's supervisory board in order to eliminate any possible abuse of authority made by the executive board.

In keeping with the idea of providing full representation to local communities and their needs at group level, LSB chairmen represent local members on the General Members' Council (GMC). The GMC has around 100 members and meets at least twice a year. It is tasked with several functions, including: being custodians of the collective values of the CB; the appointment of the members of Rabobank's supervisory board who engage the statutory members of the managing or executive board; the amendment of the articles of association or any change in the legal status of Rabobank; the approval of the annual accounts; and advisory services and the approval of major decisions taken by the managing board (e.g. acquisitions). The chairman of the GMC also chairs the supervisory board of the bank. At the operational level, the Directors' Conference also constitutes another representative body of local CBs' management. Together with the executive board and the divisional directors, the local management identifies proposals and policies concerning local Rabobanks.[17]

An interesting feature of Rabobank highlighted by De Graaf (2018) is that the professionalization of the CB's executive board was a relatively late phenomenon, possibly as a result of the idea of having top managers who represented the society they served more than the financial industry.

---

[17] See Rabobank's website. https://www.rabobank.com/en/about-rabobank/cooperative/in-practice/index.html.

Up until 2002, no chief executive officer of Rabobank had a background in banking.[18] This was consistent with the prevailing idea that "banking was seen as a means rather than an end—meaning that social returns were at least as important as financial returns" (De Graaf 2018). After 2002, the idea that it was necessary for professionals to run the banking business became dominant with the growing and pervasive financialization of economies. However, even the first banker appointed as chief executive officer, Bert Heemskerk, who held office from 2002 to 2009, made his ideas about alternative banking clear with a famous statement: "shareholder-value thinking is bullshit", as reported by De Graaf (2018). The history of the Dutch CB is characterized by an intense democratic dialogue that, along with the changes that have occurred in society and in the economic and political environment, have carried the bank toward a new organizational model which continues to give voice to its members in a bottom-up fashion.

Significant changes have also occurred in the capital and funding of the group since the second part of the 1990s. To meet the growing funding needs which could not be entirely satisfied domestically, Rabobank started to raise funds from the international bond markets and subsequently to issue member certificates between 2000 and 2005 (Groeneveld 2016b). The aim of these was to improve the core capital of Rabobank and to strengthen the member base as they were available exclusively to members. Members' dissatisfaction with CBs who were diversifying their activities and becoming more and more like commercial banks throughout the period 1980–2000 had led to a steep drop in the number of members. Groeneveld (2016b) reports that during this period the number of members decreased from 950,000 in 1979 to 510,000 in 1999. The success of member certificates was significant as membership increased. Certificates are issued in perpetuity and do not grant any voting rights. The initial certificates were not listed but could be traded internally between members. From January 2014, the certificates were listed on Euronext

[18] As reported by De Graaf (2018), "Pierre Lardinois, chairman of the executive board in the 1980s, had chaired the previous Christian Farmers Association in Noord Brabant and had served as Minister for Agriculture and as Agricultural Commissioner of the European Community. Wijffels, his successor, had been a civil servant at the Ministry of Agriculture and the General Secretary of the Dutch Association of Christian Employers (Nederlands Christelijk Werkgeversverbond). Smits had been the Director of Schiphol Airport and the highest civil servant in the Ministry of Transport. The idea had been that, since Rabobank was state owned, it was too politically involved to be led by a banker".

Amsterdam to enhance their liquidity and facilitate price transparency. Additionally, and not by chance, in the same year, the subscription of certificates was opened to institutional investors as a means of amplifying the sources for raising capital. This decision followed the Dutch Financial Markets Authority's requirement that banks disclose to those investing in certificates their non-risk-free financial nature and that investors should be advised to limit the share of member certificates in their financial portfolio to 20% (Groeneveld 2016b). Several issuances of certificates have been made over time. Technically speaking, they are issued by a foundation, "Stichting AK Rabobank Certificaten", and represent interest in a corresponding number of participations with a nominal value of € 25.00 each, issued by Rabobank Nederland. These participations are classified as Common Equity Tier 1 under the Capital Requirements Regulation (CRR) and pay a quarterly coupon linked to the interest on the ten-year Dutch government bonds plus 1.5% spread. The payment of the coupon is wholly discretionary and in the event of unpaid distributions, members do not hold any right over unpaid coupons. To assure the representation of local CBs in the foundation, the appointment and dismissal of its management is approved partly by the supervisory board of Rabobank and partly by the management of Rabobank.

Since January 2016, as a consequence of the legal merger between Rabobank and the local Rabobanks, the shares held by the CBs became void. With this merger, each CB's capital contribution to the total equity of the new Rabobank and its development is recorded in internal financial reporting and is used to determine the voting of CBs in the GMC, the highest member body in the new governance system. Local CBs voting rights are linked to their capital input.[19]

5   THE PERFORMANCE OF DUTCH CO-OPERATIVE VERSUS NON-CO-OPERATIVE BANKING GROUPS OVER THE PERIOD 2005–2017

Rabobank is one of the three biggest banks in the Netherlands, along with the ABN-AMRO Group and ING Groep. Together, the three banks hold a market share of approximately 90% (De Graaf 2018). With about 1.9 million members and more than 8.5 million customers in almost 40

---

[19] See Rabobank's Annual Report for the year-end 2015.

countries around the world in 2017, Rabobank ranks as the Netherlands' second largest bank after ING Groep. During 2018, it was rated the 25th safest bank in the world by Global Finance. ABN-AMRO ranks as the third largest bank in the country. All three banks enjoy very positive long and short term ratings. The two largest shareholder-oriented banking groups, ABN-AMRO and ING, have undergone substantial restructurings in exchange for state aid and have followed processes of cost optimization to address the economic impact of the persistently low interest rate environment.

As in the other chapters, the purpose of this section is to verify empirically the effects of the ongoing hybridization in co-operative banking. In other words, have the mitigation of the principles of mutuality pursued by CBs and the growing complementarity with markets as places of investment and funding meant that the results achieved by CBs have become more similar to those of shareholder-oriented banks? Which areas have recorded analogies and differences in results? Can a convergence in their respective performances be observed over time? To answer these important questions, we have identified a series of indicators in the form of ratios proxying bank performances. The set of indicators used to run the comparisons concerns the capitalization of banks; their activities in lending and investing in securities, including those held for trading on the financial markets; their reliance on deposits from customers; the role they play over time in the interbank market; the riskiness deriving from lending; and, finally, banking profitability and efficiency. The data used for the analysis presented here are consolidated, therefore representative of the results achieved by the banking groups. Year-end figures are used. In order to verify if, where and when there have been phenomena of convergence between stakeholder- and shareholder-oriented banking models, peer national commercial banking groups have been identified with which a comparative analysis is carried out. The Dutch co-operative banking group is compared, on a consolidated basis, with the two major shareholder-oriented banking groups, ING (€ 846.2 billion of total assets at the end of 2017) and ABN-AMRO (with € 393.2 billion), both of which are listed.

The analysis covers the period 2005–2017, which is particularly helpful since it allows the results obtained by the two groups of banks to be taken before and after the onset of the GFC. Data are collected from three databases—SNL, BankScope Bureau van Dijk, and Orbis Bank Focus—in order to minimize the potential for missing data. We provide means and standard deviations of the selected indicators in different sub-periods, covering respectively the pre-crisis period, 2005–2007; the main GFC period, 2008–2010; the period from 2011 to 2013 during which the sovereign debt crisis severely affected various countries and important regulatory and monetary policy measures were taken to restore bank financial stability; and the implementation of Basel 3 rules, the initiation of the European Banking Union with the implementation of the Single Supervisory Mechanism (SSM) and the Single Resolution Mechanism (SRM), 2014–2017.

In Table 8.4, we report the first set of indicators under investigation. The capital ratios employed consist of a regulatory proxy for the appraisal of the capital adequacy of the banking groups, the Tier 1 (%) ratio, and an accounting ratio represented by equity over assets (%). The first one stands for a measure of capital adequacy under the Basel rules to address credit risk. Broadly speaking, the Tier 1 ratio is calculated as the shareholder funds plus perpetual non-cumulative preference shares as a percentage of risk weighted assets and some off-balance sheet items. The higher the

Table 8.4 Comparison of Dutch co-operative vs. non-co-operative banking groups: capital ratios

	Coöperatieve Rabobank U.A.		ABN-AMRO Group		ING Groep	
	Mean	SD	Mean	SD	Mean	SD
Tier 1 (%)						
2005–2007	11.00	0.54	–	–	7.45[a]	0.16
2008–2010	14.08	1.49	12.90[b]	0.21	10.60[a]	1.50
2011–2013	16.95	0.30	13.74	1.37	13.19[a]	1.36
2014–2017	17.19	1.24	16.95	1.71	15.13	1.40
Equity/total assets (%)						
2005–2007	5.33	0.16	–	–	2.62[a]	0.11
2008–2010	5.99	0.46	2.77[b]	0.62	3.21[a]	0.77
2011–2013	6.01	0.12	3.34	0.45	4.14[a]	0.44
2014–2017	6.14	0.35	4.53	0.77	5.91	0.27

Source: Author's calculations

This table reports descriptive statistics (means and standard deviations—SD) of Dutch co-operative and non-co-operative banking groups. Tier 1 (%) is the ratio between primary regulatory capital and risk weighted assets; Equity/total assets (%) is the ratio between total equity and total assets. Our calculations are based on data extracted from SNL

[a]Due to missing data, figures reported refer to ING Bank NV (consolidated data)
[b]Only 2009–2010

Tier 1 value, the more capitalized the bank is, which improves its ability to face the risks arising from lending to and financing borrowers. Under the Basel 3 rules introduced in Europe in 2014 (with EU Directive 2013/36 and the EU Regulation 575/2013—CRR), the minimum level of Tier 1 permitted is 6% plus the capital conservation buffer of 2.5%.[20] The ratio of equity to total assets (%) proxies the cushion against banking risks. The higher this figure, the better the bank is able to cope with potential losses arising from its activity.

The Tier 1 ratio has, on average, been increasing over time in all the sub-periods under investigation both for co-operative and commercial banking groups. However, particularly during the crisis periods, the so-called GFC and the subsequent sovereign debt crisis, and more recently between 2014 and 2017, Rabobank performs on average better than its peer groups, resulting in being better equipped to face the risks arising from the intermediation activity. Analysis of the ratio of equity to total assets reveals a similar trend to that already seen for the Tier 1 ratio (Table 8.4). However, what emerges clearly from the reported data is the lower level of capital held by shareholder-oriented banking groups before the GFC and the subsequent periods. Only recently have commercial banking groups reported being better capitalized with ING in particular having an equity to total assets average (%) close to that of Rabobank (5.91% and 6.14% respectively).

The second set of indicators concerns the asset side of the banking groups and aims to shed light on its composition. In this regard, we employ three types of ratios: the ratio of net customer loans to total assets (%), which measures the degree of dedication to the traditional lending activity; the ratio of the total securities held to total assets (%), which provides an assessment of the banks' integration with financial markets in investment terms; and finally, the ratio of securities held for trading to total assets (%), which shows the degree of banks' active participation in the financial markets through financial instruments (i.e. bonds, derivatives, and stocks) and allows for an assessment of speculative activities within the financial markets. The data shown in Table 8.5 clearly indicate some distinctive features of the three Dutch banking groups. First of all, the propensity to finance the economy through credit is, over the entire period of observation, significantly high and very similar for Rabobank

---

[20] Prior to the Basel 3 regulations coming into force, the minimum value of the Tier 1 ratio was 4%.

Table 8.5   Comparison of Dutch co-operative vs. non-co-operative banking groups: lending and securities holdings ratios

	Coöperatieve Rabobank		ABN-AMRO Group		ING Groep	
	Mean	SD	Mean	SD	Mean	SD
Net customer loans/total assets (%)						
2005–2007	63.62	2.44	–	–	39.58[a]	2.25
2008–2010	70.80	1.04	72.66[b]	0.57	48.49[a]	1.71
2011–2013	65.95	2.31	69.07	1.43	48.18[a]	1.04
2014–2017	69.27	1.76	68.91	1.22	69.79	8.43
Securities/total assets (%)						
2005–2007	23.00	1.82	–	–	26.97[c]	2.30
2008–2010	17.39	2.10	11.19[b]	0.78	22.63[c]	2.48
2011–2013	15.82	1.61	14.44	4.20	19.20[c]	0.93
2014–2017	12.48	2.45	19.98	2.16	20.40	1.40
Total assets held for trading/total assets (%)						
2005–2007	–	–	–	–	–	–
2008–2010	–	–	5.85[b]	0.83	14.07	1.50
2011–2013	7.84	1.47	6.50	0.76	13.80	0.65
2014–2017	6.20	1.79	4.20	1.94	14.19	0.96

Source: Author's calculations

This table reports descriptive statistics (means and standard deviations—SD) of Dutch co-operative and non-co-operative banking groups. Net customer loans/total assets (%) is the ratio between net loans and total assets; Securities/total assets (%) is the ratio between total securities held and total assets; Assets held for trading/total assets (%) is the ratio between total assets held for trading and total assets. Our calculations are based on data extracted from SNL

[a]Data from BankScope from 2005 to 2013
[b]Only 2009–2010
[c]Due to missing data, figures reported refer to ING Bank NV (consolidated data)

and ABN-AMRO during 2008–2013. Corresponding figures for ING are consistently lower than those of the other two groups up until 2013: around 48%. The banks' involvement in lending to customers is mostly similar especially in the last period 2014–2017 (around 70% on average). The asset downsizing observed for ING since 2014 has led to its average becoming aligned with the other two groups.[21] In previous years, for example, during the most acute phase of the GFC, Rabobank reported a

---

[21] Had we employed the corresponding data solely for ING Bank N.V.'s consolidated data, its ratio of net loans to total assets (%) would have been aligned to those of Rabobank and ABN-AMRO Group.

relevant average value of 70.80%, an increase in comparison with the average pre-crisis value (63.62%), thus showing its firm commitment to supporting the economy during the GFC. During the phase of the sovereign debt crisis and the start of the group restructuring program, Rabobank registered an average net loans to total assets ratio (%) that was slightly lower than that of ABN-AMRO but higher than that of ING. The intense concentration in the more traditional credit activity that the three banking groups all demonstrate in the last period stands in contrast to their commitment to investing in securities. The co-operative banking group shows on average lower and steadily decreasing values for the ratio of securities held to total assets (%), while commercial banks show a slightly greater degree of integration with financial markets in terms of their allocation in financial instruments. Over the period 2014–2017, Rabobank allocates on average 12.48% of its total assets to securities, versus almost 20% in the case of the two commercial banking groups.

The investment space that the banking groups devote to financial instruments held for trading purposes is rather low. The difference with the shareholder-oriented banking groups only becomes evident and substantial if comparing Rabobank and ING (Table 8.5). For the latter, the percentage of financial assets held for trading purposes has decreased over time and is confirmed in the last period (2014–2017) at average values of 14.19%. The co-operative group has also substantially disinvested from financial assets destined for trading: from 10.46% in 2005–2007 to 6.20% in 2014–2017. ABN-AMRO consistently reports the lowest incidence of securities held for trading purposes on its total assets (4.20% in 2014–2017).

If we calculate the impact of the assets held for trading on the total securities held, we observe, for example, that the non-co-operative banking groups exhibit average values ranging from almost 70% for ING to 21% for ABN-AMRO in the last period of observation. The values reported by Rabobank lie in between with an average value of nearly 50% over 2014–2017. The trading activity, although limited, therefore absorbs about half of the CB's total investments in securities. The data analyzed to date therefore seem to highlight the emergence of similarities in the resources dedicated to lending activity among the three groups while divergences remain over time as regards the preferences of investment in securities.

A third set of selected indicators concerns the incidence of traditional funding activity through customer deposits and the role of interbank activity for the most important Dutch banking groups (Table 8.6).

Table 8.6   Comparison of Dutch co-operative vs. non-co-operative banking groups: funding and interbank ratios

	Coöperatieve Rabobank		ABN-AMRO Group		ING Groep	
	Mean	SD	Mean	SD	Mean	SD
Customer deposits/total assets (%)						
2005–2007	42.50	5.85	–	–	40.23[a]	0.26
2008–2010	47.53	1.99	54.28	1.75	40.20[a]	0.89
2011–2013	46.13	2.39	54.45	1.53	39.82[a]	3.73
2014–2017	51.81	3.64	59.40	1.27	58.47	6.73
Interbank ratio (%)						
2005–2007	64.50	24.98	–	–	33.70[a]	4.82
2008–2010	147.68	9.75	149.39[b]	58.73	51.49[a]	19.66
2011–2013	163.47	88.42	207.47	10.15	106.33[a]	48.18
2014–2017	169.50	59.98	102.54	29.93	95.24	19.73

Source: Author's calculations

This table reports descriptive statistics (means and standard deviations—SD) of Dutch co-operative and non-co-operative banking groups. Customer deposit/total assets (%) is the ratio between customer deposits and total assets; Interbank ratio (%) is the ratio between loans to banks and deposits from banks. Our calculations are based on data extracted from SNL

[a]Data from BankScope from 2005 to 2013
[b]Only 2009–2010

The difference between the two business models in terms of their dependence on funding in the form of deposits is noteworthy. Traditionally, CBs are more dependent on funding provided by customer deposits. However, in the Dutch case the opposite is true at least over the period 2014–2017. The two commercial banking groups hold a greater proportion of customer deposits, at on average 59.40% for ABN-AMRO and 58.47% for ING as opposed to 51.81% for Rabobank. In the previous periods, the average ratio held by Rabobank is lower than that of ABN-AMRO but higher than that of ING. Therefore, it seems that Rabobank's liabilities are characterized by a comparatively higher degree of diversification in its funding sources. As a consequence of Rabobank's lower reliance on deposits from its customers, its funding gap appears on average higher than that of the other groups: about 134% as opposed to ING's 119% and ABN-AMRO's 116% in the latest of the analyzed periods. This makes Rabobank more exposed to the risks arising from higher levels of maturity transformation and more dependent on funding from the financial markets.

Over time, however, all three groups display a growing focus on the funding represented by bank deposits. During the GFC, it is worth highlighting that Rabobank's ratio in this regard grew (from 42.50% to 47.53%), in contrast to the almost unaltered values registered for ING Groep. Due to the financial difficulties faced by the two shareholder-oriented banking groups which required state aid, Rabobank experienced a growth in customer deposits as a result of a "flight to quality" phenomenon in the deposit market that rewarded it as the soundest intermediary at that time.

As regards participation on the interbank markets, measured by the interbank ratio, only in the case of the Rabobank group do the data displayed in Table 8.6 show a constantly increasing trend. The two commercial banking groups record an increase in the interbank ratio till the period 2011–2013, followed by a decrease in the most recent period. Overall the data indicate the different roles of co-operative and non-co-operative banks on interbank markets: the former are more strongly positioned as fund-givers with ratio values that exceed 160% since 2011, while the latter recently hold a more neutral position.

Table 8.7 contains a proxy for exposure to liquidity risk, often used in the empirical literature, and two proxies for credit risk. The use of the ratio of liquid assets to total liabilities (excluding equity) (%), was preferred to the prudential ratios relating to liquidity risk since the latter would have been available only for the last of the periods under investigation. The ratio used looks at the amount of liquid assets available to cover all the liabilities held by banks. The higher this percentage is, the more liquid the bank is and the more generally able it is to redeem its own debts, and the less vulnerable it is to a classic run on the bank.

The data in Table 8.7 show a common trend for Rabobank and ING Groep over the whole period with liquidity decreasing between the pre-crisis period and 2008–2010. During this phase, the liquidity holdings are slightly higher for ING. However, since 2011 Rabobank has held on average slightly more liquid assets than the ING and ABN-AMRO groups. Table 8.7 reports two proxies: the ratio of impaired loans to gross loans and advances (%) and the ratio of loan loss reserves to impaired loans (%). The first one shows impaired or non-performing loans as a percentage of the bank's gross customer loans and advances (%). It indicates the weakness of the loan portfolio which increases as the percentage rises. The second of the ratios used relates loan loss reserves to non-performing or impaired loans. Higher values of this ratio, also known as the "coverage ratio", indicate that the bank is better equipped to face losses on loans. On

Table 8.7 Comparison of Dutch co-operative vs. non-co-operative banking groups: liquidity and credit risk ratios

	Coöperatieve Rabobank		ABN-AMRO Group		ING Groep	
	Mean	SD	Mean	SD	Mean	SD
Liquid assets/total liabilities (%)						
2005–2007	16.74	2.98	–	–	18.08	1.37
2008–2010	11.60	1.30	16.20[a]	0.70	12.17	0.70
2011–2013	16.56	1.04	19.96	1.86	13.51	3.63
2014–2017	19.35	1.06	14.28	1.60	16.86	8.79
Impaired loans/gross customer loans and advances (%)						
2005–2007	1.30	0.24	–	–	1.26	0.29
2008–2010	1.79	0.30	2.63[a]	0.45	1.89	0.45
2011–2013	2.67	0.78	3.09	0.12	2.60	0.38
2014–2017	4.02	0.32	2.54	0.85	2.64	0.48
LLR/impaired loans (%)						
2005–2007	51.65	2.70	–	–	43.73	5.79
2008–2010	42.73	8.22	57.70[a]	12.20	35.25	4.50
2011–2013	39.95	12.12	64.09	0.46	37.94	0.55
2014–2017	43.61	11.78	66.20	5.13	36.84	1.23

Source: Author's calculations

This table reports descriptive statistics (means and standard deviations—SD) of Dutch co-operative and non-co-operative banking groups. Liquid assets/total liabilities (%) is the ratio between liquid assets and total liabilities; Impaired loans/gross loans and advances (%) is the ratio between impaired loans and gross customer loans and advances; LLR/NPL (%) is the ratio between loan loss reserves and impaired loans. Our calculations are based on data extracted from BankScope and Orbis Bank Focus solely for the year-ends 2016–2017

[a]Only 2009–2010

the other hand, out of all accounting considerations, higher levels of the coverage rate are generally indicative of a poorer quality loan portfolio. In terms of the quality of the three banking groups' credit portfolios, the data provide evidence of increased levels of risk in Rabobank's lending since 2011. Between 2014–2017, it is Rabobank which reports the highest ratio of impaired loans to gross customer loans and advances (%): about 4% as against about 2.60% for the two commercial banks. The results recorded for Rabobank reflect losses in Dutch commercial real estate and more recently a number of large one-off items (Moody's 2018). Only during 2008–2010 did the CB's riskiness rank lower than that of ING Groep, in a period in which its average net loans to total assets (%) grew significantly (Table 8.5), possibly as a result of the selection process for debtors being less rigorous. As regards the ratio between loss reserves and impaired loans, we again detect differences between the banks. There is higher volatility (standard deviation) in the data of Rabobank compared to those of ABN-AMRO and ING over the entire period. In comparison to ING, the largest bank in the Netherlands, Rabobank holds higher coverage ratios (43.61% in 2014–2017), but lower ratios than those shown by ABN-AMRO (66.20%). The increase in Rabobank's credit risk exposure has led the bank to raise its reserves on average in order to be able to face future loan losses following the start of the banking Union, while, conversely, the two commercial banks have kept their reserves virtually stable in light of the better trends they have experienced.

The last set of indicators that we examine involves variables that are representative of bank profitability and efficiency, widely employed in the empirical literature. With regard to the profitability analysis, three indicators are taken into consideration: the net interest margin (%); the return on average assets (ROAA) (%); and the return on average equity (ROAE) (%). To evaluate the operational efficiency achieved by the bank management, we use a widespread indicator: the cost-to-income ratio (%) (Table 8.8).

The net interest margin (%) represents the profitability arising from the bank's credit intermediation activity. In the period 2008 to 2013, this was higher for the co-operative banking group (1.45% and 1.46% respectively in 2008–2010 and 2011–2013) than for the commercial banks (1.01% and 1.14% for ING and 1.25% and 1.39% for ABN-AMRO in the two sub-periods), consistent with CBs' stronger focus on traditional banking activity. Only in the last period are the results achieved by joint-stock banks better than those recorded by Rabobank which seems to have been more impacted by the prolonged low interest rate regime. Similar results can be found relative to the ROAA (%) and the ROAE (%). The profitability of Rabobank was only higher during the GFC period, but subsequently has been on average lower, with an increasing gap emerging between it and the commercial banks. Looking at the last selected measure, the cost-to-income ratio (%), we find again that the co-operative banking group was found to be more efficient in comparative terms during the period 2008–2010 but that its cost-to-income ratios have since deteriorated, being higher than those attained by the commercial banks. The latter have been able to improve their operational efficiency over the period under observation, in contrast to Rabobank, whose cost-to-income ratio stands at an average value of 68.14% in 2014–2017. In light of the data available,

Table 8.8   Comparison of Dutch co-operative vs. non-co-operative banking groups: profitability and efficiency ratios

	Coöperatieve Rabobank		ABN-AMRO Group		ING Groep	
	Mean	SD	Mean	SD	Mean	SD
Net interest margin (%)						
2005–2007	1.27	0.03	–	–	0.83	0.09
2008–2010	1.45	0.06	1.25[a]	0.14	1.01	0.14
2011–2013	1.46	0.02	1.39	0.08	1.14	0.07
2014–2017	1.50	0.04	1.67	0.08	1.58	0.08
ROAA (%)						
2005–2007	0.44	0.03	–	–	0.69	0.05
2008–2010	0.42	0.06	−0.02[a]	0.18	0.03	0.18
2011–2013	0.31	0.06	0.26	0.07	0.38	0.07
2014–2017	0.33	0.06	0.49	0.20	0.43	0.20
ROAE (%)						
2005–2007	8.54	0.19	–	–	20.98	2.19
2008–2010	7.25	1.17	−0.44[a]	5.45	0.48	5.45
2011–2013	5.28	0.75	8.08	1.92	9.06	2.65
2014–2017	5.48	0.86	10.90	3.39	7.53	3.39
Cost to income (%)						
2005–2007	67.87	1.04	–	–	59.79	1.91
2008–2010	62.54	3.59	73.05[a]	1.79	73.76	1.79
2011–2013	70.74	4.93	64.26	0.78	62.88	5.71
2014–2017	68.14	2.81	64.62	2.48	57.55	4.48

Source: Author's calculations

This table shows descriptive statistics (means and standard deviations—SD) of Dutch co-operative and non-co-operative banking groups. Net interest margin (%) is the ratio between net interest income and total earning assets; ROAA (%) is the return on average assets; ROAE (%) is the return on average equity; Cost to income (%) is the ratio between operating expenses and intermediation margin. Our calculations are based on data extracted from BankScope and Orbis Bank Focus solely for the year-ends 2016–2017

[a]Only 2009–2010

it seems therefore that the profitability and efficiency figures of the co-operative group have been worsening since 2011 in comparison with the shareholder-oriented groups.

Overall, in the Dutch case, we do not find clear differences between the co-operative banking model and the shareholder-oriented model. Moreover, after the most acute period of the GFC, the performance of the co-operative model tended to worsen, making the implementation of reorganization strategies more urgent.

In order to verify whether there are significant differences between the two banking business models, the non-parametric Wilcoxon-Mann-Whitney (WMW) (1947) test[22] is used. It is suitable for small sample sizes and for testing whether observations in one population tend to be larger than observations in the other as it tests the equality of central tendency of two distributions (Fay and Proschan 2010). The selected indicators are only subjected to the test for the period 2008–2017. It was decided to concentrate the analysis on this ten-year period, because we wanted to check whether, and if so how, the manifestation of the episodes of crisis and the start of the Banking Union in 2014, have affected the performance of the two business models, and whether this makes them more similar or not. The results of the test with the relative p-values are reported in Table 8.9.

Table 8.9   Wilcoxon-Mann-Whitney test (2008–2017)

Co-operative vs. non-co-operative banks		
	Median	*P-value*
Capital ratios		
Tier 1 (%)	16.50–13.93	0.04
Equity/total assets (%)	6.13–3.94	0.00
Lending, securities holdings ratios		
Net loans/total assets (%)	66.29–66.65	0.44
Securities/total assets (%)	15.06–18.34	0.55
Total assets held for trading/total assets (%)	8.16–12.97	0.33
Funding and interbank ratios		
Customer deposits/total assets (%)	47.30–51.11	0.38
Interbank ratio (%)	173.12–91.27	0.00
Liquidity and credit risk ratios		
Liquid assets/total liabilities (%)	17.21–15.64	0.52
Impaired loans/gross customer loans and advances (%)	2.95–2.65	0.52
LLR/impaired loans (%)	43.07–39.23	0.25
Profitability and efficiency ratios		
Net interest margin (%)	1.47–1.35	0.51
ROAA (%)	0.35–0.30	0.71
ROAE (%)	5.83–8.09	0.13
Cost to income (%)	67.10–64.42	0.29

Our calculations

[22] This test is also known as Wilcoxon ranksum test or Mann-Whitney U test.

Generally, the test results indicate that the two business models do show significant differences in their outcomes, as evidenced by the p-values obtained. The co-operative banking group exhibits a capitalization which is statistically significantly higher than that of non-co-operative banks. This implies that co-operative banking in the Netherlands retains a superior ability to face banking risks. However, if we compare the two business models, taking into account their asset and liability allocative choices, we find that there are strong similarities, both in terms of lending and deposits from customers, as shown by the insignificance in the differences in the results of the test. Holdings of securities differ, with commercial joint-stock banks devoting more funds to securities investment over the period. However, no divergences are found with regard to the allocation of assets to securities for trading purposes.

The only remaining significant difference between the two business models relates to the interbank position. CBs are active givers on the interbank and this places them in a position of extreme importance for the banking system as a whole. In terms of the exposure to credit risk and the economic performances achieved (net interest margin, ROAA, ROAE, and cost to income), we do not detect any significant difference between the two groups of banks. Accordingly, it seems that in a strong competitive climate, the hybridization of the co-operative model tends to heighten operational parallels with shareholder-oriented banks.

6   Conclusion

The Netherlands are among the European countries where domestic banks have succeeded in regaining market share soon after the crisis, domestic market power having dropped from 95% to 85% between 2009 and 2010. Three domestic banking groups dominate the market: the co-operative Rabobank and the two commercial groups ABN-AMRO and ING. While Rabobank did not need a state bailout, capital injection or guarantees during the 2008–2009 global credit crisis, the other two had to be rescued: ABN-AMRO was nationalized in 2008 and subsequently publicly re-listed through an initial public offering (IPO) in 2015, followed by further placings through which the Dutch state has progressively divested its stakes; ING was indebted to the government until 2014 due to bailout operations in 2008.

Since the 1980s, the Rabobank co-operative network was organized in line with the provisions of Art. 10 of CRR. Affiliation for any existing or newly established CB with a central institution was mandatory. The apex was empowered to issue enforceable instructions concerning the management of local CBs and the supervision of the CBs was performed on a consolidated basis, along with the reporting of results to stakeholders. After an intense debate with huge local involvement, the new governance of Rabobank was approved by the member councils of the local CBs in December 2015, followed by the approval of the merger of local CBs by the General Meeting. With the merger and the resulting demise of the independence of local CBs, local members were given direct representation on the co-operative's highest body, the General Members Council.

With about 1.9 million members and more than 8.5 million customers in almost 40 countries around the world in 2017, Rabobank ranks as the Netherlands' second largest bank after ING Groep. Co-operative banking in the Netherlands plays a key role in terms of both loans granted and deposits collected. However, as shown by reported figures, the market shares enjoyed by the CBs on the funding side decreased from 2004 (39%) to 2010 (29%) but subsequently changed direction to reach a percentage value of 34% at the end of 2017. Among the European countries under our investigation, the Rabobank group is one of the leading CBs in terms of attracting customer deposits: only France and Finland scored better in 2017. On the lending side, the bank has been able to capture a substantial gain, as its market share grew from 25% in 2004 to 39% in 2012. According to corporate presentations, at the end of 2016, the bank held a 43% share of business lending and 21% of mortgages in the domestic market.

In addition to analyzing the role and organization of the co-operative network in the Netherlands, the chapter offers an empirical investigation, aimed to verify empirically the effects of the ongoing hybridization in co-operative banking. The data reported show that overall co-operative and shareholder-oriented banking do show less significant differences in their outcomes than in other countries surveyed in this book. The co-operative banking group exhibits a capitalization which is statistically significantly higher than that of commercial banks. This implies that co-operative banking in the Netherlands retains a superior ability to face banking risks. However, if we compare the two business models, taking into account their asset and liability allocative choices, we find that there are strong similarities.

In terms of the exposure to credit risk and the economic performances achieved (net interest margin, ROAA, ROAE and cost to income), we do not detect any significant difference between the two groups of banks. So it seems that in a strong competitive climate, the hybridization of the co-operative model tends to accentuate operational similarities with shareholder-oriented banks.

References

Blok, V., Sjauw-Koen-Fa, A., & Omtac, O. (2013). Effective Stakeholder Involvement at the Base of the Pyramid: The Case of Rabobank. *International Food and Agribusiness Management Review, 16*(Special Issue A), 39–44.

Chang, M., & Jones, E. (2013). Belgium and the Netherlands: Impatient Capital. In J. Hardie & D. Howarth (Eds.), *Market-Based Banking and the International Financial Crisis*. Oxford University Press.

Cooperatieve Rabobank U. A. *Annual Report*, Various Years.

Cotugno, M. (2010). Cooperative Banking in the Netherlands: Rabobank Network. In V. Boscia, A. Carretta, & P. Schwizer (Eds.), *Cooperative Banking in Europe. Case Studies*. Palgrave Macmillan.

De Graaf, F. J. (2018). Competing Logics: Financialisation and a Dutch Cooperative Bank. *Journal of Management History, 24*(3), 316–339.

DeNederlandscheBank (DNB). (2015). *Perspective on the Structure of the Dutch Banking Sector. Efficiency and Stability Through Competition and Diversity*. Retrieved from https://www.dnb.nl/en/binaries/DNB-study%20Perspective%20on%20the%20structure%20of%20the%20Dutch%20banking%20sector_tcm47-323322_tcm47-334492.pdf.

European Central Bank (ECB). (2017, October). *Report on Financial Structures*.

Fay, M. P., & Proschan, M. A. (2010). Wilcoxon-Mann-Whitney or T-test? On Assumptions for Hypothesis Tests and Multiple Interpretations of Decision Rules. *Statistics Surveys, 4*, 1.

Groeneveld, J. M. (2016a). Rabobank Before, During and After the Credit Crisis: From Modesty via Complacency to Fundamental Steps. In S. Karafolas (Ed.), *Credit Cooperative Institutions in European Countries*. Springer.

Groeneveld, J. M. (2016b). *The Road Towards One Cooperative Rabobank*. Utrecht: Rabobank.

Groeneveld, J. M., & Wagemakers, J. M. (2004, August). *Retail Banking Strategies in Europe. The Strategic Vision of Rabobank Group*. Economic Research Department.

Hardie, J., & Howarth, D. (2013). Framing Market-Based Banking and the Financial Crisis. In J. Hardie & D. Howarth (Eds.), *Market-Based Banking and the International Financial Crisis*. Oxford University Press.

Mann, H. B., & Whitney, D. R. (1947). On a Test of Whether One of Two Random Variables Is Stochastically Larger than the Other. *Annals of Mathematical Statistics, 18*(1), 50–60.

Moody's Investors Service. (2018, October 12). Rabobank. Update to Credit Analysis. *Credit Opinion*.

Smits, H. N. J., & Groeneveld, J. M. (2001). Reflections on Strategic Renewal at Rabobank: A CEO Perspective. *Long Range Planning, 34*(2), 249–258.

Vogelaar, N. (2012). Rabobank and the Credit Crisis. In J. Mooij & W. W. Boonstra (Eds.), *Raiffeisen's Footprint* (pp. 198–216). Amsterdam: VU University Press.

Wilson, J. S. G. (1986). *Banking Policy and Structure. A Comparative Analysis.* Routledge.

CHAPTER 9

The Performance of Co-operative Banking Networks and the Challenges They Face

1   An Evaluation of the Comparative Performances of Commercial Joint-Stock and Co-operative Banks in Certain European Countries

In the previous chapters, the intermediation activity and performance of the co-operative networks in certain European countries have been analyzed to determine whether or not they come to closely resemble those of the main reference shareholder-oriented banking groups with which they compete so fiercely on a national and international scale. To date, the empirical evidence shows that, despite a growing degree of hybridization pervading the most significant European co-operative banking networks, their performances and the distinctive nature of their operational practices mostly sets them apart from those of the shareholder-oriented groups. They are distinguished from these by greater patrimonial endowments, although the gap between them has been gradually decreasing over time, especially since the introduction of the European Banking Union and the implementation of the Basel 3 regulations. At the national level, their exposure to credit risk is generally lower but only where the co-operative groups have a high degree of strategic integration. Furthermore, the indicators of a co-operative's profitability and operating efficiency are generally more satisfactory in more integrated networks.

At the country level, the activities of the co-operative groups with strategically organized networks are generally different. The focus on lending

© The Author(s) 2019   379
F. Poli, *Co-operative Banking Networks in Europe*, Palgrave
Macmillan Studies in Banking and Financial Institutions,
https://doi.org/10.1007/978-3-030-21699-3_9

and funding through customer deposits remains generally high, highlighting the importance of this business model in enabling the mobilization of savings to finance the real economy and also the confidence with which it has tended to be regarded both during and following the global financial crisis (GFC).

In the following pages, using the entire sample of the European countries analyzed, we test, over different time periods, the existence of significant differences between the co-operative banking sector and the purely shareholder-oriented banks which have been selected. We have excluded the Italian co-operative banking sector, composed of credit co-operative banks (CCBs) and popular banks, from this analysis. As previously described, the 2016 reform of the credit co-operative banking sector has given rise to two strategic groups (in line with the provisions of Art. 10 of the Capital Requirements Regulation [CRR]) and a quasi-strategic one, through an institutional protection scheme (IPS) (pursuant to Art. 113(7) of the CRR). These three organizationally more integrated networks will become operational during 2019, while the popular banking sector remains composed of loosely integrated entities with a national reference association. The comparison between more integrated co-operative networks and non-co-operative banking groups seems more appropriate given the greater degree of strategic coordination which they share. We use consolidated data where available. For co-operative banking groups, we rely on the consolidated data which are available for the following countries: Finland, France, Germany, the Netherlands, and Austria (solely for the Volksbanks Verbund). Since no consolidated data are available for the entire network of Austrian Raiffeisen banks, the consolidated data of the central institution, RBI, and the annual average values referring to the CB sample are used instead.

For each of the selected indicators, we report the median value recorded for the co-operative and shareholder-oriented groups in different periods, in order to track the evolution of that indicator and observe the effects of the GFC and the changes in prudential regulation introduced by Basel 3 and by the Banking Union from 2014 onward. Results are reported in Table 9.1. In order to verify whether there are significant differences between the two banking business models, the non-parametric Wilcoxon-Mann-Whitney (WMW) (1947) test is used. This is suitable for small sample sizes and for testing whether observations in one population tend to be larger than observations in the other as it tests the equality of central tendency of two distributions (Fay and Proschan 2010). P-values are reported in parenthesis.

Table 9.1 Comparative performances of different types of co-operative banking and peer non-co-operative banking groups (without Italian co-operative networks) (2005–2017). Medians and p-values in parenthesis

	2005–2007	2008–2010	2011–2013	2014–2017	2005–2017
	Co-op vs. commercial	Co-op vs. commercial	Co-op vs. commercial	Co-op vs. commercial	Co-op vs. commercial
Tier 1 (%)	9.94–7.63 (0.00)	11.73–10.53 (0.33)	12.84–12.95 (0.58)	16.05–14.28 (0.19)	12.73–12.47 (0.10)
Equity/total assets (%)	5.43–3.73 (0.00)	5.66–3.90 (0.00)	6.26–4.29 (0.01)	6.92–5.31 (0.00)	6.47–4.51 (0.00)
Net customer loans/total assets (%)	54.78–39.94 (0.00)	54.68–45.55 (0.04)	57.20–45.96 (0.08)	59.65–50.52 (0.01)	57.82–44.78 (0.00)
Securities/ total assets (%)	29.62–27.48 (0.18)	24.43–38.26 (0.20)	19.59–31.39 (0.10)	16.45–26.76 (0.00)	21.43–28.33 (0.00)
Total assets held for trading/total assets (%)	10.14–18.88 (0.08)	7.66–14.70 (0.07)	6.22–13.86 (0.01)	5.05–14.07 (0.00)	6.04–15.05 (0.00)
Customer deposits/total assets (%)	45.14–28.35 (0.00)	45.87–32.44 (0.00)	48.53–37.90 (0.02)	55.44–51.88 (0.00)	47.51–39.25 (0.00)
Interbank ratio (%)	69.12–52.51 (0.12)	79.13–73.09 (0.40)	87.30–90.16 (0.89)	108.00–85.46 (0.09)	82.17–73.65 (0.06)
Liquid assets/ total liabilities (%)	25.71–28.64 (0.16)	16.46–22.12 (0.11)	19.35–26.43 (0.08)	19.17–28.24 (0.00)	19.37–26.91 (0.00)
Impaired loans/gross customer loans and advances (%)[a]	1.09–3.62 (0.01)	3.24–3.73 (0.56)	4.22–4.77 (0.71)	3.79–4.25 (0.55)	3.65–3.78 (0.18)
LLR/impaired loans (%)[a]	54.36–66.23 (0.49)	58.54–59.62 (0.60)	66.54–60.80 (0.00)	59.72–62.65 (0.63)	61.63–61.35 (0.13)
Net interest margin (%)	1.80–0.88 (0.01)	1.66–1.14 (0.00)	1.45–1.11 (0.00)	1.52–1.09 (0.01)	1.53–1.10 (0.00)
ROAA (%)	0.62–0.66 (0.68)	0.36–0.27 (0.31)	0.37–0.25 (0.01)	0.38–0.35 (0.66)	0.42–0.33 (0.05)
ROAE (%)	11.49–14.91 (0.01)	5.97–6.75 (0.81)	6.09–5.37 (0.66)	5.99–7.45 (0.16)	6.16–7.52 (0.16)
Cost to income (%)	61.96–60.26 (0.20)	63.25–67.73 (0.56)	66.80–64.83 (0.37)	66.26–64.45 (0.25)	65.30–63.41 (0.12)

Source: Author's calculations

[a]Excluding Germany due to missing data

Different shades of gray are used to highlight the different levels of significance of the test, where these exist. The darker gray indicates a significance of 1%, the medium 5%, and the light gray 10%.

As can be seen, the equity held as a proportion of total assets (%) by the more integrated co-operative networks is always higher than that of the corresponding joint-stock banks, with the differences being statistically significant. In regulatory terms, much more convergence is detected between the two business models since significant differences are found only in the period before the outbreak of the GFC, whereas over the entire period of investigation, the differences are statistically weak. The regulatory harmonization process seems therefore to have led the two business models to become similar in the space of just over a decade.

The stakeholder-oriented banking sector offers a different contribution to the development of local economies and has a less intense link with financial markets, despite having apexes with generally more pronounced asset diversification than the CBs which make up their groups. This is due to the implicit mandate for specialization attributed to the central institutions which undertake financial activities that are more complementary with the financial markets. During the observation period, the co-operative banking sector's ratio of net loans to customers to total assets (%) has been constantly growing and has been statistically higher than that of joint-stock banks.[1] Thus, over time, although the allocation in securities has increased, the gap with shareholder-oriented banks has remained significant in statistical terms. The more strategically integrated co-operative banking groups invest less in securities and, above all, are constantly less focused on trading over time, thus demonstrating their lower propensity to short-term investment horizons and speculation.

At the same time, dependence on funding in the form of customer deposits is more marked among co-operative banking groups and statistically different from the values of non-co-operative banks. However, even the latter have increased their capacity to collect deposits from savers, probably due to the effects of the increase in bank deposit insurance levels after 2008.

At the national level, a significant difference has sometimes been found between the weight of CBs' interbank activity and that of shareholder-

---

[1] This result is consistent with that of Becchetti et al. (2016) who demonstrate that over the period 1998–2010, CBs hold higher loans/total assets ratios than commercial banks. They also record a lower proportion of derivatives over total assets and a lower earnings volatility.

oriented banks (for example, in France). However, in the sample analyzed here, although the values of the interbank ratio (%) are higher in the co-operative sector, the statistically significant differences are weak in the 2014–2017 period and in the long term, where the greater commitment of the CBs in the interbank market, and especially within their networks, emerges. With regard to the indicators relating to risk, profitability, and operating efficiency, the analysis identifies lower degrees of statistically significant differentiation between the two business models. The co-operatives appear to be less liquid over time, through their greater commitment to lending and this emerges especially in the last two sub-periods and over the whole 2005–2017 period. However, similarities between the two business models are found as regards their exposure to credit risk. In the long run, the co-operative sector does not prove to be more effective in taking credit risk and hedging it. It should also be noted that in the face of more recent similar levels of credit risk, there is no corresponding commitment in terms of loans, as the CBs are much more exposed.

Over time, the profitability of the CBs is higher although decreasing, both in terms of net interest margin (%) and, to a more limited extent, of return on average assets (ROAA) (%). The levels of profitability that emanate from the more traditional credit intermediation carried out by the co-operative banking sector are constantly statistically different to those of the peer non-co-operative banking. Even though in many of the countries observed, the impact of the GFC on CBs has been limited, mostly because of their lower exposure to toxic securities and speculative financial instruments, the implementation of expansive monetary policies and a prolonged low interest rate regime seem to have hit the co-operative sector precisely where it derives part of its profitability: the net interest margin (%). And although achieving a profit does not represent the main determinant of CBs' actions, there are those who do not see how in the long term this could not represent a threat to their survival or at least a factor that might alter their traditional role in supporting the development of local communities.

Since 2008, the median return on average equity (ROAE) of non-co-operative banks, although higher than that of co-operatives, has no longer been statistically different, just as there are no significant differences between the cost-to-income values (%) of the two business models. In the sample of countries where there are strong integrated co-operative networks, a certain degree of convergence seems to appear in the operating results and risk exposures achieved by the co-operative and shareholder-oriented banks.

On the one hand, the increasing harmonization of EU prudential regulation and supervision, and on the other, macro-economic dynamics, seem to have contributed to making the operational results achieved by the two types of banks more and more similar. In answer to the question of whether the progressive hybridization of European co-operative banking networks has led to a greater degree of similarity between these and shareholder-oriented banks, it can be stated that there is convergence in the operating results and in risk exposure but not in business choices. The need to preserve biodiversity in the organizational governance formulas of banking activity therefore stems from the opportunity to have institutions such as co-operative ones that, due to the elements of financial support for communities, solidarity with them, and a non-profit orientation that are embedded in their DNA, have more of a natural anti-cyclical inclination than other banking business models. Much of this reported empirical evidence remains valid even when we include in the sample co-operative networks which up until 2017 were characterized by the lowest levels of integration, such as the Italian co-operative sector and a small group of independent Austrian popular banks. In the interests of brevity, these results are not reported here.

2   An Assessment of the Performances of Local CBs According to Their Network Model

Besides the empirical results already mentioned, there is a further aspect worthy of investigation linked to the following question: which of the network models seen so far enhances the performances of its member CBs? Or in other words, which of the types of networks analyzed has the most positive impact on the results of their owners: the local CBs? To answer this question, we return to the classification of co-operative networks introduced in Chap. 2 and examine, on a comparative basis, the performances of the different networks of the individual CBs. We distinguish between CBs that belong to fully strategic networks (such as the French and Finnish ones and the network of Volksbanks in Austria), those included in so-called quasi-strategic networks (such as those belonging to the Raiffeisen banks sector in Germany and Austria), and finally, those which are part of decentralized networks (like the Italian popular banks and credit co-operative banks and the few independent popular banks in Austria).

The strategic and quasi-strategic groups include those networks that both before and after 2015 elected to adopt one of the organizational configurations mentioned above (such as the Austrian Volksbanks and the Raiffeisen banks). In the case of the Italian credit co-operative banks, they are categorized as belonging to decentralized networks until 2017. In this group there are also small-medium-sized Italian popular banks and some Austrian popular banks that have not joined the Volksbanks Austrian Verbund.

The empirical analysis that follows focuses on the 2008–2017 period and is based on the individual data of the CBs, extracted from the databases BankScope, Orbis Bank, and SNL. The analysis excludes the Netherlands due to the lack of data on local CBs.[2] Table 9.2 shows the median values of selected indicators already examined in the previous chapters, with the p-values of the non-parametric Wilcoxon-Mann-Whitney test (WMW) (1947) in brackets. The proxies of CBs' perfor-

Table 9.2 Comparative performances of different types of co-operative banking models of networks (2008–2017). Medians and p-values in parenthesis

	Strategic networks vs. quasi-strategic networks (IPS based)	Quasi-strategic networks (IPS based) vs. decentralized networks	Strategic networks vs. decentralized networks
Equity to total assets (%)	9.85–9.25 (0.10)	9.25–10.22 (0.00)	9.85–10.22 (0.67)
Net customer loans to total assets (%)	74.59–58.09 (0.00)	58.09–66.94 (0.00)	74.59–66.94 (0.01)
Customer deposits to total assets (%)	68.17–74.72 (0.15)	74.72–58.06 (0.02)	68.17–58.06 (0.92)
Impaired loans to gross customer loans (%)	2.66–4.69 (0.00)	4.69–13.47 (0.00)	2.66–13.47 (0.00)
ROAA (%)	0.46–0.34 (0.01)	0.34–0.17 (0.00)	0.46–0.17 (0.00)
Cost to income (%)	66.78–70.53 (0.00)	70.53–67.00 (0.03)	70.79–67.00 (0.46)

Source: Author's calculations

---

[2] From the 1980s onward, the supervision of Dutch CBs was performed by the central institution on a consolidated basis, along with the reporting of results to stakeholders.

mances are: equity/total assets (%), net customer loans/total assets (%), customer deposits/total assets (%), impaired loans/gross customer loans and advances (%), ROAA (%), and cost to income (%).

The CBs of decentralized networks report the highest median levels of capitalization, proxied by the equity on total assets (%). Their greater capital holdings (10.22%) may be explained by both the greater prudence of these independent banks, and by a certain degree of managerial difficulty in implementing more efficient capital allocation processes. The integrated networks around an IPS record the lowest median value of the indicator (9.25%), lower than that of strategic networks (9.85%). Comparing the median values of the net customer loans to total assets (%), it emerges that it is above all the CBs belonging to strategic groups that are most involved in lending to customers (74.59%), followed by the banks in decentralized networks (66.94%). For these banks, there is a clear strategy of specializing in the credit function to the local economy. This, however, appears more distinctly in the case of strategic networks. The CBs belonging to quasi-strategic networks (58.09%) occupy an intermediate and most distanced position.

If we consider the role of customer deposits in the funding of the CBs in the various different forms of networks, the median values are highest for the semi-strategic and strategic groups, at 74.72% and 68.17% respectively. Bank deposits from customers equal 58.06% for the CBs that form part of decentralized networks. These latter CBs are therefore very exposed in their loan activity but seem to be subject to greater competition on the liability side. Their risk, approximated by the ratio of impaired loans to gross customer loans (%), is the highest in our analysis. Their median value (13.47%) is much greater than that of the other networks, which have more effective technical and organizational controls at their disposal in terms of the risk management of individual CBs. In terms of profitability (ROAA), the best performing CBs are those belonging to strategic and quasi-strategic networks. Their profitability results are respectively almost three times higher and double those achieved by banks belonging to decentralized networks. If high levels of integration have significant positive effects on the profitability of the CBs that have opted to develop this type of organizational solution, the same emerges with regard to their degree of operational efficiency. Strategic networks achieve the lowest median levels of cost to income (66.78%), followed by decentralized networks (67.00%). For the latter, the search for operational solutions that make management more efficient is essential due to their lesser ability to achieve economic and financial results that ensure their survival in the long term and in conditions of clear independence. In the decade under consideration, it is overwhelmingly clear that increasing the degree of integration seems to be a necessary condition for preserving and enhancing the performances and skills of these banks in increasingly competitive contexts. Table 9.2 shows in brackets the significance of the Wilcoxon-Mann-Whitney (WMW) (1947) test for pairs of different models of networks. The three network models tend to perform significantly differently in the analyzed period. The strategic ones are most able to exploit the "core" competencies of their local member banks, allowing them, at the same time, to obtain superior results.

In order to capture the evolution of the performances of the CBs belonging to the different organizational and governance models, Tables 9.3 and 9.4 show the values of the selected indicators in two sub-periods, respectively covering 2008–2013 and 2014–2017. This distinction has a double meaning. On the one hand, it makes it possible to grasp the effects of the episodes of crisis that hit European economies after 2008 and that continued with greater and lesser degrees of intensity until the instigation of the European Banking Union in 2014. On the other hand, given that the reorganization of some networks into more integrated organizational models took place in the first two years of 2014–2017 (such as in Austria), it will be possible to evaluate the results of this restructuring on a comparative basis.

Without going into the details of the analysis of the individual indicators, the median values reported in Tables 9.3 and 9.4 indicate that in times of crisis the strategic and quasi-strategic groups achieved results that were decidedly better than those of the banks belonging to decentralized networks. This superiority was accentuated in the subsequent sub-period, 2014–2017. In statistical terms, however, the degree of significance of the differences in the results obtained by the three types of networks examined is attenuated in the last period under examination. The weakening of the results of the CBs belonging to decentralized networks is accentuated in comparison to those included in strategic networks. Among the latter and those with a quasi-strategic set-up, the statistically significant differences are reduced, for example, in terms of profitability and capital endowments, while the gap between the two models in their operational efficiency levels

Table 9.3   Comparative performances of different types of co-operative banking models of networks over 2008–2013. Medians and *p*-values in parenthesis

	Strategic networks vs. quasi-strategic networks (IPS based)	Quasi-strategic networks (IPS based) vs. decentralized networks	Strategic networks vs. decentralized networks
Equity to total assets (%)	9.85–8.41 (0.06)	8.41–10.86 (0.00)	9.85–10.86 (0.26)
Net customer loans to total assets (%)	70.51–56.70 (0.00)	56.70–67.67 (0.00)	70.51–67.67 (0.52)
Customer deposits to total assets (%)	67.84–72.07 (0.44)	72.07–53.33 (0.08)	67.84–53.33 (0.81)
Impaired loans to gross customer loans (%)	2.33–5.35 (0.00)	5.35–10.24 (0.00)	2.33–10.24 (0.00)
ROAA (%)	0.46–0.35 (0.08)	0.35–0.25 (0.03)	0.46–0.25 (0.00)
Cost to income (%)	68.72–67.95 (0.69)	67.95–65.55 (0.11)	68.72–65.55 (0.53)

Source: Author's calculations

Table 9.4   Comparative performances of different types of co-operative banking models of networks over 2014–2017. Medians and *p*-values in parenthesis

	Strategic networks vs. quasi-strategic networks (IPS based)	Quasi-strategic networks (IPS based) vs. decentralized networks	Strategic networks vs. decentralized networks
Equity to total assets (%)	9.94–9.93 (0.97)	9.93–10.07 (0.94)	9.94–10.07 (0.64)
Net customer loans to total assets (%)	74.59–59.75 (0.00)	59.75–57.76 (0.32)	74.59–57.76 (0.01)
Customer deposits to total assets (%)	68.17–75.25 (0.12)	75.25–63.28 (0.22)	68.17–63.28 (0.99)
Impaired loans to gross customer loans (%)	2.88–3.63 (0.05)	3.63–17.56 (0.00)	2.88–17.56 (0.00)
ROAA (%)	0.45–0.37 (0.18)	0.37–0.08 (0.00)	0.45–0.08 (0.00)
Cost to income (%)	64.46–77.68 (0.00)	77.68–69.06 (0.28)	64.46–69.06 (0.12)

Source: Author's calculations

is accentuated. Recent developments in the intra-sectorial aggregation process in the German co-operative banking sector seem to indicate the need for the entire sector to reposition itself to achieve more satisfactory levels of efficiency, given the pressures exerted by the macro-economic context and by the advancements in the digital economy.

3 What Challenges Lie Ahead for the Co-operative Banking Sector in the Near Future?

The co-operative banking sector has historically developed as an alternative form of financial intermediation, aimed at mitigating those market imperfections that give rise to the financial exclusion of both people and business ideas. To date, it has served as a complement to the public and private offer of financial activities designed to promote the formation of savings and their mobilization (Goglio and Catturani 2018). Following the outbreak of the GFC, the European co-operative banking sector has proved to be more resilient than shareholder-oriented banking, and more committed to the financing of local economies (i.e. Birchall 2013; Ferri et al. 2014; Migliorelli 2018). In recent years, banking systems around the world, as well as those in Europe, have remained exposed to several threats: the pace of digital developments, the pressures on profitability due to the persistent low interest rate environment and rigidities in the structure of bank operating costs, the restrictions imposed by regulations, and the ever-present sources of economic uncertainty at both the European and global level.

The co-operative banking system has reacted by implementing a series of organizational and operational changes that testify to the vibrancy of the sector and its ability to respond to internal and external threats and opportunities. In the decade that followed the outbreak of the GFC, we have observed the twin phenomena of an increase in the degree of integration within the networks, and the revision of governance models in order to strengthen the co-operative identity which, perhaps in the period preceding the GFC had been undermined by the flattering effects of deregulation and developments in market-based finance. As we have seen in the previous chapters, strategic co-operative networks have been formalized (for example, in Finland and Italy), and the old schemes of institutional protection of the co-operative sector have been reorganized around IPSs with the mandatory function of guaranteeing depositors (e.g. in Germany and Austria), alongside pre-existing intra-sectoral solidarity systems. In one case, in the Netherlands, integration took the form of an actual merger between the central institution and the local CBs and a thorough review of the governance model to give voice and control to the members and the community needs they represent. The recent regulations regarding capital adequacy and the resolution of banking crises have substantially influenced the organizational changes we have observed, driving their design and implementation. The weakening of the degree of independence of local banks is the price that has generally been paid in return for ensuring the greater resilience of the entire sector and its values and principles. In parallel, the progress of network reorganizations, perhaps mostly externally influenced, has required the strengthening of the co-operative identity. In terms of governance, there has been a widespread consolidation of the ownership of central institutions by local banks and a rethinking of their representation and influence over the apex companies. A variety of models have been adopted in this regard. There are cases, as in France, where the role of influencing the governance of the central banks is delegated to large second-level co-operative structures, whereas elsewhere (for example in Germany and Italy), this influence is fragmented between a large number of first-level banks. Certainly, the GFC and the regulatory reactions that followed provided an opportunity to rethink the organizational models of co-operative networks for the modern world, albeit with approaches that remain country-specific and that reflect the national historical heritage and society. Indeed, in countries where the co-operative banking movement has been more prevalent and its role in promoting widespread local economic development has been more significant, it has been clear from the very beginning that the survival of this financial idea implied organizational developments which had to be addressed along with the changes in the economic and societal environments. This has typically been achieved through the adoption of increasing degrees of integration which have also gradually incorporated market-related mechanisms, giving rise to hybrid models of co-operative banking. This was essentially necessary to support the diversification of the offer to customers and to mitigate certain limitations of the co-operative model in its participation in financial markets. The intrinsic organizational adaptability of this model of banking and financial intermediation is unquestionably functional to preserving its grounding principles of social economy and solidarity-based management. On the basis of these considerations, the European

Economic and Social Committee (EESC) approved in 2015, by a large majority, the opinion "The role of co-operative and savings banks in territorial cohesion—proposals for an adapted financial regulation framework". This clearly stated the need to preserve the biodiversity of the financial system with adequate regulations based on the principles of proportionality. As stated by Guider (2013), regulation specific to each business model is essential to preserve the diversity of the European financial system. Experience has shown that diversity, risk spreading, and distribution are good for the European financial system where co-operative banking plays a significant role (EESC 2015).

What are the next challenges for the sector? Most of the concerns of the co-operative banking model are not that different from those that European commercial joint-stock banks may face, such as:

- Pressures on margins due to increasing competition, greater demands for adaptation to capital requirements, and low interest rates
- The need to boost operational and managerial efficiency via branch rationalization, consolidation, investments in digitalization to foster multi-channel distribution and technology to promote fintech solutions complementary to social banking, and an increase in the professionalism of co-operative banking's managers
- Improvements in risk management and control at the local and central levels consistent with the specific bank missions
- The requirement to conduct the banking and financial intermediation with transparency, sound and accountable corporate governance and with clear and distinguishable social and environmental responsibility

In the following pages, we will focus on some phenomena that we consider challenging for the entire co-operative banking sector in terms of the preservation of its identity and its ability to respond effectively to economic and social needs.

3.1   Combining Digitalization and Co-operative Banking: What Are the Challenges?

In a recent paper, Pérez (2016) stated that regulatory and technological changes exert pressures on the lending-dependency of European banks, pushing them to become more focused on services. This alleviates the growing demand for regulatory capital which is aimed to absorb losses in the event of a resolution but requires substantial investment in technological innovation and digital transformation. Despite the aforementioned pressures, our empirical evidence indicates that co-operative banking has continued to support the real economy more decisively than shareholder-oriented banks, because they are more committed to their role in society and in the economy. This commitment is even more important in light of the continuing high dependence of European enterprises on bank financing (more than 75% in Europe, compared to 20% in the United States) and the lack of equity culture in Europe which makes micro- and small-medium enterprises (which constitute more than 98% of all enterprises in Europe, employing one in every three employees and creating 58% of all value added) potentially vulnerable to the risk of a credit crunch such as that which occurred during the years of the global financial crisis (EESC 2017a).

Crowdfunding, a Fintech[3] solution, for example, represents a potential source of disintermediation of banks on the asset side, but can also be a valid complement to banks' financing activities. In essence, the platforms for making loans, donations, and equity investments are inspired by principles of participatory financial democracy that blend well with those that originally motivated the first steps of CBs. Platforms may supplement or promote mainly innovative and community-related businesses, that is, through household financing and venture capital, and through their mobile applications, give customers, in real time, the financial information they need to manage their expenditure or investment choices (EESC 2017b).

In promoting and implementing these platforms, CBs can take on a role consistent with their ethical and operational principles and can intervene through providing different combinations of activities. These may range from offering support services (such as advice on projects to be financed via crowdfunding, selection of projects, rating of projects and payment services) to providing banking products such as guarantees and forms of hybrid lending. The latter implies essentially a partnership between banks and private investors in financing, which has the advantage of allowing banks to retain their business without significantly increasing their balance sheet while simultaneously sustaining their clients and their investors. Technological innovations may foster the activation of instruments such as micro-credit for small and very small production activities,

---

[3] Financial Technology or Fintech may be defined as "the application of technology to the delivery of financing, payment, investment and consulting services" (Banca d'Italia 2017).

as was originally the case for rural banks, with the use of guarantee instruments that already exist or micro-credit for people in need. Nowadays, the links between banks and crowdfunding are very different, with a focus that normally includes crowdfunding initiatives in the form of donations and less commonly also covers the other possible ways of exploiting the platforms to generate financing in the form of loans and equity investments.

Among the co-operative banking groups, those in northern Europe seem to have entered the market for crowdfunding initiatives more decisively through forms of collaboration with existing platforms and investments in their own technological financial market places. Digitalization will increasingly cover other operational areas, from payments to consulting and financial investment, and even insurance, affecting both the design of products, and their delivery. For these investments, large networks are favored, both because of their greater capacity to bear the associated costs and because of the potential to make these investments on the scale necessary to make them profitable.

Digitalization is significantly influencing the way financial services are distributed although at varying paces, reflecting several factors such as age, level of education, and occupation. In all the countries under investigation in this book, the banking systems have undergone a consistent reduction in branch numbers, a trend also shared by CBs. Over the period between 2007 and 2017, the bank branches of the co-operative networks analyzed in this book went from 46,489 to 39,665 units, representing about a 15% decrease. This percentage is lower than that recorded for the European banking sector as a whole: compared to 2007, the total number of bank branches has declined 21%, or by almost 50,000 units (from about 233,000 in 2007 to 183,000[4] in 2017, of which 53,262 belong to CBs).[5] Banking aggregations within the banking systems and the spread of remote banking channels account for the significant reduction in bank agency networks on European soil. A further critical aspect is the management of the impact of technology on the workplace and on employment levels. With regard to the latter, in the European Union, between 2007 and 2017, the total number of employees in the banking sector fell from

---

[4] See Facts & Figures for the year-end 2017 published by European Banking Federation (EBF), available at https://www.ebf.eu/facts-and-figures/.
[5] EACB's figure for the year-end 2017.

3.26 million to 2.74 million,[6] an overall decrease of around 16%. The co-operative sector employed about 26% of total banking employment in 2017 (it was 23% in 2007)[7] and has reduced the number of employees by just under 4% in the same period. This percentage rises to around 9% if we only consider the countries surveyed in this book. The lower rate of decline of CBs' branches and employees in comparison with the European system as a whole seems to indicate a certain caution on the part of this business model to proceed to rationalization processes, due to both the importance it attaches to proximity with customers and to the areas served, and because of the difficulties in reconciling the need to improve the efficiency of the sector with the degrees of autonomy and independence that these banks enjoy in some countries (e.g. in Germany and Austria). And we must not forget, employees are also typically members of the CBs in which they work and a reduction in the workforce might have some effect on the stability of the banks involved and on the trust placed in them. Bank restructures, normally involving the closure of branches located in smaller villages and municipalities, have already left numerous such places without any branch at all, with some population centers running the risk of financial exclusion and a loss of confidence in the co-operative model. An additional risk for co-operative banks is losing access to the soft information that only proximity allows them to gather. Thus, CBs are called upon to rethink their business model of local banking. For example, the heavy rationalization of the Rabobank branch network has been flanked by the implementation of a new network of banking agents who take care of the business in those areas, particularly in the countryside.

Cost rationalization and the growing demand for a multi-channel approach call for the shutting down of less efficient outlets. These trends seem inescapable and unavoidable. Digital channels increasingly act as a substitute for visits to banks' local branches which have previously been the basis for the development of co-operative banking. Hence, CBs need to adapt their business model to the new wave of digitalization in order to avoid losing significant parts of their business. According to EBF (2018), the facts show that more than half of EU individuals used internet banking in 2017, up from 29% in 2008. That said, the challenge for the co-operative sector is to be able to reconcile their firm orientation toward

---

[6] See Facts & Figures for the year-end 2017 published by European Banking Federation (EBF), available at https://www.ebf.eu/facts-and-figures/.

[7] Our calculations are based on data provided by EACB and by EBF.

people and human relationships with the growing physical distance that the pervasive development of Fintech determines.

In such a context, technology must be a complement to and not a substitute for human relationships. Rather than replacing human endeavor, for example, digitality may be designed and implemented to favor the development of smart working contexts; encourage the sharing of information on customers, activities, and so on; and free employees from low-value activities to focus on activities and services that require more skill in identifying customer needs and offering customized solutions. Digitalization may also be an effective means of conveying targeted information to bank stakeholders, a way of strengthening their voice and role, and a device for reviewing the political dimension of the co-operative status (Gorlier et al. 2018).

In today's digital world, technology challenges the way banking relationships are managed in a banking business model, including in the co-operative sector, which places relationships and inclusion at the center of its distinctive mission. To this end, the co-operative banking sector should have a differentiated and differentiating approach to technology, consistent with its values and principles. As recommended by EESC (2017b), employees, members, and the consumers of financial services should be involved, through their representative organizations, so that their practical knowledge in the field can be taken into account. And this may offer the opportunity to plan and put in place mutually useful educational programs. These would be even more valuable as a responsible way for CBs to educate their stakeholders to deal with the hidden perils of digitalization. For instance, while digitalization may make the distribution of financial products more transparent, it does not guarantee *per se* the absence of unknown deficiencies or the compliance of the products with relevant regulations. Making customers aware of this, as well as encouraging their involvement, can certainly enable trust in co-operative banking intermediation to grow.

3.2   Member Engagement and Socially Responsible and Transparent Governance

The governance of CBs ideally assigns an active role to the members based on two fundamental tenets: equality in the expression and importance of their votes (irrespective of the number of shares held) and the individual interest of members in monitoring the management of the company whose financial services they use. Theorists maintain that these incentives are not sufficiently strong to insulate CBs from managerial opportunism and episodes of moral hazard. During recent episodes of financial crisis however, these latter phenomena have proved less widespread and intense for the co-operative banking sector than for the other business models.

Active participation in governance implies the motivation and capability to exercise control over the management's conduct of business. As far as motivation is concerned, as Simmons and Birchall (2005) remind us, this involves a mixture of self-interest and concern for others, depending on circumstances. The strength of motivation may be weakened by the perception of members' marginal powers of influence through the per capita vote, with this phenomenon being amplified where membership is widely distributed. Moreover, even economic incentives (i.e. greater access to financial services or more favorable terms) could be weakened and/or fail to be clearly perceived by members in contexts where there is a high degree of competition with other business models. As a consequence, members may end up acting purely as customers, who choose the CB to obtain personal economic benefits, but do not exercise their right of involvement that derives from their property rights (Goglio and Catturani 2018).[8] Increasing levels of competition may lead to a growing homologation of the offer. Countering this to make the offer recognizable in the eyes of the members and stimulate their active participation inevitably entails high costs.

Where members' participation is weak, the management becomes stronger in response. Boards may become self-perpetuating or, in some circumstances, become solely the expression of the interests of members-employees. According to the economic analysis, the main advantage of co-operative businesses over profit-oriented ones is the possibility of enhancing worker motivation. In a world of increasing information asymmetries, having the possibility to encourage participation at reduced cost can be a great advantage. But even in this case, there is a clear risk of the co-operative business being hijacked to only safeguard the interests of employees.

The seamless alignment of the interests of members, customers, and managers is weakened if participation is low or if it is characterized by a diffuse membership's inability to understand managerial proposals and decisions and their implications for the future of co-operative banking. Empirical

---

[8] In contrast, members can try to influence the managerial decisions through their personal relationships with the administrators (Alexopoulos and Goglio 2011).

evidence on the participation rate of members at general meetings is generally scarce. However, it is alleged that participation is notoriously low (Birchall 2013). For the reasons mentioned above, member participation should be incentivized and properly managed, through *ad hoc* programs which the top management should be committed to sustaining at all levels. As highlighted by Simmons and Birchall (2005), stimulating the participation of old and new members means studying the links that form the so-called chain of participation. It presupposes connections in three areas: the resources available to members, the catalysts to mobilization and individual motivations which, as already mentioned, can range from self-interest to collective goals. The resources available to members constitute the *a priori* conditions that drive members' participation in the life of their co-operative and in taking corporate decisions. They include their degree of wealth, the time they have available, their skills, their state of health, and their confidence in the contribution that everyone can make. In respect of many of these resources, CBs can effectively act to foster participation with suitable initiatives (i.e. online voting, preparatory meetings before the AGM, courses on banking-related issues and on socially and environmentally relevant topics, etc.). The second link in the chain of participation is represented by events and initiatives that can induce participation, as it is of interest to the members. As stated by Birchall (2013), "the greater the number of opportunities to get involved, the most people are likely to begin to take part". For example, with regard to initiatives concerning health and welfare, including at the corporate level, the average age of the membership needs to be kept in mind. But in addition to welfare and health, other mutualistic initiatives could be developed in the fields of renewable energies, the management of environmental and cultural assets, education, and the interaction between generations. On this last theme, a renewed capacity to involve young members could produce many new stimuli.

In this context, the experience of the Finnish co-operative banking group, OP, in the field of medicine and hospitals (as reported in Chap. 4) is interesting. From an organizational point of view, it is also important that these initiatives come under the responsibility of the highest governing bodies. For example, in the French group Crédit Agricole, responsibility for corporate social responsibility (CSR) and governance issues is allocated to the chairman of the board of directors. The improvement of governance, in addition to requiring a higher degree of engagement from members, also requires that those who take responsibility for management and control at the various levels of the co-operative network have the necessary skills, through appropriate technical training processes, to improve the safety and psychological/physical well-being of employees. Many co-operative banking networks have intensified their collaboration with educational institutions to provide training at various levels alongside their use of digital media for training and management purposes. It will be necessary to establish rigorous codes of conduct to guarantee professionalism and ethics in the representation of different interests in the governance bodies.

Inclusive and transparent governance, aligned with management concepts such as CSR and driven by social and ethical values, is in the DNA of co-operative banking, but it is also a necessary condition for increasing stakeholder trust. The GFC has caused reputational damage and a loss of trust in financial institutions. According to estimates by the Edelman Trust Barometer (Edelman 2019), in 2018 the financial services sector is the sector that enjoys the lowest degree of trust, although this has been growing since 2015. The countries in which there is still mistrust in the banking and financial sector include some of the European countries analyzed in this book, such as Germany, Italy, France, and the Netherlands. Furthermore, the Barometer itself indicates that there is a great demand for good governance and social and environmental responsibility. The following are among the issues indicated as most important for banking institutions in 2018: the contrast between income inequality and financial security; support for social equality and human rights; and the avoidance of doing business with entities associated with social ills. The survey also indicates that there is also a strong demand for corporate commitment aimed not only at creating profits but also at improving the economic and social conditions of the communities in which they are active. In this respect, the co-operative banking sector enjoys an unquestionable advantage not only because profit represents a condition of the survival of its inspiring principles and values, but also because it enjoys the freedom to choose the destination of operating surpluses in a responsible manner, supporting its social commitment and in favor of local communities, which are the characteristics most visible to the public (EESC 2017a).

3.3   Co-operative Banking and Regulation

Both internationally and within Europe, the GFC has led to a vast process of regulation of banking and financial activity that is without precedent in terms of its intensity, pervasiveness, and cost. A complex set of rules has significantly raised bank capitalization requirements in order to make the banks more resilient in the face of financial shocks; intentionally impacted on the governance and risk control mechanisms and related organizational models; extended reporting requirements to the supervisory authorities and the wider public of stakeholders; expanded compliance regulations with regard to financial activities on the markets and the offer of investment services to customers; and made the payment system more competitive by introducing new players into the payment value chain; and so on. The list could go on because the regulatory fervor seems unending and even now, at the time of writing, a new package of measures has been approved that amends prudential regulation, namely the rules on capital requirements for the banking sector (regulation on capital requirements [CRR] and the Capital Requirements Directive [CRD IV]). Specifically, this relates to the new CRR II[9] and the CRD V,[10] approved in April 2019 by the European Parliament.

The rules recently approved by the European Parliament aim to curb certain distortions caused by the previous regulation and to help revive the EU economy by increasing bank lending capacity and strengthening capital markets. The package of measures features a greater degree of proportionality, whereby the requirements for prudential regulation are graduated in relation to the risk profile and the systemic importance of the banks. Under the new rules, the "small and non-complex institutions" will be subject to simplified requirements, in particular with regard to the reporting and provision of funds to cover any losses. Furthermore, to mitigate the regressive effects of the credit risk regulations on loans to SMEs, the backbone of the European economy, capital requirements will be lower when banks provide loans to SMEs. This represents an attempt to stimulate an increase in lending to SMEs, something that the implementation of the prudential regulations that followed the global financial crisis has somehow made less viable. This is also true for the co-operative

---

[9] European Parliament legislative resolution of 16 April 2019 on the proposal for a regulation of the European Parliament and of the Council amending Regulation (EU) No 575/2013 as regards the leverage ratio, the net stable funding ratio, requirements for own funds and eligible liabilities, counterparty credit risk, market risk, exposures to central counterparties, exposures to collective investment undertakings, large exposures, reporting and disclosure requirements, and amending Regulation (EU) No 648/2012.

[10] European Parliament legislative resolution of 16 April 2019 on the proposal for a directive of the European Parliament and of the Council amending Directive 2013/36/EU as regards exempted entities, financial holding companies, mixed financial holding companies, remuneration, supervisory measures, and powers and capital conservation measures.

banking sector.[11] Indeed, as our data also show, the lending activity of CBs, especially the smaller ones and those forming part of decentralized networks, has been significantly reduced even since the most acute phase of the GFC. The lightening of capital requirements on loans to European SMEs, largely financed by the co-operative banking sector, aims, in a sense, to boost retail banking and to encourage a greater degree of specialization of financial institutions within the financial system. But which co-operative networks will benefit most from the recent regulatory review? On the surface, it would seem to be the least strongly integrated, while those with a high level of integration, which also fulfill a systemic role, will find themselves supporting the major regulatory costs inherent to their systemic relevance. In an increasingly competitive environment, which is uncertain and demanding in terms of investments, will the greater degree of proportionality that characterizes the new amendments to prudential regulation alone be enough to guarantee the survival of small banks, including co-operative ones? In the writer's opinion, increasing degrees of integration represent a path that has proved effective, both during and since the GFC, in ensuring the maintenance of a business model, the stakeholder-centric one, that has marked the history of the economic development of many European countries. Ultimately, it will be vital for co-operative banking not to yield to the pressures of alignment in banking business and governance models, induced, in part at least, by the regulation and for the co-operative sector to make rule makers sensitive to the adverse effects (i.e. lower risk diversification, less counter-cyclicality in lending, less freedom of choice for consumers, and more social exclusion)[12] of losing diversity in banking business models.

4   Conclusion

Empirical evidence shows that, in spite of the hybridization that is increasingly a feature of the most significant European co-operative banking networks, their performances and the distinctive nature of their operational practices set them apart from their shareholder-oriented counterparts.

---

[11] This is fully in line with the requests expressed by EACB in its Manifesto (2019) relating to the co-operative banks' policy priorities for the 2019 European Parliament elections and the new European Commission. Available at http://v3.globalcube.net/clients/eacb/content/medias/publications/annual_reports/eacb_manifesto_2019_5_-compressed.pdf.

[12] In this regard, see the EACB's Manifesto (2019).

Although in recent years the introduction of the European Banking Union and the Basel 3 regulations have begun to diminish the gap, a number of clear differences persist: where co-operative banking pursues high levels of strategic integration, its focus on lending and funding through customer deposits remains higher than that of non-co-operative banks, demonstrating the importance of the co-operative model in mobilizing savings to finance the real economy. Other statistically significant differences are found in the amount of equity they hold as a proportion of total assets and, notwithstanding their links with financial markets, their lower allocation in securities. Over time, co-operative profitability was found to be higher, both in terms of net interest margin (%) and, to a lesser extent, of ROAA (%).

However, indicators relating to credit risk, profitability, operating efficiency, and cost-to-income values (%) reveal a convergence between the two models in terms of operating results, if not in business choices.

Comparing results in terms of network models, we again find some clear distinctions: profitability and operational efficiency are notably higher in CBs belonging to strategic and quasi-strategic networks, these proving most able to exploit the core competencies of their local banks to obtain superior results. Strategic networks are also found to have the highest median values of customer deposits and to be those most involved in lending to customers, pursuing a strategy of specializing in the credit function to the local economy. By contrast, decentralized networks report the highest levels of exposure in their loan activity with the highest ratio of impaired loans to gross customer loans.

In the decade since the global financial crisis, the European co-operative banking sector has proved to be more resilient than shareholder-oriented banking, as well as more committed to financing local economies. However, while the entire financial sector is affected by the pressure on profitability due to the persistent low interest rate environment and the need to boost efficiency and improve risk management, the co-operative sector faces specific challenges. These include its response to increasing digitalization, including crowdfunding and fintech phenomena; its need to mobilize its membership into greater participation; its role in restoring trust in the sector through inclusive and transparent governance and its promotion of social and environmental responsibility; and its ability to withstand the burdens of increased regulation and resist the mounting pressures of alignment in business banking models, successfully maintaining instead the case for banking diversity.

REFERENCES

Alexopoulos, Y., & Goglio, S. (2011). Financial Cooperatives: Problems and Challenges in the Post-Crisis Era. *Journal of Rural Cooperation, 39*(1), 35–48.

Banca d'Italia. (2017). *Fintech In Italia. Indagine conoscitiva sull'adozione delle innovazioni tecnologiche applicate ai servizi finanziari*. Roma.

Becchetti, L., Ciciretti, R., & Paolantonio, A. (2016). The Cooperative Bank Difference Before and After the Global Financial Crisis. *Journal of International Money and Finance, 69*, 224–246.

Birchall, J. (2013). *Finance in An Age of Austerity*. Edward Elgar Publishing.

Edelman. (2019). *Trust Barometer. Financial Services*. Retrieved from https://www.edelman.com/research/trust-in-financial-services-2019.

European Association of Co-operative Banks (EACB). (2019). Manifesto available at http://v3.globalcube.net/clients/eacb/content/medias/publications/annual_reports/eacb_manifesto_2019_5_compressed.pdf.

European Banking Federation (EBF). (2018). *Facts & Figures for the Year-End 2017*. Retrieved from https://www.ebf.eu/facts-and-figures/.

European Economic and Social Committee (EESC). (2015). Role of Cooperative and Savings Banks in Territorial Cohesion, Opinion of the European Economic and Social Committee. *Official Journal of the European Union*, (2015/C 251/02).

European Economic and Social Committee (EESC). (2017a). *Europe's Cooperative Banking Models. Study*. Brussels.

European Economic and Social Committee (EESC). (2017b). *Digitalisation and Innovative Business Models in the European Financial Sector, Impact on Employment and Customers, Own Opinion of the European Economic and Social Committee*. CCMI/147.

Fay, M. P., & Proschan, M. A. (2010). Wilcoxon-Mann-Whitney or T-Test? On Assumptions for Hypothesis Tests and Multiple Interpretations of Decision Rules. *Statistics Surveys, 4*, 1.

Ferri, G., Kalmi, P., & Kerola, E. (2014). Does Bank Ownership Affect Lending Behavior? Evidence from the Euro Area. *Journal of Banking and Finance, 48*, 194–209.

Goglio, S., & Catturani, I. (2018). The Way Forward for Cooperative Banks. In M. Migliorelli (Ed.), *New Cooperative Banking in Europe, Strategies for Adapting the Business Model Post Crisis*. Palgrave Macmillan.

Gorlier, T., Michel, G., & Zeitoun, V. (2018). The New Paradigm of Digital Proximity for Cooperative Banks. In M. Migliorelli (Ed.), *New Cooperative Banking in Europe, Strategies for Adapting the Business Model Post Crisis*. Palgrave Macmillan.

Guider, H. (2013). *La reforma financiera y la necesidad de mantener la diversidad del ecosistema*. Madrid: UNACC.

Mann, H. B., & Whitney, D. R. (1947). On a Test of Whether One of Two Random Variables Is Stochastically Larger than the Other. *Annals of Mathematical Statistics, 18*(1), 50–60.

Migliorelli, M. (2018). Cooperative Banks Lending During and After the Great Crisis. In M. Migliorelli (Ed.), *New Cooperative Banking in Europe, Strategies for Adapting the Business Model Post Crisis*. Palgrave Macmillan.

Pérez, E. (2016). El sistema financiero español: avances y retos. *Economistas,* Special Issue, No. 146/147.

Simmons, R., & Birchall, J. (2005). A Joined-up Approach to User Participation in Public Services: Strengthening the Participation Chain. *Social Policy and Administration, 39*(3), 260–283.

Index[1]

[1] Note: Page numbers followed by 'n' refer to notes.

Printed by Printforce, the Netherlands